Speaking Our Minds

Conversations With the People Behind Landmark First Amendment Cases

LEA's Communication Series
Jennings Bryant / Dolf Zillmann, General Editors

For a complete list of titles in LEA's Communication Series, please contact Lawrence Erlbaum Associates, Publishers at www.erlbaum.com.

Speaking Our Minds

Conversations With the People Behind Landmark First Amendment Cases

Joseph Russomanno

Walter Cronkite School of Journalism and Mass Communication

Arizona State University

2002

LAWRENCE ERLBAUM ASSOCIATES, PUBLISHERS
Mahwah, New Jersey   London

Lawrence Erlbaum Associates, Inc., Publishers
10 Industrial Avenue
Mahwah, NJ 07430

Cover design by Kathryn Houghtaling Lacey

Library of Congress Cataloging-in-Publication Data

Russomanno, Joseph.
Speaking our minds : conversations with the people behind landmark
    First Amendment cases / Joseph Russomanno.
        p. cm.
    Includes bibliographical references and index.
    ISBN 0-8058-3767-1 (cloth : alk. paper)
    ISBN 0-8058-3768-X (pbk. : alk. paper)
    1. Freedom of speech—United States—Cases. 2. Freedom of the press—
        United States—Cases. 3. Mass media—Law and legislation—United
        States—Cases. I. Title.
KF4770.A7 R87   2002
342.73'0853—dc21   2001051089
                                                            CIP

Books published by Lawrence Erlbaum Associates are printed on
acid-free paper, and their bindings are chosen for strength and durability.

Printed in the United States of America
10 9 8 7 6 5 4 3 2

For Julie

Contents

Foreword

*S*tromberg v. California, Brown v. Louisiana, Kunz v. New York. These are among the important U.S. Supreme Court cases helping ensure First Amendment rights in this country. We know the Court's decisions and reasoning. But we know little about the people who brought the issues to the Court in these and other free speech and media law cases. What political motivations prompted Yette Stromberg, Bella Mintz, and others in the late 1920s to display a red flag at a children's summer camp, violating a California law? Were Brown and his four friends in 1964 frightened when they remained in a Clinton, Louisiana, public library in silent protest against segregation? What caused Carl Jacob Kunz, a Baptist minister, to take all the way to the Supreme Court a $10 fine for holding an outdoor worship meeting without a city permit in 1948?

We have few answers to these questions. However, Joseph Russomanno's book, *Speaking Our Minds: Conversations with the People Behind Landmark First Amendment Cases*, allows participants in recent Supreme Court First Amendment cases to share their experiences. We learn why they brought lawsuits, what tactics attorneys used in arguing before the Court, what it is like to be sued.

Consider how valuable this is in understanding landmark Court decisions. For example, in August 1917 Charles Schenck, Elizabeth Baer, and others, acting for the Philadelphia Socialist Party, printed more than 15,000 leaflets, mailing many to men whose names appeared in newspapers as passing their draft board physical examinations. The fliers urged the men to "assert your rights" and resist being drafted into the service during World War I. The leaflets said the draft was "despotism in its worst form and a monstrous wrong against humanity in the interest of Wall Street's chosen few." In 1919, in *Schenck v. United States*, the U.S. Supreme Court upheld Schenck's and the others' convictions for violating the Espionage

Act of 1917. The law prohibits, among other things, "willfully obstruct[ing] the recruiting or enlistment service of the United States."

What did Schenck and the other Philadelphia socialists think they would accomplish by distributing the leaflets? Did they believe the Philadelphia Socialist Party's leaflet was so persuasive it would convince men to be draft dodgers? Did their attorneys think the flier was an innocuous screed by a few radicals? After the Supreme Court decision and a few years of reflection, what would the socialists have said about their actions and what might their comments have told us about free speech during wartime? How did American Civil Liberties Union attorneys Henry John Nelson and Henry J. Gibbons decide what arguments to make to the Court on Schenck's behalf? Did attorney John Lord O'Brian, representing the government, see any danger to free speech in Schenck's prosecution? We do not have interviews with Schenck and the others answering these questions.

In 1936 Alma Lovell, a Jehovah's Witness, challenged a Griffin, Georgia law forbidding the distribution of leaflets without the city manager's permission. Learning her reasons for challenging the law would add immeasurably to our understanding of the role free speech protection plays in our society. Similarly, what Jesse Cantwell would say about his Supreme Court case could help us understand the passion of those trying to express their views to others. Cantwell, another Jehovah's Witness, was arrested in 1938 for inciting a breach of the peace while telling passersby about his religious beliefs in New Haven, Connecticut.

What would Charlotte Anita Whitney have said about her First Amendment rights? Whitney was a 52-year-old philanthropist, Wellesley graduate, Communist Party member, niece of a 19th century Supreme Court justice, labor reformer and worker in the New York City slums. She was convicted of violating a law forbidding using force or violence to effect political or industrial change and for being an active member of the Communist Labor Party of California in the 1920s. Her case elicited a famous, powerful opinion from U.S. Supreme Court Justice Louis Brandeis. The participants in these and many other significant Supreme Court decisions no longer can be interviewed. Too often all we know about those involved in important First Amendment cases is a few brief comments in Supreme Court opinions. This is basic factual information, usually no more than a description of the person's actions leading to an arrest or lawsuit.

However, to appreciate more fully the importance of free speech and mass media law decisions in our society it is necessary to learn of the personal decisions made and emotions felt when an individual or company becomes involved in the legal process. People generally do not willingly hire lawyers and file lawsuits. They likely do so only when they believe themselves seriously wronged or when they have a strong belief in their right of free speech. People often are astounded to find themselves defendants in criminal cases for, as they see it, only exercising their First Amendment rights. What havoc do these people—known only by their names in legal proceedings—experience in their lives when they become part of an important case? Supreme Court opinions do not tell us. Only those before the Court—willingly or not—can provide the context that explains their actions.

In this book, Joe Russomanno allows us to learn what those involved in recent important First Amendment cases were thinking when they expressed their views or became entwined in mass communication law issues, suffered the consequences for doing so, and took their cases all the way to the U.S. Supreme Court. We also hear from their attorneys and others who were part of Court decisions that made legal history. Mary Beth Tinker recalls what she felt going to school wearing a black armband to protest the Vietnam War. Edward Cleary tells of his personal turmoil representing a youth who burned a wooden cross on an African-American family's lawn, yet realizing he had a "lawyer's dream" case. Patricia Neil Warren discusses the experience of testifying against a congressional law banning use of the Internet to send indecent materials to minors.

This book does not delve into the complex legal issues often in dispute in Supreme Court First Amendment decisions, although it provides needed background explaining the Court's rulings. Rather, it allows the people involved in key free speech and media law cases to tell their own stories in their own words. Modern-day Carl Jacob Kunzes and Yette Strombergs talk about the experience of being the centerpiece of a U.S. Supreme Court case. Their attorneys discuss legal strategy and their feelings arguing before the country's highest court.

The stories are fascinating, and we would not know them without Joe Russomanno's work in finding and interviewing these people. In this book, we learn much more than the Court tells us. For example, in the *Cohen v. Cowles Media Co.* decision the Court says only:

> Dan Cohen [working in Whitney Wheelock's gubernatorial campaign] ... approached reporters ... and offered to provide documents relating to a candidate in the upcoming election. Cohen made clear to the reporters that he would provide the information only if he was given a promise of confidentiality. Reporters from both papers promised to keep Cohen's identity anonymous and Cohen turned over copies of two public court records [concerning Marlene Johnson, a candidate for Lieutenant Governor].... After consultation and debate, the editorial staffs of the two newspapers independently decided to publish Cohen's name as part of their stories concerning Johnson. In their stories, both papers identified Cohen as the source of the court records.... The same day the stories appeared, Cohen was fired by his employer.

There must be more. What prompted Cohen to talk with reporters? Did someone in Wheelock's campaign suggest Cohen do so? Was Cohen shocked when his name appeared in two major newspapers? How did he feel about the papers breaching the confidentiality promise? Did he blame the reporters when in fact their editors revealed Cohen's name? The Supreme Court did not tell us any of this. But in this book Cohen makes clear "it was like death" when he saw his name in the newspaper articles. Cohen says that at the trial of his lawsuit against the newspapers a lawyer used "dirty tricks" to discredit him, causing Cohen to want "to kill the son of a bitch." Elliot Rothenberg, Cohen's attorney, discusses his apprehensions as a single lawyer facing the newspapers' attorneys, including Rothenberg's ex-wife, from a large law firm. Cohen and Rothenberg suggest an undercurrent of anti-Semitism ran through the trial. None of this can be discerned by reading the Supreme Court's decision, which permitted Cohen to continue his lawsuit.

Some journalists were horrified at the Court's *Cohen* ruling; some media critics thought the Court justifiably reined in the press. But Cohen's and Rothenberg's remarks in this book add immeasurably to our understanding of the Court's judgment. The story of their conflict with the Minneapolis and St. Paul newspapers is dramatic in itself, First Amendment implications aside. Reading what Cohen and Rothenberg thought and felt during the legal process makes the participants come alive. We realize the Court's decision affects real people's lives. This book is full of such dramatic tales, narratives told by the people who lived through experiences very few others ever will have. Joe Russomanno has brought life to sometimes dry—nonetheless important—Supreme Court First Amendment decisions. We will not again read a Court opinion interpreting the First Amendment—affecting our freedom of expression and the country's mass media—without asking ourselves who the participants really were, what motivated them, how the legal process and decision affected them. How much more would we understand the role of the First Amendment in America if Russomanno could have interviewed Charles Schenck, Alma Lovell, and Anita Whitney? Fortunately, in this book Russomanno allows their contemporary counterparts to talk about their cases in their own words.

—*Robert Trager, PhD, J.D.*

Preface

The study of law can be—and arguably ought to be—more than studying law. It is more than examining cases and the law that stems from them. Another perspective is to learn about the people at the center of the cases—their motivations, their beliefs, their feelings. And one method of accomplishing that goal is to talk with those people.

This project began with that premise. At its root was a simple curiosity. As its subtitle suggests, it shares with the reader conversations I had with some of the people central to some of the most noteworthy cases in our field. Cases were selected with an eye on spanning the subtopics within the province of mass communication law. Accordingly, the cases encompass freedom of expression, libel, invasion of privacy, intentional infliction of emotional distress, protection of news sources, free press-fair trial, commercial speech, broadcast and cable television regulation, and new technology regulation. Other elements in case selection were the availability and willingness of people to be interviewed and to answer questions candidly.

One goal of this book is to humanize some of the landmark cases in the field of mass communication law. The cases examined herein relate to freedom of speech and the press—those topics typically placed under the umbrella of "media law" or "mass communication law." It does not explore other parts of the First Amendment. It is also acknowledged that there is no pretense within this book's chapters of offering a complete examination of a particular case. Instead, the reader is introduced to some of the people who were at the center of these cases. Their thoughts, insights, and emotions about the case and what it was like to experience it firsthand are revealed. By doing so, it is hoped the reader's understanding of the case and its background will rise to a new level.

Each person whose words are unveiled in these pages was the subject of an in-depth interview. The interviews were conducted individually and via telephone, and occurred between December 1998 and June 2001. Each chapter is devoted to one case, and contains a brief introduction to the case, excerpts of interviews with some of the people involved in the case, explanations of key concepts, and excerpts of the court opinion(s) of the case. My questions are included occasionally for context. Interview passages are presented within these pages as oral history. That is, the interviews—both questions and answers—are excerpted here. This is a proven technique to acquaint readers with new material, particularly when it profiles people and their opinions.

Oral history tells us not only what people did, but why they did it, how they felt about it then and—with time to reflect—how they feel about it now. Although documents remain extremely important in uncovering facts, oral history recognizes that the complete and inside story is never fully revealed by the "paper trail." It offers perspectives that are often missing in histories based on written documents. Oral history offers a way of understanding motivations and feelings not reflected in statistics and records. Oral history also contributes to the creation of new contexts for established events. Rather than looking at historical occurrences independent of context, oral history examines events through the lived experience of individuals. It provides a "feel" for the facts that can only be provided by someone who lived them.

Admittedly, oral history presents a subjective perspective—that of the interviewee. People tend to remember what *they* think is important. Although the time between the events being recounted and the interview may possibly cloud the recollection of incidents, it also often enables people to make better sense of earlier events in their lives. Actions may assume new significance depending on their ultimate consequences. This method of presentation is not meant to replace other sources of information on these cases; instead, it is meant to supplement them, and to do so by providing a personal perspective told by those uniquely qualified to relate the circumstances surrounding them—those who lived them firsthand.

I would like to thank a number of people and organizations. First, I want to thank my wife, Julie, who too often endured weekends during which she saw little more of me than the back of my head while I was seated at the computer.

I also want to thank the people of Arizona State University, its College of Public Programs, and the Walter Cronkite School of Journalism and Mass Communication—all of which create an environment within which such projects are possible. I am particularly grateful for a sabbatical leave that was granted during which much of the manuscript was prepared.

I am indebted to the scholars who reviewed the initial project proposal and the first chapter. Their comments and suggestions were extremely helpful and, as they will see, many of their ideas were implemented.

I also want to thank the people at Lawrence Erlbaum Publishers who recognized the potential of the project initially. I would especially like to thank communications editor Linda Bathgate for her profound guidance and encouragement throughout the process.

Last, I am deeply indebted to the people whose words appear on the pages that follow. Their willingness to let me into a part of their lives and to share with me—and now you, the reader—some of their innermost feelings, passion, and insight is something I will never forget. Near the close of each interview, I would typically ask, "What is your lasting memory with regard to this case?" As it turns out, they were creating lasting memories for me.

—*Joseph Russomanno*

Introduction

The First Amendment has a special regard for those who swim against the current, for those who would shake us to our foundations, for those who reject prevailing authority.[1]

This is a book about people—people whose beliefs prompted them to take one kind of action or another, that led to one kind of charge or another against them, and ultimately led them into court where those beliefs and the expression of them were held up for judgment. People are at the heart of the law and the cases that are litigated in our courts. Although the opinions written by judges and Justices are vital in our understanding of the law— both its historical development and its current standing—all cases begin with people. Laws are passed and signed into law by people—sometimes with political motivations. On some occasions, an individual or group of people makes a conscious decision to take some action. When that action violates a law, charges are filed, and with the help of lawyers, the violators begin to formulate a defense. Those actions are often defended as exercises in free speech, and as expressions of their beliefs. Thus, those actions—the expression of firmly held beliefs—are measured against the First Amendment. Should the constitutional protection that the First Amendment provides against laws that abridge freedom of speech safeguard those actions?

On other occasions, media organizations may exercise their freedom, in the view of some, to a harmful degree. Those injured people may take ac-

---

[1]Steven H. Shiffrin, Dissent, Injustice, and the Meanings of America 10 (1999).

tion by filing a lawsuit, hoping not only to hold the media responsible, but also, in effect, to limit press freedom.

In other situations, people believe that newly enacted laws will, or potentially can, violate their First Amendment rights. The law itself is directly contested by individuals or groups who challenge the law's constitutionality. In all of these situations, the people at the center of the cases include attorneys who frame the case, conceptualize the argument, and lead the battle.

Chapter by chapter, this book explores 10 noteworthy legal battles. Chapter 1 explores *Tinker v. Des Moines Independent School District*. As with any case analysis, historical context is important. This case arose within circumstances surrounding the Vietnam War, American protests, and support for peace. The ruling remains a zenith for freedom of expression within the public school environment. Thirty years after the U.S. Supreme Court ruling, petitioners Mary Beth Tinker, John Tinker, and Chris Eckhardt reflected on the case.

Chapter 2 looks at a different kind of freedom of expression and efforts to proscribe it. In *R.A.V. v. St. Paul*, that Minnesota city had enacted an ordinance to forbid particular kinds of conduct which could be construed as racist. But could such conduct also be regarded as expressive activity? And if so, does such an ordinance violate the First Amendment? On the other hand, how could it be that protecting hate speech could be construed as being a good thing? These are the kinds of questions with which R.A.V.'s attorneys had to grapple.

An adequate defense for libel is that the statement in question was, in fact, an expression of opinion. But exactly how is "opinion" to be distinguished from a statement of "fact"? That question was answered by the D.C. Circuit Court of Appeals in *Ollman v. Evans*, explored in chapter 3. Professor Bertell Ollman had applied for a position at the University of Maryland but, because of his political beliefs, his credentials were questioned in a nationally syndicated newspaper column. He claimed libel; defendants Rowland Evans and Robert Novak countered with opinion. All three of them comment.

Chapter 4 will examine a case that encompassed many areas of the law, *Desnick v. ABC*. The domain of law highlighted in this chapter is privacy. At issue was the use of hidden cameras by ABC's *PrimeTime Live* producers as they investigated the practices of ophthalmologist James Desnick. To many, using hidden cameras is a questionable and controversial technique at best, unethical and intrusive at worst. But does it, by definition, rise to the level of illegal intrusion? The two defendants in addition to ABC, senior correspondent Sam Donaldson and producer Jon Entine, discuss these and other issues.

When does personal attack rise to the level of being libelous? Can a defense that the attack was parody nullify any libel claim? To what extent does the First Amendment protect parody? Can a claim of intentional infliction of emotional distress be upheld merely because the parody was hurtful? These are but a few of the questions at the heart of chapter 5's *Hustler Magazine v. Falwell*. Publisher Larry Flynt and his attorney, Alan Isaacman, offer their viewpoints.

Does it violate the First Amendment to force news media organizations to keep promises of confidentiality to a source? That question was at the heart of *Cohen v. Cowles Media Company*, examined in chapter 6. Reporters at two Twin Cities newspapers promised campaign official Dan Cohen anonymity in exchange for information about a political opponent. When editors rejected the promise and identified Cohen in print, the stage for the legal battle was set. In a remark that symbolizes this entire book, Mr. Cohen's attorney, Elliot Rothenberg, said, "[Y]ou've got flesh and blood people here. It's not just ivory tower general legal principles. People are actually getting hurt." It will be apparent that Mr. Cohen still harbors strong feelings regarding the circumstances surrounding this case. Thus, a cautionary note to the reader: the language in this chapter may be offensive to some.

Two constitutional rights that can potentially conflict are those governed by the First and Sixth Amendments—free press vs. fair trial. An unbridled press reporting about a crime and its circumstances, for example, can impair a defendant's right to a fair trial. These issues came to a head in *Nebraska Press Association v. Stuart*. When Judge Hugh Stuart attempted to ensure that potential jurors in a murder trial would remain impartial by issuing a "gag" order restricting the media, he was sued. Among others, Judge Stuart comments on the case in chapter 7—a case that also includes the issue of prior restraint.

Chapter 8 explores the issue of commercial speech and to what extent advertising is afforded First Amendment protection. In *44 LiquorMart v. Rhode Island*, a store owner wanted to include the price of some of his products in advertisements. That desire, however, was in direct conflict with a state law. The constitutionality of that law was ultimately decided by the U.S. Supreme Court. The store owner and his attorney explain their case here.

The case examined in chapter 9 encompasses a number of issues in broadcast and cable television. In *Turner Broadcasting, Inc. v. FCC*, the constitutionality of the "must carry" provisions of the 1992 Cable Act was challenged. These provisions required that virtually all cable television systems include within their array all of the local broadcast television stations in a given market. Turner Broadcasting, joined by many cable interests, claimed that by telling cable television operators what they had to carry—and, in some instances, what they could not—the legislation violated the First Amendment. It was litigation that, according to one of its attorneys, "was really a lawyers' victory." Several of them discuss their work.

A ruling that is likely to remain the starting point for any and all challenges to Internet regulation for years to come was the result of the case analyzed in chapter 10, *Reno v. ACLU*. As part of the 1996 Telecommunications Act, Congress passed the Communications Decency Act (CDA). Largely intended to target the Internet, the goal of the broadly worded measure was to deny children access to indecent or patently offensive material. Among the issues explored in this chapter is not only whether the CDA survived First Amendment scrutiny, but also how such legislation was passed in the first place.

Of the people profiled in these pages, some were courageous; some expressed views that—at least in retrospect—were righteous; others committed acts that, at best, are questionable; others wanted to hold media organizations liable for improper actions; and most were completely unsuspecting of the eventual ramifications and outcome of their actions. But all share at least one thing: They spoke not only for themselves, but also for a society that is founded on First Amendment rights, and a belief system that defends the ability to express opinions even when a majority may disagree with the specific view being proclaimed. These are the stories of what inspired them—stories that are shared with the hope that, in turn, the reader may find them inspirational. The people we meet here were speaking their minds—and in many ways, they were also speaking our minds.

"[Y]ou've got flesh and blood people here. It's not just ivory tower general legal principles. People are actually getting hurt."

—Elliot Rothenberg, plaintiff's attorney in
Cohen v. Cowles Media Co.

1 Tinker, et al. v. Des Moines Independent Community School District

"Here's this stupid little thing of just wearing an armband and all of a sudden I'm in front of the United States Supreme Court. Wow! Who thought we'd get here? Who thought a little case from Des Moines over a little piece of cloth would end up here?"

—Christopher Eckhardt, co-appellant in
Tinker, et al. v. Des Moines Independent School District

In mid-December of 1965, students across the country were eagerly looking forward to the upcoming holidays and their school vacations. In Des Moines, Iowa, several students were also anticipating another upcoming activity. On December 16, 1965, Mary Beth Tinker, a 13-year old student at Harding Junior High School and Christopher Eckhardt, a 15-year old sophomore at Roosevelt High, were among those who wore black armbands in support of a Christmas truce in the Vietnam War. They were sent home and ultimately suspended from school. The next day, Mary Beth's 15-year old brother, John, wore a black armband to North High School. He, too, was suspended.

Thus began an ordeal that would lead to the U.S. Supreme Court and a landmark decision in freedom of expression. The students contended that wearing the armbands was a right protected by the First Amendment in spite of the fact that doing so violated a school policy that had been adopted only a few days prior to the protest. That policy stipulated that any student wearing an armband to school would be asked to remove it, and if the request was refused, the student would be suspended until he or she returned without the armband.

By any measure, *Tinker v. Des Moines Independent Community School District* is a landmark case. The Student Press Law Center describes it as being "undoubtedly the most important student First Amendment case in the nation's history." In *The Struggle for Student Rights*, a detailed examination of the *Tinker* case, John Johnson writes that the decision provided an important step forward in student rights and became one of the landmarks in the American history of freedom of expression. The case established a foundation from which many subsequent cases were decided.

In the U.S. Supreme Court opinion written by Justice Abe Fortas, it was held that the armband wearing was entirely distinct from actually or potentially disruptive conduct. Accordingly, it was characterized as being closely akin to "pure speech," which is entitled to protection under the First Amendment. The ruling also advanced rights in school settings. As Justice Fortas wrote, students and teachers do not "shed their constitutional rights to freedom of speech or expression at the schoolhouse gate." As the Supreme Court's case summary states, it appeared that the school authorities' attempt to prevent protests by enacting a policy designed to prevent them was based on an urgent wish to avoid any controversy that might result from the expression symbolized by the armbands. The particular symbol of black armbands was singled out for prohibition.

In addition, the case unfolded as antiwar sentiment was growing across the country. The ruling reinforced the notion that peaceable expression of minority viewpoints was, at minimum, to be tolerated. Reading Justice Black's dissenting Supreme Court opinion in that light is particularly instructive (see Court opinion excerpts at chapter's conclusion).

That this case originated in a community not known as a hotbed of civil unrest—and with youngsters known as anything but troublemakers—not only adds to its appeal, but is significant. In order for critical constitutional tests to arise, it is sometimes necessary for the laws or regulations that are passed in a conservative environment to be challenged by individuals—some of them courageous, all of them steadfast and ardent in their convictions.

Now, more than 30 years after the Supreme Court's ruling in their case, Mary Beth is a nurse practitioner in St. Louis; John is self-employed and living in Fayette, Missouri; and Chris is living in Florida where he has undertaken a variety of activities. Their attorney, Dan Johnston, is still practicing law, but now in New York City.

PRECURSOR TO PROTEST

The armband protest was by no means the first time that either the Tinkers or Chris Eckhardt had engaged in social activism. Each of their families was involved in a number of issues, including a 1965 demonstration in Washington against the Vietnam War. In addition to the peace movement, the families were also vocal in their support of civil rights. To some extent, their involvement in these causes stemmed from their religious beliefs. John and Mary Beth's father was a Methodist preacher. That, however, did not prevent them from being the subjects of ridicule and threats in their community.

MARY BETH TINKER: One Christmas Eve someone called and threatened to blow up our house that night. One day I was getting ready for school and a woman called and asked for me and I got on the phone and she said, "I'm going to kill you." Someone threw red paint at our house. Just stupid stuff like that. The community was generally not supportive of us, but again, that wasn't that new of an experience. My family had been on the outside of other things. I got yelled at for being a nigger-lover around the neighborhood. We weren't always the most popular for our views. There was sort of this feeling that we were just kind of nuts. Because there was a lot of feeling that [the protesting] was unpatriotic at that time.

DAN JOHNSTON: Their families were really subject to a lot of ridicule in the community, and even some sort of threatening conduct. If I remember right there was some graffiti on the house. Mrs. Tinker was a teacher at a college— a little liberal arts college—on the east side of Des Moines. And I think she was the subject of quite a lot of sarcastic criticism in the school there. They called her Tinker Bell—that was the pejorative name they called her.

Do you think perhaps in some way then, as this situation unfolded and as the case unfolded, that maybe that experience actually benefited you in some ways?

MARY BETH TINKER: Sure. I think all of that went together to set the stage. It strengthened me and I also had a feeling that even though we were unpopular with some people that there was a core of supporters, and that is what makes such a big difference. I think with a lot of kids— because I've been involved with kids over the years who have been in difficult situations in their own families and they have to stand up—and if they have even one person who is supportive, it can make a huge difference as opposed to being out there completely on your own. I think that's where it really takes courage.

People have called this a courageous thing to do, but compared to some other situations that kids find themselves in, I don't think it rates real, real, high in that way compared to some of the things I've read about over the years.

Is there an argument that it was in part at least because you were children or adolescents that this happened—that children in that kind of position have an even greater sense of courage than do adults, maybe in part because they have less to lose?

MARY BETH TINKER: Yeah, I think children do have sort of a natural sense of fairness sometimes. That was certainly in play with me, I know, because I just had such a gut reaction to what I'd see on TV in reaction to the Vietnam War and the graphic scenes. It was really the first war that was televised. As kids we'd come home and watch this stuff on TV. Kids do have a hard time understanding things like fleeing families—fleeing from little huts, and napalm—children being napalmed. It's pretty hard to make that congruous with what we are doing in our lives. That may be true. Kids do some wild things sometimes.

CHRIS ECKHARDT: I would go to a Biblical quote that a child shall lead us. I would agree with your assumptions that children have the ability to have more courage if they have good self-esteem, have good role models, have encouragement from adults. Kids, because of their fewer responsibilities, have the ability—the opportunity—to be more courageous if they so desire.

A lot of people I'm sure who hear about this case assume that the three of you, as children—mature children, no question but children nonetheless— were acting only in response to their parents' wishes and desires and how they wanted you to act. How do you respond to that?

CHRIS ECKHARDT: How do I respond to those people? They're trying to cop-out and say that young people aren't intelligent enough to have opinions.

JOHN TINKER: That's a hard issue to tackle. It's obviously true that we were influenced by our parents' opinions. We had access to information and opinions that most of the rest of the kids didn't have. So we were definitely influenced, but I think our opinions were sincerely held and that we did believe them ourselves and that we were impelled by our own beliefs.

DAN JOHNSTON: There really wasn't any evidence that the impetus of it came from the parents that I recall. Now, it may have, I don't know. But I deal with what the record is, and there wasn't any evidence of that in the record. My sense is that probably the mothers were more militant than the fathers were. And if it came from anywhere, it came from the mothers.

JOHN TINKER: We were kids, you know. So we agreed as a group of kids to do that. But it was our own decision. Our parents didn't say, "You should wear armbands today." In fact, my father was very hesitant to approve of wearing the armbands after the principals had prohibited them. It was really his thoughts—you know, he discussed it with us—and he kind of convinced me to hold off a day and to try to negotiate with them first. That's, personally, why I didn't wear it the first day. I was prepared to and ready to walk out the door and he was raising these questions. And so I decided that I'll wait. There's no rush on this. Our parents were not really encouraging us to do it or putting us up to do it. They supported us when we did it, though.

THE ARMBAND PROTEST

In mid-December of 1965, word was circulating in largely conservative Des Moines that a student protest against the Vietnam War was being planned. Reactions to these reports varied, from threats made by some students in an effort to discourage participation to school district principals making a rule prohibiting any protest.

While each of the plaintiffs-to-be shared a sense of pressure and tension when they wore their armbands, each had different experiences. Chris was confronted by the football team captain who wanted to rip the armband from his sleeve. Chris explained that he was on his way to the principal's office to turn himself in. Once there, he was detained and, in his view, threatened. Mary Beth's experience was less stressful, though she admits being nervous. John wore his armband the day after the others did largely because of the cautionary words from his father. The toughest part of it, he says, "was the realization that I was going to stick out and that people would be criticizing me." Once at school that day, he removed his jacket revealing the armband, and he was sent to the school office where he talked with the principal. Like his compatriots, he was suspended from school.

Is there an argument that while the basis—the essence—of your protest may have been okay, that it nevertheless clearly violated a rule that the school board had laid down?

JOHN TINKER: The other side of that is that if the rule that the school board laid down violates the Constitution, then their rule is not the controlling rule.

CHRIS ECKHARDT: The principals of the secondary schools of Des Moines did make that rule, and then the school board backed them up a couple of weeks after they made the rule. So, yeah, the schools definitely made a rule and, yeah, I definitely broke that rule, and I definitely did it with intent. That's what civil disobedience is about.

MARY BETH TINKER: Well, I think through history we've learned that sometimes you have to violate rules and challenge things. You can't always just accept the status quo. Sometimes you just have to break the rule. Sometimes it's important. The problem is in figuring out which is which.

What about the notion that the setting of the protest was key? In other words, is it really proper to use a public school as a forum in which to make this sort of protest?

CHRIS ECKHARDT: I think in a democracy it's the *best* place to make it. If we want to teach democracy and the true principles of our Constitution that we must respect the minority, what better place to do it than in the schools of America?

MARY BETH TINKER: The public schools are where we hopefully are creating citizens in a democracy who are familiar with the concepts of democracy and free speech is one of the major foundations in our democracy. So I can't think of a better place, really, to learn those kinds of lessons and to have that kind of discourse.

JOHN TINKER: The wearing of the armbands was really designed to be nondisruptive. We wanted to let people know that we thought differently about the war. Our opinion was different, and we thought it was important that we not just acquiesce to the standard opinion on that. So we chose a method. The armband was not disruptive. I think that it's *entirely* appropriate in a democracy that students learn early to express their opinions and to go against the flow a little bit—to express their opinions even if they differ from the majority opinion. My opinion is that it's a *positive* thing to have that sort of a protest, especially a protest that is designed to be respectful of the rights of society to certain levels of decorum and order. I think for a democracy, the sort of protest that we had is very healthy and was much needed because at the time schools were sort of little Fascist enclaves, in a way (laughs). It's so evident in listening to the oral arguments—the attitude projected by the lawyer for the school board. I just don't think that's the kind of a society that we want—the control and teaching kids early on to toe the line to whatever authority decides to tell you that you have to do, then that's what you have to do. I think that's very destructive to a democratic society.

THE DECISION TO LITIGATE

Local and national attention followed the armband protest. "We were interviewed by television stations and the *Des Moines Register*," John Tinker recalls. "And I think *Newsweek* interviewed us." Also interested in the situation was the Des Moines Independent Community School District board. It was in the wake of its meetings on the situation that the decision to litigate was first considered.

CHRIS ECKHARDT: The two school board meetings upheld [the suspension], and so once they upheld it, you've got a choice. They voted against us and said, "You can't do this." Well, by the time they said that—that was January 2nd—our game plan was only to go to January 1st [with the protest]. And then you recognize that they may not be right but they've got the might. So we went back to school.

Once you returned to school after the Christmas break, was there anything that you recall about that—a marked difference in attitude amongst your classmates, anything of that nature?

JOHN TINKER: Everyone was aware of it, and I was wearing all black, and so everybody was aware of that, too. The teachers—I don't know—there was an awareness of it. It did lead to some discussions. I was invited to speak to several civics classes just to present the antiwar point of view. It wasn't a big negative. I already had shaken off the social group that would judge me negatively by that. That had happened years ago. I wasn't a loner, rejected and isolated. It wasn't a negative thing. The worst part about it was just having to keep the lint off that black sweater (laughs). That's why I quit [wearing all black] at the end of that year and didn't do it the next year. It was too much hassle.

So these are the words that will go down in history—that the most difficult aspect of this entire ordeal was keeping the lint off your black clothes?

JOHN TINKER: (laughs) What I'm saying is I wasn't bearing a heavy social burden.

CHRIS ECKHARDT:  I became more popular, more of a leader. My social development skyrocketed [although] my girlfriend dropped me. Her father was a military man. I had basically been a studious, conscientious homeboy who stayed at home and studied, and went to school and worked. Then I started developing closer friends and going to parties and developing my social side. Teachers were nice to me. Students were nice to me. I was never hit or violated in any way. The worst that happened was on two occasions. A drunk who later became a benefactor called me a Communist. On another occasion another gentleman who became a friend was playing football and yelled out, "Hey peace-boy, why don't you come a play football with us?" with the overtones of, "We'll gang up on you good." My picture was in the paper and kids were seeing that. They may not have totally understood it, but it was like I became part of a social club.

MARY BETH TINKER: There were other students those days that wore armbands that were suspended from school who were not included in the case because their parents weren't with them. So they dropped out of the case.

CHRIS ECKHARDT: At that point we were consulting with attorneys. Dan Johnston and Norm Jesse were partners and Iowa Civil Liberties Union lawyers. The Iowa Civil Liberties Union offered support and we took it. They fronted some of the money that was necessary. Out of the five students that got suspended, just John, Mary Beth, and I were willing to go to court over it.

JOHN TINKER: The other kids that were kicked out of school didn't have support from their parents, although they may have had moral support, they couldn't participate in the suit because their parents had issues with their own work. It was considered that it would harm their chances to keep their job or get promoted. We were considered to be out on very thin ice, politically and socially.

CHRIS ECKHARDT: Well, approximately 60 students were planning to wear armbands. When the rule was made, I wore it, and Mary Beth wore it, and then John wore it. And then [other students] wore them. People who had scholarships were afraid of losing them. Other parents were not as supportive as mine and John and Mary Beth's.

MARY BETH TINKER: Their parents weren't supportive of them at all. For that reason their names aren't on the case. And they would have been otherwise.

DAN JOHNSTON: There was a law professor at Drake Law School named Craig Sawyer, and Craig had represented the Tinker and Eckhardt families in front of the school board. I think when it came time to file the lawsuit, both he and the law school felt it would be better if someone else did it. So he referred the families to me. I was probably less than one year out of law school.

JOHN TINKER: We were at this meeting during the Christmas period and I believe we contacted a law professor at Drake University named Craig Sawyer, who I believe was associated with the Iowa Civil Liberties Union. He thought we had a case. I believe that Dan Johnston volunteered to do it—to take the case—and the first time I met him was during our depositions when we went down to his office. I'm really quite impressed by his work with the case. He was really quite good. [Alan] Herrick, for the school board, in contrast, was not very good (laughs).

DAN JOHNSTON: You know, I don't think I ever considered saying "No" [to taking the case]. I don't think it was ever really an issue. I thought they had a good claim and the school board was clearly wrong. People who I knew on the school board, who I respected, had voted with the students. So it just seemed to me to be the right thing to do.

CHRIS ECKHARDT: I'd say the decision to go to court was made very quickly after—it was basically, I remember talking with Dad at the time because I wasn't happy with the school board's decision and it was a process—we've got to go through a process. He was a good mentor, he was a good advisor. I chilled and I went back to school. The decision was made probably within a week or two after the final school board decision when they voted 5-to-2 against us.

JOHN TINKER: [Dan Johnston] also separated the issue and made it clear—I know my mother was pushing to challenge the legality of the war, which was really reaching (laughs). And he was good and insistent that we deal with the free speech issue only. He was right, obviously.

DAN JOHNSTON: I think Mrs. Tinker felt the trial itself should get into issues of the legitimacy of the war. I was unwilling to do that. I didn't think that had anything to do with the issues that were really under the court's consideration. So I refused to do that. And there was a little tension, I think, between us about that, but nothing that ever jeopardized the relationship among us.

At what point did you see this as a freedom of expression issue?

JOHN TINKER: Actually right from the start. But that wasn't the main point of our wearing the armbands. And we talked about that among ourselves as it became classified as a freedom of expression issue. We discussed that that is actually taking the focus away from what was compelling us to wear them in the first place which was the war in Vietnam. But we also realized that the courts weren't going to deal with the issue of the war in Vietnam because of the armband incident. I was aware right from the start, because to me it was the same as if someone had worn a cross around their neck—lots of people had the little crosses that they'd wear around their neck—or political buttons or anything like that. In my mind it was exactly the same as that. If they were going to prohibit us from wearing an armband, then they were going to have to prohibit kids from wearing crosses to school because the armband was just simply an expression of what I believed. It wasn't disruptive. It was a passive symbol of something that I believed. I guess I knew enough about constitutional law at that point just due to civics classes and so on to know that you can't prohibit the expression of a belief because of the content of the belief. I really had an instinctive understanding right from the start. I really felt we were on good ground as far as First Amendment rights goes.

The First Amendment reads, "Congress shall make no law respecting an establishment of religion, or prohibiting the free exercise thereof; or abridging the freedom of speech, or of the press; of the right of the people peaceably to assemble, and to petition the Government for a redress of grievances." The free speech clause was central to this case given its ability to protect not just the spoken word, but also "symbolic speech"—actions that contain expressive elements.

At that time, were you of the mind that the act would be and was protected by the First Amendment?

CHRIS ECKHARDT: That was my belief, and that's what I explained to [school vice-principal Donald] Blackman. This is protected, this is constitutional and what you're doing is violating my constitutional rights. I was that youthful smart-ass that challenges authority and makes you question whether *your* values are right. When you're in a position of authority, you don't want to be challenged, especially by kids.

MARY BETH TINKER: We were pretty much aware of that even from the beginning. We talked about the fact that they had [previously] worn black armbands—I'm trying to remember which school it was—to mourn the death of school spirit. They did wear things like that all the time—buttons, pins, the Iron Crosses was a big one. We knew that kids were wearing stuff. Crosses, for example, not to mention Iron Crosses—even just a regular cross. We did kind of think it out logically that way from the beginning. If these other people could wear these things that sent a message, why couldn't we wear something that sent our message? What was the big difference?

THE TRIAL

Through their fathers, the students filed a complaint in the United States District Court for the Southern District of Iowa, requesting an injunction restraining the school authorities from disciplining them. They also sought nominal damages. The trial began on July 25, 1966.

JOHN TINKER: What I remember most was the lawyer for the school board [Allan Herrick]. It was evident that he was trying to frame it as having been a decision by our parents, and so I wanted to be clear—to make it clear—that it wasn't, that it was our own decision to wear the armbands. But that's the thing I remember most about the trial was that he was trying to develop a frame to present the situation that we had some kids here who were being manipulated by their parents. And so I was consciously making the point that that wasn't what was going on. I think the argument of the school board that the school has certain prerogatives to rule by dictate in certain issues—I think that was the argument that they made—and that's the argument that was accepted by Judge Stephenson.

Judge Roy L. Stephenson was the chief judge of the Southern District of Iowa for the U.S. District Court. Prior to being appointed to the federal bench in 1960, he had been an attorney and a Republican Party leader in Des Moines. He was 49 years old when he presided over the Tinker trial. He issued his opinion on September 1, 1966.

Did you ever suspect that the judge's political orientation had a bearing on the outcome of that trial?

JOHN TINKER: Uhh, yes (laughs). I thought there was an anti-Communism and sort of jingoistic attitude toward the war … Yeah, I think it was reflected in that. But the issue that was decided on was about school authority and how much authority does the school administration really have, and so in a sense, I thought it was fair. I mean, I thought the judgment was wrong, but I thought it was dealing with an appropriate issue.

DAN JOHNSTON: Judge Stephenson, who I liked a lot—he was really a good judge—but he was a brigadier general in the

Army and was a World War II veteran and he told me during this case, "I just can't understand what position these people are taking. I just don't get it." He had been Republican county chairman, I expect he was probably an Eisenhower appointment to the court, and he just didn't get it. And he cited all these Smith Act cases from the McCarthy era, most of which have never been overruled, but are never followed any more either—nobody pays any attention to them. And he cited all of those cases that were national security cases. It was just a bad piece of work. He was just completely blind to this whole thing.

And you're suggesting that his personal politics had a bearing on this?

DAN JOHNSTON: Yeah, I think it did. In an area that's this political, I think a judge's personal views—not partisan politics, certainly—but a judge's personal views certainly do affect how the judge is going to rule in the case.

CHRIS ECKHARDT: It was a two-day trial. I was on the stand the longest. My recollection there was saying how the vice-principal threatened me with a busted nose and him getting up and walking out of the courtroom. The courtroom itself was interesting and very formal, and over two days I listened to John, listened to Mary Beth, listened to myself. Then the judge's ruling, whenever it was—a month later—that schools must have a right to make rules, but that wasn't our argument or our case, because we didn't disagree with that. We agreed that schools must have a right to make rules and schools need to be orderly and conducive to learning, but that this one rule was in violation of the First Amendment and needed to be overturned. So that's when we appealed.

MARY BETH TINKER: Yeah, I do remember being in Des Moines at the depositions and being in court. My father was grilled, and I was real proud of him—his responses. Then we came to St. Louis and I was probably about 15.

THE APPEAL

The District Court found in favor of the defendants, upholding the constitutionality of the school authorities' action on the ground that it was reasonable in order to prevent a disruption of school discipline. That ruling was appealed to the Eighth Circuit Court of Appeals in St. Louis. The case was argued before a three-judge panel in April 1967, but when a decision could not be reached the court ordered a re-hearing before all eight of the court's judges—an en banc hearing—in October. The decision was issued on November 3, 1967.

MARY BETH TINKER: It was very exciting because I got to fly on an airplane for the first time. Going to stay with some friends in St. Louis. I was young. It was an exciting trip. I remember being concerned about what I was wearing and stuff like that—things that a kid would think about. Sort of a human side of it. I remember thinking about it—just silly stuff like that—how it was so exciting just to be able to come to St. Louis just for a trip.

JOHN TINKER: I'm just kind of blank on that. I think we got in real late that night, didn't get a lot of sleep. Other than the drive to the building, I don't really have a memory of the way the questioning went.

MARY BETH TINKER: In the court in St. Louis—let's see, I'm trying to remember where it was that I was on the stand. I can't remember if it was in Des Moines or in St. Louis, but I remember I was on the stand at one point. I don't really remember a whole lot about the specifics of it. The court—I don't remember a whole lot about what was said. I remember it being a big deal, and that I had to go on the stand at some point and sit in on these depositions. Luckily there were some adults there to help out.

CHRIS ECKHARDT: It went before the Eighth Circuit Court of Appeals in St. Louis. It went before three judges and the three judges ruled that it was important enough to go before all of them. At that time there was eight of them, and the eight split four-to-four.

DAN JOHNSTON: I was really surprised when the Court of Appeals didn't reverse Judge Stephenson. But he was a very popular judge down there, too. He would go down there and sit part-time on the Court of Appeals a lot, and I think they were reluctant to overrule him. I was surprised. There were two cases from Arkansas from the Fifth Circuit which involved students who were involved in voter registration efforts. And they had pins that signified participation in the voter registration effort. In both cases, the students had been suspended for bringing these pins to school. And in one of the cases, the record shows that the students had tried to forcibly put the pins on other students. In the other case there was none of that. And the Fifth Circuit had ruled for the students in the case where there was no force, and for the school in the case where there was force. Basically, we had those two cases in the Fifth Circuit and the Eighth Circuit suppressing our case which had no evidence of disruption in it. So it made for a lead pipe for certiorari in the Supreme Court.

Appellants file a writ of certiorari with the U.S. Supreme Court when they seek review of their case by the Court. At least four Justices must agree to grant the writ for the Court to hear the case. When a writ is granted, the lower court is ordered to certify the record and send it to the higher court. If a writ is denied, the court is refusing to hear the appeal and is saying, in effect, that the judgment below stands unchanged.

THE U.S. SUPREME COURT

When the eight judges in United States Court of Appeals for the Eighth Circuit split in their ruling, thereby affirming the lower court's ruling, the Tinkers, Eckhardt, and their attorney were left with one more decision—whether to appeal to the nation's highest court.

What was the decision-making process with regard to going to the U.S. Supreme Court?

DAN JOHNSTON: At that point the ACLU gets involved in making that decision. By that time I was involved in running for attorney general in Iowa. So I lost a little bit of control at that point. The ACLU looked at the case and reviewed it, and agreed to participate in it. So we worked together in presenting the case to the U.S. Supreme Court. The heavy lifting in that process is the petition for certiorari. Once you get certiorari granted then the briefs and the arguments are almost anticlimactic.

And you're suggesting that the ACLU was instrumental in that?

DAN JOHNSTON: Yep. They had a guy named David Ellenhorn who is still a lawyer here in New York write the cert. I reviewed it, I think, and made some suggestions, but he basically did the first and final drafts on that.

Wasn't there some talk at the time that the ACLU considered replacing you as the attorney of record at the Court?

DAN JOHNSTON: Yeah.

And how did that get resolved?

DAN JOHNSTON: That got resolved by the clients.

They said they wanted you to go the distance?

DAN JOHNSTON: Yeah.

CHRIS ECKHARDT: You've got to understand that when you get to that level then they pull in the ACLU. You're always going to have your politics of, "Well, you're a young boy of 28 and you've never been here before and now you're dealing with the big boys, so you better let us take it over." As far as our families were concerned, Dan had done us justice. Personally, it was like you've nurtured this baby, and now you're going to tell me I can't deliver it? No. You can advise, you can point me in the right direction, but I'm going to play the part and I'm going to follow it through. I don't think anyone could have done a better job. I think he did an excellent job.

Had you ever argued a case before the Supreme Court before?

DAN JOHNSTON: No.

Since?

DAN JOHNSTON: No. I was the county attorney—the county prosecutor—in Des Moines for about eight years, and we had a couple of cases that went to the Supreme Court, but I had the assistants who were handling those cases do the arguments.

CHRIS ECKHARDT: We did the writ of certiorari to the U.S. Supreme Court, and they decided to hear it. Then we went to Washington and watched Dan argue that, and sat in the front row. That was fascinating.

JOHN TINKER: Well, now there's another story. I missed a flight. My flight left at 11- something p.m. from Cedar Rapids and I fell asleep when I was sitting in the lounge there waiting for the plane. When I woke up I was the only one there. And the plane was gone. I couldn't believe that nobody had nudged me or something. This was to attend the oral arguments. I took the next flight early the next morning, and I was flying stand-by, and got bumped off that flight. And so when I finally got to Washington, it was all over.

CHRIS ECKHARDT: Just sitting there in the front row and ... I remember Mom was there and I was there and such a formal procedure watching them come in and sit down. I may sound egotistical, but I had a feeling that those judges knew that a couple of these young kids sitting in the front row might have been the plaintiffs in this case. I felt good about the questions they were asking. You get a little sheet of paper and it tells you who's who sitting in which chair. It was cold. It was in November, I think, when we went up there. I was in college and I went up there. It was impressive. Here's this stupid little thing of just wearing an armband and all of a sudden I'm in front of the United States Supreme Court. Wow! Who thought we'd get here? Who thought a little case from Des Moines over a little piece of cloth would end up here?

MARY BETH TINKER: I don't remember a whole lot about it. I remember being in Washington and seeing the important sites with my family. The image of the Justices is kind of there, but I really don't remember a lot about it. We had just moved to St. Louis. I was in the middle of 11th grade. Maybe I was just caught up in this personal stress of moving. And right after we moved is when we left for Washington. So that's the only thing I can think of.

CHRIS ECKHARDT: I enjoyed reading the judges, their body language, their questions, the shaking of their heads—the little things that they did. I was counting. I felt like we had the majority. I wasn't as politically astute then on the different Justices. [William] Douglas and Earl Warren. I didn't know Abe's background that well. I didn't know Thurgood Marshall's background as well as I do today, or the other Justices. So I couldn't read them, but I had a good feel. It was like I think—I think—we're going to get some justice finally on this. It was humorous. It is justice delayed is justice denied. The process took over three years, but it reinforced my belief in America, and in our court of laws, and in our society.

DAN JOHNSTON: Obviously I was nervous, although I wasn't nearly as nervous as I thought I would be. The ACLU lawyers the night before had some former clerks of the Supreme Court Justices run me through a moot court argument, and that helped quite a bit. Although the case is not that complex. The arguments are not that complex. And you just know. You know about the case. So it really is a policy argument. To the extent that I was nervous, I felt that Earl Warren would protect me from anything that could happen. He was sort of a large, grandfatherly, white-haired figure. One of the things I was surprised about was that you are at eye-level with the Court and pretty close to them. They're not sitting three or four feet above you, and you're just eyeball to eyeball with them. It really is a fairly intimate discussion that you're having with them.

CHRIS ECKHARDT: I think Marshall said it best when he asked Herrick, "So you mean to tell me that five or seven students out of a school system of 18,000 are going to upset the educational atmosphere?" And Herrick had to respond, "Yes." That was the basis of their case. It didn't cut mustard. In a politically charged atmosphere that the Vietnam War was, there were very few people at the time standing up and saying, "This should end." Thurgood Marshall just threw that one out and just shook his head at Herrick's response. It was a look of disgust. It was like, "That's pathetic. That's your argument? That's pathetic." Even the humor. The more we learn about history the better. I think Abe even voted against hearing the case, and yet he ended up writing the 11-page—what I consider—a beautifully worded document, his opinion. (See Court opinion excerpts at chapter's conclusion.)

DAN JOHNSTON: It's intimidating. But by the time you get there you're so familiar with your case. The thing you worry about, I suppose—and it's not a rational worry—but the thing you worry about it that some Justice will look at you and say, "Well, how about the case of such-and-such?" And it's a case that you don't know anything about. But the chances of that happening are almost nil. The argument was really a policy argument. The judges who participated mostly were [Hugo] Black and [Byron] White. White ended up voting for us, but Black—who'd always been one of my heroes—was really viscous in his argument. He was obviously trying to use up my time.

And you just had to constantly get back to the issue. He kept saying, "Who runs the school, the school board or the students?" Well, the answer to that is clearly the school board, but they have to run it consistent with the Constitution. And to continually ask that question ... It just wasn't very lawyer-like for Black to be doing that because the answer to his question was obvious, but it was an irrelevant issue. He certainly knew and agreed from his prior decisions that school boards were controlled by the Bill of Rights and the Constitution. But he'd gotten so old and crotchety that he really was hostile to demonstrations by that time. It was basically his view that speech as he defined it was absolute, but he defined speech more narrowly than most of the other Justices. And to him, this was not a First Amendment case, but a reasonableness case under the Fourteenth Amendment. There was evidence in the record of discrimination—that other kinds of political symbols were allowed. And one of the reasons that was emphasized the way it was in the record in the briefs was that I thought that was an argument that might get him—might get his vote. But I couldn't get it.

Do you recall when the issue—the question—of whether the armbands themselves were disruptive arose?

JOHN TINKER: That was a justification that the school administration used to forbid them—the *potential* that they would be disruptive. In the trial it came out that they had not actually been disruptive. There was no evidence introduced at the trial that they had been disruptive except for a very minor discussion in Mary Beth's math class. Chris had gone directly to the office when he came to school because he realized that he was going to be kicked out, so there was no disruption around that. In Mary Beth's case, the disruption was caused by the teacher who used it as an opportunity to lecture to the class about the wrongness of doing that. In my case there wasn't any disruption either. I just left class and went to the principal's office. So there wasn't any disruption in the court case. The lawyer for the school board argued there was a *potential* for disruption and referred to the SDS [Students for a Democratic Society] demonstrations happening in the rest of the country around us. The school board used it as they had the right to do a pre-emptive action because it could have become disruptive. The Court then in its decision said it's the school's responsibility to deal with the disruptive element, essentially, and not try to preempt it. There's a free speech issue.

DAN JOHNSTON: Well, it really wasn't an issue, because there wasn't any evidence that it was disruptive. It was kind of hard to get your head around what the school was saying. They seemed to be saying that they needed to have the absolute right to make rules and regulations, and to have the children obey those rules and regulations in order to maintain order in the school. They never made the case—with any degree of effort, at least— that there was any danger of disruption from these armbands. There was some evidence that was available to them of reaction by other students against the armbands, but none of the teachers who testified said that there was any really disruption in their class. One of the teachers, I think in a mathematics class that one of these three children was in, changed his subject discussion on one day to talk about the worn armbands. But that was the teacher's decision. But other than the fact that other students were expected to look at these armbands and think about what they represented, and that they were worn in the classroom, there wasn't any evidence really of disruption. As a matter of fact, I think Chris went right to the principal's office and never wore it in a class. I think Mary Beth may have worn hers part of the time, and John may have worn his part of the time during the day, but none of them wore them more than one day before they were suspended. And there really wasn't any evidence of disruption.

And, in fact, the record shows that this element of the case was part of the give-and-take between you and the Court during the oral arguments.

DAN JOHNSTON: Mostly Byron White. He just kept saying that they wore the armbands, they expected other students to see the armbands and think about the armbands, and they expected them to do that while they were supposed to be thinking about arithmetic or English or science or whatever class they were in. And if you read the transcript of the argument, White really did that in a way that was, I think, more suitable for a cross-examiner in a trial than a judge. He wouldn't let me answer, really. And finally Thurgood Marshall broke in with what I thought was the right answer, and that is that the prohibition was against them wearing the armbands in the hallways and in the cafeteria and in places like that, as well as just in the classroom.

CHRIS ECKHARDT: When we walked out, Dan was as high as a kite on the job he did and felt like we had won—felt like we had at least five votes and he did a good job and he had a right to be exhilarated. It was exhilarating for the rest of us, too.

REACTION TO THE RULING

The Supreme Court ruled 7-to-2 in favor of the students. As noted previously, the opinion by Justice Fortas held that the armband wearing here was neither actually nor potentially disruptive conduct. Thus, this act of symbolic speech ought to be granted First Amendment protection. The Court issued its ruling on February 24, 1969.

CHRIS ECKHARDT: I was in my dorm room and a Minneapolis reporter called me, asked me for my opinion, and I was caught off-guard, and I said, "What's up?" And he said, "You won." And I was ecstatic, and I said words to the effect of, "Far out." I thought it was great. And then that night—I was at Mankato University in Mankato, Minnesota—it was called Mankato State College back then—about 10 of [my friends from high school who] went to college there and I partied hearty. So it was wonderful.

MARY BETH TINKER: I remember that very well because I was in school in St. Louis and it was a very big deal. It was on the news. There were reporters at the school. They came to the chemistry class and they took pictures. There was some talk at the time of maybe being on the cover of *Time* magazine, or maybe *Newsweek*, I can't remember which—which didn't happen. But just the whole idea of it ... And I had just moved to this new school not too long before then, so I was still just getting adjusted to being there, and suddenly there was all this attention. It was really great, it was exciting that we won, but I had mixed feelings because I just wanted to fade into the woodwork a little more.

CHRIS ECKHARDT: I wanted to go back through the school. It was just for personal satisfaction (laughs). In approximately March of 1969 I came home from college and I walked through the halls of Roosevelt with that black armband on, and said hello to the vice-principal and that was the only other time I think I wore it.

JUSTICE BLACK'S DISSENTING OPINION

CHRIS ECKHARDT: I think what he said was, "This would be the beginning of permissiveness in America"—words to that effect. I thought, "Far out. It's about time. Let's go for it." Yeah, we need a little more permissiveness in America. That's the direction I come from. I think we need to allow people to express themselves however they choose as long as they don't hurt themselves or others. We don't need a police state and we don't need more laws or more prisons.

Justice Hugo Black's exact words were: "[I]t is the beginning of a new revolutionary era of permissiveness in this country fostered by the judiciary." Justice Black took his seat on the Supreme Court bench in 1937 and served until 1971. He was known as a free speech absolutist, having said with regard to the wording of the First Amendment, "'no law' means no law." His view, however, did not extend to symbolic speech, where he distinguished between speech and action.

So the very thing that Justice Black was lamenting, you celebrate.

CHRIS ECKHARDT: Absolutely.

JOHN TINKER: In Black's dissent, he criticized my father as having put us up to it, and referred to him as a defrocked Methodist minister, and it was really unfair. I realized that he really did not understand what it was.

DAN JOHNSTON: It was just mean. It was mean-spirited. I just thought it was sad, based upon what his history was as a Justice, for him to have stayed on the Court that long and write an opinion like that. This was really the last really significant First Amendment case for the Warren Court. The Court, subsequent to Earl Warren being Chief Justice, has followed this case, and has not overruled it, but I'm not sure this present Court would rule this way.

JOHN TINKER: I wonder if [Black] might have been on the defensive because of the protests that were going on around the country against the war. Society did appear to be greatly disrupted by the protests against the war, especially by the time the opinion was issued in 1969. I wonder if he wasn't on the defensive a little bit in saying, "No, I don't support the way this country is going in terms of the breakdown of order. I do not take the blame for the degenerative ways that the society has broken down, or that the license or the sense that anything goes." It was nondisruptive, it was respectful of the rights of the other people in the school, it was not just a naked rebellion. If society is unable to distinguish between freedom and license, that's an issue that we need to work on. But the idea that we should become little Fascists to avoid disruption, I think, is the worse of the two ways to go. I would rather see a kind of healthy confusion and a certain degree of chaos rather than the imposition of a Fascist type of authority. To me, the lockstep is much more dangerous. A lot of the other kind of disruption is really a kind of aesthetic deal. I do need to say that in terms of gang crime and the disruption of real order, the breakdown of civil society—obviously I'm against that. I just think it's important that people be able to divide the issue and to attack the real problem and not just think that to put a lid on everything to stifle the part of it that we don't like. I think it's an important distinction that society needs to make. What is the problem here? If the problem becomes freedom, then we really need to evaluate our national assumptions—what kind of nation we really are and not be hypocritical about it. I really do believe in freedom and believe that society as a whole really has a better understanding about the way things should be than does a society without freedom.

MARY BETH TINKER: I haven't noticed [a "new revolutionary era of permissiveness" in this country]. I think the problem with our schools isn't because there's too much free speech going on around current events. I don't see the real permissiveness. I've been stopped from speaking at schools because they were concerned about—Well, one school said that they were having too much of a gang problem and if I came there to speak, then it would give kids the idea that they could wear certain clothing that was prohibited and things like that. I've worked in the schools a lot myself—I've been in them as a volunteer nurse and in different capacities and I've never seen a big rash of permissiveness going on.

SURPRISES ABOUT THE JUDICIAL PROCESS

MARY BETH TINKER: That it took so long.

JOHN TINKER: I just didn't know enough about it to realize it would take that long. Yeah, I was surprised when we lost in the first court. I thought it was open and shut. Yeah, I was surprised it took so long.

CHRIS ECKHARDT: It took longer than I thought. [Pause] Other than that … It's formal, it's politically correct, no room for humor. It served me well, it served us well, and I think it served the country well.

JOHN TINKER: Now, I don't think it should be rushed. Now, I don't see that as an inordinately long period of time. In fact, I even think of it as kind of short. I think it is important that these things be well considered and referenced to precedent. That time gives people a chance to really research what the situation is and come up with a considered opinion.

SUBSEQUENT RULINGS

JOHN TINKER: The principle established by the armband case still stands and it's still as solid as ever. We were expressing basically pure political speech in a nondisruptive way. The freedom or the liberality that developed in the schools, the kind of the looseness— the falling of the dress codes, the haircuts, and all of that sort of thing—I've got several different layers of belief on this. I believe that it's important that freedom be encouraged and respected. If that means that people are going to punch rings through their eyebrows and noses and tongues and whatever, I can live with that, and I think the schools should live with that, too. If kids are going to wear colors or dressing styles, or whatever they want to do, I personally believe that that is good. When some action or behavior by anyone is patently designed to be disruptive then the disruption is a separate issue. And I think it's important that we learn to divide the issue between the freedom of speech and the freedom of expression components and the disruption components. It's sort of like the fighting words issue that, yes, you have freedom of speech, but no, you don't have freedom to provoke someone into violence or to threaten because the threat itself becomes the crime, the issue. I'm real happy with the armband case because it was nondisruptive, it was an expression of a political view, and it still stands. The *Hazelwood* case, they were able to win because [the school] owned the student newspaper. To me, the lesson there is if you want to make a protest, do it through your own media. Develop the media yourself, don't use a medium that is provided by the authority that you're critical of.

In the 1988 ruling in *Hazelwood School District v. Kuhlmeier,* the U.S. Supreme Court upheld the right of a school district to regulate content of a school-sponsored newspaper. The case is sometimes viewed as a step backward for students' First Amendment rights and an erosion of the Tinker ruling.

MARY BETH TINKER: You have to look at it in the historical perspective. There's progress, and then setbacks. Progress, and setbacks. I think we're still going forward, but there are always setbacks. There have been setbacks in the civil rights movement. But that doesn't mean that it's all lost.

CHRIS ECKHARDT: No, I would say *Hazelwood* and some other cases limited certain things, but at the same time—I'm not happy with that, I'm not happy that students have to go through drug testing if they want to play football. I'm not happy with that. I'm not happy with searches of student lockers. But our society has concerns and sometimes overreacts. [Our case] was not a hollow victory. It was a good victory. It's still utilized and quoted frequently in various cases even today, and used as a precedent. The point was our [protest] was nonviolent.

DAN JOHNSTON: I think history ebbs and wanes. I think that *Tinker* set a certain floor that the Court has not gone below. The argument that students do have First Amendment rights in the school—which was the second time that had been said—and this case was purer than the preceding case—makes it more difficult for the schools to do what they've tried to do. As a matter of fact, I've noticed cases and incidents that get reported in the newspaper which seem to me to be clear violations of *Tinker* that the students predominate in—the students prevail. The one case I looked at more closely was the student newspaper case—censorship of a school paper. But that's a more difficult issue because somebody always censors a newspaper, and it's the publisher and that's the right of the publisher to say what goes into a newspaper. So when the school becomes the publisher, then you can make an argument that the school has a right to decide what goes in there. And you can then question whether or not a school ought to be in the business of making a newspaper, or if it has a newspaper if it's really a newspaper because the idea of a newspaper, it seems to me, is a nongovernmental publisher. But [*Tinker*] was purely private conduct, and the students would have been wearing armbands whether they'd been in school or not, and they just happened to come at a time when they were in school.

IMPORTANCE & LESSONS

JOHN TINKER: I think it's important because it affects the students. It affects kids growing up in their developmental years. When I was a kid the relationship to authority was different. It was a much more authoritarian atmosphere. I think that that kind of atmosphere is going to lead to an authoritarian society generally, which is definitely not what I want. I think it's important for kids in their developmental period to have access to the real thing—to have access to elements of democracy and get some experience with them, and leave with the notion that it's normal. The right to express your opinion is not just a special thing that you do in a time of crisis, but that it's just a normal part of life and it's expected.

CHRIS ECKHARDT: I would say, as far as civil liberties, this is one of the top cases in the 20th century in America for civil liberties.

MARY BETH TINKER: Oh, I think it's pretty important in the fight for civil liberties, especially for children. Actually, it affected not only kids, but teachers. I think it strengthened the rights of teachers also, a little bit in the public schools. I think it's important. Anytime that the rights of kids are strengthened ... It's a precedent-setting case. It's important. At least those who seem to know think it is.

JOHN TINKER: Something that I think is important is when we talk about our country and what's the nature of our country, what's the character of our country, what brings us together, what makes us a nation, we have our principles—the Constitution, the Bill of Rights. And to me that's what we offer in explanation of who we are as a nation. I think that it's important that that not just be lip service, that that not just be a front that we offer people, that we offer the world and offer history, but that we really believe it. And if we really believe in democracy, that a country should be controlled—run, governed—by its citizens, then we really have to reconcile our behavior with that, and that includes how we raise our kids and how we participate. If we're going to claim to be of the people, by the people, and for the people—if that's the nature of our democracy—then we can't really shirk our responsibility as citizens to pay attention to what's going on and to make judgments about what's going on and then to work to be active, to try to promote our points of view. To me, in the armband case, the most important thing that comes out of that is that if we're going to have a democracy, then the kids should be taught that it's a democracy and should be offered the opportunity to participate, to practice being participants in a democracy. To have the school be as democratic as possible is an important thing *if* you really want a democracy. But sometimes I'm not too sure that that's what we really want. That's what I want, and I really am a believer, but sometimes I think that the democratic rhetoric is just a cover, that it's just lip service.

CHRIS ECKHARDT: The issue was an unpopular war, a wrong war, and an over-reaction on the part of some administrators and a conflict between those who would rather suppress creativity and freedom of expression against the minority and against principled, religious, ethical individuals who believe that they're doing what their Constitution says they can do, and some authoritarians who would rather have law and order instead of democracy. Well, I think if we had more democracy it would be a better society. I think the choice is, do we educate ourselves and our children more, or do we want to become a society that continues to build prisons? I prefer education.

MARY BETH TINKER: It was having to do with children's rights partly, and if it would have taken place in an adult setting, it would have been a whole different flavor. But the fact that it had to do with children and teenagers made it have to do largely with the rights of children and teenagers and the free speech of kids.

CHRIS ECKHARDT: I think that this will be remembered as a case that helped establish and continue the humanization of America. George [Washington] and the boys basically gave white male land-owners some rights, then Abe [Lincoln] comes along and gives some African-American males some rights, then the women come along in the 1920s and give women rights. I think *Tinker* helped give children and students some rights. I see that all as a progression—and a positive progression—more respect for each other and more understanding.

MARY BETH TINKER: In my mind it has to do with raising children to be citizens in a democracy. We have to have free, active discourse with kids and encourage them to be involved in current events and to ask questions and say things that may not be popular. That's the message in my mind, is that we have to encourage kids to put themselves out, to say things, to be involved in the discussion of where we're going with the country and the world. We really need the input of our kids to solve the problems of today which are numerous. We have a lot of creative kids out there and we want them to be involved. They're energetic and creative and we need that.

DAN JOHNSTON: I think the theme of the argument that I tried to make and the theme that Fortas picked up is that it's just not good educational policy to think that you can raise kids in a totalitarian environment. The argument I made went something like this: If we're going to have the schools be a totalitarian environment where freedom of expression can be suppressed for no good reason having anything to do with education and children are going to be in that environment for the first 12 [school] years of their lives—and then the boys are going to go into the military which is obviously a totalitarian environment—and then suddenly they become mature adults and if you want them to act freely as free, responsible citizens, it just doesn't make a lot of sense. If the school is the place where people learn to be adults, then the school to the fullest extent possible ought to mimic the adult society and all of its freedoms.

JOHN TINKER: When we went back to Roosevelt High School—they had us for a 25-year reunion—and the atmosphere in the school had just entirely changed, a 180 degree reversal. It used to be a real—I keep coming back to the word—Fascist, kind of a proto-Fascist—mentality. And when we went back it was more of a collegial atmosphere and it just seemed a lot more healthy. So I think knowing the armband case is there gives kids the support to say what's on their mind, and to know that they have some rights, too. They're not just subject to the rule of the school administration. They actually come into the situation with a certain negotiating position of their own. They have something to support them. Students do. And not just students, by the way. The armband case also affects teachers. People have a right to express their opinion in a nondisruptive way.

MARY BETH TINKER: I think kids can use this as a tool to stand up for themselves in the schools. And they certainly have used this. So I think there's been an impact. When I go around and talk to kids, they feel it personally. It encourages kids to see others who have done things like that. Personally, it keeps going.

DAN JOHNSTON: I think Fortas' opinion was such a good opinion that it really raised the level that any public body, but especially schools, have to meet anytime they're going to suppress expression by students. Another more immediate benefit is that, according to Sam Brown who was one of the people organizing the antiwar movement in those days, it really opened the schools to efforts to organize students to oppose the war. It really gave a good deal of impetus to the student movement against the war.

PERSONAL REFLECTIONS

Did you have any idea when you first decided to wear that armband what would have unfolded over the rest of your lifetime up until now?

JOHN TINKER: No (laughs). No, no. I don't think any of us had any inkling of how it would turn out. I think most of us thought we would win in the first court. It really was just an extraordinary set of circumstances that led it to be a Supreme Court case because if the appellate [court] had done anything but split the way it did—it split four-to-four, they were short one judge. So if we could have won it at the appellate court, or we could have lost it at the appellate court, but with the split it became more likely that the Supreme Court would hear it. No, it seemed like an amazing thing the way it all worked out.

CHRIS ECKHARDT: No, no, no. Not at all. You know, I didn't expect them to back down when I walked into school with my armband on, but I actually thought in my own head that the school board would recognize that this was not necessary—suspending kids for expressing a political view when we allow [students] to wear Jewish stars of David, crucifixes, Iron Crosses, political buttons, etc., etc. And doing it peaceably and not disturbing anybody ... I thought they would see that this is not a threat to the educational atmosphere. So, no.

MARY BETH TINKER: Oh no. No, no. Not at all. I really didn't have any idea for a long, long time. I actually shied away from that whole part of it for years because personally I guess I just—it was uncomfortable in some way to be in the spotlight like that, especially as a teenager. But then as I got older and matured more I felt that this is an important thing and if I can use myself to promote the rights of students, I'm glad to do it.

JOHN TINKER: No, no I don't think so. Although my memory is quite strong that I did feel that we were right. I did have an intuitive feeling. It's back to that notion that if they tell us we can't wear our armband then they have to tell that person they can't wear their cross.

MARY BETH TINKER: For some reason—I have never completely understood this—the "Mary Beth Tinker" of the case has stood out, and I'm not sure why. But for some reason a lot of groups have focused on me. I don't know if it was because I was real young, or what it is. Or if it's the name "Tinker" on the case. But then my brother, John, was on the case, too. So personally, yeah, it's been a big thing for me and I used to really shy away from it, but like I said, I decided finally that if I can be a tool through this fluke of history, that if I can use myself in some positive way, that I should.

Personally, what has been the effect on you?

CHRIS ECKHARDT: I've taken constitutional law classes at the University of Florida and found that the teacher even uses the case. I remember going up to the teacher afterwards and saying, "That's me, by the way." Since then, she's had me come to a couple of her classes and give talks when they get to that part. Since then I've been a guest speaker a few times at the University of South Florida talking to groups, talking to students in San Francisco, and talking to students in Boston.

JOHN TINKER: I've had a chance to talk to a lot of people. People do interview me. I've had a lot of students interview me. I've spoken to a number of classes about it. And that's been a very enriching experience in my life. It's given me a window on the world that I feel privileged to have. There are lots of contacts like that that have really enriched my life. The negative side—I can't really think of one. I really don't see it in negative terms.

MARY BETH TINKER: To 99% of the people that I encounter I'm just the neighbor, Lenny's mom, the nurse. I was working at the VA when the *Hazelwood* case came out, and there was a big article about student rights and it said, "Mary Beth Tinker"—you know, the case had mentioned me. And I was reading the paper at a break, and I said to the other nurses, "Look, that's me." And they said "Oh, yeah, right." "No, really that was me." "Yeah, right." That was kind of the end of it. It just never comes up.

How often do you think of these events? Is there a day that goes by that it doesn't flash through your mind in some way?

CHRIS ECKHARDT: Few. But it was 30 years ago, and life goes on. I'm proud of what I did and I'm proud of what I've done since then—being a reporter, being a TV personality, for 20 years being a counselor of children and adults, working in maximum security with juvenile offenders, working in an open setting with abused and neglected and sexually abused children in residential treatment centers. You end up touching a lot of lives—we all do. It's like Jimmy Stewart in "It's A Wonderful Life." What would've happened if you hadn't been here? I consider myself blessed in many ways. I consider myself to have a guardian angel.

Would you do this again? Was it worth it?

CHRIS ECKHARDT: Oh, absolutely. Without a doubt.

JOHN TINKER: You know, looking back on it, yes, it was worth it, and, yes, I would hope that I would do it again. I realize that there are a lot of cases where I don't do what I think I should do because I'm not willing to take what the cost is going to be at that moment. So I can only say that I would hope that I would do it again. I certainly don't regret it. It stands as something that I'm proud of in my life. Yes, I would do it again if I could scrape together the courage (laughs).

MARY BETH TINKER: Oh sure. I went to a conference of students in the press in Washington. They were giving awards to people who'd written articles about students around the world. Some of these kids had done the most incredible things. One had fought during the Holocaust, one girl had challenged a policy in Sri Lanka, I think, where the girls would get attacked if they didn't marry a certain boy. They would throw acid in these girls' faces, and this girl had stood up. Kids in the civil rights movement, American Indian kids—they had some examples of things those kids had done to stand up for their people. They've really suffered. They have sacrificed physically or materially and we didn't really have to do that. There was no loss of life or limb. We had a few threats on our lives, but ...

You have a youngster of your own. Would you encourage him to partake in this sort of activity?

MARY BETH TINKER: (laughs) Oh yeah, depending on what it's about. I mean, I have my own personal views. He wears these T-shirts to school. They're semi-obscene. I don't approve of that. I don't believe there should be obscenity in the schools. I guess I'm kind of conservative in that way.

And how is that different from what you did?

MARY BETH TINKER: A lot of kids come up to me when I'm speaking and they have an example of something that has been bothering them. Oh, they won't serve enough hamburgers in the school. And I think that's important. If it's important to them, that's how things can get started. There is a list of priorities in life, and I think those are a little more important. There's kind of a funny thing: When my son was in about seventh grade he went to school and he threw an eraser at the teacher. And he was suspended and placed in detention. And he asked the principal who was in there watching the kids in detention that day, "Have you ever heard of *Tinker*?" And she told me this story later—she was taking an education class at the time, and she said, "Yeah, as a matter of fact I have"—and he said "Well, that's my mom." And she said, "That's not going to help you any, so just forget it."

So he's aware of and understands what you did?

MARY BETH TINKER: He thinks it's a good thing—a good role model. I've had a chance to talk to his friends a little bit over the years about it. The fact that it's somebody's mom makes it not that, you know—they think it's interesting. I sat down last summer with him and watched this video that was made about this case and the *Miranda* decision, and there was the flag burning case, the school prayer. So we sat down and watched it and talked about it. He thinks it's interesting.

How does that feel when you see you and your case lumped together with other landmark cases, and to know that you're categorized with those?

MARY BETH TINKER: (laughs) Well, I'm honored. I feel honored. It's just a funny thing that I've learned that ordinary people can have an impact. It's just a fluke of history that there are these historical moments and ordinary people are just going along like we were. We certainly didn't set out to do anything like that. I think in some of the major court cases in history, the plaintiffs were very simple. They were just out trying to buy a house in a neighborhood or whatever, and it turns out to be a major decision. There was a kid in this video who they interviewed—they had a group of kids who were talking about all the different cases—and this girl said, "Yeah, Mary Beth Tinker, she wore an armband. Mary Beth Tinker rocks!" And I thought, boy, I have made it to the pinnacle now. That is an honor. If some kid somewhere thinks that I rock because of this, hey, that's great.

John Tinker, Mary Beth Tinker, and Chris Eckhardt.

Tinker, et al. v. Des Moines Independent Community School District, et al.

SUPREME COURT OF THE UNITED STATES

---

393 U.S. 503
Argued: November 12, 1968
Decided: February 24, 1969

Fortas, J., delivered the opinion of the Court with which Stewart, J. and White, J. concurred. Black, J. and Harlan, J. dissented.

COUNSEL: Dan L. Johnston argued the cause for petitioners. With him on the brief were Melvin L. Wulf and David N. Ellenhorn.

Allan A. Herrick argued the cause for respondents. With him on the brief were Herschel G. Langdon and David W. Belin.

Charles Morgan, Jr., filed a brief for the United States National Student Association, as amicus curiae, urging reversal.

MR. JUSTICE FORTAS delivered the opinion of the Court.

...

I.

...

As we shall discuss, the wearing of armbands in the circumstances of this case was entirely divorced from actually or potentially disruptive conduct by those participating in it. It was closely akin to "pure speech" which, we have repeatedly held, is entitled to comprehensive protection under the First Amendment.

...

First Amendment rights, applied in light of the special characteristics of the school environment, are available to teachers and students. It can hardly be argued that either students or teachers shed their constitutional rights to freedom of speech or expression at the schoolhouse gate. This has been the unmistakable holding of this Court for almost 50 years....

...

On the other hand, the Court has repeatedly emphasized the need for affirming the comprehensive authority of the States and of school officials, consistent with fundamental constitutional safeguards, to prescribe and control conduct in the schools.

...

Our problem lies in the area where students in the exercise of First

Amendment rights collide with the rules of the school authorities.

II.

...

The school officials banned and sought to punish petitioners for a silent, passive expression of opinion, unaccompanied by any disorder or disturbance on the part of petitioners. There is here no evidence whatever of petitioners' interference, actual or nascent, with the schools' work or of collision with the rights of other students to be secure and to be let alone. Accordingly, this case does not concern speech or action that intrudes upon the work of the schools or the rights of other students.

Only a few of the 18,000 students in the school system wore the black armbands. Only five students were suspended for wearing them. There is no indication that the work of the schools or any class was disrupted. Outside the classrooms, a few students made hostile remarks to the children wearing armbands, but there were no threats or acts of violence on school premises.

The District Court concluded that the action of the school authorities was reasonable because it was based upon their fear of a disturbance from the wearing of the armbands. But, in our system, undifferentiated fear or apprehension of disturbance is not enough to overcome the right to freedom of expression. Any departure from absolute regimentation may cause trouble. Any variation from the majority's opinion may inspire fear. Any word spoken, in class, in the lunchroom, or on the campus, that deviates from the views of another person may start an argument or cause a disturbance. But our Constitution says we must take this risk ... and our history says that it is this sort of hazardous freedom—this kind of openness—that is the basis of our national strength and of the independence and vigor of Americans who grow up and live in this relatively permissive, often disputatious, society.

In order for the State in the person of school officials to justify prohibition of a particular expression of opinion, it must be able to show that its action was caused by something more than a mere desire to avoid the discomfort and unpleasantness that always accompany an unpopular viewpoint. Certainly where there is no finding and no showing that engaging in the forbidden conduct would "materially and substantially interfere with the requirements of appropriate discipline in the operation of the school," the prohibition cannot be sustained.

In the present case, the District Court made no such finding, and our independent examination of the record fails to yield evidence that the school authorities had reason to anticipate that the wearing of the armbands would substantially interfere with the work of the school or impinge upon the rights of other students. Even an official memorandum prepared after the suspension that listed the reasons for the ban on wearing the armbands made no reference to the anticipation of such disruption. On the contrary, the action of the school authorities appears to have been based upon an urgent wish to avoid the controversy which might result from the expression, even by the silent symbol of armbands, of opposition to this Nation's part in the conflagration in Vietnam. It is revealing, in this respect, that the meeting at which the school principals decided to issue the contested regulation was called in response to a student's statement to the journalism teacher in one of the schools that he wanted to write an article on Vietnam and have it published in the school paper. The student was dissuaded.

It is also relevant that the school authorities did not purport to prohibit the wearing of all symbols of political or controversial significance. The record shows that students in some of the schools wore buttons relating to national political campaigns, and some even wore the Iron Cross, traditionally a symbol of Nazism. The order prohibiting the wearing of armbands did not extend to these. Instead, a particular symbol—black armbands worn to exhibit opposition to this Nation's involvement in Vietnam—was singled out for prohibition. Clearly, the prohibition of expression of one particular opinion, at least without evidence that it is necessary to avoid material and substantial interference with schoolwork or discipline, is not constitutionally permissible.

In our system, state-operated schools may not be enclaves of totalitarianism. School officials do not possess absolute authority over their students. Students in school as well as out of school are "persons" under our Constitution. They are possessed of fundamental rights which the State must respect, just as they themselves must respect their obligations to the State.

In our system, students may not be regarded as closed-circuit recipients of only that which the State chooses to communicate. They may not be confined to the expression of those sentiments that are officially approved. In the absence of a specific showing of constitutionally valid reasons to regulate their speech, students are entitled to freedom of expression of their views.

...

The principle of these cases is not confined to the supervised and ordained discussion which takes place in the classroom. The principal use to which the schools are dedicated is to accommodate students during prescribed hours for the purpose of certain types of activities. Among those activities is personal intercommunication among the students. This is not only an inevitable part of the process of attending school; it is also an important part of the educational process. A student's rights, therefore, do not embrace merely the classroom hours. When he is in the cafeteria, or on the playing field, or on the campus during the authorized hours, he may express his opinions, even on controversial subjects like the conflict in Vietnam, if he does so without "materially and substantially interfer-[ing] with the requirements of appropriate discipline in the operation of the school" and without colliding with the rights of others. But conduct by the student, in class or out of it, which for any reason—whether it stems from time, place, or type of behavior—materially disrupts classwork or involves substantial disorder or invasion of the rights of others is, of course, not immunized by the constitutional guarantee of freedom of speech.

Under our Constitution, free speech is not a right that is given only to be so circumscribed that it exists in principle but not in fact. Freedom of expression would not truly exist if the right could be exercised only in an area that a benevolent government has provided as a safe haven for crackpots. The Constitution says that Congress (and the States) may not abridge the right to free speech. This provision means what it says. We properly read it to permit reasonable regulation of speech-connected activities in carefully restricted circumstances. But we do not confine the permissible exercise of First Amendment rights to a telephone booth or the four corners of a pamphlet, or to supervised and ordained discussion in a school classroom.

If a regulation were adopted by school officials forbidding discussion of the Vietnam conflict, or the expression by any student of opposition to it anywhere on school property except as part of a prescribed classroom exercise, it would be obvious that the regulation would violate the constitutional rights of students, at least if it could not be justified by a showing that the students' activities would materially and substantially disrupt the work and discipline of the school.... In the circumstances of the present case, the prohibition of the silent, passive "witness of the armbands," as one of the children called it, is no less offensive to the Constitution's guarantees.

As we have discussed, the record does not demonstrate any facts which might reasonably have led school authorities to forecast substantial disruption of or material interference with school activities, and no disturbances or disorders on the school premises in fact occurred. These petitioners merely went about their ordained rounds in school. Their deviation consisted only in wearing on their sleeve a band of black cloth, not more than two inches wide. They wore it to exhibit their disapproval of the Vietnam hostilities and their advocacy of a truce, to make their views known, and, by their example, to influence others to adopt them. They neither interrupted school activities nor sought to intrude in the school affairs or the lives of others. They caused discussion outside of the classrooms, but no interference with work and no disorder. In the circumstances, our Constitution does not permit officials of the State to deny their form of expression.

...

Reversed and remanded.

MR. JUSTICE STEWART, concurring.

Although I agree with much of what is said in the Court's opinion, and with its judgment in this case, I cannot share the Court's uncritical assumption that, school discipline aside, the First Amendment rights of children are co-extensive with those of adults.

...

MR. JUSTICE BLACK, dissenting.

The Court's holding in this case ushers in what I deem to be an entirely new era in which the power to control pupils by the elected "officials of state supported public schools ... " in the United States is in ultimate effect transferred to the Supreme Court.

...

Assuming that the Court is correct in holding that the conduct of wearing armbands for the purpose of conveying political ideas is protected by the First Amendment ... the crucial remaining questions are whether students and teachers may use the schools at their whim as a platform for the exercise of free speech— "symbolic" or "pure"—and whether the courts will allocate to themselves the function of deciding how the pupils' school day will be spent. While I have always believed that under the First and Fourteenth Amendments neither the State nor the Federal Government has any authority to regulate or censor the content of speech, I have never believed that any person has a right to give speeches or engage in demonstrations where he pleases and when he pleases.

...

While the record does not show that any of these armband students shouted, used profane language, or were violent in any manner, detailed testimony by some of them shows their armbands caused comments, warnings by other students, the poking of fun at them, and a warning by an older football player that other, nonprotesting students had better let them alone. There is also evidence that a teacher of mathematics had his lesson period practically "wrecked" chiefly by disputes with Mary Beth Tinker, who wore her armband for her "demonstration." Even a casual reading of the record shows that this armband did divert students' minds from their regular lessons, and that talk, comments, etc., made John Tinker "self-conscious" in attending school with his armband. While the absence of obscene remarks or boisterous and loud disorder perhaps justifies the Court's statement that the few armband students did not actually "disrupt" the classwork, I think the record overwhelmingly shows that the armbands did exactly what the elected school officials and principals foresaw they would, that is, took the students' minds off their classwork and diverted them to thoughts about the highly emotional subject of the Vietnam war. And I repeat that if the time has come when pupils of state-supported schools, kindergartens, grammar schools, or high schools, can defy and flout orders of school officials to keep their minds on their own schoolwork, it is the beginning of a new revolutionary era of permissiveness in this country fostered by the judiciary. The next logical step, it appears to me, would be to hold unconstitutional laws that bar pupils under 21 or 18 from voting, or from being elected members of the boards of education.

The United States District Court refused to hold that the state school order violated the First and Fourteenth Amendments. Holding that the protest was akin to speech, which is protected by the First and Fourteenth Amendments, that court held that the school order was "reasonable" and hence constitutional.

· · ·

I deny, therefore, that it has been the "unmistakable holding of this Court for almost 50 years" that "students" and "teachers" take with them into the "schoolhouse gate" constitutional rights to "freedom of speech or expression."

· · ·

The truth is that a teacher of kindergarten, grammar school, or high school pupils no more carries into a school with him a complete right to freedom of speech and expression than an anti-Catholic or anti-Semite carries with him a complete freedom of speech and religion into a Catholic church or Jewish synagogue. Nor does a person carry with him into the United States Senate or House, or into the Supreme Court, or any other court, a complete constitutional right to go into those places contrary to their rules and speak his mind on any subject he pleases. It is a myth to say that any person has a constitutional right to say what he pleases, where he pleases, and when he pleases. Our Court has decided precisely the opposite.

...

In my view, teachers in state-controlled public schools are hired to teach there.... [C]ertainly a teacher is not paid to go into school and teach subjects the State does not hire him to teach as a part of its selected curriculum. Nor are public school students sent to the schools at public expense to broadcast political or any other views to educate and inform the public. The original idea of schools, which I do not believe is yet abandoned as worthless or out of date, was that children had not yet reached the point of experience and wisdom which enabled them to teach all of their elders. It may be that the Nation has outworn the old-fashioned slogan that "children are to be seen not heard," but

one may, I hope, be permitted to harbor the thought that taxpayers send children to school on the premise that at their age they need to learn, not teach.

...

Iowa's public schools ... are operated to give students an opportunity to learn, not to talk politics by actual speech, or by "symbolic" speech. And, as I have pointed out before, the record amply shows that public protest in the school classes against the Vietnam war "distracted from that singleness of purpose which the State [here Iowa] desired to exist in its public educational institutions." Here the Court should accord Iowa educational institutions the same right to determine for themselves to what extent free expression should be allowed in its schools as it accorded Mississippi with reference to freedom of assembly. But even if the record were silent as to protests against the Vietnam war distracting students from their assigned class work, members of this Court, like all other citizens, know, without being told, that the disputes over the wisdom of the Vietnam war have disrupted and divided this country as few other issues ever have. Of course students, like other people, cannot concentrate on lesser issues when black armbands are being ostentatiously displayed in their presence to call attention to the wounded and dead of the war, some of the wounded and the dead being their friends and neighbors. It was, of course, to distract the attention of other students that some students insisted up to the very point of their own suspension from school that they were determined to sit in school with their symbolic armbands.

Change has been said to be truly the law of life but sometimes the old and the tried and true are worth holding. The schools of this Nation have undoubtedly contributed to giving us tranquility and to making us a more law-abiding people. Uncontrolled and uncontrollable liberty is an enemy to domestic peace. We cannot close our eyes to the fact that some of the country's greatest problems are crimes committed by the youth, too many of school age. School discipline, like parental discipline, is an integral and important part of training our children to be good citizens— to be better citizens. Here a very small number of students have crisply and summarily refused to obey a school order designed to give pupils who want to learn the opportunity to do so. One does not need to be a prophet or the son of a prophet to know that after the Court's holding today some students in Iowa schools and indeed in all schools will be ready, able, and willing to defy their teachers on practically all orders. This is the more unfortunate for the

schools since groups of students all over the land are already running loose, conducting break-ins, sit-ins, lie-ins, and smash-ins. Many of these student groups, as is all too familiar to all who read the newspapers and watch the television news programs, have already engaged in rioting, property seizures, and destruction. They have picketed schools to force students not to cross their picket lines and have too often violently attacked earnest but frightened students who wanted an education that the pickets did not want them to get. Students engaged in such activities are apparently confident that they know far more about how to operate public school systems than do their parents, teachers, and elected school officials. It is no answer to say that the particular students here have not yet reached such high points in their demands to attend classes in order to exercise their political pressures.

Turned loose with lawsuits for damages and injunctions against their teachers as they are here, it is nothing but wishful thinking to imagine that young, immature students will not soon believe it is their right to control the schools rather than the right of the States that collect the taxes to hire the teachers for the benefit of the pupils. This case, therefore, wholly without constitutional reasons in my judgment, subjects all the public schools in the country to the whims and caprices of their loudest-mouthed, but maybe not their brightest, students. I, for one, am not fully persuaded that school pupils are wise enough, even with this Court's expert help from Washington, to run the 23,390 public school systems in our 50 States. I wish, therefore, wholly to disclaim any purpose on my part to hold that the Federal Constitution compels the teachers, parents, and elected school officials to surrender control of the American public school system to public school students. I dissent.

2   R.A.V. v. City of St. Paul, Minnesota

"It was fate. I have in the past wondered how it happened in that sense, how the hand of fate put me in that position.... I felt it was professionally a gift of sorts from a superior being, I suppose. Not in the sense that it enriched me financially in any sense because it certainly didn't, but because it was probably every lawyer's dream in an intellectual exercise. And I got to do it."

—Edward J. Cleary, co-counsel in *R.A.V. v. City of St. Paul*

"Am I crazy, or is this unconstitutional?" With those words, attorney Edward J. Cleary embarked on a journey that would take him through a maelstrom of issues, gross misperceptions and misunderstandings by members of the public, and culminating with his eloquent presentation before the U.S. Supreme Court and a unanimous ruling in his favor. Cleary's question about constitutionality, directed to co-counsel Michael F. Cromett, concerned the St. Paul Bias-Motivated Crime Ordinance. That law read:

> Whoever places on public or private property a symbol, object, appellation, characterization or graffiti, including, but not limited to, a burning cross or Nazi swastika, which one knows or has reasonable grounds to know arouses anger, alarm or resentment in others on the basis of race, color, creed, religion or gender commits disorderly conduct and shall be guilty of a misdemeanor.

Cleary's newest client, Robert A. Viktora (R.A.V.), had just been charged with violating that ordinance. On the first day of summer in 1990, R.A.V. was one of several teenagers who burned a crudely made cross on the front lawn of Russell and Laura Jones, an African-American family in St. Paul, Minnesota. Ed Cleary, an attorney on contract with the Ramsey County Public De-

44

fender's office, was assigned the case. Within minutes of receiving the case file, he began to question the constitutionality of the ordinance.

R.A.V. v. St. Paul was—and in many ways remains—a controversial and highly charged case. Any case that has a racist act of expression at its core tends to engender controversy. Add to the mix an attorney who sees something wrong with the law that the cross-burner is charged with violating—and who then tries to right it—and fuel is only added to the fire. Even the members of the U.S. Supreme Court, unanimous in their belief that the ordinance was unconstitutional, were sharply divided and passionate in their convictions as to the reasons why. As Justice Antonin Scalia wrote for the Court, there is no mistaking that burning a cross in someone's front yard is "reprehensible." No one, including R.A.V.'s attorneys, ever defended that act. What was on trial as much as the defendant himself, however, was the St. Paul Bias-Motivated Crime Ordinance. As structured, it was constitutionally flawed. According to Justice Scalia's opinion of the Court, it was a law that not only attempted to silence speech on the basis of its content; it also endorsed some viewpoints by prohibiting others. It was a law that at its core was in direct conflict with the spirit of the First Amendment because it tried to limit thought (and the expression of it) to those deemed "acceptable" by a majority. Moreover, it was a law that St. Paul prosecutors did not have to use in this case given that they had at their disposal other measures less intrusive of First Amendment rights to prosecute R.A.V.

When Ed Cleary was interviewed for this book, he was director of the Minnesota office of Lawyers Professional Responsibility, a quasi-judicial arm of the Minnesota Supreme Court which essentially regulates the 22,000 lawyers in that state. Mike Cromett was a Minnesota assistant state public defender. Attempts to contact Rob Viktora were unsuccessful. As Cleary says, however, after the cross-burning incident occurred, the story was no longer about R.A.V. or what he did. "It's an issue much larger than the incident itself," he said. It is an issue that encompasses the constitutionality of laws that attempt to regulate whether particular viewpoints are expressed.

GETTING THE CASE

ED CLEARY:

The very first awareness of the incident came early morning one day when I went out to get the paper on my step—I was getting ready for work—and it was a headline up here because that type of activity—that is to say, cross burning on someone's lawn—was to my way of thinking virtually unheard of up here, although I heard from others later that it wasn't as isolated as I thought. But in any case, that was the first I'd heard of it. It was splashed on the front page of the daily newspaper up here. I think that was on perhaps a Friday, and then I happened to have court on Monday, and just happened to be given the petition—which is what it's called when it's an underage person—charging him with the cross-burning violation. I wasn't too pleased, as I recall.

MICHAEL F. CROMETT: I received a call around noon time on the day that R.A.V. first appeared in juvenile court. Ed gave me a call and said, "What do you think about this ordinance that they've charged him with?" And so we talked about it a little bit. And that was the first that I became aware of it. We'd known each other a long time, but I guess three or four years earlier we had teamed up to represent an individual charged with first-degree murder and we tried the case for three-and-a-half or four weeks. I think I asked him to help me represent that client, and then when he got his murder case, he asked me to help him. And we kinda began that kind of relationship. So probably over the three years before that—three-and-a-half years—we were pretty close.

ED CLEARY: Because I was the attorney on intake that morning, I got the case. It was just that simple. Had I been on Tuesday instead of Monday, I wouldn't have been on the file, and I certainly wouldn't have reached out for it. It was fate. I have in the past wondered how it happened in that sense, how the hand of fate put me in that position. I know a number of lawyers early on consistently said things like, "Better you than me" because of the impact of hours and so forth that was taking place. And nobody at that time, of course, knew where it was going. So at first I felt burdened by it. Later I felt it was professionally a gift of sorts from a superior being, I suppose. Not in the sense that it enriched me financially in any sense because it certainly didn't, but because it was probably every lawyer's dream in an intellectual exercise. And I got to do it.

MICHAEL CROMETT: There was never any question that it was Ed's case and I was helping him. And that was fine with me. I had the best of both worlds—being involved in a case like that and not having the pressure on me to do the argument. Ed had more time and spent more time getting geared up for the First Amendment. I'd done a lot of criminal appellate work, but only tangentially had I been involved with the First Amendment, and that

was a long time ago. I don't know that I would have
had the time to become a First Amendment expert
which I think Ed did. So there was never any question
about that.

ED CLEARY: So that's when I first became aware, was when I read
the petition—that is, when I first became aware of
the details. That was also my first conversation with
Mr. Viktora. [H]e was a very slight young man and at
that point had a shaved head and we just exchanged a
few words. He was a troubled—clearly *appeared* to be
troubled, just physically. And bright. And inquisitive,
and angry. Clearly not of the intelligence level that I
was used to perhaps in some of the juveniles that I
represented over there. He grasped some concepts
relatively quickly that others wouldn't, I think. But he
was clearly confused and angry, probably the classic
rebellious kid that gets in this kind of trouble. I guess
past that point, we never established the kind of relationship that we ever saw each other outside of the
courtroom situation or consultations or my office, of
course. [H]e held some very unpopular views and was
a very angry and misguided young man. The emotion I
probably felt most was saddened, which is generally
how I feel when you go from that initial emotion of an
ger when somebody holds a view different than your
own, and then generally you think "What, a waste."
But I was never intimidated. Nor, frankly, was he ever
intimidated by me, I don't think.

Cleary had minimal contact with R.A.V.'s parents. Both of them, he
says, were concerned about their son, and they were cooperative
throughout the legal process. He kept them informed as best he could. As
far as personalities were concerned, however, the focus, remained on
R.A.V. himself.

ED CLEARY: I think it's fair to say that he enjoyed the celebrity
status—the limo coming and picking him up to be on
the satellite on the "Today Show" [after the U.S. Supreme Court ruling]. I think he became a kind of local
hero to certain elements because he was so
well-known at that time, at least his initials were.

*It sounds as if to some extent he reveled in that celebrity. Were you surprised,
for example, that he even agreed to that "Today Show" interview?*

ED CLEARY: No, I wasn't (laughs). I wasn't. Because my problem was just the opposite—to try to get him to not talk. The *Life* magazine article, for example. He had pictures taken without me ever knowing it. And he made some comments in there without me ever knowing it. And most of my anger there was aimed at the reporter—not the reporter, because the reporter was straight with me. But the pictures were never mentioned. And you could say, "Well, he's an adult. He should object to it himself." Actually, he wasn't an adult yet. Knowing that he was represented, I'd have preferred they'd gone through me. But that kind of thing was going on. He was getting contacts from the media. And he generally learned his lesson after a couple of unfavorable articles. After that he pretty much shut up, but it was always that willingness to grab the spotlight. I think any lawyer with a client who's in the eye of the media has a problem—explaining to them the dangers and trying to keep them from saying too much.

In terms of evaluating the case initially, at what point did you begin to see it as a First Amendment issue and, in fact, what turned out to be a significant First Amendment issue?

ED CLEARY: Well, I did see it right away as a First Amendment issue—not because I'm any sort of an intellectual genius, but because if you go back in time and recall when I received the petitions. It was in June of 1990. And *Texas v. Johnson* had come out in '89. I don't know if *U.S. v. Eichman* had come down yet—the second flag burning case. But I believe it had. I was very much aware of those cases, and the combination of my awareness of those cases led me to read it and think that this was, quite honestly, unconstitutional. In fact, I got on the phone and called Mike Cromett, who eventually became my co-counsel on this case, and said, "Am I crazy, or is this unconstitutional?" And he still remembers that phone call. It was within 10 minutes of receiving the petition. So it wasn't like it hit me over the head. I will say that I did not see all the angles of it. I had not walked into the maelstrom of hate speech and what that all entailed at that point. I simply saw it as an unconstitutional infringement on unpopular, symbolic speech.

In *Texas v. Johnson*, 491 U.S. 397 (1989), a sharply divided U.S. Supreme Court ruled that a Texas flag desecration statute—and Gregory Johnson's conviction of violating it after he publicly burned an American flag as part of a political protest—were inconsistent with the First Amendment. In *U.S. v. Eichman*, 496 U.S. 310 (1990), a flag burning measure was again on trial. After *Texas v. Johnson*, Congress passed the Flag Protection Act which criminalized the desecration of the United States flag. The Supreme Court ruled the Act violated the First Amendment. The ruling was issued 10 days prior to the cross burning on the front lawn of the Jones family in St. Paul.

PUBLIC PERCEPTIONS

In taking a case such as this one, R.A.V.'s attorneys had a myriad of challenges before them, not the least of which was dealing with public perception. Oftentimes, it was misperception. Even other lawyers failed to grasp just what Cleary and Cromett were doing and why. Their attempts to explain that they were *not* defending R.A.V.'s action—but rather that they were challenging the constitutionality of the law being used to prosecute him—frequently went unheard or misunderstood. The misperceptions grew, with Cleary being labeled at various times a racist, a Fascist, and—in spite of the fact that he was not paid for his work in this case—a lawyer who would do anything for money.

ED CLEARY: I knew right away [our defense of R.A.V.] was going to be misunderstood. And I certainly knew right away that it was going to be misunderstood by minority people, particularly nonlawyer minority people. And I was right. And that's why the media became so important, because the way the media covered it was crucial to anyone who bothered to take the time to read the articles. Now early on, of course, the media weren't covering it at all. All that was known was that I had gone in and suggested that a law that said you couldn't burn crosses was wrong somehow—and therefore the logical corollary to that was that it was okay to do. But it didn't shock me. I was disappointed, but it didn't shock me.

MICHAEL CROMETT: I guess the biggest hurdle was getting people to look beyond the conduct to the language of the ordinance. That forever—and still is—the legacy of *R.A.V.* When Ed wrote his book and they came up with the title *Be-*

yond the Burning Cross, it seemed so natural. That's
what we were fighting to do the whole time—get people to see beyond the burning cross. That was the
biggest hurdle. Everybody could really follow the prosecutor saying the First Amendment doesn't allow a
person to burn a cross in someone's yard. It was really hard to get people to see that we were coming at
the challenge from a different angle, a different plane.

*When you say the biggest challenge was to get people to see beyond that,
what "people" are you referring to? People in the judicial system, or outside
of it?*

MICHAEL CROMETT: Both. The most interesting thing—or perhaps for us
the most frustrating—was some of our colleagues.
And not to me so much, as to Ed. Some of our colleagues were just incensed about what we were doing, and couldn't imagine why we were spending so
much time on the case. It really showed what later
became clear—the rift between the civil rights part of
the First Amendment and the civil liberties part. We
were never asked by any of our colleagues if we believed in murder when we represented people charged
with murder, but here they were asking, "Do you believe in cross burning?" Those kinds of comments. A
lot of it was pretty emotional and hostile.

ED CLEARY: Locally here, I knew a number of the reporters so I
could trust them to—even if they didn't understand
it—they wouldn't take an easy shot. They would at
least try to outline the issue involved to the degree
they understood it. And I don't mean to say that in a
mean or rude way, but a number of local reporters
never really did grasp what was going on, I don't think.
And as time wore on, and the *New York Times* and the
Washington Post and papers like that got involved, you
could see the difference in reporting, quite honestly. I
don't know how many of those reporters had law degrees, but they clearly were able to educate the public in a way that wasn't happening locally. So that was
kind of a relief when we got to that point. These reporters were flying into town and interviewing us. The
initial reaction was fear that these reporters would
somehow take a shot. Underlying all of that, which I
probably really didn't grasp then but I grasp more
now, is that because I was on the First Amendment

side—that is to say I was a First Amendment champion of sorts—I think that there were a number of reporters who tried to understand it because they were obviously First Amendment people themselves, a lot of them. Even if they didn't necessarily like it, they tried to understand it. And obviously those in the national press were better at it. But there were some ugly episodes and that really didn't get going until right before the argument and after the decision. There was the terrible experience of going on "Sonya Live." And that has stayed with me through these years. That to me was one more sign how lucky I had been with the media and how fair so many reporters had been with me, and what it was like to fall under the power of the media when you didn't have someone who bothered to read the pre-interview or bothered to study the issues and take cheap shots. I mean, it just kind of grew. The media left a bad taste, but that comes with the territory.

How would you respond to someone who would ask you, "How can it be that protecting hate speech is a good thing?"

ED CLEARY: Boy that kind of gets to the core of it, doesn't it? I guess first and foremost, if somebody asked me that, I'd challenge their belief that we can always tell what hate speech is. So it's first a matter of definition. And if we can ever get to the point of agreeing what hate speech is—one man's hate speech is another man's free speech—but let's just say that we can all agree on a very small core that is very clearly hateful in nature. Then I think it would be a further line-drawing problem of what degree of "disturbing" or "offensive" or any of those—where do we draw that line? And most importantly, who decides? So even in the most blatant examples, by protecting it we've left the door open to very disturbing speech. And I think history has shown that core political speech—just to put it aside for a minute from hateful speech—is often very disturbing and offensive, and some would call hateful. And no one would argue that core political speech isn't protected. So I guess my attitude simply is it's a matter of protecting all speech, and if that makes me a First Amendment absolutist—I mean I'm not a total absolutist in the sense that I agree with some of the lines that the Supreme Court has drawn—but "hateful" is just one of those words that causes a lot of people, including me, a lot of concern as a line-drawing criterion.

MICHAEL CROMETT: The thing that I've always tried to say—and really, it's something that we fell into pretty early on—was the whole idea that you need to protect the Devil's free speech in order to protect your own free speech. One of the things that we put in the brief to the United States Supreme Court was the quote from Robert Bolt's play *A Man for All Seasons* where Sir Thomas More has a discussion with a young lawyer about that principle. And it turned out that Justice Scalia really likes that quote. We didn't have any clue about that at the time we did it. But it seemed to summarize the position so well. If you're going to allow people to regulate speech that you don't agree with, it can't be too long before *your* speech—speech that *you* agree with—will be limited, too. I think it's probably that slippery slope that we're afraid of. Once you decide that, where does it end? It's that kind of idea that seems to make sense to me. It really seems to me that the defining principle that distinguishes the United States from most other countries is that we allow speech we disagree with, with the hope that it's going to be other speech that wins out in the marketplace of ideas. Now it's at this point that it starts to get a little crumbly for me in terms of the First Amendment part. People say, "Well, what values does a burning cross have?" And I'm not sure that a burning cross does [have value]. But it's the idea of racial supremacy or separatism—those kinds of things—that carry that principle forward and, despite what we may think about it, they have some currency.

ED CLEARY: I'd say in the first year, when it was still kind of a local issue, to the degree that it was known, you'd be introduced as, "The lawyer that's involved in that cross burning." And with nothing further, you can imagine how people reacted. They reacted like maybe you were a little crazy, or a little off, or more importantly, hiding a racist or political agenda of some sort. So that just made it very uncomfortable. But I knew that what I believed in politically was in strong contrast to what the person who I was defending did. But quite clearly I

understood that it was my job to do so. The contradiction never bothered me probably because I embrace
as much as I do the Sixth Amendment right to counsel. With one of my friends, I used to interrupt her
and change the conversation to something else just
because I didn't want to get into it. You find yourself
just not wanting to try to explain to *everybody* what
the issue was. Then afterwards, after it hit, I had
more credibility in the sense that the U.S. Supreme
Court had taken it. For nonlawyers, they were impressed with the hoopla—that is, that somebody in
Washington wanted to talk about it. But they still
didn't understand and thought that it was a very bad
thing to do—that you were making the world safer for
racists. Therefore you were, in a sense, aiding and
abetting the racists and Fascists in this country. I
remember very distinctly after the Supreme Court
agreed to take [the case], I felt a chill like I had read
my obituary—being referred to as the cross-burning
lawyer, which would not be the nicest epitaph.

Does some of this sentiment exist to this day?

ED CLEARY: I think so. I mean, I don't get crank calls, or anything.
[But] I still get sideward glances and apprehensive
looks, particularly when I'm dealing—as I must in this
position—like when I go talk to the Black Lawyers Association, for instance. Pretty clearly, in the back of their
minds—as lawyers, they know what it was I did and
why. But as members of a minority race, they're not
necessarily trusting of someone who would do that.

The case developed within this contentious sort of environment.
Misperceptions and misunderstandings abounded. The cost of representing someone like R.A.V. was often heavy. It was something that not only
Cleary had to deal with, but also his father—himself an attorney—and his
mother did as well, as the case moved through the courts.

The case existed on one of three levels at various stages. First, it was
heard in the Ramsey County District Court in July 1990. Judge Charles
Flinn agreed with Cleary's argument that the St. Paul Bias-Motivated Crime
Ordinance was unconstitutional. Prosecutors then appealed to the Minnesota Supreme Court which, in January 1991, unanimously overturned
Judge Flinn's judgment. Its ruling was issued on the Martin Luther King, Jr.
holiday weekend, which, given the racist overtones of the case, Cleary believes was not coincidence. It was a difficult time for Cleary, who firmly be-

lieved he was right. His father echoed that sentiment, and urged his son to continue the fight.

ED CLEARY: I remember when I first got this case he wouldn't say much at all. I'm sure he was probably thinking that it was going to be a real mess in the sense that if it went past the initial level—again, nobody had any idea what this was going to do, that it was going to explode like it did—that people would misunderstand me. But we never really discussed the constitutional side. I didn't tell him why in great detail as to all the different cases and why it was clearly right being wrong. But once I'd lost, he knew that hurt bad. The unanimous decision coming down on Martin Luther King, Jr.'s birthday was kind of a double whammy for me. I thought it made a political statement. It may have been accidental, but I didn't really think it was. And it left everybody with the idea that I'd been way off. [My father] was protective even at that age enough to know that it hurt and we talked about that, and that's when I suggested to him that deep down I knew I was right but there was no more funding. It seemed like spitting in the wind. And I was still trying to do my other work, my other defense work, maintaining my practice. And he *did* suggest that I shouldn't give up. "If you feel that strongly about it, then you should do it." And that was one of the last conversations we had. That conversation only had real significance later. I certainly wasn't thinking about that conversation during those dark days when he suddenly died and I was dealing with all of that. But it did come back to me in the sense that I did petition shortly thereafter, and his advice was certainly a factor in that. My mother did not understand the legal issues involved, quite honestly. She only understood that I felt strongly about it, and that was good enough for her—unlike my father who would have understood more of that other side. And it was very hard on her. She was 85 years old. She had a number of incidents with women her age. If they were close enough friends to her, and they didn't understand, they weren't going to criticize me. They weren't going to do that to her. But there were other women who made comments to her. She felt this was clearly the kind of behavior that you wouldn't want to spend a lot of time defending. But she understood that this is what I had to do.

PREPARATIONS

Why do you think the Supreme Court agreed to hear the case?

ED CLEARY: I think timing is everything, personally. I think we sized up the issues well in our front page. I was very much aware that that's about as far as the clerks that do the initial reviewing of the initial certs. that are filed get. In other words, the framing of the issues is extremely important. And I spent some time on that beforehand and drafted a rather short and I thought concise petition. So I think the way we framed the issues to give it a national scope helped get the attention of whoever it was that saw it, whatever clerk it was. And I also purposely did try to broaden the issue to one of speech codes and what I considered a national move to censor hateful or offensive speech. I was aware of the Court's ideology and felt that we had a better chance than maybe we would have in some other instances, although I've come to think since that the First Amendment is pretty nonideological. I think it was the timing, considering the sweeping move across the country in 1991 on political correctness—although that's usually over-used now. At the time it was less so. And I think it was probably members of the Court who read it and viewed it that way after having a clerk bring it to their attention. That's probably why they took it. I do remember the *U.S. Law Week* reported that there were 90 petitions that week, and that was the only one granted. So obviously it stood out of the pile.

MICHAEL CROMETT: I think the timing that we had was everything. There were so many things going on related to the hate speech idea. We looked back at the petition for cert. that we did and found a lot of different things going on that we could point to and say this is an important issue that you should review and decide. It's hard to believe that 10 years ago there was still discussions

Appellants file a writ of certiorari—sometimes referred to as "cert"—with the U.S. Supreme Court when they seek review of their case by the Court. At least four Justices must agree to grant the writ for the Court to hear the case. When a writ is granted, the lower court is ordered to certify the record and send it to the higher court. If a writ is denied, the court is refusing to hear the appeal and is saying, in effect, that the judgment below stands unchanged.

about the rebel flag in South Carolina. There were campus speech codes in *Newsweek* and *Time* it seemed every week. There were newspaper articles within the months while we prepared the petition about things going on across the country related to the hate speech idea. A number of states had enacted legislation like the St. Paul ordinance, including Minnesota. So it just seemed ripe for a decision.

As you were assembling the case and formulating a strategy, what kinds of challenges were you presented with in terms of staying focused in the face of mounting opposition in the community and beyond?

ED CLEARY: Well, our first challenges were more mundane than that in the sense that early on—that is to say, when we were dealing with the local district court—the coverage was minimal and the impact on us was fairly minimal as well. By the time it got to the Minnesota Supreme Court up here, it had become covered more and therefore it was more of a burden. But then the burden that really started to mount, frankly, was an economic one for us as much as anything. We worked on the Minnesota brief without compensation. We petitioned the U.S. Supreme Court in the same way. And, again, those were not heavy burdens at that point. One could argue that any lawyer should do that as part of a pro bono practice. But after that point, by the time the Minnesota Supreme Court agreed to hear it, the impact came on all fronts (laughs). It came from the misunderstanding that the public felt. Initially, the misreporting that a number of media outlets conducted and the economic impact—of really having to put everything aside—we had to put everything aside in our civil practice, our criminal practice and, frankly, our other public defender cases. So the impact was such that—and I can't speak for Mike, but I'm sure he felt the same effect as I did— [there was] a sizable drop in gross revenues combined with clients falling away, partially because you weren't available and partially because some clients don't want to be connected with that kind of notoriety.

You conducted a lot of research for this case.

ED CLEARY: Right.

Part of the preparation was to learn the Supreme Court, to learn the Justices, and to, in fact, go and hear them speak at times. On that latter point, what was it that you hoped to gain from that?

ED CLEARY: That was fairly remote, and I knew that, in terms of public speaking and in terms of just having the chance to go and listen to Justice Kennedy or Justice Stevens in Chicago and hear them expound on topics. I guess part of that was trying to size up each individual. Actually, I don't think the speech I heard from Stevens helped a hell of a lot. But the speech from Kennedy really did, because he reiterated once again— it wasn't even the topic, I don't think, that he was necessarily going to speak on—but he once again reiterated free speech issues. I don't think everyone knew that, but it's become more obvious that he fashioned himself more of a First Amendment advocate than people realized initially. The aftermath of his concurring opinion in *Texas v. Johnson*—and he mentioned it again in his speech, which was only once before I was to argue—did give me some more faith that he was going to be a willing listener to what I had to say. So did it give me great insight in terms of the argument? No, it didn't in the sense that it didn't give me specifics, but it did give me an overall feel for where their lines were at in terms of the case in front of them.

In fact, you've said that without Justice Kennedy's opinion in Texas v. Johnson, *you'd have had a much different kind of challenge.*

ED CLEARY: Actually I may have even stated that we may not have even reached Washington at all because the initial judge that heard it, district judge Charles Flinn—you know, he spent 20 years in the reserves and was a conservative man—and generally I think he would have sided with the dissenters in *Texas v. Johnson*, but for that one-page concurring opinion [by Kennedy]. If I didn't read it in the record, then I read portions of it in the record and I gave it to Judge Flinn. And I'm sure he would acknowledge, as he has since then, that that was what made him throw out the law. It gave him the strength to do so anyhow. So that kind of set off a whole chain of events. Now had he not thrown it out, I would have appealed, but in terms of procedural posture, it would have been totally different. It may never have gotten there.

An Associate Justice since 1988 and considered to be a member of the Supreme Court's centrist bloc, Justice Anthony Kennedy's concurring opinion in *Texas v. Johnson* is viewed by many as a key swing vote in that ruling. Among the statements in his concise opinion: "The hard fact is that sometimes we must make decisions we do not like. We make them because they are right, right in the sense that the law and the Constitution, as we see them, compel the result."

The time when you heard Justice Kennedy speak— Is that the time when you ran into him in the men's room?

ED CLEARY: (laughs) Yeah, one of those odd things. He was about to speak and I had just finished my dinner, and we'd both walked out. Neither one of us had seen the other one. It was a long hallway. It was just the two of us. I certainly didn't identify myself as someone who was going to see him in a month or two. But we did chat a little bit and you know how odd men's bathrooms can be in terms of space anyhow. We just chatted very briefly. He was very outgoing and friendly. You know, sometimes people change when they're one-on-one, but he talked about seeing the Twins—at that time they were a good ball team—win the World Series. At least he'd seen them win a game. How he missed sports because he taught con[stitutional] law and missed Monday Night Football because of his class. So we did chat about certain things that weren't relevant to this issue. Again, one more of those examples of just trying to see the person behind the office.

And how important is that? It seems as if you put a lot into getting to know the Justices and their personalities in addition to where they stood on this particular issue and those issues on the tangent. To what extent is that important, to what extent does that impact your strategy?

ED CLEARY: I'm not the first one to delve into the decisions of the Justices prior to arguing their own case. But this case was an unusual one, as commentators have noted at length because it wrapped in so many different things: race, obviously, free speech, campus speech codes, federalism, the flag burning cases. I think Chief Justice Rehnquist was an example of someone who I tried my best to figure out. I knew how he felt about the flag-burning cases. He and Stevens were very, very angry about that decision. He was considered a conservative when it came to race issues. But I also knew that he was adamant about not overturning state and local laws if there was a way to avoid doing that. So we had all these conflicting things going on. So you tried, either by their readings or if you could hear them speak, or I saw Scalia on TV on Channel 2 a few times—on PBS. You just tried to discern some of the beliefs or opinions they might have short of a written opinion—something that might give you a little gleaning that you might not have otherwise. So I did try to do that within the time frame that I could and within the lack of resources. So it wasn't that I had this huge master plan, it was just that things fell into place—that the more I worked on it, and the more I studied readings on the various Justices, the more opportunities seemed to arise to either hear them speak—either live or on TV—or in one or two cases, talk to their ex-clerks. Obviously they're not going to reveal anything confidential, but to try to get a feel for their feelings about their former bosses. After awhile you start to put it together.

MICHAEL CROMETT: The bottom line was that we didn't want to get bombed out (laughs). We wanted to know what we were doing. And for me—I had done quite a bit of appellate work throughout the years in association with the State Public Defender's Office primarily. But I had never been to Washington, I'd never seen the Supreme Court in action. It's quite a difference, I think, between state and federal courts and going to the United States Supreme Court. It's really the big leagues. From a certain perspective, it was some experience of what we were about to be doing, to figure out the lay of the land a bit so when you walk in there on argument day it's not something completely new and so that you're not prepared for it. I think we were always concerned about what votes would be there and what sympathetic ears would be there and what approaches to take. That's part of the fun of a big case like this—trying to figure things out. The Court had changed a bit just prior, and left a lot of unknowns for us. Again, it was trying to get a feel for what we're doing, what we got ourselves into, and how to make the best of it. Clerks know perhaps more than many lawyers who have appeared before the Court. I think Ed talked to a couple of lawyers who had argued in front of the Court, but the one meeting I attended was the lunch with the former [Scalia] clerk. It was a chance for us to bounce our questions: Why do you think they granted review? How do you think they're going to approach it? What kinds of things should we watch out for? What should we do in preparation? Those kinds of things.

You've alluded a couple of times to the flag-burning cases. Would you comment on their role in this case, and on two levels? First, from the Court's standpoint, and perhaps how that may or may not have played into the granting of cert. and their eventual analysis of the case. And secondly, in your strategy.

ED CLEARY: Our strategy from the very beginning was to seize on those cases. As I mentioned, the judge in the district court who eventually threw it out did so primarily because of *Texas v. Johnson* and Justice Kennedy's concurring opinion. I think that we were less successful at the Minnesota Supreme Court level in trying to find out that the inconsistency was that those cases were controlling in terms of a review of this ordinance, but that court, of course, disagreed with us. As to the U.S. Supreme Court, in the end, I don't know how much it played in the Court's approach. I know, again, on a superficial level, I've read one or two books that said that they thought it was the conservative Court's way of evening out the score, quote-unquote, for what they considered initially a liberal decision on *Texas v. Johnson*. But again, that is superficial, particularly when you consider that Kennedy and Scalia were in the majority in *Eichman* and *Johnson*. I purposely tried to move away from it because I did not know where Justices Souter or Thomas were going to come down. They were unknowns. They had not voted on those cases. So I wanted to move away from it thinking that I did not want a close vote to go the other way if they joined in with Stevens and Rehnquist and White, etc. So I think my attempt in oral argument was to seize on the language that the dissents had used in *Texas v. Johnson* suggesting that the burning of a flag *could* be suppressed because it was a unique symbol. By definition, a unique symbol to me is just that—there aren't any others. My attempt, then, was to suggest to the Chief Justice—and I remember looking into his eyes when I said it—that that case could be distinguished because it was a unique symbol. So even the dissents in *Texas v. Johnson* could find differently in this case and still be consistent.

AT THE U.S. SUPREME COURT

ED CLEARY: I ate breakfast and I sat with my closest friends and my sister, and at this table nobody else ate (laughs). One of my memories is eating a blueberry muffin and having them stare at me like, "How can you do that?" And I answered them, "Because I'm hungry." So I wasn't totally out of it, but by the time I got in the taxi—and this is probably because I was the son of a military man—the fact that you need to be prompt was drilled into me, and I can't think of anything that I wanted less to be late for. So the fact that we went in the opposite direction and I thought I knew Washington very well—I'd been there a number of times. So I was just sure he was going the wrong way, and we were going to be late, and he didn't speak English. So I just thought this was it. And I couldn't imagine coming in late to the Court. Just get there. That was the big thing. Just get me there.

MICHAEL CROMETT: Ed was pretty nervous. He swore we were going in the wrong direction. He said it was some plot. I'm maybe adding a little bit about the plot. But he was pretty nervous that we were going in the wrong direction. I hadn't been to Washington that much, but I knew there was a loop going around. So I just said, "Relax. I think we're going the right way, or the quick way." But that was easy for me since I didn't have to worry about getting up [before the Court] and talking.

ED CLEARY: There's a little procession that everyone goes through once you get there. You go downstairs and through the clerks' office and they warn you. And I think that's a nice service. They tell you to be responsive because maybe some of these lawyers have not seen a prior argument and the one thing you cannot do is hedge your answers. If you have to give an answer, you have to do it. And if you don't know the answer—if you don't know it—to do the typical lawyer thing that we're all trained on—just to kind of weave along while you try to find the real answer isn't going to work

with this crowd. They're too bright, they're too sharp,
and they're too impatient. And they're too well prepared. They don't hear that many cases now and they
certainly have bright clerks and they're bright themselves and so they really zero in. So that whole process of being reminded was important. There was a
certain atmosphere that day. When I came upstairs,
they had all the folding chairs out which I'm told they
only do five or six times a term. So there's a full
crowd. Seeing that atmosphere through those chairs
actually has a strange effect on you. In one sense it
makes you proud because it means that the topic and
the issue that you think is so important, obviously
other people do, too. On the other hand, it's intimidating because you realize that you have a packed
house and the media on the left is full in that area,
and on the right, it had been group portrait day so
the families of the Justices were there. Clarence
Thomas had just gone through his hearings, so his
wife was sitting there, and I could see her. And so you
see all of these different people back there as well as
your friends and family. You're very much aware that
for better or for worse in the next hour or so you're
in the midst of making history whether you succeed or
don't succeed. And whatever else you do, this is a
moment to treasure. And I think most lawyers probably do. But you think about those lawyers that get to
go there and the few that get to go there sometimes
don't get to argue very interesting cases, so to get
to argue an interesting one and an important one was
something special.

In the audience that day—December 4, 1991—were Russ and Laura
Jones, the St. Paul residents on whose front yard the cross was burned
nearly 18 months beforehand. Cleary does not recall when he first met
them, but says they had not been present at the initial court proceedings or
at the Minnesota Supreme Court. While it had been a challenge to explain
to others his role and his passion for the First Amendment cause he represented, the challenge grew exponentially with the Jones's.

ED CLEARY: Seeing them there that day made me feel the same
way that I usually felt when I saw them, which was
bad. I'd heard from other people—because one of the
prosecutors was a friend of mine and they talked and
tried to explain to them that I wasn't a bad guy. And I

think they understood that, but as they told the prosecutors second-hand, they didn't understand why I fought so hard. I think their attitude was, "Sure, go ahead and throw up your argument and just sit down and shut up." And the fight all the way to Washington made them question my motives, I'm sure. So I didn't really have the luxury at that point of being distracted, so I didn't spend a lot of time concentrating on the fact that they were there. I expected that they would be because [lead prosecutor] Tom Foley told me that they would be.

Before the arguments began, and you are waiting for the Justices to enter, and then they do so, can you describe to me what that is like knowing that they are coming in to listen you?

ED CLEARY: Frankly that whole morning and even up to that moment I suppose, I was thinking about my Dad as much as anything. He had been a lawyer, I had grown up at his side watching him practice law, and I was just thinking how exciting and hopefully how proud he would have been to get to that moment, regardless of what happened.

MICHAEL CROMETT: We both wrote [on different notepads] right about at the same time "carpe diem" which was our saying about seize the day. We had talked about that in the past and it was kind of the theme for what we were doing which was going for it, taking our moment, doing the best we could.

ED CLEARY: They have the long, velvet curtains behind the various chairs, so when they come out, and the marshal calls out, I think it's an intimidating point for anybody in the room, much less the person who's going to argue. Generally speaking, that's how they come out. The bench is such that there isn't a lot of curve to that bench. I won't say it's straight, but it's very close to straight so it makes it hard for whoever is arguing. Because you're very close up there. You're not very far from them. The mics are such that you really need a few seconds to ascertain who it is asking a question. You can't distinguish voices that easily. When they came out, and we all stood up, and the Chief Justice says down, by then I had a—one might call it unnatural—but I had a calm. I was very calm, frankly. My

stomach was not doing somersaults. I think you simply get to the point where you've done all you can and
what's going to happen now is you're going to give it
your best shot, and you really have, to a certain degree, do not have control. You have a *certain* amount
of control. But some of it is out of your control. And I
think even if you're right in the sense that your argument is correct, the Court can still embarrass you or
humiliate you or do whatever they want with you. They
can bat you around in front of the audience. And I'm
not saying they do that, although one or two Justices
do seem to do that every once in awhile. So you're
aware of that and you just hope that it all goes well.
That was what I was thinking. But you really don't
have much time other than to think, "Okay he's now
going to start speaking and in a few minutes I'm going
to go up there." So you're kind of going step by step
at that point.

*The word "profound" does not do justice in describing your opening line be-
fore the Court. How did you come up with it?*

ED CLEARY: Well, you know, it's been so long since I wrote that
kind of preamble, as I thought of it. I wrote it down
the night before, sitting in the Embassy Suites, just
thinking out loud. Obviously, the roots of it came from
First Amendment cases and decisions. It came from
Holmes and later Douglas. And Brandeis. And I was
just taking snippets, frankly. "With each generation,"
of course, is my own mind. I was very much aware
that it was a generational case. In my own mind it
was. There was a generation that grew up in controversy, and when we think of the First Amendment in
the '60s and on, it occurred to me that we're a very
definable generation, and that we had relied on the
First Amendment for a lot. The power of the Bill of
Rights as we grew up and were educated. In my own
mind I felt that some of the same people whose politics I agreed with over the years had kind of turned
and stopped believing in the Bill of Rights. I think people left-of-center and with the speech codes, etc.,
had turned their back on it, thinking that they knew
what was best, just like people on the right did. That's
probably why I started out the way I did—just a reminder that there will be more cases long after we're

gone, and there will be more fights on this topic with a different group listening. And hopefully again it will be defended, and it will succeed in the sense that the First Amendment will not be eroded.

Cleary began his opening statement as follows: "Each generation must re-affirm the guarantee of the First Amendment with the hard cases. The framers understood the dangers of orthodoxy and standardized thought and chose liberty. We are once again faced with a case that will demonstrate whether or not there is room for the freedom for the thought that we hate, whether there is room for the eternal vigilance necessary for the opinions that we loathe. The conduct in this case is reprehensible, is abhorrent, and is well known by now. I'm not here to defend the alleged conduct, but as Justice Frankfurter said forty years ago, history has shown that the safe-guards of liberty are generally forged in cases involving not very nice peo-ple. He might as well have said, involving cases involving very ugly fact situations."

As you're making your oral argument, are you totally focused on what you're saying, or is there also some reading of the Justices that is occurring?

ED CLEARY: You can't be focused on what you're saying because if you were, you'd essentially be giving a speech, and that would be the worst thing to do there. So I wrote a preamble with the thought that I'd give as much as I could that I could get out. So I did go up and down and looked into their eyes as I spoke to see if there was any—oh, I don't know what I was looking for. I suppose initially it was just to let them see my eyes. But it was also to see if any of them were kind of grimacing or feeling like this was not the issue and, "What are you doing?" And what I got mostly back, was interest. "Where are you going with this?" Clearly not going through the facts of the case, but facts weren't important to this case. I mean they were—certainly to the people involved—but not for their decision. I guess I was trying to pick up where they were going— whether they were looking down, whether they were looking at me, whether they were looking around the courtroom. Obviously, they were concentrating on the case before them, and it was early enough that they were just looking at me. You know, this case had gotten a lot of coverage out in

Washington, too—the *Life* Bill of Rights article had been out and the *Washington Post* and *USA Today* and the *New York Times* that Sunday did a cover story. They might very well presumably have read some of the background on this case before them. So initially I was thinking—at least for 10 seconds or so—whether if I had been an object of interest, wondering about me because a lot of those articles had talked a little bit about how I'd gotten there. So I looked around, and what I saw mostly was initial interest and no animosity that I could detect, which was important. Then I distinctly remember finishing what I thought would be the maximum before there would be questioning, and realizing I had to move on because nobody had asked me questions. And starting in on the next portion of the argument, and that's when Justice O'Connor spoke. As it develops from there, you find your mind racing to understand, not the question—well, obviously you want to understand the question—but you have to discipline yourself to let the question finish, which is an age-old problem in litigation or advocacy because, particularly Justice O'Connor had this tendency to talk very slowly and you're racing like a grade-school kid trying to get the right answer out. I tried to discipline myself because I'd talk quickly. And after those first few questions, I remember distinctly realizing that I needed to do more than answer the question now. I needed to detect patterns, which is kind of advanced oral advocacy. And trying to do that and answer the question properly—there are probably one or two questions that I didn't answer in the amount of depth I should have. And once or twice with Justice Souter I misunderstood. And part of that was I had thought he was attacking what Scalia just had said, but he wasn't. So you need to change your attitude. And then you need to decide whether you can see blocs forming. Doing that all in such a short period of time does take quite a bit of concentration. After awhile you can see the blocs forming. Of course it's easier looking back to detect exactly what blocs are forming. But at the time it was still clear that certain Justices were in agreement while others weren't. And what we didn't know was that they were all against the law, but that they had different objections to it.

I am interested in something you said in response to my previous question with regard to the opening statement. I think you said something along the lines that the Justices let you do it. What would have happened otherwise?

ED CLEARY: That Court, like any court at that level, I presume, doesn't suffer fools gladly in the sense that when a lawyer starts to speak in too flowery of a manner, you'll get a question right away because it would be like, "We don't have time for you to give us a speech." Or, "That might be fine and well, but what about this?" The arguments I've seen now—and I've probably seen eight or ten—I haven't seen anyone quite allowed to give the preamble they allowed me to give in that fashion and not interrupt me. And it could have been they were waiting for meat on the bone before they attacked. But I don't think so. Justice O'Connor could have gone in and just knocked me out right away. I think they figured I'd fought damn hard to get there—to the degree they gave it that much attention, but to the degree they did—I think they thought I'd fought very hard to get there. And it turned out they were sympathetic to my position overall, and they thought I probably deserved another chance to state what this was all about in my mind.

In spite of the preparation of trying to get to know the Justices, did any of them offer any surprises?

ED CLEARY: Certainly having seen five or six arguments, their mannerisms and their reported- on techniques were pretty well known—Justice Scalia's in-your-face approach, and Chief Justice Rehnquist is like that at times, too, as opposed to Souter's more gentlemanly approach—he still had been there only a year or two. Justice Thomas was an unknown, very quiet. Justice Blackmun, we knew would bring in Minnesota somehow. So there are always different things that you see happening that you expected in terms of the general rotation, but you're not really sure where they're going to come from in terms of the actual precedents. In other words, I didn't know how much this was going to be a *Chaplinsky* case, and how much they were going to rely on fighting words, and how much they were going to move it into another area. So I guess when I look back in my work preparation in terms of individual Justices and what I saw when I got up there, I think probably the biggest surprise to me was the Chief Justice. The one nightmare that every lawyer has, I'm sure, that's ever argued there is that they're all going to say, "You're an idiot. Sit down," or just excoriate you in some other fashion. For me, I had the flip side. For the most part I could tell that as the argument was developing that they were, in fact, pre-conditioned to my position. And that surprised me. That it was as widespread as it was, that was a surprise. I think probably the biggest surprise was for me that I had misjudged the Chief Justice. I thought he would be much more against me. That was probably my biggest surprise, once we started jousting. Because he's so law and order, and remember I'm a criminal defense lawyer, and criminal defense lawyers don't do well up there—as opposed to prosecutors. Prosecutors do well up there. A lot of the tables were turned on this one, but it didn't become obvious until things started to really move.

In *Chaplinsky v. New Hampshire*, 315 U.S. 568 (1949), the U. S. Supreme Court established the "fighting words" doctrine, ruling that a verbal assault—in this case calling a police officer a "damned fascist" and a "God damned racketeer"—by their very utterance inflicted injury and tend to incite an immediate breach of the peace. Such fighting words, it was ruled, are not protected by the First Amendment.

In the oral arguments, and then in the aftermath, did you sense that any one particular Justice was key in trying to win him or her over?

ED CLEARY: In approaching the oral argument, I suppose deep down I was looking to the left—physically to the left—of the Court, and that would be Souter and Scalia. I think Scalia was, in fact, important because even though he had voted in the majority in *Texas v. Johnson*, I felt that whether or not you agree with him ideologically, he was the intellectual force of the Court at that point, and his opinion would carry some weight. Although at the same time his opinion would probably alienate one or two Justices, including Justice O'Connor. So trying to keep everybody together was part of it. And I also was curious as to how Justice Souter might approach it because by then there were a few signs at least that he

might be more moderate than people originally thought.
I can't say there was one in particular that I thought if
I could get, I'll get the Court. My hope was to fend off
the Chief Justice if he was very critical of our position
and to hope that I could still form a majority from the
rest of them.

MICHAEL CROMETT: I remember thinking that I'm glad it's Ed up there answering those questions and not me. They're such
deep questions and difficult questions because of the
difficulty of the issue (laughs). I was glad it was Ed
and not me.

ED CLEARY: [After my presentation] I felt pretty good, sitting
down. You know, you think that a half-hour is not that
long, but a half-hour up there—and I saved, I think,
four minutes, so I'd been up there 26 minutes—and I
felt pretty good sitting down. And as Mr. Foley stood
up I did take an opportunity to look around at the Justices. But they weren't really showing anything at
that point. I actually felt bad for him a little bit because he was never actually able to get in any kind of
flow. And then my next memory was of Tom saying—I
can't remember his exact language, but—"there are
four parts to this and this is how I'm going to do it."
And I remember thinking he was not well-advised because it had a paternalistic air to it, like a lecture.
"I'm going to explain each part of this to you in this
order." As soon as he did that he was dead. I don't
mean in the sense that they were not going to let him
go near that. Justice O'Connor hit him right away
with, "So what are you saying, to what your opposing
counsel says about viewpoint discrimination?" So he
never really got any kind of flow. I remember thinking
as the questions started to develop for Foley and particularly when Justices Scalia and Souter went after
him a bit—in different ways (laughs), one a little bit
more gentlemanly than the other—that I was in
pretty good shape and he wasn't. By that I mean the
arguments and positions. And that was what I felt as
his argument went along—that I would be surprised
at that point if we lost, although I did not at all foresee a unanimous outcome.

*And then at the very end, once it was all wrapped up in there, what kinds of
feelings did you have then, what were you sensing at that time?*

ED CLEARY: Relief—that I hadn't made a fool out of myself—was the first emotion. A certain amount of exhilaration that it was over and had apparently had gone well. And I think Mike felt that way, too, because we both started to leave the table there. When you turn around and realize exactly how crowded the room was and all the hallways were crowded, too. It was kind of an unreal experience. One of my strong memories was as I went out and around and tried to avoid going through the main crowd, there was Tom Foley's uncle, who was a former congressman who approached me before he approached Tom. And he congratulated me and we talked at some length. And I was very impressed with that—meaning perhaps that he agreed with my own position more than he did his own nephew's. I don't know. In any case, I had never met him before and I was impressed by that. That was the first person I talked to. And other than that, just a good feeling that it had gone well, that whatever happened, I had done my best. Then, of course, I went out and my friends and relatives were out there. And I did my press pool thing, then left and went to lunch with all my friends and relatives.

SUPREME COURT AFTERMATH

ED CLEARY: Initially in the few days right after—of course, it was right before Christmas—there was the media barrage. There were the interviews—some of the sillier ones like *People*—and some of the more important ones like the *Times* and the *Post*. And then literally I came home for three days and got in a plane and then went to New York to do the "Today Show." So it was a very unreal period immediately following it. It settled down by Christmastime. So then it was just a waiting game. Then it was kind of hurrying back into the practice, frankly. I talked to other people who have argued, and they felt the same way. Periodically I'll get calls from people who I have worked with who argued after me that I consulted. It's like this one, unique episode, and I think it's hard for people to withdraw from it. It's very exciting in its own way, intellectually. I don't mean just because of the pomp and circumstance, I mean the intellectual challenge. So that was it. Time just went on. I won't deny that I was wondering every

day when I was going to get the call. Then I had a little
health issue there, and then got out.

While awaiting the Supreme Court's ruling, Cleary began experiencing
pain in one of his legs. Eventually it was diagnosed as a major blood clot
that could have led to severe problems. Cleary was admitted to the same
hospital in which his father had died 14 months beforehand. Among his
visitors one day was another person who had a vested interest in the *R.A.V.*
ruling, his opposing counsel in the case, Tom Foley.

ED CLEARY: You know, we hadn't just opposed each other on this
case. I had actually been the campaign manager for
somebody who challenged him early in his career. So
there was no real love lost there. [But] I think the experience of having gone through all this and going
through all our joint interviews when we did our dog
and pony show, we got to perhaps grow to like each
other a bit more than we would have otherwise. I was
impressed that he came over one day at lunch and sat
over on the other bed when nobody was there, and we
just talked. Yeah, people would be surprised, but you
can argue and advocate very strongly and still *usually*
remain on good terms with your opposition. I think for
nonlawyers, that comes more of a surprise because I
think that means it's an inside job somehow, that you
can still be on good terms with somebody who clearly
is in your face at times. I won't deny that we looked at
a few TV interviews where we weren't real warm to
each other because of how we went after each other.
But that comes with the territory.

THE RULING

Events over the previous couple of years had reminded Cleary that there
were no guarantees in life. In spite of the fact that the ruling had yet to be issued and that there were only a few dates left on a list of likely Supreme
Court "decision dates" that he had been provided, Cleary decided to proceed with a long-awaited vacation to Greece. In fact, he says that the idea of
being out of the country when the decision came had some appeal given
the opportunity to escape some media coverage. The tension built until
June 22, 1992 when, during another in what had become a series of routine checks, Cleary got the word.

ED CLEARY: I was over there for at least a week before it hit. And
one of my memories is getting to places like Santorin

and trying to find the one phone on the island that was public that I could get to and check—because I knew the days when there would be issuances. So I probably wasn't the best traveling partner because of the tension. It just kept building and building and building. So when I did call—I just called the Court directly that day—I was sitting in the hotel in Delphi looking out at this valley, and heard it, my feeling again was tremendous relief, frankly. I just remember sitting down. I didn't scream or jump up and down, or say, "Let's go out and get blasted" or anything. It was just flat-out relief. And a great feeling of satisfaction. You know, I'd seen it through over a two-year period from beginning to end and regardless of what happened now, that I always had that. I'd fought hard for what I believed in and had been proven right. And that was really the primary emotion. I remember calling home and I ran up a $600 bill on faxes and phones that night because I needed to get the decision. I remember my mother in tears because I hadn't really considered then how much emotion she had tied up in it because of her friends not understanding. So it was a highly emotional event, but primarily my feelings were relief and great satisfaction. There was no arrogance to it, no "I told you so"s. I just knew I was right and I'd been proven right, and that felt very good.

In the opinions themselves, did anyone surprise you?

ED CLEARY: I thought there'd be some people who'd try to save [the law] in some fashion. Although most people who observed it who were with me thought it would be unanimous. I was not surprised there was the division on how to get there, although I was surprised by how vitriolic the language was between the Justices. For instance, Justice Blackmun's dissent said you can say what this is about, but it's really about political correctness. In the back of my mind I thought that shouldn't be a surprise because that goes back to the granting of the cert. because I had originally and literally invoked that as why one of the reasons the Court should see it as a broader issue than just cross burning. He seemed to feel that was a bit of a blindside. I didn't think it was. In any case, as to how everyone voted, I couldn't have predicted that. I don't think any-

body could. I think even now, if you look at the group-
ings, it's an unusual group—that Souter and Kennedy
would be on one side of that vote, and that O'Connor,
for instance, would be on the other. That's interesting
to me. The other blocs are not that surprising—
Stevens and Blackmun on one side and Thomas and
Scalia and Rehnquist on the other. But the people who
joined them were unusual, particularly Souter disagreed with the others. And then that O'Connor
would go in with the minority viewpoint, that surprised
me a little bit.

*And then once you got back home, what kind of reactions did you experi-
ence in the community, in the media there, and so forth?*

ED CLEARY: I had done the media, some of it from [Greece]. I went
to Athens and did the "Today Show" and felt that the
message was getting out. And from calls home I really
didn't get a taste for the climate until I got here and
realized from looking at the tapes how hostile the response had been. I guess I shouldn't have been
shocked, but I was really disappointed ... in the mayor,
for instance—not the mayor now, but the mayor
then—holding a press conference with some minority
people who were screaming about violence and he
stood there and Foley stood there, and they didn't say
a word. I was very disappointed in the local government leadership here and the climate they let develop,
rather than approaching it quietly and suggesting
that they'd been wrong—which they never acknowledged—and suggesting that the Court had spoken and
they'd do what they have to do. There was none of
that. And so they stirred it up, and that's what led to
that letter of opinion suggesting that we got all this
money that we didn't get. And that was a very hostile
environment that I came back to. That was not pleasant. Perhaps one could say that I should have expected it, but I didn't. I was surprised. I certainly
didn't expect, as I said, everybody to jump up and
down when I came home, but I was surprised at the
overall public approach. Having said that, there were
other examples of the other side. The lawyers were
obviously very supportive and complimentary, and I
even got a note from Esther Tomljanovich [the Minnesota Supreme Court Justice who wrote that court's

opinion upholding the constitutionality of the St. Paul Bias-Motivated Crime Ordinance] saying you were right and I was wrong. Within the legal community, it was what I would have hoped in the sense that there was a very favorable reception. Otherwise it was very hostile with a lot of misinformation out there.

MICHAEL CROMETT: I received a number of letters from classmates and people who I hadn't seen for a number of years. A lot of them had the tone of congratulations—I think (laughs)—and a couple of people wrote really nice notes realizing what we had done and why we had done it. A couple of public defenders said that's what public defending is all about.

ED CLEARY: Probably the most shocking incident for me was coming back and seeing the paper published headlines about the money and the picture of the Jones family and a letter to the editor, leaving everyone with the impression that we had done it for the money when we hadn't been paid—literally hadn't been paid—except expenses. To this day it rankles me. It really fit into everyone's stereotype of lawyers which is that they can say this and they can say that but what they're really talking about is material compensation—that's what they want. They'll do anything for a price. The correction, in my letter, was printed within a few days, but the harm had been done. And that still angers me. At the very least I want people to know I didn't do it for material reasons. I did it because I believed in it. By this time, now, the Supreme Court had found 9-zero that we were right, you know. And yet here we are in my hometown with a big article and a big picture of the Jones family and a big headline decrying my fee—which didn't exist. So that was the low point. You'd think you had credibility after every Justice up there had agreed in one fashion or another that the law was wrong. And even then, people didn't understand it. And to this day, I'd guess that there are plenty of people who don't understand it. I think most lawyers realize that after what had happened at the Supreme Court, it was pretty clearly a defective law. But I don't think most nonlawyers to this day understand it totally. They just think the Court is a little out there. I think that's kind of the general consensus. It was kind of interesting because I guess I expected, if I did succeed in Washington, my credibility would rise considerably back here. And it did—in the legal community. But it certainly did not in the nonlegal community. I think I was still viewed with skepticism. And I probably still am locally, particularly with some minority community members. It comes with the territory, I guess.

And how long did it take for that sort of sentiment to die down?

ED CLEARY: It took a few months, but there's always going to be some of it here. There are people who hear my name and remain confused. That's just the price you pay. I still see occasionally when people connect it. That's just the way it goes. I don't expect everybody to clearly understand the issues because they are complex and they're not easy to understand unless you give it the time and effort to do so. Once you win unanimously before the U.S. Supreme Court, I can't tell you how many lawyers came up to me and said, "I knew all along you were going to win" (laughs) whereas there were very few who had ever indicated that before.

SIGNIFICANCE, IMPACT, & LEGACY

Bottom line, what was really at issue in this case?

MICHAEL CROMETT: A fundamental First Amendment principle: Is there room for speech that we hate, that we disagree with? The city of St. Paul tried to legislate tolerance. And tolerance is a good idea. I'm for it. But the way they went about it was to say we recognize a certain core thought that we disagree with and we want to prevent it. And we're going to do it with this ordinance that takes disorderly conduct and incorporates the idea of these selected symbols and try to punish it that way and legislate it that way. In the Minnesota Supreme Court's decision, when they said, "We're going to narrow this down to fighting words only," there were a couple of footnotes or sentences or phrases in the text that to me said this ordinance can prevent or regulate speech that people disagree with or causes harm or injury that's not a physical injury. And it seems to me that one of the ideas that was referred to was racial supremacy. It seems to me that with the First Amendment, you

can't rule out the idea—even though you may disagree with it—you can't rule out the idea of racial
supremacy. It needs to be out there and aired. The
antidote is not regulation but more speech. The idea
of why the prosecutor chose that particular ordinance is one that still troubles me. I guess the best
explanation for it that I've heard is that when a law
says you can't burn a cross and someone burns a
cross, use that law. That's never been very satisfying to me in explaining what happened. It was more a
question of the state trying to use the ordinance to
make a political statement. And I'm not sure that's
what the criminal or juvenile courts are for. It's
whether a person has violated the law or not. The
way they steadfastly clung to that—that stupid ordinance (laughs)—is really beyond me. In retrospect, I
guess I'm glad they did because of where it took us,
but I just don't understand why at some point they
didn't abandon it and deal with the case appropriately in some other fashion.

ED CLEARY: It's a complex decision, obviously. But if you boil it
down, to me it really came down to the right to dis-
sent. I realize that a lot of people think that really
wasn't what it was. But it was. You take some of the
most serious issues that also happen to be group
identities—race, religion, gender, etc.—and you attempt to stifle unpopular expression on one of those
topics or group identities, and you could literally, I
think, undermine the whole concept of freedom of expression. And I think there was a movement to do
that. I think it was blunted. I think you'll still see it
now in some places. There are still issues in the workplace—how far discrimination laws and harassment
laws can go constitutionally. Bottom line: it was the
right to say unpopular things on hot topics. That's extremely important. Political speech isn't always going
to be Democrat-Republican. Sometimes it's going to
be on topics that we think, when we're at certain
points in our history, are too sensitive to talk about.
You have to make room for people to talk about them,
even if that means putting up with the hateful diatribes that we get. So to me that was it: the right to
dissent on sensitive topics and express yourself on
those topics.

The phrase "landmark case" is certainly a subjective one, but by any measure this case certainly qualifies. In your view, what was it that made R.A.V. a landmark case?

ED CLEARY: It showed nine people in power in one branch of our government struggling with these issues. If you think back to Madison, and their discussions as to what is even at issue make it, I think, a fascinating case. And then I think the five [Justices] who come out and actually find the viewpoint neutrality issue—I find that alone makes for an extremely significant case in that whether it's a conservative Court or a liberal Court doesn't matter. It shouldn't matter. People shouldn't always read it in that context, in this case or the flag burning cases. What it is, is a group of Justices that disagree a lot and are divided a lot seem to get together—not always, but seem to get together—mostly over the First Amendment. And I find that that's interesting that when they put on the robes, Scalia can vote, for instance, to strike down the flag-burning statutes. I find that interesting that people who are generally ideological manage to put it away when it comes to basic First Amendment issues. Not always, but often they can. I think they did in this case, even though Justice Blackmun obviously didn't. He felt it was a matter of political correctness, as he put it. And it might have been to a certain degree. But I think it was one of those cases that really addressed a number of issues that were important at that period of our nation's history. And I think they still are. I think it is fascinating to read the decision and see how these Justices worked. There's a certain amount of anger in this decision, I think, in the language that's used by the various Justices.

Anger directed at who or what?

ED CLEARY: At each other. At each other. I see it. I think Blackmun is angry in it, and I think White is angry in it. And maybe one or two that are gone. Because I think they felt the Court reached out. I mean, everyone agreed that it was an unconstitutional law. They felt they were reaching out to make a statement. And I think they were, too, to a certain degree, but I had asked for that, frankly. I'm not a fan of speech codes, and they were using language to try to knock down speech codes. And they still use those words now regularly. And I think a constitutional law professor would suggest that the way that they went about talking about fighting words in terms of specific viewpoints was important—was a different way of looking at things. It's been a long time since I looked at it. I think it will be studied. I know it is in a lot of casebooks now, and I think it will continue to be studied as an important decision that adds to the breadth of the First Amendment.

For any law or regulation to be constitutional it must pass a First Amendment test of being "viewpoint neutral." That is, it cannot discriminate on the basis of a viewpoint that an individual holds—no matter how distasteful most people may find the viewpoint. As Justice Scalia wrote in his *R.A.V.* opinion (see Court opinion excerpts at chapter's conclusion), the St. Paul ordinance went beyond mere content regulation to actual viewpoint discrimination by singling out specific disfavored subjects: "St. Paul's desire to communicate to minority groups that it does not condone the 'group hatred' of bias-motivated speech does not justify selectively silencing speech on the basis of its content." Scalia believed that the ordinance suggested that certain viewpoints (and the expression of them) were unacceptable—a concept clearly in violation of the First Amendment.

Does this case demonstrate an anti-majoritarian aspect of the First Amendment ?

ED CLEARY: Boy, I hope so. I think that's what it really was about in the end—the flip side of majority rule in the sense of how a single voice should be protected and should it continue to be protected. And that there's an anti-majoritarian [element] when it comes to the Bill of Rights. I think clearly the anti-Federalists understood that way back when, when they put those protections in. To me, a lot of this all comes down to power. Even the media comes down to power—access to the media and all the rest of it. To the degree that a group wants a special law thinking that it will protect them at the expense of the First Amendment, not only ignores the danger of the Bill of Rights, likewise ignores the power structure in America. Speech codes backlashed against the minorities that wanted them. The very fact that they were enforced against the

very minorities that sought the protection. I think
there are a lot of issues there that are clearly
thought of in the heat of the moment—the passion of
the moment.

*Given the nature of the case, this may seem to be a ridiculous question,
but—To what extent was this case about race?*

ED CLEARY: Well, that's more interesting than ridiculous, frankly,
because certainly the pull on the case—the attraction
that everyone felt toward the articles and the sympathy that everyone felt for the family—was, I think,
based on race. The message that was sent by the juveniles involved clearly was a race-hate message. So
in that sense it was obviously about race. Obviously
also, as it grew it became much more than that, I
think, in the sense that by the time it got to the Supreme Court it wasn't just based on race any more. It
had taken on much more. Just look at the amicae
briefs that came in and how wide and varied they
were, and they were way past race. It started out as
a race-hate message that invoked a hate speech law
that led to the U.S. Supreme Court addressing the
larger issue of free speech on issues involving group
identity past race.

*Does this case illustrate the notion to some extent that perhaps we need to
abandon labels such as "conservative" when we analyze cases like this and
their opinions.*

ED CLEARY: I totally agree with you when it comes to First
Amendment law. I really do not think there's an ideological basic for the votes. Occasionally there is. You
can't ever say never. But I think we should abandon labels when we look for votes on First Amendment issues. There was a lot—particularly back here and
some nationwide—a backlash that this was a conservative and racist Court, giving the green light to cross
burning, which was simply inaccurate. Those same
people probably didn't even realize that Scalia, for instance, had voted in the majority in *Texas v. Johnson*
and *U.S. v. Eichman*—clearly against his own ideological beliefs. I really do think they check that at the
door for the most part when it comes to First
Amendment law. I think it shows up in some other

cases. But in First Amendment law it might be one of those very specific areas where they put on those robes and realize it's for the ages and they really do have to set aside their opinions, and I think they do for the most part really work hard at that.

In the aftermath now of this case, what is different in the world—or at least in this country—in its wake?

ED CLEARY: It put an end constitutionally to the speech aspects of the move to censor in the sense of offensive speech and hate speech. The codes that are out there now— the speech codes, for instance—that haven't been challenged could be challenged and knocked down. And they started to fall by the wayside. Wisconsin backed off, Stanford's went down. And that's important be- cause I can't think of anything more opposed to the notion of freedom of speech than restricting expres- sion in a university setting. So I think it's just showing that the First Amendment cases that protect the right to speak your mind, even offensively. So I do think it's had an impact in that sense and it is taught regularly throughout the country in law school and in college law courses.

Well-meaning attempts by some universities to limit hate speech on their campuses often include issues similar to those in *R.A.V.* in that their regu- lations are content based and lacking in viewpoint neutrality—and there- fore they violate the First Amendment. For example, the University of Wisconsin's code was ruled unconstitutional by a federal district court in 1991 for that reason. Similarly, a Stanford University hate speech code was declared unconstitutionally overbroad by a California Superior Court in 1995.

The possible impact of *R.A.V.* is still being measured. One barometer is the attempt to regulate speech and the efforts to fight those attempts. Relying on the U.S. Supreme Court's ruling in *R.A.V.*, the Wisconsin Su- preme Court invalidated a hate crime statute in that state that provided for increased punishment for a crime when a victim was selected because of his/her "race, religion, color, disability, sexual preference, national origin or ancestry." One year after *R.A.V.*, however, the U.S. Supreme Court re- versed and upheld the statute, ruling that the law was not unconstitutional, in part because it was aimed at conduct unprotected by the First Amendment. This ruling, Wisconsin v. Mitchell, 508 U.S. 476 (1993), served to clarify *R.A.V.* and the circumstances under which similar rulings may and may not occur.

Is there a common thread that runs through this case and through other landmark First Amendment cases?

ED CLEARY: It often involves people like R.A.V. or people like him whose history shows that they often fade into the background in terms of the fact that they were a willing party, but they were a tool of history just like everyone else involved in the case. I think the common thread very often is that the people who pursue it do pay a price of sorts. In any case, I think the common thread is very often a controversial position that, with hindsight, is the right position, that it takes a certain amount of courage for whoever goes forward with it, that there's often misunderstanding during the case, and oftentimes that misunderstanding never totally dissipates except to the degree that young lawyers and law students and college kids are taught how this is consistent certainly throughout the 20th Century in terms of First Amendment law, and how if you go back 80 years or so you will find that thread, and you will see the Court fall down now and then—particularly during times of war—but overall that branch of government protects the essential freedom of speech very well.

MICHAEL CROMETT: The First Amendment protects speech that the majority doesn't agree with and that the majority would like to regulate and control. The Supreme Court recently—and that's the thing that I didn't realize at the time and that's how recent that First Amendment law really is—stood up and said the majority doesn't have the right to control ideas that it disagrees with. When people are afraid they want to do what they think they can to prevent what they're afraid of. We tend to forget that we are the United States and we have this free speech right. If we lose that idea we lose everything.

ED CLEARY: I think the mistake is to minimize the impact [of this case] by suggesting that it's just about—whatever you want to say—burning crosses, or it's just about hate speech, although it certainly is directed at hate speech laws and ordinances and codes. But that it has a bigger impact. It goes to the very aspects of whether a local government or a larger unit of government can censor unpopular expression on a given topic and what that might mean for everything—music, art, theatre, books. And I think that's why you see the American Library Association or other groups jumping in. Because the impact of these types of cases is much larger than people realize, particularly if they're decided wrong (laughs). You know, First Amendment law oftentimes, once it's decided right, people might not see the impact as readily because things are going well in terms of expression. But when they go bad, they'll feel the impact over time and they'll look back and see where it started. And that's what everyone who takes on these cases is trying to avoid. We want to keep it into a situation where we maintain freedom of expression. And I sincerely believe that America is virtually alone on that to the degree it does. And I realize that Canada and some other countries have some provisions for it. But I think America is really unique.

When you get involved with a case like this and all the issues that permeate it, did it ever strike you that in some ways you're carrying the same torch that originated with people like Madison and Jefferson, and passing it on to future generations?

ED CLEARY: It sounds less than humble to say that that happened, but it did. It didn't early on. Clearly I was just swimming, trying to make my way. And it didn't really even when the U.S. Supreme Court decided it. When after the brief was over and I was preparing for the oral argument and I'd go to Washington and I'd come back here—that's when it started to happen, that you started to feel a certain pride in what you were doing that would outlive you, that a case at that level would, in fact, become something that would be studied. I didn't know that it would be studied as much as it has been. Simply that you were fighting for a good cause. And [a friend] would talk about Madison a lot. Initially I thought that was a little out there. But the more I read and the more I studied, I was very proud of that, and to this day I am. I remember buying Jefferson's and Madison's correspondence and reading a lot of those letters and really getting into that side of it— seeing how short a time period 200 years is, and how the Federalists and anti-Federalists really went at it over some of these issues, and how to this day all of it ties in. I even feel that way to this day when I pick up the paper and see the U.S. Supreme Court has a First Amendment case of any sort now. Because I see it as a kind of giant tree with all these different branches coming from the same trunk of issues that Madison and Jefferson dealt with. So, yeah. That's very observant of you. And it sounds, I think, presumptuous of me to say that, but I'm not the only one to feel that. You do see the tie-in if you give yourself the time and permission to do it. You start to feel the historical context. Frankly, it's exciting and something to be proud of.

R. A. V. v.
City of St. Paul, Minnesota

**SUPREME COURT
OF THE UNITED STATES**

---

505 U.S. 377
Argued: December 4, 1991
Decided: June 22, 1992

COUNSEL: Edward J. Cleary argued the cause for petitioner. With him on the briefs was Michael F. Cromett.

Tom Foley argued the cause for respondent. With him on the brief was Steven C. DeCoster.

JUDGES: SCALIA, J., delivered the opinion of the Court, in which REHNQUIST, C. J., and KENNEDY, SOUTER, and THOMAS, JJ., joined. WHITE, J., filed an opinion concurring in the judgment, in which BLACKMUN and O'CONNOR, JJ., joined, and in which STEVENS, J., joined except as to Part I-A. BLACKMUN, J., filed an opinion concurring in the judgment, post. STEVENS, J., filed an opinion concurring in the judgment, in Part I of which WHITE and BLACKMUN, JJ., joined.

OPINION: JUSTICE SCALIA delivered the opinion of the Court.

In construing the St. Paul ordinance, we are bound by the construction given to it by the Minnesota court. Accordingly, we accept the Minnesota Supreme Court's authoritative statement that the ordinance reaches only those expressions that constitute "fighting words" within the meaning of *Chaplinsky*. Petitioner and his amici urge us to modify the scope of the *Chaplinsky* formulation, thereby invalidating the ordinance as "substantially overbroad." Assuming, arguendo, that all of the expression reached by the ordinance is proscribable under the "fighting words" doctrine, we nonetheless conclude that the ordinance is facially unconstitutional in that it prohibits otherwise permitted speech solely on the basis of the subjects the speech addresses.

The First Amendment generally prevents government from proscribing speech, or even expressive conduct, because of disapproval of the ideas expressed. Content-based regulations are presumptively invalid. From 1791 to the present, however, our society, like other free but civilized societies, has permitted restrictions upon the content of speech in a few limited areas, which are "of such slight social value as a step to truth that any benefit that may be derived from them is clearly outweighed by the social interest in order and morality." We have recognized that "the freedom of speech" referred to by the

First Amendment does not include a freedom to disregard these traditional limitations.

We have sometimes said that these categories of expression are "not within the area of constitutionally protected speech." Such statements must be taken in context, however, and are no more literally true than is the occasionally repeated shorthand characterizing obscenity "as not being speech at all."

What they mean is that these areas of speech can, consistently with the First Amendment, be regulated because of their constitutionally proscribable content (obscenity, defamation, etc.) not that they are categories of speech entirely invisible to the Constitution, so that they may be made the vehicles for content discrimination unrelated to their distinctively proscribable content. Thus, the government may proscribe libel; but it may not make the further content discrimination of proscribing only libel critical of the government.

The proposition that a particular instance of speech can be proscribable on the basis of one feature (e. g., obscenity) but not on the basis of another (e. g., opposition to the city government) is commonplace and has found application in many contexts. We have long held, for example, that nonverbal expressive activity can be banned because of the action it entails, but not because of the ideas it expresses—so that burning a flag in violation of an ordinance against outdoor fires could be punishable, whereas burning a flag in violation of an ordinance against dishonoring the flag is not. Similarly, we have upheld reasonable "time, place, or manner" restrictions, but only if they are "justified without reference to the content of the regulated speech." And just as the power to proscribe particular speech on the basis of a noncontent element (e. g., noise) does not entail the power to proscribe the same speech on the basis of a content element; so also, the power to proscribe it on the basis of one content element (e. g., obscenity) does not entail the power to proscribe it on the basis of other content elements.

In other words, the exclusion of "fighting words" from the scope of the First Amendment simply means that, for purposes of that Amendment, the unprotected features of the words are, despite their verbal character, essentially a "nonspeech" element of communication. Fighting words are thus analogous to a noisy sound truck: Each is, as Justice Frankfurter recognized, a "mode of speech," both can be used to convey an idea; but neither has, in and of itself, a claim upon the First Amendment. As with the sound truck, however, so also with fighting words: The government may not regulate use based on hostility—or favoritism—towards the underlying message expressed.

...

Applying these principles to the St. Paul ordinance, we conclude that, even as narrowly construed by the Minnesota Supreme Court, the ordinance is facially unconstitutional. Although the phrase in the ordinance, "arouses anger, alarm or resentment in others," has been limited by the Minnesota Supreme Court's construction to reach only those symbols or displays that amount to "fighting words," the remaining, unmodified terms make clear that the ordinance applies only to "fighting words" that insult, or provoke violence, "on the basis of race, color, creed, religion or gender." Displays containing abusive invective, no matter how vicious or severe, are permissible unless they are addressed to one of the specified disfavored topics. Those who wish to use "fighting words" in connection with other ideas—to express hostility, for example, on the basis of political affiliation, union membership, or homosexuality—are not covered. The First Amendment does not permit St. Paul to impose special prohibitions on those speakers who express views on disfavored subjects.

In its practical operation, moreover, the ordinance goes even beyond mere content discrimination, to actual viewpoint discrimination. Displays containing some words—odious racial epithets, for example—would be prohibited to proponents of all views. But "fighting words" that do not themselves invoke race, color, creed, religion, or gender—aspersions upon a person's mother, for example—would seemingly be usable ad libitum in the placards of those arguing in favor of racial, color, etc., tolerance and equality, but could not be used by those speakers' opponents. One could hold up a sign saying, for example, that all "anti-Catholic bigots" are misbegotten; but not that all "papists" are, for that would insult and provoke violence "on the basis of religion." St. Paul has no such authority to license one side of a debate to fight freestyle, while requiring the other to follow Marquis of Queensberry rules.

What we have here, it must be emphasized, is not a prohibition of fighting words that are directed at certain persons or groups (which would be facially valid if it met the requirements of the Equal Protection Clause); but rather, a prohibition of fighting words that contain (as the Minnesota Supreme Court repeatedly emphasized) messages of "biasmotivated" hatred and in particular, as applied to this case, messages "based on virulent notions of racial supremacy." One must wholeheartedly agree with the Minnesota Supreme Court that "it is the responsibility, even the obligation, of diverse communities to confront such notions in whatever form they appear," but the manner of that confrontation cannot consist of selective limitations upon speech. St. Paul's brief asserts that a general "fighting words" law would not meet the city's needs because only a content-specific measure can communicate to minority groups that the "group hatred" aspect of such speech "is not condoned by the majority." The point of the First Amendment is that majority preferences must be expressed in some fashion other than silencing speech on the basis of its content.

Despite the fact that the Minnesota Supreme Court and St. Paul acknowledge that the ordinance is directed at expression of group hatred, JUSTICE STEVENS suggests that this "fundamentally misreads" the ordinance. It is directed, he claims, not to speech of a particular content, but to particular "injuries" that are "qualitatively different" from other injuries. This is wordplay. What makes the anger, fear, sense of dishonor, etc., produced by violation of this ordinance distinct from the anger, fear, sense of dishonor, etc., produced by other fighting words is nothing other than the fact that it is caused by a distinctive idea, conveyed by a distinctive message. The First Amendment cannot be evaded

that easily. It is obvious that the symbols which will arouse "anger, alarm or resentment in others on the basis of race, color, creed, religion or gender" are those symbols that communicate a message of hostility based on one of these characteristics. St. Paul concedes in its brief that the ordinance applies only to "racial, religious, or gender-specific symbols" such as "a burning cross, Nazi swastika or other instrumentality of like import." Indeed, St. Paul argued in the Juvenile Court that "the burning of a cross does express a message and it is, in fact, the content of that message which the St. Paul Ordinance attempts to legislate."

...

Let there be no mistake about our belief that burning a cross in someone's front yard is reprehensible. But St. Paul has sufficient means at its disposal to prevent such behavior without adding the First Amendment to the fire.

The judgment of the Minnesota Supreme Court is reversed, and the case is remanded for proceedings not inconsistent with this opinion.

It is so ordered.

JUSTICE WHITE, with whom JUSTICE BLACKMUN and JUSTICE O'CONNOR join, and with whom JUSTICE STEVENS joins except as to Part I-A, concurring in the judgment.

I agree with the majority that the judgment of the Minnesota Supreme Court should be reversed. However, our agreement ends there.

...

But in the present case, the majority casts aside long-established First Amendment doctrine without the benefit of briefing and adopts an untried theory. This is hardly a judicious way of proceeding, and the Court's reasoning in reaching its result is transparently wrong.

...

This Court's decisions have plainly stated that expression falling within certain limited categories so lacks the values the First Amendment was designed to protect that the Constitution affords no protection to that expression. *Chaplinsky v. New Hampshire*, 315 U.S. 568 (1942), made the point in the clearest possible terms:

"There are certain well-defined and narrowly limited classes of speech, the prevention and punishment of which have never been thought to raise any Constitutional problem ... It has been well observed that such utterances are no essential part of any exposition of ideas, and

are of such slight social value as a step to truth that any benefit that may be derived from them is clearly outweighed by the social interest in order and morality."

Today, however, the Court announces that earlier Courts did not mean their repeated statements that certain categories of expression are "not within the area of constitutionally protected speech." The present Court submits that such clear statements "must be taken in context" and are not "literally true."

To the contrary, those statements meant precisely what they said: The categorical approach is a firmly entrenched part of our First Amendment jurisprudence. Indeed, the Court in Roth reviewed the guarantees of freedom of expression in effect at the time of the ratification of the Constitution and concluded, "In light of this history, it is apparent that the unconditional phrasing of the First Amendment was not intended to protect every utterance." In its decision today, the Court points to "nothing ... in this Court's precedents warranting disregard of this longstanding tradition." Nevertheless, the majority holds that the First Amendment protects those narrow categories of expression long held to be undeserving of First Amendment protection—at least to the extent that lawmakers may not regulate some fighting words more strictly than others because of their content. The Court announces that such content-based distinctions violate the First Amendment because "the government may not regulate use based on hostility—or favoritism—towards the underlying message expressed." Should the government want to criminalize certain fighting words, the Court now requires it to criminalize all fighting words.

To borrow a phrase: "Such a simplistic, all-or-nothing-at-all approach to First Amendment protection is at odds with common sense and with our jurisprudence as well."

...

Therefore, the Court's insistence on inventing its brand of First Amendment underinclusiveness puzzles me.

...

Any contribution of this holding to First Amendment jurisprudence is surely a negative one, since it necessarily signals that expressions of violence, such as the message of intimidation and racial hatred conveyed by burning a cross on someone's lawn, are of sufficient value to outweigh the social interest in order and morality that has traditionally placed such fighting words outside the First Amendment.

...

JUSTICE BLACKMUN, concurring in the judgment.

I regret what the Court has done in this case. The majority opinion signals one of two possibilities: It will serve as precedent for future cases, or it will not. Either result is disheartening.

In the first instance, by deciding that a State cannot regulate speech that causes great harm unless it also regulates speech that does not (setting law and logic on their heads), the Court seems to abandon the categorical approach, and inevitably to relax the level of scrutiny applicable to content-based laws. As JUSTICE WHITE points out, this weakens the traditional protections of speech. If all expressive activity must be accorded the same protection, that protection will be scant. The simple reality is that the Court will never provide child pornography or cigarette advertising the level of protection customarily granted political speech. If we are forbidden to categorize, as the Court has done here, we shall reduce protection across the board. It is sad that in its effort to reach a satisfying result in this case, the Court is willing to weaken First Amendment protections.

In the second instance is the possibility that this case will not significantly alter First Amendment jurisprudence but, instead, will be regarded as an aberration—a case where the Court manipulated doctrine to strike down an ordinance whose premise it opposed, namely, that racial threats and verbal assaults are of greater harm than other fighting words. I fear that the Court has been distracted from its proper mission by the temptation to decide the issue over "politically correct speech" and "cultural diversity," neither of which is presented here. If this is the meaning of today's opinion, it is perhaps even more regrettable.

I see no First Amendment values that are compromised by a law that prohibits hoodlums from driving minorities out of their homes by burning crosses on their lawns, but I see great harm in preventing the people of Saint Paul from specifically punishing the race-based fighting words that so prejudice their community.

I concur in the judgment, however, because I agree with JUSTICE WHITE that this particular ordinance reaches beyond fighting words to speech protected by the First Amendment.

3 Ollman v. Evans and Novak

"The freedom of the press in this case is the freedom of the people who own the press."
—Bertell Ollman, plaintiff in *Ollman v. Evans and Novak*

"You get sued for $6 million, and you think, 'Jesus Christ! Six million! What happens if we lose? What happens if that judgment comes down against us?' You're very uneasy. It leaves you feeling pretty clammy and cold."
—Rowland Evans, co-defendant in *Ollman v. Evans and Novak*

"When the suit was filed, the greatest concern was from my son who was then 10 years old. He said, 'Daddy, do we have $6 million?' I said, 'Don't worry.'"
—Robert Novak, co-defendant in *Ollman v. Evans and Novak*

"It's a terrific high in some ways ... but it really takes something out of you, especially if you lose. You don't feel that great."
—Isidore Silver, plaintiff's counsel in *Ollman v. Evans and Novak*

In 1977, the University of Maryland was in the process of trying to fill a vacancy for chair of its Department of Government and Politics. A political science professor at New York University, Bertell Ollman, was contacted and invited to apply. Initially reluctant to do so, he ultimately relented. After the typical interviews and give-and-take, Ollman was offered the position, and he accepted. But after that, events were anything but typical.

The news that Professor Ollman was a Marxist began to spread, in his words, "like wildfire," first across the University of Maryland campus, into the community at large, then to nearby Washington, D.C. Maryland's acting governor was among those who denounced the appointment, and the issue became a political football. The news media took an interest, and columnists began expressing their views. Among those were Rowland Evans and Robert Novak, whose jointly written syndicated column was published in newspapers nationwide. In particular, Novak had his interest piqued by this situation. "I'd gotten close to the University," he says. "I knew a lot of the administrative people—the president of the University, the chancellor of the College Park campus. And I am still close to the University. It struck me as an interesting column of why in the world this state university would hire a Marxist, and what kind of Marxist he was. I didn't know anything about him until I started doing some research on him."

The column (see court opinion Appendix at chapter's conclusion), authored primarily by Novak, was published by a number of newspapers, including *The Washington Post* on May 4, 1978 and was entitled "The Marxist Professor's Intentions." It questioned Professor Ollman's qualifications to assume his new role at Maryland. But Ollman thought it did more than that. He believed it damaged his reputation and contributed to the ultimate withdrawal of the job offer. In February of 1979, Ollman filed a $6 million libel suit against Evans and Novak, charging that their column contained statements "false both on their face and in their intended innuendo." Thus began what proved to be a circuitous path of a case in which a battle was waged over what constitutes a statement of fact versus an expression of opinion, and ultimately yielded a four-part test to distinguish between the two. The case is also noteworthy for those judges at the U.S. Court of Appeals in Washington, D.C. who participated in the ruling, including Kenneth Starr, Robert Bork, and Antonin Scalia.

Today, Robert Novak continues to write columns as well as serving as a host and commentator for CNN. Rowland Evans retired from regular column writing in 1993 at the age of 72, but continues his association with Novak on CNN and in two newsletters that they write. Bertell Ollman remains a professor of political science at New York University. He was represented in this case by Isidore Silver, who is a professor emeritus of constitutional law and history and now retired from the practice of law.

THE BACKGROUND

ROBERT NOVAK: It was a news story that the University [of Maryland] had hired a Marxist as the head of the political science department. Ideologically, I thought it was improper. Marxism has caused a lot of havoc in the world, so I thought it was ideologically improper. I found that there

was a good deal of concern—a lot of people wouldn't go on the record—in academic circles about this. I found out that Professor Ollman—there was a rather low opinion of him in his own profession. He had run for office in the American Political Science Association and hadn't done very well. I'd got his books out and read them and I thought they were doctrinaire Marxist diatribes. So the question that was put forward in the column was rather, "Why in the world would they do a thing like this? It doesn't make any sense."

ISADORE SILVER: Bertell and I had been friends for many years, since college actually, which goes back to the mid-50s. God, that makes us sound ancient, doesn't it? Bertell has a way of getting notoriety (laughs), and I kind of gave him advice periodically on various matters of business, et cetera. He's a bit litigious—I wouldn't say he's a maniac on the subject. And then one day out of nowhere, Evans and Novak write a column about him.

ROBERT NOVAK: Our column—my column today—is still based a great deal on reporting. I don't just sit down and say, "Gee, I think this is so-and-so." So I called a great number of people. I talked to a number of people connected with the University, connected with the board of regents. Some of them defended it. I did a lot of research about him. And you see what the product was.

ISIDORE SILVER: [The column] is subject to some interpretation. It's largely opinion. But one fair reading, I suppose, would be that he said his main point was that when a student understands Marxism, taught objectively, he will naturally and rationally become a Marxist. So it's not a matter of indoctrination, but the student's own logical reflection. So Evans and Novak took that, and I don't know why—who knows why?—they did the column. They zapped him in a hundred-and-something newspapers with this charge of using the classroom to indoctrinate which, of course, under libel law— apart from First Amendment issues—is an imputation of the highest unprofessionalism given the fact that indoctrination is a "no-no" academically.

What was the intent of the column?

BERTELL OLLMAN: To keep me from assuming the chair. And I suppose this was the goal of not just Evans and Novak, but

others who got involved in criticizing me at that point—to try to convince the President [of the University of Maryland] that he should use his power to not approve of the offer. I think there was obviously a lot of hostility to the position that I hold in political science—the approach that I take to studying American society—and they were very determined to keep students from having a chance to hear that approach. It was surprising. I think the reason there was such a stir was the University of Maryland is really a part of Washington, D.C. College Park is a suburb of Washington, D.C. And the University has many connections with politicians and the media in Washington, D.C. So a lot of the people there took a personal interest, too, in what was happening at the University of Maryland.

ROBERT NOVAK: The local press in the Washington-Baltimore area had been very passive about [the story], kind of treated it as though it was a little odd, but as if [the University of Maryland] had selected a birdwatcher, or something like that. "Isn't it odd that they selected a birdwatcher to head the political science department?" I thought it was much more serious than that. So my intention was to call attention to the case. Now at that time the column was, I guess, about 17 years old. I had called attention to a lot of things in which absolutely nothing happened (laughs). I don't consider myself an activist in any way. I just try to put on the public record some aspects of things that don't get published elsewhere. I really didn't think it would have any effect. I would have been delighted if it had the effect that it perhaps had, but I didn't really expect that this decision could be reversed.

To your knowledge, did the column directly have impact on the ultimate decision on Ollman's hiring?

ROBERT NOVAK: I think it did have some impact. Yes, it did. I can't prove that, but my column was followed by a number of other columns. There were several other commentaries. Some of the conservative publications wrote things about it. We were the only ones that got sued for some reason.

ISIDORE SILVER: Probably, yeah. Yeah. Oh, sure it did.

BERTELL OLLMAN: I think their column probably had more influence on the outcome than many of the other things which were said and written opposed to my coming to Maryland around the same time.

What kind of immediate reactions do you recall having to the column?

BERTELL OLLMAN: My reactions to it were not based upon who wrote it, although I was familiar with who they are. But it was what was said which I found so objectionable that led to my reactions such as they were. I guess the main points of the article, if I can try to summarize, was 1) that I was very dishonest, 2) that I was really about brainwashing my students into Marxist positions, 3) that I admitted to doing this. Not only was I doing it [according to the column], but that this is something that I admitted to do. They had some quotations taken out of context from one or two works that I had written. And finally and most surprising—I guess it was shocking in a way—is they quoted who they described as a leading liberal political scientist from a major Eastern university who said, "Ollman has no reputation as a scholar, only as a political activist." And so here it was quite clear that it wasn't simply them stating their opinions about the kind of person I am and all the terrible things I would do if I came down to Maryland in the position of chairman, but here they were supporting their opinion with the authority of someone who was in a position, according to their general description, to really know about my standing in the profession. Of course, individuals can have a view about what another person's quality is—the quality of his work—and that is certainly an opinion. But if we talk about what is an opinion of a whole group of people, that is something that you can verify and see whether, in fact, that group of people hold such an opinion or not. As you may or may not know, political scientists have over the years conducted a number of reputational polls. And there was a reputational poll taken just shortly before that happened in which I came in very high—in fact, perhaps higher than any political scientist in the city of New York. So this was a statement of fact saying what was the case about how people in the profession regarded me, and it was a false statement. Yet it was terribly important to the whole article because it seemed to give a factual basis to someone who was presented as knowing—and not only knowing, but someone who was presented as being not too far from me politically—he was a *liberal* political scientist, not just *a* political scientist. So that gave a great aura of authority to the other things that they were charging, and as a result, reading this in a column with those kinds of charges and such misstatements, I was really quite angry. This article, perhaps more than any other of the ones which were written—and there were, oh maybe as many as eight or ten columns which were written in that period in newspapers dealing with the issues and dealing with me—many of them were quite unfriendly. But that was just his opinions. And there were some which were moderately on my side. So not only was I angry, but a number of my supporters were very angry because they thought this was a severe distortion of who I am and what the facts were about things like my reputation and what I do in class and with and to my students. They were also very disturbed because it was something which was quoted a lot by people in and around the University who were opposed to me.

Going a bit back to your method and then, touching on what the gist of the case turned out to be, would you say that the column contained opinion, did it contain facts, or perhaps a combination …

ROBERT NOVAK: A combination.

… where opinion was supported by facts?

ROBERT NOVAK: The latter. That's the way my column has always worked and I'm not going to get into the legal questions, but I think that was part of the whole legal question, of whether this was fact or opinion. The quote that was the gravamen of the case by an unnamed political scientist was, "Ollman has no status within the profession but is a pure and simple activist." The whole question of the case as I remember it was that having an anonymous quote like that was an indication of malice—an unprovable fact—which under the *Sullivan* decision, would make us liable.

In *New York Times v. Sullivan*, 376 U.S. 254 (1964), the U.S. Supreme Court ruled that the First Amendment protects criticism of public officials—even if the remarks are false and defamatory—unless "actual malice" is proven. That is, that the press acted with knowledge of falsity or with reckless disregard for the truth. The case is generally regarded as the starting point of contemporary libel law analysis.

ISIDORE SILVER: To a certain extent, one of their arguments, which was perfectly legitimate, was that a columnist should have more leeway. And I'm sympathetic to that argument that when it's labeled opinion or it's clearly opinion then maybe the First Amendment should recognize that. But they're not journalists. In this case they weren't journalists. They were guys that had a forum. They had a perpetual op-ed piece going. We thought they went a little too far.

Isn't it good journalistic technique to support the expression of opinion with facts?

ISIDORE SILVER: As a general proposition, that's true. But the rule about opinions is that if you have an opinion based on stated and non-defamatory and non-false facts, you can say anything you want. To come within that rule, the statement has to be true. Our argument is that they did not state the truth. An opinion based on true facts which may or may not be defamatory is libel-proof, and should be. But when you twist the underlying facts, as we contend they did, then those are "facts" that color the opinion—false and defamatory facts.

When and how did you first begin to learn of possible problems stemming from the column?

ROBERT NOVAK: When they filed the lawsuit (laughs).

So you hadn't heard any rumblings prior to that point?

ROBERT NOVAK: No. And I might say, a lot of people—when this was filed and we got into court—they said, "Boy, I guess you guys are used to this." I've written millions of words, a lot of them controversial, and a lot of facts.

This is the only lawsuit that actually went to court. Some people have threatened them over the years, but this was the only lawsuit I've ever had to defend.

ROWLAND EVANS: It's a very sinister reaction that you have. What have you done? You thought you were writing a strong column—no question about it, it was a strong column—but that you had the facts on your side. And you get sued for $6 million, and you think, "Jesus Christ! Six million! What happens if we lose? What happens if that judgment comes down against us?" You're very uneasy. It leaves you feeling pretty clammy and cold. If you get a judgment against you for $6 million and you're in our position, you don't have much left. You don't have anything left. So it's an uneasy feeling and a very uncomfortable feeling.

ROBERT NOVAK: When the suit was filed, the greatest concern was from my son who was then 10 years old. He said, "Daddy, do we have $6 million?" (laughs) I said, "Don't worry."

ROWLAND EVANS: I don't recall having a strong feeling one way or the other as to whether we were going to win or lose it. I know that I was very concerned about the possibility of losing it because $6 million is a lot of money.

What was it in your view that made the piece defensible?

ROBERT NOVAK: I think you're asking the wrong question. I think the questions is, "What made it actionable?" because I didn't think there was any case there whatsoever. I thought it was all free comment. And, indeed, the only thing that made it—according to our attorney and to other attorneys I talked to—that they had any case at all was that there was an anonymous quote in there, quoting an unnamed professor. All the rest of the stuff was very straight. But the anonymous quote by a professor at a prestigious eastern university saying [Ollman] has no standing in our profession—something like that. That was the whole of the case. That was the only thing they had to hang their hat on. Was this an attempt to defame him by using an anonymous quote? That was the question. I called this professor when the suit was filed and I asked the professor whether he would be willing to let me use his name. And he said, for a lot of personal reasons, absolutely not. So if this had ever gone to court, my lawyer told me, this would have been a very difficult situation for me where the case would have been in jeopardy. They would have claimed that I made this quote up if I had not disclosed the identity of the professor. But if I disclosed the identity of the professor, I would have violated one of the tenets of journalism. That was a tremendous dilemma that would only be reached if it went to trial. It was very important to us, apart from the time and expense involved, that the case not go to trial. When I say this was not an actionable case, the case never went to trial and it was finally determined through the judicial process that there was not merit in the case, and these issues never had to be resolved.

PUBLIC REACTIONS

In response to the column and then in the subsequent legal action, what kinds of reactions were you getting from colleagues, from friends, from the various communities in which you work?

BERTELL OLLMAN: I got a lot of support from most of the academy—from the people in the University of Maryland, including the administration, with the exception of the President. At NYU, also, I think people were very sympathetic with what I was going through, and in many ways showed that they supported me. The AAUP [American Association of University Professors] also supported me with money to help fight the case against the University. There were very favorable things written in their publications. At conferences I attended I got nice statements of support from colleagues, including many who I had never met before. So at that level, I think there was a great deal of sympathy for me, and again, not because of who I am but because of the kind of forces that were lined up against me and the kind of tactics that they used. Even *The New York Times* had an editorial on the subject of Maryland in which they said this was a matter for the people of Maryland to decide and everyone else should stay out of it. And Maryland, for better or worse, *did* decide, and therefore, that's what should happen.

Along the way, from the moment the suit was filed up to its conclusion and even beyond, what sort of reaction were you getting from colleagues in the media and beyond as far as support, things of that nature?

ROBERT NOVAK: Oh, almost none (laughs). Really none. I think I'm relatively well liked in my profession, but I am a conservative and this is a liberal profession. I don't think many people approved of this column, so I don't think they were going out and having benefits for me. And I also think most of my colleagues thought I could take care of myself which I think I can. There was a fellow named Jack Landau who was involved with the Reporter's Committee for the Freedom of the Press, which was kind of a liberal group which for many years oddly I served on its advisory committee without doing anything. He worked for the Newhouse papers and he was down the hall from me and he came in. He saw that the suit had been filed, and he said, "Be sure you get a lawyer and respond to it." Apparently when some reporters are sued they just let it go. Of course that means it's just settled by default. That was about the only assistance from colleagues that I got.

THE LIBEL SUIT

ISIDORE SILVER: [Bertell] called me about the column because I hadn't even known it had occurred. We decided that it would be better to sue in the District of Columbia. He brought suit, claiming libel. I had conflicting feelings on this. I had qualms about it in terms of First Amendment values. [That conflict] was there at all times. My feeling was to a certain extent, a guy like Ollman, who is a radical and is kind of on the fringe and fairly despised anyway, probably had a case for making a claim that would be an exception to the First Amendment. These were two well-known, rich columnists who were getting their jollies zapping a Marxist. I thought they had really treated him unfairly and it was a low blow. And it seemed that he needed a weapon. He was taking it all cheerfully and he wasn't getting fired, there was no threat. I thought that in terms of evening the score a little, maybe teaching them a lesson or at least getting some kind of publicity that you should not use the First Amendment to attack the politically defenseless.

This column was one of several that were published around this time. Why was it that you chose this one as your target in court?

BERTELL OLLMAN: Because the others were, I think, clearly opinions of the writers. Some of them were as harsh as the Evans and Novak column. But they were presenting their opinions. They described what had happened and they thought it was a terrible thing that the University had offered such a position to someone with my views. And I thought that's a fair thing to write about in this context. I disagreed with them, but I didn't get terribly angry with what they said. It was the Evans and Novak column which I think was trying to present some certain facts which were relevant to their opinions, which made their opinions seem more believable and more acceptable—that's what triggered an exceptional response on my part. I never considered suing anyone else for libel. And in the case of Evans and Novak, I was kind of even a bit surprised that I decided to sue them because I never saw myself as someone who would ever sue anybody for libel. This was a big surprise to me as the victim in a libel suit trying to secure an apology and damages—that this was a very unusual position to find myself in. For someone who believes in the First Amendment, someone who is in discussions and debates, always on the side of freedom of the press and the need for the press to have considerable freedom to do its necessary work. And feeling that, unfortunately, almost always they don't take sufficient advantage of the freedoms that they do have.

Typically in libel suits, we see the defendants being not only the author or authors of a piece, but usually the newspapers in which the piece was published. And yet you did not do that. Why was that?

BERTELL OLLMAN: Why was that? I can't remember thinking about that decision. If I tell you it's because I didn't want to put pressure on the paper, that it's about the authors, it sounds like that's what I would have thought, but I can't remember actually thinking that.

ISIDORE SILVER: We said, "These guys said it. We think *they* committed libel. We want *them* to be held accountable. The newspaper—we don't want to raise that kind of First Amendment issue." And we honestly felt that the people directly responsible were the proper defendants.

ROBERT NOVAK: Let me suggest a couple of interesting things in who he filed suit against. The column ran in several newspapers. The paper they used and the version they used in the filing was *The Washington Post*. But they did not sue *The Washington Post*. That's extraordinary because they have the deep pockets and the two columnists did not. Now, we are not employees of *The Washington Post*. The only connection with *The Washington Post* is that it buys the column from the syndicate. We are, however, employees of *The Chicago Sun-Times*. That was our old newspaper. I thought it was extraordinary that they brought suit against us instead of us and the newspapers or, as is usually the case, just the newspaper that prints it. That's extraordinary because they have the deep pockets and the two columnists did not. We thought that this was an attempt to destroy us financially.

Do you feel that this was also an effort to discredit you?

ROBERT NOVAK: That's the conclusion I drew, yes. I don't know that for a fact. But the fact that he sued us instead of the newspaper—as I remember, he asked for $6 million. My partner and I combined didn't have $6 million. *The Washington Post* and our syndicate at *The Chicago Sun-Times* had millions and millions of dollars. So if you're really interested in collecting money you don't sue the journalists with only modest financial assets.

Is there any truth to the notion that one aim of the structure of the lawsuit— that is, suing only the individuals and not any of the newspapers—was to financially cripple Evans and Novak?

BERTELL OLLMAN: (pause) No, I didn't think in terms of crippling them. The figure that was mentioned in the suit—that was suggested to me by my lawyer. I don't remember how we came to that figure. But I think we all knew that it's a jury that decides, with the help of a judge, what the figures are going to actually be if you win. I had no idea what the actual figures would be. That was presented as a kind of ballpark figure. I think also maybe they were as high as they were to show what we took to be the seriousness of what they had done. I wouldn't have minded too much if I had won and that figure had been seriously cut. I could have lived with a much, much smaller figure if the point would have been made that they had lied—if I had won the case.

ISIDORE SILVER: Oh no, no, no, no, no, no! No. First of all, what damages is a Marxist going to get? It was a losing case in a tactical trial sense, even if we had gotten to trial. It's a losing case. I mean you might get some kind of—well, I won't say nominal damages. For one thing, apart from the Maryland job, which was tenuous, he did not lose his job at NYU, he was still speaking—doing lecture tours, all of that. Oh, no, we didn't want to cripple anybody. We wanted them to retract it. That would have been fine. I remember writing a very specific, detailed letter pointing out where they had gone off base and wildly interpreted what was said, and please retract.

ROBERT NOVAK: There was nothing to retract, there was nothing inaccurate about it. There were no inaccuracies in the whole column. I'm not a lawyer, but the old English law—The reason you had all these criminal libel suits in England was that truth was not a defense. But in the United States, almost from the very beginning after a hard fought battle, truth is a defense. There was nothing to retract. We did have a private luncheon with the lawyer from *The Washington Post* who gave us some of the options we had. Retraction was certainly the option that would be easiest to lead Ollman to not file the suit. But it certainly would be a question of self-humiliation and, we made clear to this lawyer, it was not true. He said if there's nothing to retract, you shouldn't retract.

If somehow a retraction had been issued, would the lawsuit have gone forward?

ISIDORE SILVER: No. I mean, I don't know what Bertell would have done, but I wouldn't have pushed it.

BERTELL OLLMAN: I would have looked carefully at the retraction, what exactly it said, and whether it was made in a column which got the same amount of publicity—was seen by roughly the same number of people who saw the original column. It *could* have stopped me from going ahead with the lawsuit, but I'm not sure it would have. I can't say from the perspective of today.

With 20/20 hindsight, knowing all the legal machinations that would result from this, was there ever any time where you said, "Gee, I just wish we had issued a simple retraction and that would have been that?"

ROBERT NOVAK: Oh no. Never. Never, ever that. Now what the question was, "Did I really have to write this column?" That sometimes went through my head because obviously we write several columns a week, and it's all a matter of picking and choosing. We're not a column of record. We don't write about everything. We write about some oddball things—this was in the oddball category—and some mainstream things. And so that went on in my head. "Boy, I really didn't have to write this column. This is not the end of the world." But never, ever were there second thoughts about a retraction.

BERTELL OLLMAN: I think there were a number of things in the column which were stated as fact and that were false. But the most obvious one: was this quotation taken from somebody who may not exist? I should mention that in the subsequent period, we discovered that the Evans and Novak column had been dropped by *The L.A. Times*, and the editor mentioned—it may have been in *Time* magazine where I saw this—the editor mentioned he dropped their column because he could never be sure of their facts, even implying that they made up things. We suspected that this person may not have existed, and that this was just something they did in order to make their charges sound more believable. But when they said, for example, that I admitted to brainwashing my students, or trying to brainwash my students, this was taking half a sentence out of context. I think the sentence began with "Some people might think that ... " and that I'm trying to brainwash my students, and to this I reply—and I forget the exact wording of it—but I'm quite clearly not *admitting* it. They say, "Ollman even admits to doing this." So that clearly for me was a false statement as well. Then there were a few others. But I thought I saw four, maybe even five, false statements that went beyond opinion.

ISIDORE SILVER: I was outraged by the district court opinion. I kind of got more turned on to the issue because of the district court opinion dismissing the complaint. Against my will, by the way—I had other things to do, I was writing one of my legal treatises and I knew this case

would be a hot one that would consume a lot of time—
[I agreed to represent him]. Bertell didn't have the
money. He was not going to give me big things or anything. So to a large extent it was my sense that the
district court had misread the whole thing that ani-
mated my commitment to carry it forward.

After Professor Ollman filed his libel suit in February 1979, a U.S. district
court in Washington, D.C. granted summary judgment in September of
that year, dismissing the suit and ruling that the statements in dispute qualified as "opinion" and were therefore protected by the First Amendment.
Nearly 4 years later, however, a three-judge panel of the U.S. Court of Appeals ordered the lower court to reconsider its previous decision. In its review, the panel questioned several elements of the Evans and Novak
column including the possible omission of information that could be found
by a jury to be a "culpable omission of error." But 2 months later, in October
1983, that same U.S. Court of Appeals set aside the three-judge panel's decision to remand the case to a district court. Instead, it granted a petition by
Evans and Novak for a rehearing before the entire Court of Appeals—an *en
banc* hearing.

ISIDORE SILVER: When the case was dismissed [by the district court],
I read the opinion and I thought it was very shoddy.
We appealed through the normal appellate procedure.
And we won with the panel—the three-judge panel,
with one dissenting opinion. The two "liberal" judges,
said that a) he's not necessarily a public figure. We
can't assume that, at least on a motion to dismiss.
And b) there's a statement of fact here that he says
he indoctrinates. So I said, "Oh, we won." We got the
complaint reinstated. And then they moved to *en banc*
it [on appeal], which I understood. There was a First
Amendment issue. I would have loved to get a positive
decision. To realize that the full court is going to hear
it gave it a certain importance—I'm not sure I thought
it warranted it.

BERTELL OLLMAN: In the views of the various judges, most of them who
agreed with me—that is to say, the five who dis-
sented from the Court of Appeals opinion—all focused
on the claim that there was a political scientist who
made a statement about my reputation and that was
a factual claim, and we can see whether it was true
or false. And if it was false, then it was a libelous
statement. I think [Judge] Robinson found one or two
other statements which he thought were false state-

ments. So it's not that there was just one false statement, although Scalia—in what was I think a brilliant and very hard-hitting opinion—said that I shouldn't have claimed that there were a number of false statements. I should have focused on the one which, for him, was obviously false. Incidentally, it's interesting that even Bork, who has this very creative opinion, admits that if we take the words at their face value and don't introduce his unusual criteria of my being a political person—whatever that means—into the picture, if you just take the words at their face value, then that seems to be a factual statement. He seems to disagree with the majority opinion written by Starr who emphasizes the importance of contextualizing the statements. If we contextualize even that statement, for him it is an opinion. But Bork, who comes down on the same side of the fence [as Starr], seems to think that this is a factual statement, and he has other reasons to believe that I should not be given the chance to have a jury trial.

If the judges on the Court of Appeals had ruled in Ollman's favor—or had deadlocked, thus affirming the lower court's ruling—the case would have gone to a trial court where a jury would have decided whether the Evans and Novak column was libelous. Instead, the Court of Appeals ruled 6-to-5 against Ollman (see court opinion excerpts at chapter's conclusion). The court's majority opinion was written by Judge Kenneth Starr, who acquired perhaps his great notoriety in the late-1990s as the independent counsel in the Whitewater investigation of the Clinton Administration. It was in that opinion that Starr outlined the most noteworthy element to stem from this case—a four-part test to distinguish fact from opinion, the "*Ollman* test." A concurring opinion was written by Judge Robert Bork, whose 1987 nomination to the U.S. Supreme Court was rejected by the Senate amid a storm of political controversy. A dissenting opinion in *Ollman* was authored by a judge whose Supreme Court appointment in 1986 was approved, Antonin Scalia. He referred to the column as a "classic and cooly crafted libel."

ROWLAND EVANS: Of course, I disagreed with him. I thought [what Scalia wrote] was a cooly crafted attack on us.

ROBERT NOVAK: The Court of Appeals breakdown of the judges—the final decision of the judges *en banc*—was 6-to-5 in our favor. The breakdown was almost entirely opposite to what it usually is in a libel suit. The normal breakdown is that the liberal judges—and you can tell liberal and conservative judges, believe me—the liberal judges are very attentive to First Amendment rights and the conservative judges are not. This was, with one notable exception, almost completely flipped in the Court of Appeals where the conservative judges supported Evans and Novak and the liberal judges supported Ollman, which is just opposite to the normal way the situation would come out.

And why do you think that was?

ROBERT NOVAK: Because politics was stronger than their legal ideology, with one exception. Antonin Scalia joined the liberals in writing the most strident dissent against the decision saying our column was a "cooly crafted libel." I'm a great admirer and, I think, a friend of Nino Scalia, but he really disliked the First Amendment. He hates it, as a lot of conservatives do. On the other hand, the opinion was written by Ken Starr. And the very, very effective concurring opinion was written by Bob Bork which was used—not successfully, unfortunately—in his [U.S. Supreme Court] confirmation hearings to show he was a civil libertarian. The strong liberals—the knee-jerk liberals, if I might say—on the court all voted against us and for Ollman. This was not the case on the Supreme Court as far as it went. But this was the case on the Court of Appeals. The only event that I attended was the oral arguments at the Court of Appeals. On the Court of Appeals, sitting *en banc*, were not 11 judges, but 12. The 12th was Abner Mikva who was an old acquaintance of mine. He had been a former member of Congress—a Democratic member of Congress. We had had a little bit of a falling out, more on his part than mine. But we had been quite friendly. I had been a guest in his home for dinner. But I think he took exception to some things I wrote near the end of his congressional tenure. Immediately after the oral arguments, he recused himself because, he said, of his personal contact with the defendant in the case. He never made it clear whether he recused himself because he was prejudiced for us or against us, and I have never asked him that. Maybe sometime I'll ask him that. To continue this line of thought, when they asked for cert. from the Supreme Court, they immediately got it—reversing what had happened in the Court of Appeals—from the conservatives. They got agreement for cert. from the Chief Justice, Burger, who didn't like the First Amendment much and from Justice Rehnquist, the future Chief Justice. You only need four for cert., and my attorney said if you have the Chief Justice and another Justice, you have got cert. and we're before the Supreme Court and we're in trouble. But they didn't get a single other Justice for cert. Just those two.

And why do you think that was?

ROBERT NOVAK: I think the case was without merit! It was so totally without merit. But I thought Burger and Rehnquist were—unlike Starr and Bork, who I think were looking at it politically, maybe as good lawyers—so anti-media and so anti-First Amendment that any case that came up to them asking for cert. on a bench decision to throw a case out, they were going to ask to review it.

ISIDORE SILVER: I went to the court to pick up the opinion, and the clerk said, "This is the most confused case I've ever seen." [But] I was kind of heartened, in a way. There were five judges [on our side], it was a high-profile decision, there were five judges who said let this case move forward. Bertell wanted to, so I said let's take a shot at the Supreme Court. Let's take a shot. What do we have to lose? And we did and they denied cert. Rehnquist and one other Justice wanted to hear the case. And I said, "Well, with only two others, we would have gotten to the Supreme Court." Which would have delayed my book (laughs). All it would have done is cost me more money, more time—preparing for a Supreme Court argument is incredibly time-consuming—and delayed a book that I made a lot of money on. So I was of two minds again. I would have loved to argue it.

Why do you think the United States Supreme Court denied cert.?

BERTELL OLLMAN: I haven't the faintest idea. See, I start by thinking that judges are human beings like the rest of us, and like the rest of us have views—usually strongly—about social and political matters. And I don't think there's anyone on the Supreme Court who's close to sharing my social and political predilections. So I start by thinking these people were quite happy that this

Marxist who's terribly advocating all these outrageous things, that he got his comeuppance. Now,
they also have to find legal reasons to justify what
they want because of their personal biases. There's
something to this effect in Justice Douglas' autobiog-
raphy. There's a discussion he has with the then-Chief
Justice whose name escapes me. And the Chief Justice is trying to explain to this new member of the
Court how it works, and it's something to the effect
that it's our predilections which determine how we
vote. And we use our reason mostly to rationalize
what we want to do because of our predilections. And
he was a little shocked when he heard this, but after
some time on the Court, he comes to realize that this
is the way it works. So this is where I start in trying
to understand why judges vote the way they do. And
then their arguments are an attempt to support
that. There are exceptions to this, and there are all
sorts of nuances and this is how someone like Scalia
can find himself supporting my position in the Court of
Appeals. So I don't want to present that as law of nature which applies to every judge equally, but it applies
to enough judges most of the time so that this is an
important part—maybe the most important part—in
explaining any particular decision. And not the particular principles that they draw upon when they rationalize what it is they want to do.

ROBERT NOVAK: What made it close [at the Court of Appeals] was
Scalia. If it had broken down on ideological grounds, it
wouldn't have been 6-to-5, it would have been 7-to-4.
Secondly, [if the court had ruled the other way], this
would not have been a ruling for Professor Ollman. All
it would have meant is it would have gone to trial.
What would have happened in a trial? Well, again, the
question of would I have taken a bullet for the anonymity of this professor? Would I have said, "Okay, I'm going to lose this case because I can't prove this is
what he said?" Or would I produce my notes and name
the professor? Nobody's ever going to know that, are
they? But I don't think if I had revealed the source, I
don't think they could have won the case. If they had
won the case in a jury trial—this is something that's
been going on for years—this would have been appealed. I'm sure you're aware that many of these libel
suits are won by the plaintiff at the jury phases, and
reversed on appeal. So it's a long, long stretch to say

that if the 6-to-5 vote were reversed we would have lost the case. It would have prolonged the case, but the outcome was still very much in doubt. I think we still would have won.

Did anything about the judicial process surprise you?

ROBERT NOVAK: Yes, just how slow it was. It was agonizingly slow. The decision by the district court judge who threw it out was agonizingly slow. It took forever. Then we had the three-judge panel which ruled 2-to-1 against us, again on political grounds—two liberals and one conservative—and overruled the district judge. And then we appealed to the Court *en banc*, and let me tell you, although our lawyer thought we had a very good case— he thought it was very rare that you got an *en banc* reversal of a three-judge panel on this kind of a case, which is whether to hear the case or not. The fact that we were heard and then they reversed the three-judge panel would indicate to me that there was very little substance in the case. But it was an agonizingly slow process. This column was written in '78 and the Court of Appeals decision came in 1984. Don't forget that we had no discovery, we never got to that point. There were no depositions taken. All this was strictly whether the case should be heard. That was the only thing that was ever decided. And it took 6 years for that. And the *Sun-Times*, which in the middle of this underwent a change of ownership, picked up all our legal bills. I have no idea what they cost. I haven't the faintest idea. And they were prepared to pick up the legal bills for the trial, which I'm sure would have been considerable.

BERTELL OLLMAN: Well, at each stage there was something that surprised me. I was surprised that the district court judge threw it out as quickly and easily as he did. It seemed to me that I was certainly going to have a trial and that it would all be decided there. And so when the first judge threw it out, it was a surprise. It was a surprise that the committee of the Court of Appeals found in my favor—and I think it was a unanimous decision. And that was a surprise, too, that they would find in my favor. And then it was a surprise—so you see I'm being surprised at every stage—that the Court of Appeals agreed to hear the case *en banc* because I thought then, and my lawyer thought, that Evans and Novak were going to appeal to the Supreme Court. But instead they decided to try to get the Court of Appeals to hear it *en banc*. And apparently that hardly ever, if ever, happens. So the fact that the Court of Appeals agreed to hear it *en banc* was very surprising. And then that the vote was so close was something of a surprise. There, I was also surprised by one liberal judge, Abner Mikva. Mikva heard the case. And I've heard from a friend of a friend of a friend who Mikva spoke to indicating that he took my side in the case. But he recused himself before the vote. That surprised and angered me to no end, because if he had voted, then it would have been a 6-to-6 vote—which would have confirmed the decision of the panel of three. I did appeal to the Supreme Court and two Justices wanted to hear it, but you need at least four who want to hear the case. So the case never got to the Supreme Court. But Mikva turned out to be the difference and the reason that he didn't vote, it was suggested to me, is that he had been a congressman from Illinois a couple of decades earlier. When he was a congressman, Evans and Novak had written something critical of him, and he didn't want it said that he was getting revenge for something they had said critical of him many years before. That seems foolish to me, but in any case, whatever his reason was he changed the balance. It would have been, as I say, 6 to 6. And then in terms of surprises, I was very surprised by Bork's arguments. The first time I saw them I couldn't believe them because I know, from teaching political science, I know about Bork's reputation. I know what judicial restraint is and I know that Bork was supposed to be one of the main philosophers in favor of judicial restraint against judges who try to make new laws. And this was a grotesque example of a judge making a new law. He was, in fact, creating a category like a political person who was little different than a public person. Someone who consciously enters the political fray, as I was supposed to have done, is without any protection in libel law. I think this was one of the things which so shocked Scalia and some of the others who dissented. So this surprised me, that he could come up with such a cockamamie theory in order to support what I think was his pressuring for political and philosophical reasons.

AFTERMATH & LEGACY

Given the way that the case turned out, what signal do you think that sent?

BERTELL OLLMAN: That the rich and powerful can do what they want and that the courts will support them in this even when what they're doing goes against what seems to be the letter of the law.

ISIDORE SILVER: The [four-part *Ollman*] test has survived. You see it in a lot of opinions. That test is pretty much the standard test in fact–opinion issues. In general, I would agree with it. I don't find anything wrong with the test. It's just that I'm not sure how clearly it applied to our particular case.

ROBERT NOVAK: I think that there is no dividing line between the column and the news story. Certainly a columnist has a wide berth of freedom to render judgments about public people who are in controversial positions. To libel someone, you really have to tell a basic untruth about them.

ISIDORE SILVER: Well, I think it did have the effect of clarifying later— not in this opinion which was muddled and nobody agreed on a single rationale—[but] in a case like *Milkovich* where the Supreme Court said not everything is opinion. It may have had the ironic effect of making conservatives—apart from the politics of the case—more aware of the First Amendment and more interested in it. That's why the Rehnquist Court has been quite good on First Amendment issues. *Milkovich* is the direct descendant of *Ollman*. My impression is that modern libel law works pretty well in terms of protecting First Amendment values and media independence. *Ollman* contributed to that in the sense that it somewhat balanced the issue.

Milkovich v. Lorrain Journal, 497 U.S. 1 (1990), is a U.S. Supreme Court ruling in which the evolution of the opinion libel defense further developed, and which utilized the four-part Ollman test. In *Milkovich*, the Court rejected the opinion defense, holding the assertions in question to be statements of fact in spite their journalistic context—a newspaper column.

BERTELL OLLMAN: I hope that we try to go beyond generalizations regarding the press, and to see who owns the press and why someone with the point of view of Evans and Novak get to write a column which is distributed to several hundred newspapers across the country and have the kind of power that they do and how that is important to understand before we discuss in a general way what the freedom of the press should be. In our country, it's a matter of what the freedom of *this* press should be—what the freedom of *these* people should be, what the freedom of the people who own the paper, therefore what the freedom of their money should be. I guess in the last analysis, it's really the money which has the freedom. This has to be grasped to some degree before one can go on to see why anyone should contest this freedom. What is being contested is not freedom in the abstract, but the freedom of *these* people with *these* interests to do anything they want including breaking their own laws. And this is what I think my case is really an example of. They were willing to agree to Evans and Novak breaking our own laws. This goes back to the way my case is path breaking. It's path breaking because it shows that a certain interpretation which seems to be a standard of libel law no longer is. Therefore a new interpretation comes into being. But it no longer is because the old libel law was being used by someone who is socially an outcast—by someone who is so opposed to those who run our society. The freedom of the press in this case is the freedom of the people who own the press, through Evans and Novak, to break the laws of the land as they were at that point in our history in order to service all the better their interests. If someone has to be hurt, well that's small potatoes, that's unimportant.

ISIDORE SILVER: In a sense I think we were lucky to get as far as we did. I was so personally torn by what I was doing, I said, "Look, Bertell got a fair airing of his position, he got [some] judges to see the merits of the position, and in the next case Evans and Novak might lose." Maybe they will cross that line into fact rather than opinion. In retrospect, in a sense, they were lucky.

Do you in any way feel that the First Amendment protection of the press is too great today?

ROBERT NOVAK: Oh no. I really don't. I think it is a basic of a democratic society.

ROWLAND EVANS: This goes back to the age-old argument about the First Amendment. When you get down to the bottom of it, it's very hard to find serious flaws in the First Amendment because of its importance.

Has this case changed your mind in any way about how much freedom the press ought to have?

BERTELL OLLMAN: Well, how can I put this? I acquired a deeper understanding of something which I already had a general understanding of, which is that one must always contextualize particular problems. Contextualize means to put it into the context of which groups have power in the society and how that power manifests itself—to what kinds of institutions, and what the people with power do in order to reproduce the conditions which give them their power and enable them to serve their needs. I think this is where one must begin in trying to understand any particular event in our society. I suppose this is the A-B-C's of Marxism. What that means is one wants to see what the press is doing. One doesn't want to direct as much attention as I think most people do in discussing First Amendment issues to things like principles and rights and the amendments to the Constitution. One wants to spend time early on in such an analysis on who owns the press and what their interests are and what they do with the power of the press to promote their interests. I think this is crucial because what you have here is conservative newspaper columnists representing the elite and the rulers in our society taking off against a small, relatively powerless individual who has views which are opposed to theirs, and who would prefer to have society organized in another way. I think that this needs to be brought forward early on in making sense of what happened. And then, it's a matter of asking if I had access, as someone who holds opposing views, to other media where I might have presented another point of view where I might have engaged them in open debate about some of the questions—where I might have denied some of what they were accusing me of before the same audience. Of course, that wasn't the case. So first of all, it's a question of looking at the power relations between the parties in the dispute and not to move immediately to what principles are involved, because as we see in the kind of strange interpretation that the majority of judges, and particularly Judge Bork, gave to the principles, they were able I think to seriously twist not just the meaning of the law, but of the meaning of the various precedents established by earlier rulings in order to come out on the side of someone who they agreed with politically and philosophically. I think that was clear not just to me, but clear to members of the minority on the court. I was very struck with the kind of language used by normally restrained people like Judge Scalia. Scalia and the other people who were in the minority really are outraged—if you look at the language—and shocked and can't believe some of the reasons that the majority and particularly Bork are giving for deciding against me. It's not simply they're saying the majority is taking one view and we disagree. Scalia descends to irony in describing what Bork is saying. This is because they realize they can't possibly believe those reasons that their conclusions come from somewhere else. They come, I believe, from the political biases which they share with Evans and Novak and there wasn't any way that they were going to find against Evans and Novak on behalf of someone whose ideas they oppose so totally as me.

ROBERT NOVAK: I think what was really at issue was whether a columnist could give a fair opinion, using sources and giving justification, on someone who is a private citizen or a public figure. Again, I think that Justice Scalia in his dissent came very close to the old English position that if you say anything nasty about anybody, that's libelous. And that would make it very hard to do fair comment on public figures.

ISIDORE SILVER: For me, it was an intellectual challenge to see how our judicial system would deal with two questions: Are the weak going to be protected a little more than the strong in this context? And the genuine issue of whether something that's labeled as opinion can be dissected and found to be libelous nevertheless. There's always an issue in a case when a client comes to you and says, "Hey I want to sue this son of a bitch. Find an issue." For me the issue was this kind of pretty direct accusation of unprofessional conduct that, by common law standards, was clearly libelous. I thought they were hitting a man when he was down.

BERTELL OLLMAN: The press is an institution owned by real human beings who have strong points of view, and who use the press in ways which support their point of view—promote it. And, of course, some do this more than others. The result is you can't really talk about the freedom of the institution. It's really the freedom of the people who own the institution which becomes, in the last analysis, the freedom of money. I really don't think that money should have as much freedom as real human beings. And especially when us real human beings who don't have money are so much more numerous than those few human beings who have a lot and who with that enormous amount of money can buy up most of the media and have scribblers like Evans and Novak who are not given their order to write what they write.

PERSONAL REFLECTIONS

How do you respond to criticism that lawsuits such as this one place an undue chilling effect on the press?

ISIDORE SILVER: All lawsuits place a chilling effect. I don't like most lawsuits against the press. But we weren't suing the press. These guys were columnists who had time to reflect. That's another thing. All the time pressures of writing that's emphasized in the daily newspaper business where people get their facts wrong here and there. I don't think it applies to columnists. And we weren't suing the media. We were suing these two SOBs. It's true that every lawsuit has that potential. But these truly flimsy suits that are brought by people who are clearly victims of opinion, unlike Bertell, where juries give them $40 million is crazy. So in a way, if we had a small role in that, I do regret it. But I think there are so many more outlandish examples of people trying to zap the media, I wouldn't put Ollman's case in that category.

BERTELL OLLMAN: Given the actual content of the article that I was suing them over, I think this would have made people in the media more careful 1) of making up things, if we discovered that that's what had occurred as we strongly suspected that that was the case here, 2) it would make them very careful about making clear, factual statements of the kind which they made about that this professor was supposed to have made about my reputation. Be very careful about making those and damaging the reputation of people who are in areas of work where reputation is so important. So it would have made all people more cautious against doing something which people in the media, no matter what their politics, should not be doing. And I don't consider that a bad thing.

ROBERT NOVAK: Has [the lawsuit] made me more cautious? I think I'm cautious anyway. I thought this was a cautious column. In the early years of the civil rights movement, we did a great deal of columns on the Communists and the far left infiltration of the civil rights movement which were much more inflammatory than this—the student nonviolent coordinating committee being infiltrated from the left and the antiwar movement being infiltrated from the left. They were much more inflammatory than this. And this was one column, by the way, on Bertell Ollman. On the other subject, we had dozens of columns, and never had a libel suit against us. I don't think this column had any effect whatever on my writing.

ISIDORE SILVER: Maybe they were warned "Gee we had a close one, we had a little scare here. Next time we won't be wildly making accusations."

ROWLAND EVANS: No, I don't think so at all. I can't recall that we suddenly got cautious. I don't think so.

Are you of the mind that this lawsuit was an effort to place an undue chilling effect on the press?

BERTELL OLLMAN: On the contrary. I would like to have a really free press. I would like to have it free not just for the people who are rich enough to own it, I'd like to have people with a variety of positions able to express their views in the media and to exchange ideas with large numbers of people. And I would like them to have great freedom in expressing those views. That is one of one of my social and political goals. I certainly would like to be more associated with a critique of the narrow range of people who have access to the media and how they use them to promote their social and political position rather than with some kind of principle which some have suggested that I have which is to limit the freedom of the press. That certainly is not my goal. It just never has been, never would be.

ROBERT NOVAK: If we had lost at the end of this long procedure, I think that would have had the chilling effect on columnists on what they could write and particularly on the use of anonymous quotes.

In some circles, this is regarded as a landmark case and a landmark decision in this area. What, in your view, makes it so?

ROBERT NOVAK: What makes it so is that the idea that [just because] you're making commentary in a column on an individual is not per se an indication of malice. I think why this is a landmark case is that it indicates that certainly just reporting opinions about a controversial figure in the context of a critical essay is not a matter of libel. I think it takes some freedom from worry for columnists. I don't think there was a chilling effect. I'd say [the ruling] prevented a chilling effect.

BERTELL OLLMAN: I tried very hard to protect my family. My wife, in particular, worried about me. And maybe I should ask her what the toll was, but I don't think it was all that great on her, although she suffered with me when there were difficult moments. Otherwise, I was very lucky in never quite resigning from NYU, even when I thought, as I did for a couple of weeks, that I really was going to go to Maryland in the Fall—this all happening in April and May of '78. And I had indicated to many people, including the president at NYU who I had a meeting with, that I was going to resign, that I was going to Maryland, but I never actually wrote the letter. Once controversy emerged about my appointment, I was even more careful not to write the letter. So that I was able to fall back on my feet, as it were. I still had my job, I still had my duties here, I still had my salary. In this way, I wasn't in the position of someone who was fighting that kind of injustice from the outside having been fired from a job—which is often the case where one doesn't have another activity and doesn't have an income. I was terribly involved in each of the steps that we took at each stage of the case, and was concerned about the outcomes when we were preparing for some judgment to come down. But I can't say that it had any dramatic effect on the kind of life I was leading at the time.

ROBERT NOVAK: It's hard to analyze. Don't forget that nobody assigns me columns to write. I decide what I'm going to write. I am perhaps less inclined to pursue offbeat subjects involving personalities. That might be the case with me. I'm not sure. I think maybe the column has changed a little bit in 22 years. I don't think I would write this column now, not because I'm afraid of the libel suit, but I just don't write these kinds of columns now. Maybe it's had that effect. I'm not sure. I didn't write many columns like this before this one, and I didn't write many afterwards. So it's hard to tell. Otherwise, as far as writing harsh things about public figures, it hasn't bothered me.

BERTELL OLLMAN: I was involved in writing books and other things. I didn't have my emotions that much bound up in the case. I would have loved to win, and it hurt a lot when the news came down at each stage that I lost. But it didn't last very long. I have good friends and family that supported me so I was able to weather the blows when they came. In terms of the cost, my lawyer in the suit was a dear friend of mine, Isidore Silver, who was doing it on spec—that is to say, if I got damages he would get a percentage. Otherwise, I was just liable for the costs, which I forget what it was—maybe in the area of $10,000.

How does it feel to have your name personally linked to a landmark case in this area, knowing that it is brought up on a regular basis in university classrooms and so forth?

ROWLAND EVANS: Oh, it doesn't make me feel anything one way or the other. That's fine with me. I don't know what they're saying in classrooms about the case.

ROBERT NOVAK: I haven't thought about it much. Of course, it's always referred to as *Ollman v. Evans* and, of course, Evans had almost nothing to do with this column (laughs). During the 30 years that we wrote [the column] together, the general rule would be that one of us would write the column and throw it over to the other guy and he would edit it or re-write it. Sometimes the editing and rewriting was substantial if it was a subject that the other person was also engaged in and had some ideas. In this case, my recollection is that Evans kind of raised his eyebrows and he wasn't much interested in it and didn't know anything about it and made some minor pencil editing changes and threw it back at me.

Although, of course, it didn't turn out to your liking, how does it feel to know that your name is forever in the title of a case that has come to be regarded as landmark in this area and that is studied to one extent or another with regularity in classrooms across the country?

BERTELL OLLMAN: Well, it feels very strange because I think I like what is the lesson that I think most people take out of it which is that the press should be free to say what they want even if some people don't like it, and we should understand opinion in a very broad way so that it stretches into what some people might think of as the area of fact. And I don't mind that, except that I would rather be on the other side. I'd rather not be in the position, I think, of the villain of the piece—the one who is trying to restrict the press. I don't think I was trying to restrict the press. I think I was trying to restrict a very powerful conservative member or duo in the press who were using their political power and their media power to clobber a small person whose views they were hostile to, and who were willing to use lies and possibly to make up quotations in order to have that effect. This is the struggle I was in. I fear that there's not too many Marxist professors dealing with the case. It's mostly lawyers and professors in journalism who do treat the case narrowly in terms of what was actually said in the opinions and what actually appeared in the column. They don't try to contextualize it in terms of who has power in the society and who doesn't, and how those who have power use that power in order to preserve their ends.

ISIDORE SILVER: Bertell loved it. He loved it. Everybody was calling him, and here was the most famous man in America—for two seconds—a real McLuhan kind of phenomenon.

How often do you think of these events?

BERTELL OLLMAN: How often? Whenever I hear someone from Maryland (laughs). Less and less. It does come up in ways when I meet someone who has some connection to Maryland or when I see Evans and Novak on TV or happen to read one of their columns. It's usually provoked an incident, which doesn't happen all that often. It's not something that I think about on my own. I'm too busy doing other things.

If you had to pick out one lasting memory of your work on this case, what would that be?

ISIDORE SILVER: The sense of that colloquy, the sense of that "seminar" at the *en banc* [hearing]. I'll always remember that. Was it genuine? Were people—the 12 judges—genuinely exploring the deeper issues? That appealed to the academic in me. I love to sit down with people. And the fact that I wrote what I considered a good brief, and that the issues—however they were resolved—were significant ones that required a lot of analysis. I was happy to be involved in that whole process. It wasn't a simple case. I think that all in all, a lot of it did get explored. It didn't come out the right way, I think in some ways. But the intellectual [experience] was terrific.

ROBERT NOVAK: The lasting memory was when this political scientist who was the hub of the case and a very, very famous person—famous!—if I ever write my memoirs I'll reveal who it was. He refused to give me any assistance on this at all. It was just shattering to me. I had the column in front of me. He said, "Ollman has no status in the profession ... " I asked would he say that publicly. "No chance of it." Okay. "Our culture does not permit the raising of such questions." I thought, because I had considered this person a friend, that when I had a lawsuit against me—there were some further reasons which I can't give you because they would reveal the identity. It's that memory that will stand out for a long time.

When these events first started, could you have possibly imagined that they would have unfolded as they did?

BERTELL OLLMAN: Not in a million years. Everything was such a big surprise from the very beginning—that they were encouraging me to apply for this job, my getting the offer, and then the way things came to pieces—the various attacks on me and how the dissident people at the University responded. Eventually what happened was the President of the University, who had never gotten involved in such decisions—he was to retire in the summer. He then didn't act at all and retired before taking action on my appointment. His successor came in and immediately took action and decided I wasn't the best candidate for the job. He retracted the offer.

ISIDORE SILVER: It impacted my life very significantly in one way. I said I can't go through this again in terms of time. It was the sense of, "Do I want to be an academic, and a writer primarily, or did I want to get involved in this kind of grinding, endless appeal?" ... It's a terrific high in some ways—much more so than writing—but it really takes something out of you, especially if you lose. You don't feel that great.

Could you have imagined that the events would unfold as they did when they first began?

ROBERT NOVAK: (laughs) No, I never did. I'll tell you quite frankly, I was stunned when the suit was filed because to this very day I can find nothing even faintly libelous about [the column], and secondly, I was disappointed how long it took the trial judge to throw it out, but I assumed when he threw it out that that was the end of it. For this case to go on through two appellate processes, I never dreamed that that would be possible or that it would be making some kind of permanent contribution to libel law.

Bertell Ollman v.
Rowland Evans, Robert Novak

**UNITED STATES COURT
OF APPEALS FOR
THE DISTRICT OF
COLUMBIA CIRCUIT**

242 U.S. App. D.C. 301
Argued
En Banc March 6, 1984
Decided
December 6, 1984

COUNSEL: Isidore Silver, a member of the Bar of the Supreme Court of New York, pro hac vice, by special leave of Court, with whom Alan Dranitzke was on the brief, for Appellant: A. Daniel Feldman, for appellees. Ronald A. Jacks also entered an appearance for Appellees.

JUDGES: Opinion for the Court filed by Circuit Judge Starr. Concurring opinion filed by Circuit Judge Bork, with whom Circuit Judges Wilkey, Ginsburg and Senior Circuit Judge MacKinnon join. Concurring opinion filed by Senior Circuit Judge MacKinnon. Opinion dissenting in part filed by Chief Judge Robinson, with whom Circuit Judge Wright joins. Opinion dissenting in part filed by Circuit Judge Wald, with whom Circuit Judges Edwards and Scalia join. Statement concurring in part and dissenting in part filed by Circuit Judge Edwards. Opinion dissenting in part filed by Circuit Judge Scalia, with whom Circuit Judges Wald and Edwards join.

OPINION BY:
STARR, Circuit Judge:

…

This case presents us with the delicate and sensitive task of accommodating the First Amendment's protection of free expression of ideas with the common law's protection of an individual's interest in reputation. It is a truism that the free flow of ideas and opinions is integral to our democratic system of government.

…

At the same time, an individual's interest in his or her reputation is of the highest order.

…

In *Gertz*, the Supreme Court in dicta seemed to provide absolute immunity from defamation actions for all opinions and to discern the basis for this immunity in the First Amendment. The Court began its analysis of the case by stating:

Under the First Amendment there is no such thing as a false idea. However pernicious an opinion may seem, we depend for its correction not on the conscience of judges and juries but on the competition of other ideas. But there is no constitutional value in false statements of fact. Neither the intentional lie nor the careless error materially advances society's interest in "uninhibited, robust, and wide-open debate on the public issues."

...

Gertz's implicit command thus imposes upon both state and federal courts the duty as a matter of constitutional adjudication to distinguish facts from opinions in order to provide opinions with the requisite, absolute First Amendment protection. At the same time, however, the Supreme Court provided little guidance in *Gertz* itself as to the manner in which the distinction between fact and opinion is to be discerned.

...

In formulating a test to distinguish between fact and opinion, courts are admittedly faced with a dilemma. Because of the richness and diversity of language, as evidenced by the capacity of the same words to convey different meanings in different contexts, it is quite impossible to lay down a bright-line or mechanical distinction.... While this dilemma admits of no easy resolution, we think it obliges us to state plainly the factors

that guide us in distinguishing fact from opinion and to demonstrate how these factors lead to a proper accommodation between the competing interests in free expression of opinion and in an individual's reputation.

...

While courts are divided in their methods of distinguishing between assertions of fact and expressions of opinion, they are universally agreed that the task is a difficult one.

...

The degree to which such kinds of statements have real factual content can, of course, vary greatly. We believe, in consequence, that courts should analyze the totality of the circumstances in which the statements are made to decide whether they merit the absolute First Amendment protection enjoyed by opinion. To evaluate the totality of the circumstances of an allegedly defamatory statement, we will consider four factors in assessing whether the average reader would view the statement as fact or, conversely, opinion.

...

First, we will analyze the common usage or meaning of the specific language of the challenged statement itself. Our analysis of the specific language under scrutiny will be aimed at determining whether the statement has a precise core of meaning for which a consensus of understanding exists or, conversely, whether the statement is indefinite and ambiguous.

...

Second, we will consider the statement's verifiability—is the statement capable of being objectively characterized as true or false? ... Third, moving from the challenged language itself, we will consider the full context of the statement—the entire article or column, for example—inasmuch as other, unchallenged language surrounding the allegedly defamatory statement will influence the average reader's readiness to infer that a particular statement has factual content.... Finally, we will consider the broader context or setting in which the statement appears. Different types of writing have, as we shall more fully see, widely varying social conventions which signal to the reader the likelihood of a statement's being either fact or opinion.

...

[O]nce our inquiry into whether the statement is an assertion of fact or expression of opinion has concluded, the factors militating either in favor of or against the drawing of factual implications from any statement have already been identified. A separate inquiry into whether a statement, already classified in this painstaking way as opinion, implies allegedly defamatory facts would, in our view, be superfluous. In short, we believe that the application of the four-factor analysis set forth above, and drawn from the considerable judicial teaching on the subject, will identify those statements so "factually laden" that they should not receive the benefit of the opinion privilege.

...

Now we turn to the case at hand to apply the foregoing analysis. As we have seen, Mr. Ollman alleges various instances of defamation in the Evans and Novak column. Before analyzing each such instance, we will first examine the context (the third and fourth factors in our approach) in which the alleged defamations arise. We will then assess the manner in which this context would influence the average reader in interpreting the alleged defamations as an assertion of fact or an expression of opinion.

From the earliest days of the Republic, individuals have published and circulated short, frequently sharp and biting writings on issues of social and political interest. From the pamphleteers urging revolution to abolitionists condemning the evils of slavery, American authors have sought through pamphlets and tracts both to stimulate debate and to persuade.

...

The reasonable reader who puruses an Evans and Novak column on the editorial or Op-Ed page is fully aware that the statements found there are not "hard" news like those printed on the front page or elsewhere in the news sections of the newspaper. Readers expect that columnists will make strong statements, sometimes phrased in a polemical manner that would hardly be considered balanced or fair elsewhere in the newspaper.... That proposition is inherent in the very notion of an "Op-Ed page." Because of obvious space limitations, it is also manifest that columnists or commentators will express themselves in condensed fashion without providing what might be considered the full picture. Columnists are, after all, writing a column, not a full-length scholarly article or a book. This broad understanding of the traditional function of a column like Evans and Novak will therefore predispose the average reader to regard what is found there to be opinion.

...

Evans and Novak made it clear that they were not purporting to set forth definitive conclusions, but in-stead meant to ventilate what in their view constituted the central questions raised by Mr. Ollman's prospective appointment.... Prominently displayed in the Evans and Novak column, therefore, is interrogatory or cautionary language that militates in favor of treating statements as opinion.

...

Nor is the statement that "[Mr. Ollman] is widely viewed in his profession as a political activist" a representation or assertion of fact.... While Mr. Ollman argues that this assertion is defamatory since it implies that he has no reputation as a scholar, we are rather skeptical of the strength of that implication, particularly in the context of this column.

...

Next we turn to Mr. Ollman's complaints about the column's quotations from and remarks about his writings.... When a critic is commenting about a book, the reader is on notice that the critic is engaging in interpretation, an inherently subjective enterprise, and therefore realizes that others, including the author, may utterly disagree with the critic's interpretation.... The reader is thus predisposed to view what the critic writes as opinion.

...

Evans and Novak's statements about Mr. Ollman's article clearly do not fall into the category of misquotation or misrepresentation.

...

Professor Ollman also objects to the column's posing the question, prompted in Evans' and Novak's view by Mr. Ollman's article, of whether he intended to use the classroom for indoctrination. As we noted previously, the column in no wise affirmatively stated that Mr. Ollman was indoctrinating his students. Moreover, indoctrination is not, at least as used here in the setting of academia, a word with a well-defined meaning.

...

Finally, we turn to the most troublesome statement in the column. In the third-to-last paragraph, an anonymous political science professor is quoted as saying: "Ollman has no status within the profession but is a pure and simple activist."

...

We are of the view, however, that under the constitutionally based opinion privilege announced in *Gertz*, this quotation, under the circumstances before us, is protected.... [H]ere we deal with statements by well-known, nationally syndicated columnists on the Op-Ed page of a newspaper, the well-recognized home of opinion and comment. In addition, the thrust of the column, taken as a whole, is to raise questions about Mr. Ollman's scholarship and intentions, not to state conclusively from Evans' and Novak's first-hand knowledge that Professor Ollman is not a scholar or that his colleagues do not regard him as such.

...

[W]e are reminded that in the accommodation of the conflicting concerns reflected in the First Amendment and the law of defamation, the deep-seated constitutional values embodied in the Bill of Rights require that we not engage, without bearing clearly in mind the context before us, in a Talmudic parsing of a single sentence or two, as if we were occupied with a philosophical enterprise or linguistic analysis. Ours is a practical task, with elemental constitutional values of freedom looming large as we go about our work. And in that undertaking, we are reminded by *Gertz* itself of our duty "to assure to the freedoms of speech and press that 'breathing space' essential to their fruitful exercise." ... For the contraction of liberty's "breathing space" can only mean inhibition of the scope of public discussion on matters of general interest and concern. The provision of breathing space counsels strongly against straining to squeeze factual content from a single sentence in a column that is otherwise clearly opinion.

...

The judgment of the District Court is therefore: Affirmed.

...

CONCUR: BORK, Circuit Judge, with whom WILKEY and GINSBURG, Circuit Judges, and MacKINNON, Senior Circuit Judge, join, concurring:

...

[T]he statement challenged in this lawsuit, in terms of the policies of the first amendment, is functionally more like an "opinion" than a "fact" and should not be actionable. It thus falls within the category the Supreme Court calls "rhetorical hyperbole."

...

Ollman, by his own actions, entered a political arena in which heated discourse was to be expected and must be protected.

...

Plaintiff Ollman, as will be shown, placed himself in the political arena and became the subject of heated political debate.

...

[I]n order to protect a vigorous marketplace in political ideas and contentions, we ought to accept the proposition that those who place themselves in a political arena must accept a degree of derogation that others need not.

[T]he core function of the first amendment is the preservation of that freedom to think and speak as one please which is the "means indispensable to the discovery and spread of political truth." ... Necessary to the preservation of that freedom, of course, is the willingness of those who would speak to be spoken to and, as in this case, to be spoken about.

...

Ollman has, as is his undoubted right, gone well beyond the role of the cloistered scholar, and he did so before Evans and Novak wrote about him.... Professor Ollman was an active proponent not just of Marxist scholarship but of Marxist politics.... It was plain that Ollman was a political activist and that he saw his academic post as, among other things, a means of advancing his political goals.

...

Ollman was not simply a scholar who was suddenly singled out by the press or by Evans and Novak.... He had entered the political arena before he put himself forward for the department chairmanship. [H]e must accept the banging and jostling of political debate, in ways that a private person need not, in order to keep the political arena free and vital.

...

Ollman entered a first amendment arena and had to accept the rough treatment that arena affords.

...

[I]t is indisputable that this swirling public debate provided a strong context in which charges and countercharges should be assessed. In my view, that context made it much less likely that what Evans and Novak said would be regarded as an assertion of plain fact rather than as part of the judgments expressed by each side on the merits of the proposed appointment.

...

When we come to the context in which this statement occurred, it becomes even more apparent that few people were likely to perceive it as a direct assertion of fact, to be taken at face value. That context was one of controversy and opinion, and it is known to be such by readers. It is significant, in the first place, that the col-

umn appeared on the Op-Ed pages of newspapers. These are pages reserved for the expression of opinion, much of it highly controversial opinion. That does not convert every assertion of fact on the Op-Ed pages into an expression of opinion merely by its placement there. It does alert the reader that he is in the context of controversy and politics, and that what he reads does not even purport to be as balanced, objective, and fair-minded as he has a right to hope to be the case with what is contained in the news columns of the paper.

...

SCALIA, Circuit Judge, dissenting, with whom WALD and EDWARDS, Circuit Judges, join:

More plaintiffs should bear in mind that it is a normal human reaction, after painstakingly examining and rejecting thirty invalid and almost absurd contentions, to reject the thirty-first contention as well, and make a clean sweep of the matter. I have no other explanation for the majority's affirmance of summary judgment dismissing what seems to me a classic and cooly crafted libel, Evans and Novak's disparagement of Ollman's professional reputation.

...

[T]o say, as the concurrence does, that hyperbole excuses not merely the exaggeration but the fact sought to be vividly conveyed by the exaggeration is to mistake a freedom to enliven discourse for a freedom to destroy reputation. The libel that "Smith is an incompetent carpenter" is not converted into harmless and nonactionable word-play by merely embellishing it into the statement that "Smith is the worst carpenter this side of the Mississippi."

APPENDIX

"The Marxist Professor's Intentions"
by Rowland Evans and Robert Novak
The Washington Post
May 4, 1978

What is in danger of becoming a frivolous public debate over the appointment of a Marxist to head the University of Maryland's department of politics and government has so far ignored this unspoken concern within the academic community: the avowed desire of many political activists to use higher education for indoctrination.

The proposal to name Bertell Ollman, professor at New York University, as department head has generated wrong-headed debate. Politicians who jumped in to oppose Ollman simply for his Marxist philosophy have received a justifiable going-over from defenders of academic freedom in the press and the university. Academic Prince Valiants seem arrayed against McCarythite [sic] know-nothings.

But neither side approaches the central question: not Ollman's beliefs, but his intentions. His candid writings avow his desire to use the classroom as an instrument for preparing what he calls "the revolution."

Whether this is a form of indoctrination that could transform the real function of a university and transcend limits of academic freedom is a concern to academicians who are neither McCarthyite nor know-nothing.

To protect academic freedom, that question should be posed not by politicians but by professors. But professors throughout the country troubled by the nomination, clearly a minority, dare not say a word in today's campus climate.

While Ollman is described in news accounts as a "respected Marxist scholar," he is widely viewed in his profession as a political activist. Amid the increasingly popular Marxist movement in university life, he is distinct from philosophical Marxists. Rather, he is an outspoken proponent of "political Marxism."

He twice sought election to the council of the American Political Science Association as a candidate of the "Caucus for a New Political Science" and finished last out of 16 candidates each time. Whether or not that represents a professional judgment by his colleagues, as some critics contend, the verdict clearly rejected his campaign pledge: "If elected ... I shall use every means at my disposal to promote the study of Marxism and Marxist approaches to politics throughout the profession."

Ollman's intentions become explicit in "On Teaching Marxism and Building the Movement," his article in the Winter 1978 issue of *New Political Science*. Most students, he claims, conclude his course with a "Marxist outlook." Ollman concedes that will be seen "as an admission that the purpose of my course is to convert students to socialism."

That bothers him not at all because "a correct understanding of Marxism (as indeed of any body of scientific truths) lead automatically to its acceptance." Non-Marxists students are defined as those "who do not yet understand Marxism." The "classroom" is a place where the students' "bourgeois ideology is being dismantled." "Our prior task" before the revolution, he writes, "is to make more revolutionaries. The revolution will only occur when there are enough of us to make it."

He concludes by stressing the importance to "the movement" of "radical professors." If approved for his new post, Ollman will have a major voice in filing a new professorship promised him. A leading prospect is fellow Marxist Alan Wolfe; he is notorious for his book "The Seamy Side of Democracy," whose celebration of communist China extols the beneficial nature of "brainwashing."

Ollman's principal scholarly work, "Alienation : Marx's Conception of Man in Capitalist Society," is a ponderous tome in adoration of the master (Marxism "is like a magnificently rich tapestry"). Published in 1971, it does not abandon hope for the revolution forecast by Karl Marx in 1848. "The present youth rebellion," he writes, by "helping to change the workers of tomorrow" will, along with other factors, make possible "as socialist revolution."

Such pamphleteering is hooted at by one political scientist in a major eastern university, whose scholarship and reputation as a liberal are well known. "Ollman has no status within the profession, but is a pure and simple activist," he said. Would he say that publicly? "No chance of it. Our academic culture does not permit the raising of such questions."

"Such questions" would include these: What is the true measurement of Ollman's scholarship? Does he intend to use the classroom for indoctrination? Will he indeed be followed by other Marxist professors? Could the department in time be closed to non-Marxists, following the tendency at several English universities?

Even if "such questions" cannot be raised by the faculty, they certainly should not be raised by politicians. While dissatisfaction with pragmatism by many liberal professors has renewed interest in the comprehensive dogma of the Marxists, there is little tolerance for confronting the value of that dogma. Here are the makings of a crisis that, to protect its integrity and true academic freedom, academia itself must resolve.

4   *J.H. Desnick, M.D. Eye Services, Ltd., et al. v. American Broadcasting Companies, Inc., Jon Entine, and Sam Donaldson*

"I felt enormous pride as the story was going on the air. I just felt, 'Wow. I know this is going to do some good. I know this guy is finished. I know that he will not last as a doctor. His operation is over.' Overnight he went from $120 million in revenue to within about a year he was out of business and bankrupt.... [W]hat I really thought it would do is destroy his reputation, and I had no sorrow about that."

—Jon Entine, *PrimeTime Live* producer and co-defendant in
Desnick v. ABC, Entine, and Donaldson

"I think the signal has to be that if you do an honest job of investigative reporting, it's going to stand. If you work for an organization that can stand the expense of defending it in court, it's going to stand. And it would then say to other news organizations and journalists, if they can stand the expense of a Desnick assault in court, that they have nothing to fear from doing this kind of investigative report."

—Sam Donaldson, *PrimeTime Live* correspondent and co-defendant in
Desnick v. ABC, Entine, and Donaldson

"We begin tonight with the story of a so-called 'big cutter,' Dr. James Desnick." With those words, Sam Donaldson began a segment of the ABC News program *PrimeTime Live* on June 10, 1993. "In our undercover investigation of the big cutter you'll meet tonight," Donaldson continued,

134

"we turned up evidence that he may also be a big charger, doing unnecessary cataract surgery for the money."

Based both on the content of the 18-minute report and the newsgathering techniques employed—including the use of hidden cameras—Dr. Desnick, an ophthalmologist, and two of his associates filed suit against ABC, Donaldson, and the segment's producer, Jon Entine. The doctor's claims included trespass, invasion of privacy, and defamation. The report was highly critical of the Desnick Eye Center and its practices. The allegations made by *PrimeTime Live* included the claims that elderly patients were recruited for eye examinations, that they were told they required cataract surgery even when they did not, and that Medicare—and thus, the taxpayers—was defrauded in covering the cost of the operation. According to a court record, the report also included

> [a] former marketing executive for the Center [who] says Desnick took advantage of "people who had Alzheimer's, people who did not know what planet they were on, people whose quality of life wouldn't change one iota by having cataract surgery done." Two patients are interviewed who report miserable experiences with the Center—one claiming that the doctors there had failed to spot an easily visible melanoma, another that as a result of unnecessary cataract surgery her "eye ruptured," producing "running pus." A former employee tells the viewer that Dr. Desnick alters patients' medical records to show they need cataract surgery—for example, changing the record of one patient's vision test from 20/30 to 20/80—and that he instructs all members of his staff to use pens of the same color in order to facilitate the alteration of patients' records.

Desnick himself was no stranger to the field of law and regulation—or, as *Modern Physician* put it in its May 1, 2000 issue, "no stranger to controversy." In 1995 he was fined $100,000, placed on probation for five years, and banned from practicing medicine for two years as part of a settlement in a case alleging illegal marketing of eye care services. This followed an 18-count complaint that was filed against him by the Illinois Department of Professional Regulation. In 1997, a jury awarded $3 million to a Chicago man who claimed Dr. Desnick was negligent in treating the patient's eye condition. In June, 2000 he was fined $5000 and placed on probation for another 5 years when accused of lying to Indiana officials about the status of his medical license in Illinois. Later in 2000, he agreed to pay $14 million to settle allegations that he defrauded Medicare and Medicaid programs while operating a Chicago hospital. Neither Dr. Desnick nor his attorney would agree to be interviewed for this book.

Sam Donaldson is a 40-year ABC News veteran and remains an anchor and correspondent for that network. Highlighting his resume are two appointments as chief White House correspondent, interviews with Presidents and world leaders, co-anchor of *PrimeTime Live* and *This Week*, and anchor of the first network webcast. Jon Entine is a former NBC News and ABC News producer where his work won numerous awards. He is now a television producer and author of many articles and a book, *Taboo: Why Black Athletes Dominate Sports and Why We're Afraid To Talk About It*. It was with him that the Desnick story began its journey to becoming a *PrimeTime Live* report.

JON ENTINE:

I kept a file at work where I would dump interesting articles that I read here and there, and then would peruse it every month or two to see if it was appropriate timing to do that story or whether it needed more research. I had come across some references to Desnick in some articles. I had also recalled that Desnick had been the focus of a number of news stories in Chicago by Pam Zeckman, a well-known investigative reporter for the local CBS station. Those were two things. Those two things came together and I did some research on it, and I think there were some new standards that were just going into effect in the ophthalmology community—national standards about this. Some controversies that had been coming up in the press about so-called mills—cataract surgery mills. So I decided it was something I wanted to explore. Ultimately after doing some preliminary research on it, it was quickly clear that the number one, highest volume center in the United States was Desnick's. I didn't really know how I came down on the issue. I didn't know particularly anything about his operation, but I did know that I did want to take a look at his operation and kind of see—were the critics right, were the critics wrong, and where did I come down on this issue, and whether this is something we wanted to address for *PrimeTime*.

SAM DONALDSON:

Well, as a correspondent on this story, it was brought to me. I cannot recall—but the records will show—whether it was the guy in charge of the old *PrimeTime* investigative unit, whether it was Jon Entine himself—I do not recall. But someone within the unit came to me and said, "We want to do the story about this eye doctor, etc., etc., etc. Would you like to do it?" They obviously gave me some precis of it, and I said, "Yes, I would like to."

JON ENTINE: I did this story with Sam. And Sam is not so involved initially. He tends to be more involved later on. I sent it to Sam and got Sam's approval on it.

SAM DONALDSON:  I don't believe that we had done, previously, a full *Prime Time* piece together. But we had, from time to time because I think [Entine] worked at ABC News before we started *PrimeTime Live* in 1989. I think he'd worked in another department at ABC News where I'd encountered him. In other words, I knew who he was and I had some belief from personal experience that he was an honest, skilled producer. But, no, he would not have been one of my regular producers with whom I'd worked on a number of stories.

As best you recall, what can you share with me with regard to your association with him, particularly on this story?

SAM DONALDSON: [M]y personal experience with Jon Entine was just fine. [A] producer and a correspondent always have differences as the story progresses. "Well, I would do it this way." And particularly when it comes to the script. "Well, should we say this? Should we say that?" I'm sure we had those kinds of minor discussions. But the word is "minor." I don't recall any major thing at which we were at loggerheads one way or the other. Now, you know the famous sequence when we were trying to reproduce the refractor machines' false readings. That's all there in the transcript of what I said and all of that. But that wasn't, to me, either at the time or later, anything that impugned Entine's work on this piece.

The court record documents that in the *PrimeTime Live* report, Donaldson tells the viewer that "the Desnick Center uses a very interesting machine, called an auto-refractor, to determine whether there are glare problems." Donaldson then demonstrated the machine, saying that an optometrist who worked at the Desnick clinic from 1987 to 1990 claims the machine was regularly "rigged" and that he saw a technician tamper with the machine. The one-time optometrist maintained that the "rigging" happened routinely with elderly patients. Donaldson also reported that four other former Desnick employees who were interviewed claim that almost everyone "failed" the refractor machine's glare test for cataracts.

Do you recall what it was about the story that intrigued you and/or your producers?

SAM DONALDSON: What it was, was the allegation—at that point, of course, to me, that's what it was—that this was a "cataract mill"—the kind of the slang term used. The allegation that the Desnick Eye Clinic was more interested in the Medicare money than in supplying advice to patients who didn't need the operation—that in fact, they didn't need the operation. Anything—when you're an investigative reporter, and while I don't consider myself primarily that—I'm a political reporter—have been for 40 years in Washington—I've done a fair amount of this type of work. Anything that looks like there is some sort of—again, I'm using the slang term—rip off of customers, of the public and particularly—since I've done a number of these stories—in the health care field. We all have our health problems, right? I'm a member of the cancer club. I wasn't back then, though, so I shouldn't do a post facto explanation. I'm intrigued by it and I enjoy doing those stories, and I still do to this day.

What was it specifically that caught your attention about that operation?

JON ENTINE: That it was a high-volume surgery that was done in just a few minutes. And the dollars generated were just absolutely enormous. Most of the criticism was not about performance but should the Medicare reimbursement be so high because it was such an easy surgery? It's much different than when the standards were set up. Essentially it permitted doctors the expense of the public treasury to do relatively easy surgeries at outrageously exorbitant payments just because the system lagged in taking into account all the developments you'd gotten in surgery. To me, I saw it as a kind of fleecing story. I thought it was worth exploring to see if, in fact, this was true.

As the investigation proceeded, were you satisfied with the extent to which these hypothetical suppositions were borne out?

SAM DONALDSON: Well here's the way it works, and I know I'm telling you what you already know. Once I said, "Yes, I'd like to do the story," then Jon Entine and people who worked for him were responsible for the initial collection of further information, the debriefing in the field of potential interviewees. When they come to me and say, "Alright, we think we're ready to go ahead with a shooting schedule, then I sat down with him, and we went over what he had." "Okay, what do you got?" "Alright, we've got this, we've got this, this person would testify because we've already talked to them about this. We have two people who are former employees who we would have to use in shadow because they're afraid of retaliation, but they will tell us this. This doctor who worked at the clinic for some period of time, but resigned even though he had the opportunity to make a lot of money—he will tell us the following. And this man will, with the use of a machine exactly like the one used at the Desnick Eye Clinic, will show us how he is going to tell us Doctor Desnick personally jiggered the machine so as to be able to do operations for the Medicare money when it was not actually necessary." We went over all of this. At this point, I'm obviously taking Entine's word on the fact that he has these people and the story is as represented. So I said, "Fine, let's set up a shooting schedule." And we did.

JON ENTINE: The story started out much broader. Originally I had it set up to profile a doctor. I was going to show different kinds of doctors in different settings. It only became focused on Desnick as he emerged as such an interesting figure the more research I did. Frankly, it ended up serving as an interesting contrast to what most high-volume surgeons in that area are, which is pretty good.... [We interviewed] a lot of people who worked for him. I did a good dozen interviews of people who worked for him—everyone from doctors to recruitment officials. The general feeling was that he operated on the edges. I think it was reflected in the research, and it was also reflected in the people who spoke on camera. There was a general feeling in the community that was negative toward him, but I have to say that I didn't take that fully at face value. In his case I felt where there was smoke there was a forest fire.

The Desnick Eye Center had 25 offices in four Midwestern states and performed more than 10,000 cataract operations a year, mostly on elderly persons whose cataract surgery is paid for by Medicare. In March of 1993

Entine telephoned Dr. Desnick and told him that *PrimeTime Live* wanted to do a broadcast segment on large cataract practices.

JON ENTINE: [N]ot only had I been in touch with [Desnick], I led off [a meeting with him] saying he was a controversial person. All the documents show this. We wanted to do the story on high-volume surgery, and we weren't going to prejudge high-volume surgery. When we approached him, we presented the situation, we recognized that we wanted to be candid with him that this was a controversial story. The very first meeting with him, they called in the former U.S. attorney who had represented him—one of the heaviest hitters in all of lawyerdom in the United States. We had a very candid meeting where I outlined some of the controversies involving him and the charges against him. I mentioned in the original meeting that I wanted to get his view on the number of malpractice suits because I hadn't researched that before I went into him. So all of this was laid out. He knew this was not going to be a puff piece. He knew this was going to be a serious piece of journalism where we were going to discuss the pros and cons of high-volume surgery. I told him we were going to find some patients who were critical of him. I was very candid about that. And I asked him to supply some patients who had a very good experience, and he said he would do that, and ultimately they did do that. I thought we were extremely above board from the very beginning. There was no question that this was going to be a pretty interesting complex piece on a controversial man doing a very controversial medical technique.

According to the plaintiffs, Entine offered to make an agreement with Desnick Eye Services such that, if Eye Services cooperated with the preparation of the *PrimeTime Live* segment, the program would not focus exclusively on the Desnick Eye Center and would not use "undercover" surveillance techniques or "ambush" journalism. Dr. Desnick claims he accepted Entine's offer and cooperated with Entine and his crew for the preparation of the *PrimeTime Live* segment by allowing the defendants to videotape the interior of the Desnick Eye Center's Chicago office, to interview doctors, to videotape live cataract surgery, and to view Eye Center's informational videotape used for patient education. Desnick alleged that the defendants breached their agreement by focusing the show exclusively on Desnick Eye Center and by using "undercover" surveillance techniques and as a result of the breach, Eye Services lost patients, profits, and revenue.

JON ENTINE: In the original [story] proposal, even though it did have undercover with Desnick, I never imagined that we'd find the breadth of problems that we did find and document.

When you say "undercover," tell me what you mean by that.

JON ENTINE: Undercover takes on different forms in different stories. Specifically in this story it meant using a hidden camera. That was the only undercover dimension. You don't always have to use cameras in undercover work. In this case we did. The idea was, we debated this. I had to send the idea to the ethics department at ABC where this was debated very carefully beforehand at a number of different levels. The question always asked is, "Do we need to do undercover in this case, or is it just sensationalizing it? Does it add to the knowledge that we're going to bring to the viewer, or is it just a gimmick?" I think we got down to the point where the reason that the ophthalmogical controversy exists is because the evidence about whether surgery is necessary or not is destroyed in the very act of surgery. It's all based on the claims of the doctor who saw the patient before they went into surgery, or the claims of the patient. And all these things were subjective to a certain degree. You had no hard evidence which is the eye—the cataract—itself since it's essentially emulsified. So everyone agreed that the only way you could capture what was really going on and what representations were made was not through interviews afterwards where you get a "He said," "She said" but in this case a hidden camera undercover which should capture accurately what was exchanged between the patient and the doctor in terms of their need for surgery and the representations about the seriousness of their eye problems.

As you well recall, the use of hidden cameras was central to this story, I think it's fair to say.

SAM DONALDSON: Yes. Well, let me put it this way. It certainly was a major element in the story, but had we not had hidden cameras—which was a very effective and dramatics and, yes, controversial method—the things that we had, which we took to experts outside of that, the re-

fractor machine alone, I think, would have made the
story very important. But I'm not going to quarrel
with you over that except to say that I don't think it
was the only or the central element.

I'm wondering what the decision making was like on this story, and in general, anytime that they're going to be used—what the debate is like—the pros and cons of using them.

SAM DONALDSON:　We always had a policy concerning hidden cameras. I
think the policy was further defined—and perhaps the
word would be "tightened"—I'm not the expert—after
the *Food Lion* case which came subsequent to the
Desnick case. But before that, we still had a policy
about the use of hidden cameras. I don't have it in
front of me. To try to characterize it now, I'm sure I'd
leave out something and you'd say, "Well, you didn't
follow that or that." But it was not something that
Entine and I just dreamed up without management input and without following what we believed was then
the policy of ABC News.

The "*Food Lion* case" stemmed from another *PrimeTime Live* report. It
aired on November 2, 1992 and uncovered unsanitary practices in two
Food Lion grocery stores. The grocery chain sued ABC not on the content
of the report—although outside the courtroom it disputed the veracity of
the segment—but over the network's newsgathering techniques. As with
the Desnick report, those techniques included the use of hidden cameras.
After a jury initially found ABC guilty and awarded Food Lion $5.5 mil-
lion in damages, a federal appeals court reversed on all but one claim in
1999, and left Food Lion with $2 in damages.

On this issue of hidden cameras, would you say that they were a commonly used technique at ABC?

JON ENTINE:　At *PrimeTime* they were commonly used and in investigative stories. That was the qualification. They weren't
used for noninvestigative stories. It was part of a sig-
nature of the investigative unit.

In your opinion, were they overused?

JON ENTINE:　Absolutely. No question about it. I think that they
were overused.

SAM DONALDSON: (sigh) Ohhh, no.

JON ENTINE: The thing that I tried to do when I used them was to ask, "Is there something you can get from this that you can't get otherwise." That has to be the criteria. I think that in the beginning they were over-used, but I think by the time that I was there in the end, that they had reigned it under control. They seemed to use it everywhere in every situation in the beginning, but I think they got it under control, clearly. The danger is not in using hidden cameras, it's in the editing process. That's like in the Food Lion incident. You can selectively edit what goes in the hidden camera to present a certain point of view which is really at odds with the facts. That's the real issue, I think less than the fact of using the hidden camera itself.

SAM DONALDSON: I suppose you can always go back and look at a piece and ask, "Did you really need it there? Was that really necessary? Was the main thing that you had to have the information to prove the point, or was it more of the element of an interesting piece of video for the viewer?" I think second guessing—anybody in this life who goes back and says, "I would do everything I ever did in my life exactly the same" is some sort of a fool. So in general, I think I can defend our general use of hidden cameras, and not say to you, "I think 60% of the time we were right, but maybe 40% we weren't." No, I think a much, much higher percentage can be defended even in retrospect.

At that time, would you say that hidden cameras were commonly used at ABC?

SAM DONALDSON: Well, they've been used, mainly by us, meaning mainly by *PrimeTime Live*. I think *20/20* did some, but we were not the pioneers of hidden cameras. *60 Minutes*, as you know, was the pioneer newsmagazine using hidden cameras. But I think in the period 1990 to 1993–4–5—in there—we probably did more hidden camera work than any other single newsmagazine. We, at one time, I think had a reputation of using hidden cameras. When you thought of hidden cameras in the business, you thought of *PrimeTime Live*. But again, the record will show whatever it shows. My characterization of it is just my poor recollection, not a definitive answer to your question.

I'm curious about your personal opinion about the pros and cons of hidden cameras.

SAM DONALDSON: The policy as I understand it today is the right one, although frankly I'm not certain how often we use hidden cameras today. As you know, once *PrimeTime Live* died, in a short period of time I left the 20/20 effort. So I'm not really up on what we're doing today. But as I understand the policy, a) we only use the hidden camera when there is no other equally effective way to prove a central point to the story. Second, we don't use a hidden camera to squash a fly. It's the old saying, "You don't use the atomic bomb if you're going to try to prevent the bank robber from robbing the bank." Third, obviously we follow all applicable federal and state laws. The state laws, as you know, vary from state to state. And fourth—and this ties in with the fly business—there has to be a general feeling that the viewer is going to take away that we were fair, that this use of the hidden camera which met the other objectives, was a fair use. That can be a subjective evaluation, obviously. But we can all take any given type of illustration and on many of them I think most of us would agree that either "That's fair to use a hidden camera," or "That's not fair to use a hidden camera." And does the wrong that we're attempting to spotlight rise to the level of a serious, major wrong? That ties in with the question, "Is it fair?"

Some people would say that by definition, the use of a hidden camera invades someone's privacy—maybe not rising to the legal definition of it, but just practically speaking. How would you react to that belief?

SAM DONALDSON: I think it's case by case, quite obviously. Where is the camera? What is the activity that the person is doing? So when you ask me whether any use of a hidden camera invades someone's privacy, yes, I would think that to some extent that has to be a true statement. But whose privacy? Under what conditions? And who is the person from the standpoint of a wrong whose privacy we're invading? I can't give you a general rule. This has to be case by case. Obviously, if we invaded the privacy of Doctor Mengele at Auschwitz, it would have done a service to the world. I obviously use the strongest and most ridiculous case, but as you come towards center and then on the other side, I think this is all open to discussion.

As you know, one of the many counts that Desnick filed suit over is the invasion of privacy.

SAM DONALDSON: I suppose that if a bank robber is in the process—in the dead of night—of invading a bank, and the security cameras that are there, his privacy is being invaded. And you'd say he's a trespasser. I understand that circumstance. I would think most people would say his trespass takes precedence of the bank's invasion of his privacy. Now, if you come to a Desnick case, we could discuss or argue and maybe disagree—and, company policy was followed—as to whether the wrong that we think we illustrated using a hidden camera was a lesser consideration or a greater consideration than the so-called invasion of privacy. If you try to lay down a hard-and-fast rule, we're not going to get anywhere. I don't mean you and me—we're having a great conversation, you and I. But it's not going to be possible. The First Amendment has exceptions, as you well know.

You're suggesting that it's a matter of trade-offs, to some extent?

SAM DONALDSON: I am suggesting that it is a matter of judgment as to where the public interest lies. Again, I'm not talking about the breaking of the law. I've told you we're going to follow the laws. But if the law says this is permissible legally, then we do have an obligation to explain in discussing my understanding of our criteria at ABC News for the use of hidden camera—we have an obligation to go beyond that. But I am not going to go to the other extreme and say, "Hey, any use of a hidden camera has *ipso facto* per se an invasion of an individual's privacy connected with it, therefore we cannot do it." Sorry, I can't do it. I don't feel that way.

In his suit, Desnick used what might be called a shotgun approach, trying several claims and seeing what stuck to the wall. With regard to the trespass and privacy invasion claims, why, in your view, were you and ABC News not in violation of those?

JON ENTINE: In terms of trespass and being on private property uninvited, we *were* invited. The public was invited. It was a walk-in clinic. So there's no "uninvited" there, so I don't see there's trespassing. He invited people in to get looked at as prospective patients. So there's no trespassing there. The real issue is did we violate some patient–doctor privacy relationship. But the reality of it is, that's a two-part relationship in which the patient grants to the doctor that right. I don't see any violation in that sense. The patient was someone who was prepared to—if the patient leaves a doctor's office and spills the beans about what went on in a discussion, there's nothing illegal about that. All we did was record that rather than just the person representing that orally.

What about the counter to your contention that, yes, the public is invited in—patients are invited in—but these folks who came in were not legitimate patients?

JON ENTINE: I think you're splitting hairs here. These were prospective patients. They could have gotten surgery if they wanted. I wouldn't have stopped them. What I did was actually recruit people who were of age and could go in and might or might not need surgery. I didn't see any advertisement that said, "Only people who definitely need surgery are allowed to come into this office." Instead it said, "Come to the Desnick office. We're offering surgery and we'll give you a free exam." We fit—by any measure if you read their advertising—the patients who went in fit every single qualification that was offered in their advertising. There was no fine print that said, "You can come in here unless you're accompanied by a hidden camera, or you have motivations other than getting surgery." It just said, "Come in for a free exam." We went in for a free exam.

By the way, how did the people have the hidden camera on their person?

JON ENTINE: They didn't. We sent in everyone with a "son" or "daughter" or "cousin" or something like that. We didn't want them to have to worry about that. They were somewhat old and in some cases they were erratic and might have panicked. So what we did was to recruit people to act as hidden camera carriers. And we sent them in posing as their son, daughter, and so forth with the idea that they might need someone to drive them home afterward.

Desnick and his co-plaintiffs asserted that the defendants and their agents "intruded into the private spaces of the Desnick Eye Center in a highly offensive nature." The plaintiffs further claimed that their facilities, especially the examination rooms of the Desnick Eye Center, were places that any reasonable person would consider private. Finally, Desnick claimed that the defendants' intrusive invasion of privacy violated the doctor–patient relationship and jeopardized their ability to communicate openly with their patients.

The U.S. Court of Appeals, 7th Circuit, held that a corporation cannot bring action for invasion of privacy. As for Desnick's associates who claimed their personal privacy had been invaded, the court labeled it "strange" that the alleged intrusion was offensive because it violated the doctor–patient relationship. "The privacy and privilege of the doctor–patient relationship is for the benefit of the patient," the court ruled, "not the doctor.... While the doctor–patient privilege would be violated and communications between doctors and patients chilled if the doctor clandestinely filmed and recorded a medical examination or consultation, the same cannot be said when the patient chooses do the filming or recording." Thus, the court dismissed the invasion of privacy/intrusion claim.

Wasn't another Desnick technique to pick up patients and drive them to his clinic?

JON ENTINE: They had vans that went out. They had full time Desnick Vans that would go out. We had a picture of one unloading that had swept past a home.

And that practice of theirs with the van was routine?

JON ENTINE: Oh yeah.

When did you first get an inkling that a lawsuit was brewing?

JON ENTINE: I got it before the piece came out because they basically said, "We're going to sue you if you air this piece."

When did you get that word?

JON ENTINE: In the 2 weeks before. They kind of let us know. They felt that we'd be committing a slander against him and the company if we aired this piece. We were quite on guard in recognizing that that was indeed a possibility.... I was almost certain that we were going to be sued, and so was ABC. It had nothing to do with any of the individual things on this. They just knew of Desnick's litigious reputation. When you bring in [the Chicago law firm of] Winston and Strawn, you're bringing in one of the heavy hitting corporate lawyers in the country. I think everyone anticipated that was a more than likely conclusion of what was going to happen.

Given that, did you ever face any pressure in terms of the content of the piece?

JON ENTINE: I'm not sure the word is "pressure," but the piece was heavily scrutinized. We went through a couple of weeks of daily conversations about every single line in the piece with the legal department, internally, with Sam, with Rick Kaplan and Ira. Everyone wanted to make sure we dotted every "I" and crossed every "T." But there was a general belief that this was an enormously important story, a good story for *PrimeTime*, a good story for Sam, and that we'd really make a difference with it. I think that everyone was really willing to go the extra nine yards. We realized that there were some areas that [Desnick] would try to exploit. But we ultimately felt, as the courts ended up agreeing, that this was a pretty seamy operation. It wasn't paradigmatic of what was going on in the industry, but it definitely represented a certain trend at the extremes of what was going on in cataract surgery.

Did you ever, with this piece in particular, face any pressure—covert or overt—in terms of the content of the piece out of fear of being sued?

SAM DONALDSON: No, not that I recall. Entine might be the best judge. In defending the piece to the lawyers, once the script had been completed, he was the one who went over line by line the script. I only heard of things if the lawyers were insisting on changes. Now you say, "Alright Sam, which changes did they insist on?" I don't remember that they insisted on any major changes. But knowing lawyers, I'm sure that they said, "Oh, can you change this word." "Don't show that picture." I'm sure they did that. But whatever it was does not stick in my mind as being something that I remember as I do with some other pieces in the 10 years we did *PrimeTime Live* where I violently objected, or I thought, "Well, that is an untoward watering down." Whatever changes they might have insisted on were fine with me from the standpoint that I still thought we were telling the story, doing it effectively, and not pulling punches that should not be pulled.

On a personal level, what is it like to learn of the fact that you have been named as a defendant in multiclaim, multimillion dollar lawsuit?

SAM DONALDSON: It's part of the business. It's easy for me to say that now, and you'll say, "Yes, in retrospect what else would you say?" From the very first, I knew that we would prevail. How did I know? I had no lock. The judge was not a personal friend of mine. But we had the facts. And I was persuaded when we put the piece on the air—or we would not have put it on the air because I do have the understanding that the only way I can stay in this business is to preserve a reputation for at least *believing* that I have the facts. And I thought that we did have the facts. And the fact that this man who had a reputation—had a history—of defending his ability to do what he was doing by suing, by the use of a weapon which has with it, as you suggest in your question, a certain intimidating value, that he was going to do this. When I say he was going to do this, when we put it on the air I didn't know he was going to do this. But when you ask me when I'd heard he'd done this, my reaction was, "Okay, here we go!" But it's going to cost the company money. I'm sorry, but in this business we all know that that's one of the costs of doing business if you're going to put on investigative reports.

JON ENTINE: I react on a number of different levels. I'm generally perturbed that ABC is going to have to defend something like that. It doesn't help the news business—especially the news business at ABC—to have cases of this magnitude, and in this case, a case of this legal importance, that they have to face. On the other hand, I relish it. I am very proud of the work that I do.

The idea of having to go into court and testify and give depositions on all that was something that I looked forward to with utter sincerity and expectation. I was more than thrilled to go into court and lay out the case and lay open my record. I always say to people that my record as a journalist is absolutely open to scrutiny. I wouldn't do investigative journalism if I didn't feel that way. I couldn't wait for this case to get to go forward with Desnick. I couldn't wait. I was so confident that we had captured a snapshot that was as honest and fair as could be. By that I don't mean the pseudo-notion of objectivity—that you have to balance everything 50–50. In this case, I thought we had been fair. I couldn't wait—couldn't wait. I thought the first deposition was fun. My lawyers weren't so excited about everything. Neither was ABC. But to be honest with you, that's what I live for—doing stories that are meaningful and if need be, to ruffle feathers to get the truth out.

Had you ever been named a defendant before this?

SAM DONALDSON: You know, I don't think so—which may speak badly of me, I don't know. But I can't recall ever before.

JON ENTINE: I have since been named in one [case] involving an undercover story that's still pending, involving surgical scorecards. It was a story of doctors who were ranked by a state surgical scorecard system set up by the state of New York. We did undercover with doctors and saw how they would represent themselves based on their surgical scorecard.

Has it occurred since?

SAM DONALDSON: I don't believe so.

Once the segment aired, were you satisfied with it?

JON ENTINE: I was thrilled by it.... It was a good story for Sam. It was a good story for me. I was proud of the story. It was one the stories I'm most proud of. All along, I think ABC was willing to take their lumps with this. They recognize that the very nature of investigative reporting is to take those lumps. I think that they're much more cowed now in a different corporate environment than they were years ago.

Would you say that in some respects, the practice of journalism was on trial here?

JON ENTINE: Some of the techniques, yeah, the tactics. Sure, in the sense of the use of hidden cameras and the whole question of representation—if I had misrepresented myself—would that have been an issue in this case? Ultimately, I think all the judgments ruled that we're not going to decide whether you misrepresented yourself or not—we're not going to address that. But if you *had* misrepresented yourself, it wouldn't have necessarily constituted a slanderous misrepresentation on your part. So, yes, there are serious issues here. The First Amendment is pretty delicate and a lot of these issues are important for journalists, but I also believe that privacy rights are pretty important. I think a good percentage of investigative journalism is pretty sloppy and it's based on anecdotal moments rather than hard research that honestly tries to accurately portray a pattern of things. With that in mind, I think on both sides of the equation, this ended up being a pretty revealing and important story.

Do you think to some extent that journalism—or certain techniques of journalism—in addition to you and ABC News, were on trial here?

SAM DONALDSON: Well, I didn't think of it this way at all. My memory of this whole period—and I've now mentioned it once or twice to you—revolves around the dispute over the refractor machine and whether we had cooked the test more than the hidden camera aspect of it. Yes, I think I knew at the time that was one part of Desnick's suit—one part of his alleged claim of wrong—wrongful action, all of that. But to me, unlike the *Food Lion* case which came later, where clearly from the outset the central proposition was the hidden camera—the trespass allegation and the hidden camera. I never thought of it in this one as that at all.

Your lead attorney was Mr. [Michael] Conway. Describe your association with him.

JON ENTINE: He's a very low key, straightforward guy. I felt he's honest with a capital "H." He genuinely cares about First Amendment issues. He absolutely did not want me to ever say or do anything that misrepresented the facts of the situation, even if it meant losing the situation. He never wanted me to go beyond the facts. He was just so good. He's the essence of what I'd want out of a lawyer in this type of case. He became—I don't want to overstate it as a personal friend—but let's say a professional friend. I respect him immensely.

Your attorney was Michael Conway out of Chicago. Any recollections about your association with him on this?

SAM DONALDSON: They were all pleasant. They were all terrific. We talked on the phone a number of times, even until recent days (laughs), but the main association was when he came to Washington with an associate of his to prepare me for the deposition. We sat down and we reviewed the video of the piece. We talked about the script. He suggested to me the kinds of questions I'd probably face. He said all the right things to give—give honest answers, stuff like that. He gave me the good advice that most of us who are not adept at this almost never take, and that is keep your answers short, answer the question asked, don't sit there and volunteer your life's history if the guy asks how old you are. I broke it, I'm sure, although Conway later said I did a good job. I can remember rambling on (laughs). Again, the central questions to me—oh, they were all over the lot, and they were up and down and all that— had to do with the refractor incident. Let me just say—maybe it's my ego working—with some pride, I look upon the transcript of the raw interview, the raw discussion there, as being something I'm rather proud of because it is clear from the transcript and the video that when we first tried it, I still could see fine. And instead of saying, "Oh yes, I see, oh yes, it's blurred," I said, "This is ridiculous. We can't do this. I'm not going to do this." I think I even one time said, "Where's the effect? We're not going to fake it." I may not have used the word fake. And Conway told me later that he thought with the judge who was weighing the merits, that that was something that the judge should have found very much in our favor against Desnick's claim. Now the man who did this test for us, the former employee, we disclosed in our piece that he had sued Desnick and lost, although as I recall the reason he lost was that he had missed a filing deadline. At least that's what we thought. My memory dims now to the extent that it turned out exactly that way. But we disclosed that there was bad blood between them in addition to his claim that Desnick did all of this.

To what extent, if any, were you involved in legal strategy?

JON ENTINE: I was involved in the sense that I loved my lawyer and we got along great. The case was based on the information that I gave them. So the case got underway, so to speak, when I went to Chicago and I met with them for a week giving everything I knew about the case. They built the case and the defense based on all the information I gave them. My deposition was clearly key to this. Every deposition that was done, they would ask me to read it and comment on it. So I was involved in being the information source for them, but I don't think I gave them legal strategy at all. They were really smart and I respected them. I never felt that I needed to stick in my two cents. Informationally, they were very interested in every way that I would view a certain aspect of testimony, for example, that Desnick would give or testimony that an expert witness would give. So based on my reaction to that, I would show them why someone's expert testimony was really fallacious. Then they'd decide what to do with that information.

SAM DONALDSON: Overall, I understand allegations made by Desnick throughout the long process of the trial—the filing of the suit. And when I say understand them, our lawyer in Chicago kept me abreast of it. I gave a deposition.

Tell me a little bit about Desnick.

JON ENTINE: I don't really know him that well. I just know him in his business dealings. I found him incredibly smart. By reputation he was an incredibly good technician in what he did, but he really wasn't doing surgery when

I was there. He decided he wanted to be a business-man. It was clear he wanted to be a well-known pub-lic figure. He loved the limelight, and he loved being a power baron. He made that quite clear in conversa-tions. He liked to drop names. I found him very typical of people like him in that they're very self-absorbed. You have a conversation with them and they hold 90% of the conversation, and then at the end they say, "You're such a good conversationalist." It's very typical of that egocentric personality type. I think it really came up in the very first interview that I had with him. Here I was to give a presentation and out of the hour that we were together, 50 minutes was them talking about who they are and what they are and how great he is and all this kind of stuff—which is just fine by me. That's the best kind of pre-inter-view I could ever do. But I expected it to be exactly the opposite ratio. I didn't know if he was seamy. I had no sense that he dealt with individuals in a seamy kind of way. But when I started doing research and talked to people who had worked in his office and so forth, pretty much everyone felt it was an ethi-cally questionable operation. But I have no personal judgment against him. I didn't see anything bizarre about what he was doing. I just found him walking the ethical edge on something that he thought he had the cover of a very loose government Medicare sys-tem that would continue to allow him to operate with a very wide latitude.

SAM DONALDSON: I only met him once. It wasn't the best of meetings because having gone through the routine of asking for interviews and all of that and having been told "No," we staked him out, as you know from the piece. He came back from overseas to the airport. I was waiting for him at the gate with two cameras and began a running questioning of him as he vainly tried to get away. He crossed the street and made his way. What we have in the piece is a matter of re-cord of what I said to him and he said to me. He made his way to a small table in a coffee lounge or a bar or something. Of course we didn't follow him with the cameras, but I went in and sat down with him and tried to convince him to do a nonrunning inter-view with me, but he was having none of it.

One of the claims he later made in the lawsuit was that promises were made to him that were not kept including that there would be no such attempts to interview him in that manner.

SAM DONALDSON: Well, of course, that falls on the face of it. None of us in an investigation like this will ever say to a person, "We will not ever attempt to talk to you in a public place about this" (laughs). That promise in return for what? If we had made that promise, what do we get in return? Usually there's a *quid pro quo* if people make a promise to someone else. Tell what it was that if we had made such a promise, we were getting from Desnick in return for not staking him out. It's just silly. I can assure you—and I speak only for myself. Entine can speak for himself. I made no such promise by any method of communication to Desnick or any of his people about that. Now, I'm sure—I don't remember our conversation—but I'm sure as I often have with people where we've done this kind of stakeout—said to them, "Look, if you will sit down and do a formal interview with me, we will not use this video of us running across the street." I'm sure I must have said something like that to him. But, of course, he never agreed to a sit down interview.

As you know, he later made the claims that there were promises made to him that were not kept, i.e., that it would be a positive story, fair and balanced, no ambush interviews, no undercover surveillance. Is that true?

JON ENTINE: First, you've got to see where he said those things were represented. We had a very long and candid meeting with the lawyers present. If you go through the court briefs, you'll see that the lawyers say that none of those things were said in those meetings. What was said in those meetings was exactly what I said to you now. I always said it would be fair and balanced, and I believe it *was* fair and balanced. But I never made any representation about undercover or anything like that. We would never make that. And, in fact, all those claims come from a meeting I had at his office with just him and me. Those claims are just fictitious. I wouldn't suddenly make any claims there that I didn't make in front of the lawyers. In fact, when the lawyer was asked about this in the case, he admitted that I had made none of those claims in front of him, anyway. I think that was a post hoc example of Desnick trying to maintain this. Not only can I represent this personally, but I was so concerned about making even one statement even directly to him where I could claim that I never made it, that before the meeting with him in his office, I was at a Denny's in Chicago. In fact, I had just come from a meeting with another doctor who had supplied me with background information about Desnick. I had stopped at a Denny's to make a call to call my office. I talked to Ira Rosen, who was the head of that unit at that time. I said, "Ira, what do I say if he asks are we gonna do any undercover? We've been very, very straight so far. We haven't over-promised, but we've been very sparse in what we've said." I was frankly surprised from the initial meeting at how uninquisitive [Desnick] and his lawyer were about techniques and so on and so forth. They did not raise anything. He said, "Under no circumstances should you misrepresent us and say that." And I agreed. I just wanted him to know that I would not deny that we would do it. I would just say that we do not discuss how we execute a story. I don't want to give him the false impression that we will or we won't. We just don't discuss that. That's ABC policy. We do not discuss those things. And that's what I was prepared to say, but the question never came up. I know he definitely pushed the envelope. He was aware that high volume surgery as he was doing it was questionable. And I also think he was aware that the recruitment process that he was doing was questionable. It's like taking a net to fish instead of using hook and bait. You're going to sweep in a lot of stuff that shouldn't be. He knew that's the nature of that. I guess he figured what the heck. So you give someone who doesn't need cataract surgery cataract surgery. It's a harmless operation. In essence, they're probably gonna need it soon enough so it's a benefit to them. No skin off their nose because the government is going to pay for it. In his mind, it was very easy to rationalize it. It's not like he's bringing people in to take out all their teeth and not put any replacement in. He's actually bringing a benefit to them that the government is going to pay for and they're not. The fact that the population in general is being scammed by this, I think, was less of a concern to him. He didn't see it as a negative. It was a win-win situation for everybody except the taxpayers.

Did anything surprise you about this case and the way it unfolded?

SAM DONALDSON: Yes, but it has nothing to do with our script or our presentation. I understood, as I've told you, from his background, that he loved to sue—that it was a method he used in order to intimidate and also to say to the public, "Hey, I'm suing this guy!" So the public wouldn't immediately be left with the impression that, yeah, what we'd said was absolutely correct. But I was surprised how long he kept on after losing time after time in his presentations to the judge. Time after time, long after it would seem to me that a reasonable person—had they been honestly thinking they were wronged and wanting redress and even if they had been using it as a tactic—would have said to themselves, "You know, I gave it the college try, but it didn't work. I lost." He simply kept on. I told you it cost the company money. It must have cost him lots and lots of money. And that surprised me. It really did.

Dr. Desnick's case against ABC, Entine, and Donaldson was not confined to the trespass and privacy claims. For example, a defamation claim against the same group of defendants was put to rest in October, 2000. The Seventh Circuit of the U.S. Court of Appeals ruled that Desnick had failed to present enough evidence to pursue a defamation claim against these defendants.

What about his run for the U.S. Senate [in 1995]?

JON ENTINE: I think that was a desperate, last minute attempt to rehabilitate his reputation. He had enough money that I think he thought he could buy his way in.

Given the outcome of the case, what kind of signal do you think this sends?

SAM DONALDSON: When I think of signals from investigative reports in the last 15 or 20 years, I don't think of Desnick. I think of *Food Lion*. I can think of some other cases, some done by ABC, some done by other news organizations, which to me are landmark type questions. I don't use that as a legal term, but I use it as a conventional term. I don't think of *Desnick* as being in that category. But if it is in that category—if people are paying attention to it, if people now look at the *Desnick* case—I think the signal has to be that if you do an honest job of investigative reporting, it's going to stand. If you work for an organization that can stand the expense of defending it in court, it's going to stand. And it would then say to other news organizations and journalists, if they can stand the expense of a Desnick assault in court, that they have nothing to fear from doing this kind of investigative report. And I think—since I still absolutely believe in the integrity of what we found and said, that we did some sort of a service to some people—can I give you their names? Obviously not—by exposing a wrongful action by the Desnick Eye Clinic. So I think it sends a salutatory message, frankly.

How do you compare these circumstances to a situation like Food Lion?

JON ENTINE: In general, I think the Food Lion piece was mis-edited. Their overall story was fairly accurate, I think. I think it had a lot of truth in it. But they opened themselves up to raise questions about their zeal. I think they were over-zealous. There's a real danger in all of television news, especially *60 Minutes* type of investigative stories. This was said to me once by Don Hewitt: "We're in the business of white outs and black outs. We're looking for heroes, and we're looking for victims, and we're looking for enemies." There's the danger of rubbing out the grays in stories. Any time that the perpetrator, so to speak, is complicated—where the circumstances are complicated—it makes them less willing to do the story because you don't have that simplistic television drama that is true of investigative reporting. The problem with *Food Lion* was that it was a little bit more complicated. There were motivations of employees. I don't think it was nearly as systematic as they claimed it to be. And the editing was very selective to make the problems more gross and dramatic than they were. They took anecdotes and they turned them into facts. Even though they had a

story there, the story wouldn't have been as re-
motely as dramatic as it was by the way it was for-
mulated.

Given the outcome, what kind of signal does this send?

JON ENTINE: Unfortunately, it probably sends the opposite signal
than I would hope. Aggressive individuals can cost corporations a lot of money to defend the public's right
to important and critical information. There's no winner here. ABC is not the winner here, and the public is
not the winner here. This cost ABC a ton of money.
I'm not arguing for the British system where the
plaintiff has to reimburse the system if they can't
prove their claim. I think that would be chilling to people who were wronged by the system. On the other
hand, I don't think this is a win for journalism, I don't
think this is a win for anybody. There's definitely a
chilling effect as a result of this even though it was ultimately a slam dunk victory.

*If somehow—and I know you expressed confidence in the way this would
turn out, but with the courts you never know—conversely, if this had gone
the other way, what kind of signal would that have sent?*

SAM DONALDSON: Just turn on its head what I just said to you. I don't
think it was a close case, and the way it turned out,
the courts agreed. If therefore, we put the same report on the air and had it exactly right and somehow
the courts, through the appeal process which we
would have certainly taken from some lower court decisions against us—if the courts had found at the end
of the day that we were liable, it would have been a
terrible, terrible message and a terrible chilling on
journalism because again, we had it right. If you can't
get it right and follow the rules, and be held harmless,
then you can't do a report, you can't do anything.
We're at the mercy, then, of people who can do anything they want to and unless the legal system gets
them, they can't be exposed by the press at all. I just
can't conceive of it turning out the other way.

*On the first point that you raise—regretting that ABC had to defend itself in
this situation—have you seen any kind of chilling effect surfacing?*

JON ENTINE: Since I was leaving ABC right as this thing was evolving to go to do some writing and some other things, I never saw the chilling effect, but I understand that it's there, from what people have told me. They've really pulled back on undercover, for instance, and they're much more careful with litigious stuff. But most stories are not black and white, so I find there's an intrinsically ideological chilling effect, and it happened at *PrimeTime* as well. You tend to go after the smaller fry because the story is easier—the easier it is to form it as a black-and-white. So you go after small time crooks who do unnecessary car repairs, but you rarely go after Medicare fraud of this magnitude, or you rarely go after complicated stories in which a person might be wrong 55% versus 45%, instead of 90 versus 10. So I think the chilling effect is that you go after only easier stories, and by going after only easier, more black-and-white stories, they tend to be less consequential. So that's the chilling effect. You're still going to see the same volume of stuff, but the stuff that's uncovered is the kind of roll your eyes exposing of the local astrologist rather than serious journalism. So that's always been the nature of these things. *PrimeTime* actually bucked that for a while, but now I think like *Dateline* and all the rest, they've fallen into line to doing silly exposés or ones that have real no merit.

Bottom line, what was this case really about?

JON ENTINE: This is a story of someone who could have been enormously good to society getting so caught up in his own—he went up his own backside. He really thought that he was more important than his patients and his responsibility to the government through the Medicare program. That's the scam that I was exposing. The real scam is human nature. The best of this is to arm people to be more thoughtfully skeptical about every aspect of their life. That doesn't mean cynical at all, but just recognize that you can be taken and it can have real serious consequences financially and otherwise.

SAM DONALDSON: I think our case proved—and I think in rejecting Desnick's claims of injury the courts agreed—that we did a report on an eye clinic that wrongfully did cataract surgery for the money from Medicare in many instances—not in all, but in enough instances—so that this wrong rose to a level of a truly public matter. And it was about exposing—and we were not the original ones; there had been a local station in Chicago and other news media that had done stories on Desnick, as you know—but in exposing it nationally, we did a service and the case was about a wrong to elderly people and to the taxpayers of this country. And over our report, which ultimately the courts agreed had done a service—or at least they agreed in the sense that they turned back Desnick's claim that he had been wronged.

A moment ago you raised the idea of the chilling effect. Have you noticed anything along those lines at your workplace in the wake of this case, or any others? Certainly it came out correctly, as far as you're concerned, but you have mentioned the tremendous cost associated with this defense.

SAM DONALDSON: Well I can only speak generally to you because in the wake of this case the record is clear that *PrimeTime Live* and other news organizations continued to do investigative reports and continued to use hidden cameras, just as you questioned me about that part of our report. I think now today again—forgive me but I'm frying other fish and therefore I'm not in the middle of what's going on in the magazine shows today, alright? But my impression is that across the board we're doing fewer and fewer hidden camera investigations. I can't tell you why that is. I know of no memo or meeting or directive from the management of ABC News which says, "We're going to cut down on hidden camera investigations for the following reasons ... " I'm simply saying that my impression is that we're doing fewer. I can't tell you why. Is that a chilling effect? Or is that simply moving on to other ways? I don't know. As far as investigative journalism is concerned, I think it's alive and well in the overall sense. But let's face it—I took maybe one economics course in college, and I learned about something called Gresham's Law: bad money drives out good. In the news business, with a small amount of time, stories that are of not great consequence but for one reason or another we've decided we want to do, simply drive out the time to do other stories. And while I think in an overall sense investigative journalism is alive and well, my impression is that the business—I'm not talking primarily or necessarily about ABC News—but the overall business—television—is doing fewer of the Desnick-type of investigative report. I'm sure you can point to something and say, "Didn't you see such-and-such?" "Didn't you see so-and-so?" No. But that's my impression. And, again, why that is—is it a chilling effect? "Hey, we think one more diet pill story is going to get the viewers." I don't know. I'm not in charge of that.

As a journalist, when you do a piece such as the Desnick piece …

SAM DONALDSON: It's very satisfying.

I'm wondering when you do a piece like that or one of the many other investigative pieces you do, while, yes, it's satisfying and certainly there's tremendous pride in doing good, solid work and good journalism, how do you as an individual deal with the fact that that story has consequences for another human being?

SAM DONALDSON: Well, let's go back to our discussion of the invasion of privacy that we had. I'm going to replay it. Which human being? When we put it on the air, I was certainly aware that the story would have consequences perhaps for Desnick. I was aware, I suppose, that the story would have consequences for some of the people we interviewed that were part of the story—again, the two women who were the ex-employees that we shaded in black so they wouldn't be seen—they were *afraid* to be seen—and it could have consequences for them. I also believe—and I hate to sound priggish, so high and mighty—but I also believe that the story would have consequences for these elderly people who Desnick was rounding up by the busloads to bring in. And we did stress the money. Again, I'm sounding very high minded, but you're asking me—for the taxpayers! Which people do I feel more for, or that I worried more about? Well, clearly Desnick was low on my list, as long as we treated him fairly and we were accurate. The consequences to Desnick, if they were adverse, was *not* something I was going to spend a sleepless night over.

As a journalist, yes, there's tremendous pride on putting a good piece on the air. But how do you deal with the fact that you've done that to another human being?

JON ENTINE: Almost in every piece I feel that and I think about that. I recognize that. Oddly, maybe I was just so hardened by what he had done that this is the only investigative piece that I didn't feel personally concerned about this issue. One, because I didn't think it would destroy him financially. I thought it would nick him financially. And what I really thought it would do is destroy his reputation, and I had no sorrow about that. There are other investigative stories that I've done where I felt enormous qualms even as it was going on the air. I think about that all the time. Journalists are leeches to a certain degree. We have enormous personal consequences. I think a lot of us, especially investigative journalists, don't take into account the fact that once you attach a person's name or profession or reputation to a point of view— whether it's legitimate or not, exaggerated or not— it's pretty unshakable. But you know something? I just didn't feel it in this case. I really didn't. And I can't think of any other story I've ever done, even non-investigative stories, that it hadn't either crossed my mind or I'd become obsessed by that. I've cancelled a number of stories that I'd completely done. I once cancelled a story for a year because I thought it would have bad consequences for the people involved that outweighed the news value and journalistic value of putting it on the air. Ultimately, I was forced to put it on by my bosses.

What sort of reaction along the way, if any, did you get from colleagues or, in fact, even competitors in the TV news industry with regard to this suit?

SAM DONALDSON: I got some good comments from people in the business. My phone didn't ring off the hook from everyone from Mike Wallace on down. But I heard from people outside of ABC who are in this business as well as some of the people here. And you can always tell. Your friends always say, "Good piece the other night." But if they go the extra mile, you can always tell they really mean it. And if they talk about what it's like. So the personal reaction was satisfying on that score.

JON ENTINE: I know that people at NBC News were humiliated because their report [on a similar topic] was so bad....
We really realized that this was a "dot your I" and
"cross your T" kind of piece, so we took an extra
month. They rushed theirs.

Is there anything with regard to this case that is often overlooked?

JON ENTINE: Yeah. A number of people misportray this that a judge
found that we had violated certain legal principles
when, in fact, when judgments were made, they said
we are not going to rule on whether this was a violation. It's portrayed as if we did something wrong but
got away with it because the law allows us to do
something that maybe legally is on the edge of things
but is ethically over the line. I don't think that's what
any ruling said. They would just say we're going to rule
on the merits of whether we had made promises. I'm
appalled that it's misrepresented that way. They don't
realize how careful the judge was and how careful my
lawyer was in arguing. His intention was always to argue, "Let's put aside for the moment whether misrepresentation is right. Can it even be adjudicated on
the principle itself?" He managed to get it thrown out
on the principle rather than on the merits. They never
got to the point of evaluating the merits because that
wasn't even an issue. That appalls me because it goes
right to my reputation.

On a personal level, did it have any negative effect?

JON ENTINE: No, not in the slightest. If anything, it gave me a little
caché among certain people. I just had my eyes
lasered by a well-known laser surgeon in L.A. They
knew about the piece. It got a lot of play in ophthalmology journals. He shook my hand and said, "I'm glad
you put that guy out of business." If anything, it's kind
of brought an extra luster to it. People in Chicago definitely know about it.

When this began, could you have imagined how it would have unfolded?

JON ENTINE: Of course not. I definitely thought it was a good story
and I thought he was potentially litigious. Although the
more I got into it, I realized it was more than poten-

tially litigious. When he hired who he hired, a big heavy hitter, I knew that this was going to be a big story, meaning that it was going to have repercussions, but I never would have imagined that 10 years later we'd still be talking about this.

If I asked you to pick out one memory from your involvement with this case that is most lasting, what might that be?

JON ENTINE: Doing a grueling, three-day deposition with Desnick there staring at me the whole time—and finding it scintillating, fun and frightening at the same time. I was constantly monitoring every word I said to make sure I was saying things as exactly as I wanted to say them and not as I have a tendency to do and that is to be too enthusiastic and offer more than is asked for which, as my lawyer says, will only get me in trouble. I felt enormous pride as the story was going on the air. I just felt, "Wow. I know this is going to do some good. I know this guy is finished. I know that he will not last as a doctor. His operation is over." Overnight he went from $120 million in revenue to within about a year he was out of business and bankrupt. I knew the process was in place for that to happen. I don't think I'd ever done something in journalism before that had that much impact. That was one of the proudest moments of my career.

J.H. Desnick, M.D., Eye Services,
Ltd., et al. v. American
Broadcasting Companies, Inc., Jon
Entine, and Sam Donaldson

UNITED STATES COURT
OF APPEALS FOR
THE SEVENTH CIRCUIT

Argued
November 1, 1994
Decided
January 10, 1995

COUNSEL: For J.H. DESNICK,
M.D., EYE SERVICES, LIMITED,
MARK A. GLAZER, M.D.,
GEORGE V. SIMON, M.D., Plain-
tiffs—Appellants: Dan K. Webb,
Julie A. Bauer, Steven F. Molo,
WINSTON & STRAWN, Chicago,
IL. Rodney F. Page, ARENT, FOX,
KINTNER, PLOTKIN & KAH,
Washington, DC.

For JOHN ENTINE, SAM
DONALDSON, Defendants—Ap-
pellees Michael M. Conway, Mary
Kay McCalla, James M. Falvey,
HOPKINS & SUTTER, Chicago, IL.

JUDGES: Before POSNER, Chief
Judge, and COFFEY and MANION,
Circuit Judges.

OPINION: POSNER, Chief Judge.

...

The plaintiffs' claims fall into
two distinct classes. The first arises
from the broadcast itself, the second from the means by which ABC
and Entine obtained the information that they used in the broadcast.
The first is a class of one. The
broadcast is alleged to have defamed the three plaintiffs by charging that the glare machine is
tampered with. No other aspect of
the broadcast is claimed to be
tortious. The defendants used excerpts from the Desnick videotape
in the broadcast, and the plaintiffs
say that this was done without Dr.
Desnick's permission. But they do
not claim that in showing the videotape without authorization the
defendants infringed copyright,
cast the plaintiffs in a false light, or
otherwise invaded a right, although they do claim that the defendants had obtained the
videotape fraudulently (a claim in
the second class). And they do not
claim that any of the other charges
in the broadcast that are critical of
them, such as that they perform unnecessary surgery or that Dr.
Desnick tampers with patients'
medical records, are false.

...

The fact is that consent to an entry
is often given legal effect even

though the entrant has intentions that if known to the owner of the property would cause him for perfectly understandable and generally ethical or at least lawful reasons to revoke his consent.

There was no invasion in the present case of any of the specific interests that the tort of trespass seeks to protect. The test patients entered offices that were open to anyone expressing a desire for ophthalmic services and videotaped physicians engaged in professional, not personal, communications with strangers (the testers themselves). The activities of the offices were not disrupted ... [n]or was there any "inva[sion of] a person's private space."

...

No embarrassingly intimate details of anybody's life were publicized in the present case. There was no eavesdropping on a private conversation; the testers recorded their own conversations with the Desnick Eye Center's physicians. There was no violation of the doctor–patient privilege. There was no theft, or intent to steal, trade secrets; no disruption of decorum, of peace and quiet; no noisy or distracting demonstrations.

...

[T]he entry was not invasive in the sense of infringing the kind of interest of the plaintiffs that the law of trespass protects; it was not an interference with the ownership or possession of land.

...

The right of privacy embraces several distinct interests, but the only ones conceivably involved here are the closely related interests in concealing intimate personal facts and in preventing intrusion into legitimately private activities, such as phone conversations.

...

The defendants did not order the camera-armed testers into the Desnick Eye Center's premises in order to commit a crime or tort.

...

Telling the world the truth about a Medicare fraud is hardly what the framers of the statute could have had in mind in forbidding a person to record his own conversations if he was trying to commit an "injurious act."

...

[P]romissory fraud is actionable only if it either is particularly egregious or, what may amount to the same thing, it is embedded in a larger pattern of deceptions or enticements that reasonably induces reliance and against which the law ought to provide a remedy.

We cannot view the fraud alleged in this case in that light. Investigative journalists well known for ruthlessness promise to wear kid gloves. They break their promise, as any person of normal sophistication would expect. If that is "fraud," it is the kind against which potential victims can easily arm themselves by maintaining a minimum of skepticism about journalistic goals and methods. Desnick, needless to say, was no tyro, or child, or otherwise a member of a vulnerable group. He is a successful professional and entrepreneur. No legal remedies to protect him from what happened are required, or by Illinois provided. It would be different if the false promises were stations on the way to taking Desnick to the cleaners. An elaborate artifice of fraud is the central meaning of a scheme to defraud through false promises. The only scheme here was a scheme to expose publicly any bad practices that the investigative team discovered, and that is not a fraudulent scheme.

Anyway we cannot see how the plaintiffs could have been harmed by the false promises. We may assume that had the defendants been honest, Desnick would have refused to admit the ABC crew to the Chicago premises or given Entine the videotape. But none of the negative parts of the broadcast segment were supplied by the visit to the Chicago premises or came out of the informational videotape, and Desnick could not have prevented the ambush interview or the undercover surveillance. The so-called fraud was harmless.

One further point about the claims concerning the making of the program segment, as distinct from the content of the segment itself, needs to be made. The Supreme Court in the name of the First Amendment has hedged about defamation suits, even when not brought by public figures, with many safeguards designed to protect a vigorous market in ideas and opinions. Today's "tabloid" style investigative television reportage, conducted by networks desperate for viewers in an increasingly competitive television market constitutes—although it is often shrill, one-sided, and offensive, and sometimes defamatory— an important part of that market.

AFFIRMED IN PART, REVERSED IN PART, AND REMANDED.

5   *Hustler Magazine and Larry C. Flynt v. Jerry Falwell*

"Jerry Falwell once made a remark that I didn't save the First Amendment; the First Amendment saved me. And I said, 'Jerry, that's the first thing you've ever said that I agree with.'"

—Larry Flynt, publisher, *Hustler* magazine

"[B]y defending his rights, we were defending everybody's rights.... I believe that there is a constant tension in our society between those who want to curtail freedom of speech and those who want to expand it. If those who want to expand it stop doing anything to help that, then those who want to curtail it will gain the upper hand, and pretty soon free speech will be a thing of the past."

—Alan Isaacman, Larry's Flynt's attorney

In its November 1983 issue, *Hustler* magazine published what looked like another in a series of advertisements that were a part of a national campaign by Campari, a liqueur. The campaign had been a series of endorsements in which celebrities—in an interview format—spoke of their "first time"—the first time they drank Campari. This time, however, the full-page spread was not a paid advertisement at all, but instead a parody designed by *Hustler*. The "endorsement" was from an unlikely source, Rev. Jerry Falwell, a nationally-known pastor and head of the Moral Majority. Moreover, besides suggesting that Rev. Falwell drank often and preached while intoxicated, the "interview" stated that his "first time" was an incestuous relationship in an outhouse.

Jerry Falwell talks about his first time.*

FALWELL: My first time was in an outhouse outside Lynchburg, Virginia.

INTERVIEWER: Wasn't it a little cramped?

FALWELL: Not after I kicked the goat out.

INTERVIEWER: I see. You must tell me all about it.

FALWELL: I never really expected to make it with Mom, but then after she showed all the other guys in town such a good time, I figured, "What the hell!"

INTERVIEWER: But your mom? Isn't that a bit odd?

FALWELL: I don't think so. Looks don't mean that much to me in a woman.

INTERVIEWER: Go on.

FALWELL: Well, we were drunk off our God-fearing asses on Campari, ginger ale and soda—that's called a Fire and Brimstone—at the time. And Mom looked better than a Baptist whore with a $100 donation.

INTERVIEWER: Campari in the crapper with Mom . . . how interesting. Well, how was it?

FALWELL: The Campari was great, but Mom passed out before I could come.

INTERVIEWER: Did you ever try it again?

FALWELL: Sure . . .

lots of times. But not in the outhouse. Between Mom and the shit, the flies were too much to bear.

INTERVIEWER: We meant the Campari.

FALWELL: Oh, yeah. I always get sloshed before I go out to the pulpit. You don't think I could lay down all that bullshit *sober*, do you?

© 1983—Imported
by Campari U.S.A.
New York, NY
48° proof Spirit
Aperitif (Liqueur)

Campari, like all liquor, was made to mix you up. It's a light, 48-proof, refreshing spirit, just mild enough to make you drink too much before you know you're schnockered. For your first time, mix it with orange juice. Or maybe some white wine. Then you won't remember anything the next morning. **Campari. The mixable that smarts.**

CAMPARI® You'll never forget your first time.

Rev. Falwell was horrified to the point where he felt like weeping. He filed suit against *Hustler* and its publisher Larry Flynt, seeking damages for libel, invasion of privacy, and intentional infliction of emotional distress. The case proceeded down a judicial path in which a jury delivered a "split verdict," an appeals court then affirmed that ruling, followed by the United States Supreme Court reversing. But it was even more than that. It was a case that produced a landmark First Amendment ruling. The *Harvard Law Review* described it as a classic First Amendment case in which the "antagonists could have been selected by central casting to embody the fundamental constitutional tension between anarchic self-expression and strict civil virtue."

These antagonists were Larry Flynt, publisher of *Hustler* magazine and well known for his run-ins with the law over his attempts to distribute a variety of pornographic materials. He continues to pursue a variety of business interests, including the publication of *Hustler,* from his Beverly Hills, California offices. His adversary in this case was Rev. Jerry Falwell, then and now a well-known public figure, pastor, head of the Moral Majority, a television and radio evangelist, and president of Liberty University. Through his publicist, Rev. Falwell turned down repeated requests to be interviewed for this chapter. Mr. Flynt's case was argued by Alan Isaacman, who still practices law and is based in Beverly Hills, California. One of his clients continues to be Larry Flynt.

BEGINNINGS

ALAN ISAACMAN:

I started to represent Larry Flynt in 1978, about 6 months after he got shot. He got shot in March of '78. He moved his business operation from Columbus, Ohio to Los Angeles. I was practicing law here. I was with a firm and had been practicing for about 10 years or so and tried a lot of cases in the interim. He sent his in-house general counsel around to interview some law firms. The attorney interviewed us. I met with them and we started doing some business. He had just had a very large verdict against him back in Ohio in one of the Guccione cases. It was something like a $39 million jury award which a judge reduced to about $10 million, and put a special master in charge of all his affairs. So he was really kind of reeling from that in a kind of financial sense. He had been sued by Hervé Villechaize, who's now deceased. Villechaize played "Tattoo" on "Fantasy Island." There was a libel claim there and I began to represent Flynt in that case. That's pretty much the first case I had for him.

And then as time went on, I took on more and more.
We did cases, not just in California, but started to
take them on all around the country. Over the years,
we became his primary counsel and, in effect, his general counsel.

How would you characterize your association with him over the years?

ALAN ISAACMAN: (laughs) It's been a very interesting association. Most
of the time we have gotten along very well. We've had
our battles. He's a very strong-willed individual. In my
own way, I'm a strong-willed individual. So every once
in awhile we have a little run-in. But most of the time
we've gotten along better than a lot of people would
ever expect, I think, particularly since we've had such
a long run together through a lot of ups and downs in
his own life.

LARRY FLYNT: I said [to Alan], "I'm your dream client. I'm the most
fun, I'm rich, and I'm always in trouble."

*Is there an additional challenge or obstacle when it comes to representing
someone like Mr. Flynt who—shall I say?—is typically viewed as something
less than a standard bearer for morality?*

ALAN ISAACMAN: Yes, there is. There are extra dimensions to the problem of it. Part of my background—it's an unusual back-
ground—I spent just about 5 years in a federal public
defender's office early in my career. I've had a lot of
criminal cases. I've been involved in and over the years
I've also represented people beyond those criminal
cases. All my clients haven't been the most savory individuals. Some of them have fine reputations. But he's a
guy that clearly sought publicity—and still does, for
that matter. In earlier years, he was looked on with
greater disfavor than he is today. That was something
to be aware of. To me, my attitude was as long as I'm
performing ethically, then I'm not going to care a whole
lot about what other people think about it. As long as
I'm true to myself in this, I'm not really that concerned. I figure it's a lawyer's plight in life to have a
thick skin. If he doesn't, that's his own problem.

*In a similar vein, how would you respond to someone who would ask you,
"How can it be that protecting the rights of a pornographer is a good thing?"*

ALAN ISAACMAN: You've hit on something that made it a lot easier for me to represent him. And that is I always could see that by defending his rights, we were defending everybody's rights. And particularly in the First Amendment area—the free speech area—where it's so easy to fall victim to the attitude that, "Well, this is so outrageous that what this person is saying, the courts or the government should stop them from being able say it." Pretty soon you go down that slippery slope and they're telling you what you can say. So the battles, to a large extent during my career—or at least this time of my career—were being fought in the First Amendment area. They were being fought with people like Larry Flynt or in pornography as far as free speech is concerned. If you were going to fight for free speech, you were going to fight it in that area to a large extent—not exclusively, but to a very large extent. All you have to do is go back and look at the appellate cases and see where the First Amendment comes into play, you'll see Larry Flynt's name very often. So I didn't have any problem defending what he was doing. To me, it's a lot easier to defend his right to say things than it would be to defend someone who's charged with murder or something much more physically injurious.

Does it take somebody like a Larry Flynt to push the envelope of the law?

ALAN ISAACMAN: It does. I don't say that he does it because he's trying to protect everybody's rights. You can draw your own conclusions about his motivations. But I believe that there is a constant tension in our society between those who want to curtail freedom of speech and those who want to expand it. If those who want to expand it stop doing anything to help that, then those who want to curtail it will gain the upper hand, and pretty soon free speech will be a thing of the past. I really think that that's true. I don't think you can sit back and let inroads be made on freedom of speech. And somebody like Larry Flynt is there—for whatever his purpose—he's there serving as a kind of foil to those who want to curtail speech. He's out there making a case in some peoples' minds that speech ought to be curtailed, but as long as the courts are there in place, I think that people will recognize over time that this is what we have to tolerate even if you don't like what he's saying.

THE CASE

ALAN ISAACMAN: What happened in the Falwell case—this case came about during a very volatile period in [Larry's] life. He was actually going to court on a daily basis on the DeLorean matter. John DeLorean was charged with conspiracy to distribute cocaine. Flynt got hold of some videotape and then some audio tape. The videotape was actually a piece of government evidence where DeLorean was looking at the cocaine and saying it was better than gold. He gave it to Dan Rather. It was on the news for four or five nights in a row on the national news. The press was all around him and he was doing kind of bizarre antics. I think he had some kind of a manic phase that he was going through at the time. But in any event, he was going to court every day because the court was insisting that he disclose the source of his tape. He was being fined $10,000 a day in order to come in every day and either perjure himself or pay the fine. The fine was later raised to $20,000 a day. There was just constant press around. He was traveling here and there in violation of court orders. One of the things that happened around the same time was his magazine published an ad parody of Jerry Falwell. This Campari liqueur ad, which was actually an authentic ad that was part of a nationwide advertising campaign, was spoofed in *Hustler* magazine.

LARRY FLYNT: There was, in the '70s, all sorts of celebrities appearing in the Campari ads. Everybody from movie stars to people like Johnny Carson. We just thought it would be great to use Falwell in the ad parody because he would be an unlikely person that you would see doing a liquor ad. So we all thought it was funny. Apparently Falwell didn't.

ALAN ISAACMAN: Falwell filed suit immediately after it came out. And then *Hustler* re-published it, and then he filed an amended complaint, doubling his claim for damages. I got word of it the first time he sued. He actually got hold of [attorney Norman Roy] Grutman, who was *Penthouse's* lawyer at the time and who had had a series of battles with Flynt, some of which I had been involved in. Flynt was sued. We just started defending the thing. When Falwell went out and sent these million copies of the ad parody to his supporters, we sued Falwell for copyright infringement. It was a running battle on both coasts.

Whatever became of that copyright suit?

ALAN ISAACMAN: That was an interesting case. The federal district court granted summary judgment against us. That was in Los Angeles. We went up on appeal and the appellate court affirmed that on a 2-to-1 vote. I was actually back in either New York or Virginia trying a case at the time. I didn't argue that one. I would have liked to argue it, but I didn't argue it. From an anecdotal standpoint, the panel was composed of three judges out here, one of whom was Harry Pragerson, for whom I had been a law clerk some time before, and remained a good friend. But he was not the vote [that went] my way (laughs). He voted the other way. So it was 2-to-1 against us on that one. The argument was whether he made a fair use or not. They claimed it was a fair use to re-publish our whole ad parody.

Why did Hustler publish the ad parody in the first place? What was the intent?

ALAN ISAACMAN: The reason that *Hustler* published the ad parody, in my view, was because Falwell was the public figure who repeatedly went on television and on the radio and spoke out against pornography, spoke out against *Hustler* in particular, and Larry Flynt in particular. He would constantly talk about the Big 3—*Playboy*, *Penthouse*, and *Hustler*—and Larry as being one of the kings of pornography. He was quoted as saying, for example, that when a DC-10 airplane went down out of Chicago and had a couple of *Playboy* executives on it, that that was God's will. It was a ridiculous thing. *Hustler*, for its part, would publish cartoons about Falwell. There was one in particular where they had a little old lady sitting in a dark room with a light bulb hanging down from the ceiling and writing a letter to Falwell saying, "Here is my Social Security check. You need it more than I do. Keep doing God's work." You know, he's on TV all the time soliciting money. So it was basically two ends of the political spectrum and two people who were out in the public arena going at it with each other.

LARRY FLYNT: Falwell had preached against me on his "Old Time Gospel Hour" for 15 years. We had done a lot of cartoons about him in the magazine and he just really seemed like an appropriate candidate.

How did you feel about the parody being published a second time?

ALAN ISAACMAN: I actually had no input in it. I didn't even know about it until after it happened.

Did it make your case more difficult in any way?

ALAN ISAACMAN: It certainly did in the sense of the emotional distress claim—to the extent that there was not an attempt to cause emotional distress, to the extent that there was any argument on that—that certainly undercut that. Of course, by the time [Larry] got through testifying in his deposition (laughs), there wasn't anything we could say in terms of his intent anyway. And he was the publisher of the magazine. Yeah, but on the other hand, if there was a right to publish it, it didn't matter how many times. In fact, they even published it a third time after the Supreme Court decision.

LARRY FLYNT: I was in prison at the time because I had refused to give up my source in the DeLorean cocaine case—the tapes that I had. I was more or less isolated from the outside world. I didn't really know [Falwell filed suit] until my attorney came and told me.

Over the course of this case—not just at trial, but on appeal, too—to what extent were you in touch with Mr. Flynt? Was he contributing in any way to legal strategy?

ALAN ISAACMAN: He always puts his 2 cents in. He always contributes his ideas. But he has always deferred in terms of legal strategy to what we thought, what we wanted to do. You know, when it came time to determine whether he was going to pay money or not—that kind of thing, whether we were going to settle or not—he would

make the call on that. We would make recommendations, but he always gave a lot of deference to what
we had to say. But in terms of legal strategy, my nature is not to have the client determine legal strategy. I think that's the lawyer's job to do that.

LARRY FLYNT: Alan has remained my attorney and done most of my
litigation work. That was his big day, too. He tried the
case very well, I thought.

THE TRIAL

*What kinds of particular challenges did it present you when your adversary
was a highly- respected, well-known man of the cloth?*

ALAN ISAACMAN: Very difficult. A very difficult situation. The case was
filed in Lynchburg, Virginia. The population of
Lynchburg at that time was about 63,000 people as I
remember the number, because we had done a check
on it. Falwell was the presiding pastor at the Thomas
Road Baptist Church that had a membership of
21,000. So kind of a quick, easy arithmetic—it
seemed like everybody was either a member or the
next door neighbor of a member of this church. Of
course, he was certainly a powerful figure there. He
ran the Liberty University. He was all over the TV and
he was a major, major figure—maybe the biggest one
in the area. We tried to get the case transferred. We
filed a motion to change venue and get it to California.
But we got it as far as Roanoke (laughs). I wasn't terribly successful, but we did get it out of Lynchburg
which was a help. After that, it was very difficult, even
from things that happened outside the courtroom. We
would get to the courthouse, and the first 2 days we
were basically taken to a room that the defense
team—although Flynt wasn't with us the first few
days—where they had metal detectors run over us
and it was really very intrusive—much more so than
any courthouse I'd ever been in—an intrusive procedure. And I didn't get the sense that that was applied
to the plaintiff's side. It looked like it wasn't, at all.
But by the end of the trial, which wasn't that long—it
was a 6-day trial finishing on a Saturday night—the
courtroom staff and the people around the courthouse had really become much more friendly to us and

less friendly to Falwell's side. I think a lot had to do with his counsel. He was a pretty arrogant fellow.

Was that Mr. Grutman at that time?

ALAN ISAACMAN: Yes. Yeah. One of the interesting things about the trial was that there was a surprise witness in the case—a surprise witness for Falwell—and that was Jesse Helms. He came in unannounced and got on the stand and testified for Falwell as a kind of character witness. It was kind of a strange thing. It was in federal court in Virginia, but the judge was not making either side disclose witnesses. So he came in and shook Falwell's hand, he went up and shook some of the jurors' hands. He tried to shake the judge's hand. He got on the stand and he said what a great guy Falwell was and what a terrific reputation he had. In cross examining Jesse Helms, we took him down the road of saying how great [Falwell's] reputation really was and how everybody knew where he stood on drinking, everybody knew where he stood on sex outside of marriage, and that nobody in the country would think that he would actually have incest—this was all to the libel claim—or actually get drunk before he goes on the pulpit or drink Campari at all, for that matter. We compared him to several notable people including the President of the United States who at the time was Reagan. In every instance he said that people would be less likely to think that Falwell would do any of these things than even the President. By the time he was done, he had basically made our case that a reasonable person could understand about the actual facts about Falwell, or actual events in which he participated. I think that was a very significant factor in our winning the libel claim. Losing the intentional infliction of emotional distress was easy to explain because Flynt, in his deposition, said he intended to assassinate the character of Falwell—tried to hurt him in his profession and that was his whole purpose. He also said in his deposition testimony that he meant it as a factual statement, and it wasn't intended to be a parody. He said he had witnesses to Falwell having sex with his mother in an outhouse. He did everything he could to make it tough for us to win the case.

Did Rev. Falwell take the stand during the trial?

ALAN ISAACMAN: He was on the stand. He was very vocal on the stand. He was very strong about how much emotional stress he suffered. He tried to make it sound like this was something attacking his saintly mother—who had passed on a year or so before—and how unpleasant it was for him. He felt so much anger that had Flynt been near him he thinks he would have physically struck him, which is something for Falwell to admit. [W]hat we asked Falwell was something that actually happened in the weeks and months leading up to the trial. Once this publication came out, Falwell ran off about a million copies of the ad parody and he sent them out to all his supporters—Moral Majority people, Old Time Gospel Hour people. And he asked them to send money so he could fight Larry Flynt in court. In discovery, I tried to get into what kind of money he raised and I got as far as finding out that he raised over $700,000. But the judge wouldn't let us get beyond that in terms of what he did with the money, where it was, that kind of stuff. When he was on the stand, I went into a bunch of that—what he did with the money, where is it? Part of the uncomfortable part about it for Falwell had to be that here he was, the plaintiff himself. It wasn't Moral Majority, it wasn't Old Time Gospel Hour, it wasn't anybody else. So any monetary award that would have come down would have gone to him personally. When we asked him the questions to point that out, he had difficulty and he was uncomfortable saying that he was really trying to raise money for his own purposes. He said he hadn't spent it yet and didn't really know what he would do with it, and he hadn't decided to use it in his case, and he wasn't going to use it for himself, and all this kind of thing. So then we had fun asking whether he ever sent the money back to the people he had so-licited from for one purpose, but now planned to use it for another purpose. Did he ever ask permission to use it for another purpose? We tried to make him as unsympathetic as we could. I actually think it helped.

At trial, the judge dismissed Rev. Falwell's invasion of privacy claim. The jury found for Flynt on the libel claim, accepting the defense argument that the "advertisement" was a parody, that it could not be taken seriously by a reasonable person, that it was therefore not a statement of fact and therefore not libelous. But the jury found for Rev. Falwell on the intentional infliction of emotional distress claim. In spite of what the jury believed about the nature of the parody with regard to its believability, it said it was published with intent to cause Rev. Falwell emotional distress. Flynt's admission that his objective was to "assassinate" Falwell's character with the parody was apparently dispositive. Rev. Falwell was awarded $100,000 each for actual and punitive damages.

THE APPEALS

After the ruling at the district court, were you immediately thinking appeal, or were you generally satisfied with the ruling?

ALAN ISAACMAN: First of all, I was thinking appeal. But we were immensely satisfied. Everybody—me less than most people—was unbelievably surprised that it came out as well as it did. I say myself less, because by the time I'm done with the trial, I really believe in our case. I expected to win that case. I don't think anybody else around there believed we were going to win the case. We had a huge victory at the trial court level by winning that libel claim. And I think that Flynt and others thought that that could have been just an astronomical award against him, dwarfing anything else that he had suffered.

LARRY FLYNT: I was happy at the trial level when they found no libel. I would have gladly paid the $200,000. But I felt these jurors wanted me to pay Jerry Falwell $200,000 for hurting his feelings. That's just not right. That's why I told my attorney that I wanted to appeal it.

The appeal of the intentional infliction of emotional distress ruling was heard by the Fourth Circuit of the U.S. Court of Appeals based in Richmond, Virginia. Isaacman argued that recovery for intentional infliction of emotional distress should be denied whenever a libel claim within the same lawsuit fails. However, on August 5, 1986, the three-judge panel there unanimously affirmed the trial court ruling on all counts. While the court ruled in favor of *Hustler* on the libel and invasion of privacy claims, it upheld Falwell's award for intentional infliction of emotional distress. Once again, the record of Flynt's admission that the parody was meant to "assassinate" Rev. Falwell's integrity was key. The court inferred that such an acknowledgment from Flynt meant that his magazine's publication of the parody rose to the level of intentional infliction of emotional distress.

Freedom of expression had taken a severe blow. A federal appeals court had ruled that liability could be based on the intent to induce stress even though the published material was neither libelous nor an invasion of privacy. This apparent inconsistency would be resolved once and for all by the United States Supreme Court.

Why do you think the Supreme Court granted cert. on this?

LARRY FLYNT: Because we had lost at the trial court, and we had lost at the Fourth Circuit. If they hadn't agreed to hear that case, that would mean the Fourth Circuit [ruling], in effect, would have become law. I think they wanted to make a determination.

ALAN ISAACMAN: I hoped that they granted cert. because they recognized the consequences of this decision. To me, it had just terrible ramifications which we pointed out in our briefs—the petition for cert. You had a situation where a jury had made a specific finding that nobody could believe what was said here as being factual. All it is, is poking fun at a person. We didn't defame him, we just poked fun at him. We might have ridiculed him, and might have hurt his feelings in the process, but if you can't do that to a celebrity—to a public figure—then that applies not just to Larry Flynt and *Hustler* magazine, but to everybody else—Jay Leno, David Letterman, the newspapers, cartoonists, and sportwriters. Every day we run into that a dozen times. Political campaigns. We just thought it had far-reaching consequences. I think one of the other surprising things about the case is that the pundits around at the time—the people who we went to for help to try to get them to file friends of the court briefs when we sought cert.—didn't want to join in on this because they thought we were going to lose if we got to the Supreme Court. They thought the best we would do would be a 4–4 split. There were eight Justices at the time. Kennedy hadn't been confirmed yet. Once they granted cert., then they came in and helped us out because, of course, at that point they were concerned that since the Court was going to make a decision, they wanted to weigh in on it. I think they also weren't very anxious to be involved in the beginning on Flynt's side. That was probably a factor. But I think what they thought in reality was that we wouldn't win at the Court of Appeals. The best we would get is a tie, if we got that far. Then we'd be struck with a nationwide precedent as opposed to something they would argue was a Fourth Circuit precedent.

LARRY FLYNT: I don't think the press was fair in covering it the way they did. I think they were somewhat embarrassed because they didn't come to our support initially, and did so only when the Supreme Court agreed to hear oral arguments in my case.

ALAN ISAACMAN: It is, I think, really something that I won't forget. When we went to people that you'd expect to jump in there and say, "This is a very important issue. We're going to fight for it even though we may not like your client a whole lot"—and it wasn't anything personal. I had gotten to know some of these people because of my practice in the area. We were on friendly terms. But they didn't want to join in asking the Supreme Court to hear it largely because they were afraid the Supreme Court would affirm. They were convinced that was what the Supreme Court was going to do.

And these were media organizations?

ALAN ISAACMAN: Media organizations and their counsel. And really very well-respected individuals.

THE U.S. SUPREME COURT

A lot of people are very impressed when they're at the United States Supreme Court. What was your reaction to being there?

LARRY FLYNT: Well, I had been there before. I've been there three times (laughs).

ALAN ISAACMAN: It was a very exciting time. It was unlike anything that I had experienced. I had argued a number of appellate cases before and had a lot of trials, but never before in front of the Supreme Court. I really hadn't even been to the Supreme Court before this. A lot of people important in my life were there. My family came to see me in court there. They live in the East and they had never seen me before in court. A bunch of relatives. Other lawyers. Other clients. It was a very well-attended event. They had to shift people in and out, it was so crowded. We had all the news media there—you know, the HBOs and those people were

there. They were all interested in the case. The courthouse itself—I ran into secretaries and people in the
elevator who were all so excited about this. They were
waiting for this case, I guess primarily because it was
Flynt and Falwell. It was unlike other cases. It could
have easily been an overwhelming thing. I remember
thinking about it as I was watching the clock in the attorney's lounge waiting for the 10 o'clock hour. You
know, I could just get up and take off and never come
back again (laughs). Maybe that's not a bad idea. Or
just get up and try to have fun at it. I said, "Well, I'll
just go up and try to have a good time and see what
happens." You never know what's going to happen. I
absolutely really enjoyed the experience. I was sad to
see the clock show it was time to end.

*In fact, very early within your argument the give-and-take began, starting
with Justice O'Connor.*

ALAN ISAACMAN: Right.

How do you keep your composure when that begins to happen?

ALAN ISAACMAN: It's *very* tough, I'll tell you. I don't mind the give-and-
take. I like that. To me, that's the most fun of it. But
you have points you want to make and you're kind of
figuring while you're talking there, it was like an out-
of-body experience to me. I was kind of watching myself. I was very conscious of it—kind of watching myself and my arms move and talking and listening to
myself and to them—and thinking, "Oh, I want to get
this point in, is this the opportunity?" You know that
they don't want you to duck the questions. They don't
want you to take control and say, "You can't ask this
question." So you try to answer their questions, you
see the clock running on you, you know that the yellow
light and the red light are going to go off in no time,
and it did. I said [to myself], "I'm happy that they're
so interested in this." So we got in a lot of colloquies
there. I felt that we were really doing well, I really did.

*In spite of what I'm sure is a wealth of preparation on a variety of levels, in-
cluding getting to know the Justices, did any one of them particularly surprise you?*

ALAN ISAACMAN: Yes. Marshall is the one that caught me a little by surprise. It was because—I don't know if I didn't under-
stand him very well or he was just not understanding
this case very well. He asked a question. I'll tell you the
question. We're going back a lot of years, so I might
have it a little bit off. But the question was, "Isn't this
libelous because we accused [Falwell] of a crime—the
crime of adultery?" I answered him with a point that we
made and that we were trying to make here, and that
the jury found, was that we're not accusing him of any
crime, we're not accusing him of *doing* the things in
there that we're describing. This was a parody. This
was hyperbole, in a sense. This wasn't saying that
Falwell really had sex with somebody outside of marriage. He said, "Well, he wasn't married to this woman.
It was his mother. Isn't that a crime?" It's kind of like is
he all there? Is he holding onto his seat because he
just doesn't want to give it up, or what? It was the
Reagan era. That's really about all that Marshall said
the whole time. I remember thinking that I hope his law
clerks straighten this out. And he voted the right way.
They all did. The others were all a lot of fun. Scalia and I
had a little—well, you heard the thing. That was just
like [Marshall] was missing the point. He didn't understand. I wasn't getting through.

During the oral arguments, while in a colloquy with Justice Scalia, Mr.
Isaacman cited one of Scalia's previous opinions: "What you're talking
about, Justice Scalia, is a matter of taste. And as Justice Scalia, you said in
Pope v. Illinois, just as it's useless to argue about taste, it's useless to litigate
it, to litigate about it. And what we're talking about here is, well, is this
tasteful or not tasteful. That's really what you're talking about because nobody believed that Jerry Falwell was being accused of committing incest."
Mr. Isaacman was referring to part of Justice Scalia's opinion from just a
year before: "Just as there is no use arguing about taste, there is no use liti-
gating about it," *Pope v. Illinois,* 481 U.S. 497, 505 (1987)(Scalia, J. concurring).

*Did you sense that any one particular Justice was really key in trying to win
him or her over?*

ALAN ISAACMAN: That's a good question. In preparing for the oral argument, I had help from a significant number of First

Amendment lawyers—media attorneys. I met with them for about a month or so before the argument back in Washington. They came from surrounding places—from New York—and just all over the country, for that matter. We had panels. There must have been 20-some attorneys there, or more. They acted as a moot court. I just stood up and made the argument and then the panel would step up. And we did this a few times. You know, then after it was all done, they all said this is the way they thought it should be argued. Everybody basically had a different idea, which kind of left me with the conclusion that I might as well just do what I was going to do in the first place. If these guys can't agree, there must not be a right way. I asked them, "Who do you think we should be trying to win over?" "Well, you'll never get Rehnquist." "You'll never get Scalia." "Forget about O'Connor." On and on. You have at least four you're going to lose, and then you've got a few others. White was one of them, too. If you listened to them, you felt it was hopeless. So I went in there without any idea of trying to go after anybody in particular. I do remember when Scalia made some comment about deterring good men from going into politics, or something like that. I remembered some quote in one of his cases that I was able to say back to him, that it is useless to litigate taste. He had made that comment. Other than that, I wasn't very personally directed to any of them. I'd read their opinions in the area so I had an idea where they're coming from. I wasn't surprised about White having his own actual malice position—not thinking that it made much sense in this whole area. He would just as soon dispense with it. I'll tell you the one thing that immediately—very early on—was encouraging to me. It was the first time at any level in this case—the trial level, the Fourth Circuit, or here at the Supreme Court—that I had perceived this. And that is they seemed to see that there was some humor surrounding this thing. At least that was the intention. The big problem we had—and I felt this from the very beginning—what I did with this ad parody when I went back to take Falwell's deposition in Lynchburg, I walked around the street there the day before, and just showed it to some people. I just stopped and they must have thought I was nuts or something. I showed them this ad parody and asked them what they thought. And almost every one of them stopped, read it, looked to see that nobody was looking, they started laughing and shaking their head. Some of them, at least, thought it was funny. They thought it was humorous. But in the courtroom, it was like, "This was a terrible thing to do to somebody." Nobody thought it was funny the whole trial. And they certainly didn't think it was funny when we argued before the Fourth Circuit. I wasn't trying to get them to disrespect Falwell and laugh at this thing. The argument was this was intended for *Hustler* readers, they would recognize it as being humorous and not a factual assertion. You've got to take it into context in deciding what it means. But when we got to the Supreme Court and the way the colloquy went, they asked what my client is trying to accomplish. And I said some comment about trying to bring [Falwell] down to his level. And then I said, "Well, maybe not quite there." Rehnquist doubled over. It doesn't show up on a tape. But he absolutely just—I can still picture him bent over at the waist laughing. He's got a sense of humor. And then Scalia got into it, and he was joking back and forth. There was good humor around, and I said, "Boy, this is finally an encouraging sign in this case."

LARRY FLYNT: You know, supposedly nobody laughs at the Supreme Court, but in my case it was totally different because there were some things said about various cartoons involving everything from George Washington to Franklin Roosevelt. It just really broke the gallery up. One guy at the Supreme Court told me, "In the 15 years that I've been here, I've never seen anybody laugh."

ALAN ISAACMAN: [I]n talking to people beforehand, I would say, "You know what? Maybe I ought to go in there and try to say something funny to lighten the mood." And everybody said, "You don't joke in the Supreme Court. That would be a terrible thing to do. Don't even try it." [But] to me, if they're going to laugh at this thing, it's going to be a lot harder for them to affirm the lower court, I thought, in this.

On February 24, 1988, the U.S. Supreme Court ruled unanimously for Flynt and *Hustler*. In an opinion written by Chief Justice William Rehnquist (see Court opinion excerpts at chapter's conclusion), the Court held that in order to protect the free flow of ideas and opinions on matters of public interest and concerns, the First Amendment prohibits public figures from recovering damages for intentional infliction of emotional distress. In balancing First Amendment interests against those of protecting public figures from emotional distress, the Court ruled that when the expression in question can not reasonably be interpreted as stating facts, free speech wins.

THE RULING

Once the ruling came down, what kind of reaction did you and Mr. Flynt have?

ALAN ISAACMAN: We were both very, very happy. I was happy and he was happy. I actually thought when I walked out of the courtroom that day that we had won the case. That sounds a bit arrogant, but I really had that feeling from the response that we had in the courtroom and the difficulty the opposing side had in dealing with the questions that were asked of them. Flynt was overjoyed. He ended it basically with a lot of very favorable publicity. He was on "Nightline" immediately and other talk shows. He was kind of a hero in a sense, having won this First Amendment case. He threw a victory party at the Bel-Air Hotel in Los Angeles. It was a very high time.

LARRY FLYNT: I was very happy.

ALAN ISAACMAN: He started this case—whether he'll ever admit it or not, I don't know—but he started this case, I know, thinking that he was in for a *very* rough road. He stood to lose a tremendous amount.

LARRY FLYNT: I actually thought I was going to lose the case, and I'm not just saying that. I saw it as the preacher versus the pornographer, and I felt that there was no way I would win that case. But after being able to analyze it since, I realized what happened. First of all, had they come down on the side of Jerry Falwell, the mainstream press would have been in chaos. That means that in order to collect damages, you didn't have to prove libel, you only had to prove intentional infliction of emotional distress. So what would that do to Jay Leno's monologue or David Letterman or "Saturday Night Live"? I think that the Justices could see far enough ahead to realize what a ruling the other way would have meant.

ALAN ISAACMAN: Now recognizing what this is all about, if you take this away from *Hustler* and they can't do [a parody], then as far as I'm concerned then nobody else can do it.

Does the ruling cast any doubt on the validity of this concept of intentional infliction of emotional distress?

ALAN ISAACMAN: It certainly makes it clear that you cannot get around First Amendment limitations on legal actions by calling the action intentional infliction of emotional distress. If you're really talking about something where the gravamen of the complaint is defamation, it doesn't do you any good to say it's intentional infliction of emotional distress and therefore I don't have to meet the First Amendment problems. It does, without any question, undercut what the action of intentional infliction of emotional distress would be in a vacuum. Clearly, when somebody talks about another person in an attacking manner, he knows that what he's saying is calculated to cause emotional distress. If he did not have protections for speech, and if this ruling went the other way, then the intentional infliction of emotional distress tort could give rise to a lot more actions than we've seen.

REFLECTIONS & AFTERMATH

LARRY FLYNT: There had never, in the history of our country, been a case where parody was challenged as protected speech. It was always thought to be [protected speech] from time to time throughout the years, but there was no constitutional protection. So I would say my case with the Reverend was probably the most important case since *New York Times v. Sullivan* in 1964 where you had to prove actual malice to collect damages.

One of the things that always struck me about this case is what a slippery slope we would have stepped onto had this gone the other way.

ALAN ISAACMAN: Exactly. I agree.

What if it had gone the other way? What sort of signal do you think that would have sent?

ALAN ISAACMAN: Either people would have ignored it at their peril, and said this is idiosyncratic or unique to Flynt. Or you can paint scenario after scenario. You can say forget about Leno's monologue. He starts the show where he's making fun of politicians or celebrities. Forget about Herblock or Conrad or any of these cartoonists. Forget about all the columnists, these guys who are making fun of athletes or other people. The point is that if you hurt somebody's feelings you're subjecting yourself to legal action, then you've got to watch that what you say doesn't hurt anybody's feelings— whether or not you're making a factual assertion. How do you defend yourself? To me, it would just to- tally change the way we engage in discourse in this country, and much to our detriment.

Mr. Isaacman's closing words to the Supreme Court are worth noting: "If Jerry Falwell can sue because he suffered emotional distress, anybody else who's in public life should be able to sue because they suffered emotional distress. And the standard that was used in this case—does it offend gener- ally accepted standards of decency and morality—is no standard at all. All it does is allow the punishment of unpopular speech."

What would you say is your single most lasting memory about your work on this case?

ALAN ISAACMAN: That's a good question. I guess on a personal level, what was probably the most inspiring part of the case to me was finishing up the argument in the Supreme Court—just looking around and seeing this hallowed place, this historically significant place, and the Jus- tices sitting up there. And everybody very much inter- ested in what's going on, and knowing we're fighting about concepts that I thought were central to our de- mocracy. It was just a very, very exciting moment. That's what has stuck with me over the years.

What was the most difficult aspect of your work on the case?

ALAN ISAACMAN: The most difficult aspect was probably at the trial level—the preparation for the trial and the trial it- self—where there was an awful lot of animus in the case. There was a lot of hostility. Norman Roy Grutman, who was representing Falwell, was a very difficult guy. Great hatred for Flynt. I don't think he felt any more fondly towards me, frankly. So we had a lot—*a lot*—of big battles. There was a witness in the trial—a witness who was paid $10,000 to give a one-page declaration and a deposition saying that Flynt came up with this idea to go after Falwell and he came up with it at a poker game. And he [supposedly] said I'm going to really destroy this guy, and I've got this great idea to do this, etc., etc. This was totally false. It wasn't the way the idea came up at all. When we uncovered this in deposing this guy, we tried to get Grutman to tell us, "What were you giving him the money for?" Basically he said he wanted the guy to do some investigation. It was a whole crock. We reported him to the U.S. Attorney. They actually looked into the matter. Nobody ever did anything, although I think they got a grand jury to look into it because they did call some witnesses on it. We went to the court about it—to the judge—and tried to get him disqualified. He was violating a federal statute, as far as we were concerned. He was paying a witness for testimony. That's what the witness said, and he actually did pay the witness. We got the check. This was kind of typical of the intensity. Emotionally, it was a very, very draining kind of experience.

LARRY FLYNT: You know, compromise is not part of my vocabulary. Heroes die for their country. I wouldn't have given my legs for anything or anyone. And I think if you could lift some of those boys' faces out of the mud in Vietnam today and ask them if they had it to do over, would they give their lives for their country, and I think many of them would feel the same as me.

ALAN ISAACMAN: The pressures were so great. I had a young lawyer working with me, a guy named David Carson, who is a very bright young guy. He'd been out of Harvard for 2 years, maybe 3. He was working closely with me on a number of cases including this one. He was feeling the pressure of all this, too. He got sick right before the trial started. I went back a couple of days early, and he got sick, and I just got on the phone with him and said take a day or two, stay back in L.A. But come when you can and you'll have a good time. Some day you'll have a story to tell you grandkids about these two cult figures and the issues. I didn't have any idea it was going to be like this. But I re-

member saying this to David and he came and participated very well in the trial and did a great job. He
wrote a lot of work on the briefs. Today he's general
counsel for the copyright office, so he's gone a long
way. In the beginning I had this sense that here we
had Larry Flynt who was so controversial on the one
hand. And we had Jerry Falwell, who in his own way
was equally controversial.

*How do you respond to criticism that in situations like this, you and people
like you are hiding behind the First Amendment?*

LARRY FLYNT: You bet your ass that I am, and I'm thankful that it's
there. Jerry Falwell once made a remark that I didn't
save the First Amendment; the First Amendment
saved me. And I said, "Jerry, that's the first thing
you've ever said that I agree with." I've always said
that if I hadn't been a pornographer that I'd probably
have been an evangelist.

ALAN ISAACMAN: I always thought that these guys really needed each
other. It was a very interesting sociological phenome-
non that I was watching. Falwell needed Flynt to rail
at. Flynt needed Falwell to try to keep everybody telling him you couldn't look at Flynt's magazines. [That
way,] Flynt could sell more magazines. Since then,
these guys have actually become friendly and have exploited each other by going on talk shows together
and doing other things together.

LARRY FLYNT: In 1998 I was scheduled to do "The Larry King Show"
with him when the movie "The People vs. Larry Flynt"
came out. I was looking for a real lively debate but
Falwell immediately comes to me and says, "We've
been fighting each other for years. Why don't we just
bury the hatchet?" So it was sort of disarming because for me to come out and be the bad guy at that
time, I don't think it would have gone over very well. I
just sort of refocused and said, "Look, he knows what
he's selling and I know what I'm selling." Although
what he's selling has done more harm than any other
idea since the beginning of time. So that kind of dialog
went on.

*As I understand it, you have a pretty good relationship with him today, do
you not?*

LARRY FLYNT: Yes, I do. I've always known where he's coming from. I talk to him regularly. I've gotten to know him very well.

ALAN ISAACMAN: I think that what makes it a landmark case are several factors. One is the personalities involved that are so well known and basically are such apparent opposites that have many similarities. So their being involved in the case attracts a lot of attention to the case. Secondly, the issues involved—at least the ad parody itself—to a lot of people it's shocking. It's easy to understand. It's not some kind of complicated economic analysis. It's not highly technical. You can look at that ad parody and you have an immediate reaction to it, one way or the other—you think it's funny or terrible or it's whatever. And, you know, these people are representing very strongly felt interests in our society. One is the moral, righteous side that is now representing a person's right to be left alone or a person's right not to be attacked or to be made fun of by others. The other is representing the right to freedom of expression—and if you want to dignify it a little bit—talked about very important political issues or sociological issues. The argument that we tried to make about the ad parody is that it was attacking somebody who was always on TV and telling people how to live their lives and what they should or should not do, and talked against sex and trying to preserve an awful lot of what Flynt thought was unfounded and dangerous sexual inhibitions in a society. Then we had it in a kind of classic battle of the gladiators of our day with the lawyers, and the arena being the courtroom that we all recognize. And it went all the way up. By some kind of quirk in the outcome of the trial we had this strange situation where the jury had come back our way in this libel claim and had made specific findings that we were able to get them to do. From a technical or professional standpoint, that was a big victory in a charging conference where we convinced the judge to let us ask these questions with the special verdict being submitted. So now we had this issue framed. We had this finding of fact that nobody could understand this [ad parody] as describing actual facts about Falwell. And yet here it was, the defendants were being ordered to pay money for intentional infliction of emotional distress. Everything worked out from the standpoint of making this a landmark case. It went the distance. And then we had a conservative

Supreme Court who did what to many people was a surprise. In hindsight, it looks obvious, but at the time I can tell you that there were wiser people than I in Supreme Court practices who thought that this was never going to turn out the way it did. And yet, as far as I'm concerned, they all adhered to the rule of law and did not make a special rule for Larry Flynt.

LARRY FLYNT: You know, there's an old saying that there's no such thing as justice. All you've got is a shot at justice. I got a shot at it, and I hit the bull's eye because they did the right thing.

In 1997, "The People vs. Larry Flynt" was released by Columbia Pictures. Directed by Milos Forman, the highly acclaimed film highlighted this case, and portrayed many of the people central to it.

LARRY FLYNT: Any time they reduce your life to two hours on the silver screen a lot gets left out. But what was there was accurate. I think Milos did a very good job.

ALAN ISAACMAN: The film was quite accurate with respect to the way I think it portrayed Larry Flynt, and pretty accurate as well—maybe even more accurate—the way it portrayed Althea Flynt [Larry's wife]. The lawyer in the picture was very much a composite type of character. There were actually different lawyers at different times in Flynt's life. I've been in his life since about 1978, so that's a pretty long time. The character of the lawyer, at least the description that you would make if you were saying what this lawyer is about, wasn't exactly like any of the lawyers in real life. It was basically a composite picture as viewed by either the writers or Milos Forman. The issues came across, I thought, pretty well. I thought from the standpoint of it being a biographical type of picture that was designed to have some sort of appeal to the mass audience, that he did a pretty good job—Forman did a pretty good job.

In terms of the accuracy of the events as they unfolded, with maybe the exceptions that you've just alluded to, was that pretty much on the mark?

ALAN ISAACMAN: Yes, I think that's right. I guess that everybody sees things from his own perspective. From the very beginning in talking to Milos about it, I thought there could have been improvements in the way the cases were portrayed and were depicted. And a more clear way of

presenting the issues involved. And the background of
the lawsuits and what actually happened in the courtroom, particularly the Falwell case. As it was, by the
time the film was done, they had actually made it substantially more clear from the way it was originally in
the script. A couple of writers who had gone to U.S.C.
and who were out pairing up together for some years
drafted a screenplay on this thing. In actuality what
happened was they had gotten hold of Oliver Stone, or
Oliver Stone got hold of them, they together went to
Sony Columbia and made a deal on this thing. Nobody
talked to us about it. We got wind of it and tried to
track it down. Finally I spoke to somebody at Columbia
who was fairly high up who confirmed that they were
making a picture on this thing. They thought they could
deal with it all as public domain material, and we convinced them that they were better off trying to get our
cooperation and input in this thing. We were concerned
about accuracy. We weren't concerned so much about
how it was going to make Larry Flynt look, we were
more concerned how accurate it was going to be. I
think once we convinced them of that and they understood that they would be treading on thin ice if they did
his biography, in effect, or did a story about real char-
acters without our cooperation, they agreed to work
collaboratively on that picture. And they did. [Larry] had
a big influence, and I had some influence in it. One of
the things that was obvious to me from the beginning
was the way they were portraying the Falwell case,
particularly the trial aspect of it. The jury's decision
would not have been understood by a lay audience, or
even any audience, the way it was being portrayed. In
reality, the case was a libel case and attached to it had
claims for intentional infliction of emotional distress
and invasion of privacy. The jury returned a defense verdict on the libel claim. The judge threw out the invasion
of privacy claim. And the jury returned a plaintiff's claim
on intentional infliction of emotional distress. The
screenplay really never indicated why the jury returned
that kind of a verdict. It seemed like an inconsistent
verdict. It never really indicated what was involved in
this thing from a legal standpoint or what the importance of the First Amendment issues were. So Edward
Norton, who was selected by Milos to portray me in
this case, came to California a few days before they
started shooting and spent several days with me get-

ting background and finding out what was involved and what happened and what the legal issues were. He's a bright young actor and he's a guy who went to Yale and graduated in, I think, the history area there. His father is a lawyer. His father practiced law and went to Harvard Law School. So he's got a background with some academic accomplishment in it. He seemed very interested in the legal issues involved. When I explained to him that the jury's decision would be totally incomprehensible and the issues weren't being portrayed accurately, he listened to me. Nothing else happened until the middle of principal photography—about two months later—when he called me from the set and said they were going to shoot the courtroom scene. He said he had read through the script and agreed that the way it was portrayed was really very difficult to understand, and he was troubled by that.... [A] lot of the questions that were asked of Falwell in the movie were really asked of Jesse Helms.... But to me, for some inexplicable reason, they left Helms out of the script. I thought he was a great character and from a commercial appeal would be somebody useful to have given that he had importance in the way the story actually developed. When Edward called me from Mississippi where it was being shot to a large extent and said that this was something that he was troubled by in terms of the script, because it jumped from the trial to the jury's returning this crazy, inconsistent verdict. I said, "Why don't you ask Falwell the questions that I asked Jesse Helms?" I kind of dictated that to him for the next hour or so. I got a call from the director after that. I got a call from Sony Columbia who was worried about that maybe there would be some lawsuit on this thing. I assured them, "Don't worry about it. We'll defend you if you have a problem on this. He's not going to sue you for doing this." That's what happened. They rewrote the script. Edward asked Milos to do it. Milos agreed. So that actually got changed right in the middle of production. That's the kind of guy Milos is, in a way. He likes to get average people or unknown people—not necessarily unknown, but unknown to the film world— like he had James Carville and that kind of thing.

And, of course, Mr. Flynt himself.

ALAN ISAACMAN: That's right. Exactly.

In a touch of irony, Milos Forman cast Larry Flynt himself to portray a trial judge in "The People vs. Larry Flynt."

I was particularly impressed with the performance of the actor who played the trial judge.

LARRY FLYNT: (laughs) Yeah, I had no idea they wanted me to do that. I was on the set one day and Milos Forman asked me to do it. I said, "Well, I'm not an actor." And he said, "We'll help you through it." And then I was told what an arrogant S.O.B. the guy was, so it wasn't much of a stretch for me to play him.

I am reminded of how the film portrays your relationship with Mr. Flynt and, in fact, according to the film, you resigned as his counsel. Is that accurate?

ALAN ISAACMAN: That is not accurate. No, that's not accurate. The way Edward portrayed the lawyer in that case was that he was much more excitable than I ever was. With Flynt providing so much volatility in and out of court, my role was often to calm the situation. That just happens to be my style anyway—to be much more low-key and not flamboyant, shall we say? I really didn't get terribly excited about him. I always advised him. If he did something bizarre, it was him doing it, it wasn't me. I didn't get caught up in any of his incidents that he was getting a lot of attention for. I had to deal with him and get him out of trouble a lot. The line that he gives in the movie where he's on the plane about he's wealthy, he's got interesting cases, and he's always in trouble was really what I would say to other members of my profession in the judiciary out here when they would say to me during the most crazy period back in the early '80s, "How can you represent this guy?" That's exactly what I would say. And it's true! I always recognized the separation between my client and myself, and I think that's the way it is with most lawyers. As long as I was behaving in a proper fashion in representing my client, then I didn't have a problem with it. My other clients didn't seem to have a problem with it either, which was of more concern to me, frankly.

*Hustler Magazine
and Larry C. Flynt, Petitioners
v. Jerry Falwell*

SUPREME COURT
OF THE UNITED STATES

485 U.S. 46
Argued: December 2, 1987
Decided: February 24, 1988

COUNSEL: Alan L. Isaacman argued the cause for petitioners. With him on the briefs was David O. Carson.

Norman Roy Grutman argued the cause for respondent. With him on the brief were Jeffrey H. Daichman and Thomas V. Marino.

JUDGES: REHNQUIST, C. J., delivered the opinion of the Court, in which BRENNAN, MARSHALL, BLACKMUN, STEVENS, O'CONNOR, and SCALIA, JJ., joined. WHITE, J., filed an opinion concurring in the judgment. KENNEDY, J., took no part in the consideration or decision of the case.

OPINION BY: REHNQUIST

This case presents us with a novel question involving First Amendment limitations upon a State's authority to protect its citizens from the intentional infliction of emotional distress.

We must decide whether a public figure may recover damages for emotional harm caused by the publication of an ad parody offensive to him, and doubtless gross and repugnant in the eyes of most. Respondent would have us find that a State's interest in protecting public figures from emotional distress is sufficient to deny First Amendment protection to speech that is patently offensive and is intended to inflict emotional injury, even when that speech could not reasonably have been interpreted as stating actual facts about the public figure involved. This we decline to do.

At the heart of the First Amendment is the recognition of the fundamental importance of the free flow of ideas and opinions on matters of public interest and concern.

…

We have therefore been particularly vigilant to ensure that individual expressions of ideas remain free from governmentally imposed sanctions.

…

The sort of robust political debate encouraged by the First Amendment is bound to produce speech that is critical of those who hold public office or those public figures who are "intimately involved in the resolution of important public questions or, by reason of their fame, shape events in areas of concern to society at large." ... Justice Frankfurter put it succinctly ... when he said that "one of the prerogatives of American citizenship is the right to criticize public men and measures." Such criticism, inevitably, will not always be reasoned or moderate; public figures as well as public officials will be subject to "vehement, caustic, and sometimes unpleasantly sharp attacks."

...

Of course, this does not mean that any speech about a public figure is immune from sanction in the form of damages.... False statements of fact are particularly valueless; they interfere with the truth-seeking function of the marketplace of ideas, and they cause damage to an individual's reputation that cannot easily be repaired by counterspeech, however persuasive or effective.... But even though falsehoods have little value in and of themselves, they are "nevertheless inevitable in free debate," and a rule that would impose strict liability on a publisher for false factual assertions would have an undoubted "chilling" effect on speech relating to public figures that does have constitutional value.

...

In respondent's view, and in the view of the Court of Appeals, so long as the utterance was intended to inflict emotional distress, was outrageous, and did in fact inflict serious emotional distress, it is of no constitutional import whether the statement was a fact or an opinion, or whether it was true or false.

...

[I]n the world of debate about public affairs, many things done with motives that are less than admirable are protected by the First Amendment.

...

Thus while such a bad motive may be deemed controlling for purposes of tort liability in other areas of the law, we think the First Amendment prohibits such a result in the area of public debate about public figures. Were we to hold otherwise, there can be little doubt that political cartoonists and satirists would be subjected to damages awards without any showing that their work falsely defamed its subject.

...

Respondent contends, however, that the caricature in question here was so "outrageous" as to distinguish it from more traditional political cartoons.... "Outrageousness" in the area of political and social discourse has an inherent subjectiveness about it which would allow a jury to impose liability on the basis of the jurors' tastes or views, or perhaps on the basis of their dislike of a particular expression. An "outrageousness" standard thus runs afoul of our longstanding refusal to allow damages to be awarded because the speech in question may have an adverse emotional impact on the audience.

...

We conclude that public figures and public officials may not recover for the tort of intentional infliction of emotional distress by reason of publications such as the one here at issue without showing in addition that the publication contains a false statement of fact which was made with "actual malice," i.e., with knowledge that the statement was false or with reckless disregard as to whether or not it was true.

...

Here it is clear that respondent Falwell is a "public figure" for purposes of First Amendment law.... The judgment of the Court of Appeals is accordingly Reversed.

6   *Cohen v. Cowles Media Company*

"[W]hat really was at stake here, so far as I was concerned, was my life. I was not going to let these arrogant bastards get away with that."

—Dan Cohen, plaintiff in *Cohen v. Cowles Media Co.*

"[Y]ou've got flesh and blood people here. It's not just ivory tower general legal principles. People are actually getting hurt."

—Elliot Rothenberg, Dan Cohen's attorney

In 1982, Dan Cohen was a 46-year-old advisor to the gubernatorial campaign of Republican Wheelock Whitney in Minnesota. Just 1 week prior to the election, campaign officials had acquired documentation indicating that the candidate for Lt. Governor on the Democratic ticket, Marlene Johnson, had a misdemeanor arrest record. During a meeting of select members of the Whitney campaign staff, Cohen volunteered to approach members of the Twin Cities media with copies of the documents. In exchange for a promise to keep his identity confidential, Cohen provided the information to each of the four media representatives with whom he met privately. Two of the promises were kept. But after deliberation inside their newsrooms, two of the organizations—the *Minneapolis Star Tribune* and the *St. Paul Pioneer Press*—concluded that Cohen's identity was an essential part of the story, and decided to identify him as the source of the information in the articles they published. In response, Cohen's employer, an advertising firm, fired him. Thus began a series of events that culminated in a landmark decision that the First Amendment does not immunize the press from the requirement to adhere to generally applicable laws.

When Dan Cohen filed suit against the newspapers, the case began its long journey through the courts—from the Hennepin County District Court, to the Minnesota Court of Appeals, to the Minnesota Supreme Court, to the U.S. Supreme Court, then back to the Minnesota Supreme Court. Virtually every step of the way, the rulings were by razor-thin margins.

Cohen's lawyer was Elliot Rothenberg, like Cohen a graduate of Harvard Law School. When Rothenberg took over the case in January 1986 (Cohen had accepted the resignation of his previous counsel after a dispute over whether to accept a settlement), he was a 46-year-old former Minnesota state legislator who had also run (unsuccessfully) for state attorney general. His courtroom demeanor was described by Franklin Knoll, the judge who presided over the trial phase of this case, as akin to Jimmy Stewart's in "Mr. Smith Goes to Washington." Ironically, this case and its participants did go to Washington when they presented the case to the United States Supreme Court.

Today, Rothenberg remains out of the political arena and continues to practice law, based in his home office in Minneapolis. Dan Cohen works on a freelance basis in the advertising business in Minneapolis. The two newspaper reporters with whom Cohen met in 1982, Lori Sturdevant of the *Star Tribune* (who remained true to a self-imposed policy of not commenting on this case because, she says, she does not want to be put in the position of having to be critical of her employer) and the *Pioneer Press'* Bill Salisbury are still with those publications, as an editorial writer and a political reporter, respectively. It is Cohen's meetings with them where the roots of the case lie.

PRE-TRIAL CIRCUMSTANCES*

BILL SALISBURY: It was in the fall of 1982, about a week before the election for governor in Minnesota. I know I was working on a Sunday story to wrap up the pre-election coverage. I got a call fairly early one morning from Mr. Cohen who asked if I would be willing to meet with him. And I said, "Yes." I recognized the name. He had been a Minneapolis alderman previously. He was active in Republican politics. I knew that he was an advisor to the campaign of Wheelock Whitney, the Republican nominee, and I actually had interviewed him once years previously for an article about the Minneapolis mayor's race. So he came over to the State Capitol where my office is located.

NOTE: This chapter includes language that may be offensive to some readers.

DAN COHEN:

Well, first of all I called them and said I have some information. I developed a little litany. And the litany went like this: "I have some documents which may or may not relate to a candidate in the upcoming election, and if you will give me a promise of confidentiality—that is, that I will be treated as an anonymous source, that my name will not appear in any material in connection with this, and you will also agree that you're not going to pursue with me a question of who my source is—then I'll furnish you with the documents."

Yes, yes, yes, yes, yes. So I went over there. The meetings with the reporters, which I tried to engage each of them privately, despite the fact that they were all kind of clustered in small offices in a little warren down in the basement [of the Capitol building].

BILL SALISBURY:
He came into the Capitol press room that morning and stuck his head into the office of the *Pioneer Press* where there were two or three other reporters working at the same time, and [he] motioned for me to come out with him and asked if we could meet somewhere privately. So I took him to the State Capitol cafeteria, found a quiet corner there, and we each had a cup of coffee and sat down. As I recall, he reached into his pocket, pulled out some papers, and told me that he had some information regarding a candidate that I might be interested in, and he would offer it to me if I would guarantee him anonymity—if I would promise not to reveal his name as the source of the material.

DAN COHEN:
I recited another little litany: "I have in my hands some information that represents a public record which may or may not pertain to one of the candidates ... " (Since her name was Marlene Johnson, and that's about as common in Minnesota as John Smith, I wasn't at all certain that it was the same Marlene Johnson. That was their problem, it wasn't my problem as I saw it.) " ... which may or may not pertain to one of the candidates." (But her birth date was identical.) "I'm giving you this information which is a public record on the basis of the following promise on your part. And the promise is that my identity, in passing this information on to you, is not going to be disclosed to your readers in any way, shape, or form."

BILL SALISBURY:
As I recall, I asked a few questions to find out what the material was, but he made it very clear that he

wasn't going to say anything about it until I made the promise to treat him as a confidential source. So I promised to do that and he handed over papers. I opened them and looked at them, and there were a couple of court documents regarding Marlene Johnson who was the Democratic Farmer Labor party candidate for Lt. Governor. One of the documents said that she had been arrested for—it was some kind of a demonstration-related charge like trespassing or something like that. The charges—I think there were three counts—had all been dismissed subsequently. So I thought to myself, "Well, that's not news." But the second document to be handed over showed that she had been convicted of a petty misdemeanor for theft several years earlier. I thought that was certainly newsworthy. I just assumed that any conviction for a candidate for that kind of office—even a misdemeanor—is worth reporting. I thought the voters had a right to know about it, and they had the right to make the decision whether that should be a factor in their decision who to elect.

Did you find the fact that Mr. Cohen was adamant about a promise of anonymity and stating that up front and wanting to secure that promise from you before he even revealed exactly what the information was that he had—did you find that unusual?

BILL SALISBURY: No, not terribly. That happens occasionally in this business. It's fairly widely used in politics and in covering government. Typically, I experience it mostly with government employees who are unhappy with the actions of their supervisors or policymakers and want to expose what they think is bad policy or mistaken decisions or just something which they oppose politically.

Let me ask you a question that I know came up several times over the course of the litigation, and that is ...

DAN COHEN: Why didn't you slip it under the door, Dan?

Exactly.

DAN COHEN: The answer is—and this was asked by a judge of the Minnesota Supreme Court, it was asked by a judge at the United States Supreme Court. The answer is because I thought I could trust the representations of the *Minneapolis Star Tribune* and the *St. Paul Pioneer Press* in saying that they would observe their promise of anonymity.

BILL SALISBURY: I immediately went back to my office, called my editor and said I had this document and we need to sit down and talk about it. So I went to the newspaper office in downtown St. Paul and met privately with the city editor at the time. We decided that we should proceed with the story. My next effort after that was to try to reach Marlene Johnson to talk about the issue. I reached Marlene Johnson that afternoon, and she acknowledged that she had indeed been arrested and convicted for theft and explained the circumstances. It was something that happened while she was grieving her father's death. So she had an explanation for her behavior. Once she confirmed that it did indeed occur, I had another discussion with the editor and we decided that I would write a story. While I was writing the piece, I got a call from the editor of the paper— David Hall, the top guy in the newsroom, he called the shots—telling me that *he* decided that we should publish Cohen's name. And we had an argument about that. I told him that I made a promise and that I strenuously objected to breaking the promise. And we went back and forth for a while, but ultimately he ordered me to write the story saying that Cohen provided the material. And I did. Several of my colleagues were also very upset with his decision and complained to him as I did. He decided to have a staff meeting, basically to clear the air. At that meeting I once again raised my objections and several other reporters did. But he explained his reasoning, and told us that he had no regrets about making that decision, and defended it.

ELLIOT ROTHENBERG: Right around the time it happened in October of 1982, I do remember vaguely reading about it in the *Star Tribune*. That's the newspaper I get on a daily basis. There was a front-page article originally saying Dan Cohen was the source of the information. The interesting thing was that it didn't really make clear that he was a confidential source, that they had promised him confidentiality. And then there were a

series of articles and columns and a cartoon on virtually a daily basis excoriating the guy.

Would you say that granting anonymity to sources is, in fact, commonly used and is a necessary ingredient in the mix of performing journalism and carrying out its mission?

BILL SALISBURY: Yes it is.

Given that what you did is a commonly occurring practice in the newspaper industry and across the board in journalism, why do you suppose it was this one incident when they decided to go against the grain?

DAN COHEN: Because they hate Republicans. Because they are bi-
ased against Republicans. Because Republican Jews are
an even greater anathema to them than Republicans.

ELLIOT ROTHENBERG: [The possibility of anti-Semitism] is something that's
a very incendiary topic. I think this issue permeated
the case. There were undertones, or overtones,
throughout the case. Minnesota has a very bad history in that regard, for what is known as a very liberal
state. I do think this was an underlying factor in what
was going on [during the trial], and something that
could not be ignored.

DAN COHEN: I believe they used it, to the best of their ability they
used it without outrightly making the charge. If you
read the transcript of this case, their lawyers contrast my background to Lori Sturdevant's background,
to Marlene Johnson's background—it was evident in my
mind what they were attempting to do here. They
thought I was an easy target. They could rub my nose
in this fine mess by emphasizing the Scandinavian background, which their attorney did, of Miss Johnson in
contrast to my nefarious background. While they didn't
call me a dirty Jew, they just said I was a dirty trick
artist, which was close enough for their purposes. They
thought they had an easy target, and they were wrong.

So was there a personal vendetta at work here?

DAN COHEN: Oh, yes! By all means.

ELLIOT ROTHENBERG: We had some testimony in the case that the newspapers did not like Cohen. They didn't like it that they

weren't given the story exclusively. Why did they hound him and why did they go ballistic on the guy after they dishonored the promise? I have to feel that there was something personal, there must be some sort of intense personal animosity that was involved in this situation. It never really came out directly. Of course, they all denied that it had anything to do with him. But none of their explanations, none of their excuses, held up under the examples of previous and subsequent treatment. So I feel there had to be some deep-seated animosity there.

BILL SALISBURY: Back then, I think there was a tradition of newspapers allowing themselves to be used and manipulated by political campaigns. It used to be more common for newspapers to accept dirt from one campaign about their opponents, and publish it without saying where it came from. Dave Hall strongly objected to that practice and I think that's what prompted his decision. [But] we argued that there were other ways to do it. We said we didn't have to name Dan Cohen. We had never agreed to say that the information was provided by a Republican source or we could have identified in general where the information came from without identifying Dan Cohen individually, thereby breaking that promise to him. Dave Hall's response to that was that if we did that then everybody in the Whitney campaign would have been suspect and he contended we should identify the specific source.

Was your byline on this article?

BILL SALISBURY: Yes it was. In retrospect, I thought it was a mistake. Under our guild contract, I had the right to pull my byline off a story, and I simply didn't think about that. Had I remembered that clause in our contract at the time, I would have pulled my byline.

What was it like when you actually saw the articles with your own eyes, with yourself identified in them?

DAN COHEN: It was like death. By their having done that, I knew that I had to litigate that or I would die. And I was going to litigate it and win no matter how long it took, what I had to do, how I had to do it, I would take these fuckers' pants down in front of the whole United States of America—which I did. The response around my [work]place was overwhelmingly negative. Terrible. I was in the advertising business. It's overwhelmingly Democratic. I think I ran a straw poll at one time. There were a handful of Republicans there. It was overwhelmingly Democratic. The article was very sympathetic to Marlene Johnson. There was no mention of the agreement they had with me because that would be embarrassing to them, if they were to have admitted that they made me a promise which they broke. The article itself was a lie by omission, by failing to mention that. I was a pariah. I was canned from my job. I had calumny heaped upon my head. I was characterized in an editorial cartoon as climbing out of a garbage can. It was unpleasant.

ELLIOT ROTHENBERG: I thought he got screwed. I thought that they had made promises to him, they'd broken the promises, then proceeded to hound the guy. So I felt there was a grave injustice that was done to the man. This became perhaps the most interesting story of the whole campaign. I think it's wholly illegitimate what they did. They always denied it, naturally. Their position was that they were serving the public interest somehow by exposing a dirty campaign trick. That was their argument. They saw a story, they saw a way to sell newspapers. The judge made this point, too, occasionally, especially in the latter parts of the case—Judge Frank Knoll, the trial judge when they had a motion for a judgment not withstanding the verdict. He was making that point as well.

PRECURSOR TO LITIGATION

ELLIOT ROTHENBERG: The first time we met was when we had lunch. And we were talking about my writing an article to get published somewhere on the case. The case at that point, although it had been going on since late 1982, had gotten virtually no coverage anywhere. So after meeting with him, I did write the article which eventually got published in the *Columbia Journalism Review*. So that first meeting was not a meeting to explore possible representation. He, or course, still, was working with his first lawyers. Then I got a call [from Cohen] right around the time the article was published. It was, oh, around January of 1986. And he said that he and his lawyers at that time had reached a parting of the ways, and that he would like me to represent him in the case.

DAN COHEN: Without my authority, my first attorney attempted to settle the case for $4,000 at which point I was sufficiently unhappy with him so that when he suggested that if I did not accept his advice on this, that he might feel compelled to resign. I said, "Your resignation is accepted."

ELLIOT ROTHENBERG: We had known each other before, too. We lived about a mile from each other, and frequently took the same bus to downtown Minneapolis where we had our offices—at least I had my office there at that time. He had his office there then and still does. And we would talk about the news of the day. So we had gotten along well even before that.

DAN COHEN: I've known Elliot for many years. We're both Harvard Law School graduates, we live within a mile of each other. We used to ride the bus downtown to work together. He was a Republican office holder—a state legislator—I was a Republican office holder—a city councilman. We are a rare breed—Jewish Republicans. We used to run around Lake Calhoun, which is a lake in this neighborhood, at about the same time. In fact, to this day I see him most mornings when I go out because I'm a crack-of-dawn runner. He stopped running. He's walking now. I see him. We talk. We are still in frequent contact. Right now, I'm trying to assist him in getting his book converted into a screenplay and sold to the movies. I think it's marketable as a small film of some kind because it's two guys against a couple of big bullies, and that's always a good story—particularly when the bullies are as obnoxious and as crooked as these people.

You felt from the start that this was a potential landmark First Amendment case, and possibly a Supreme Court case.

ELLIOT ROTHENBERG: Yes. It was the conflict between the rights under a contract—under an agreement—versus the First Amendment rights of a newspaper, or First Amendment *claims* of a newspaper. And particularly where you have the conflict between rights under a contract and the newspaper's right to print the truth. Because all the way through this case, one of the big issues was that they had a tougher standard when they were telling the truth than they would have if they were lying about the guy, under the *New York Times v. Sullivan* rule. So that's why I thought that—and this is the first case that proposed the issue of a deliberate violation of a contract claiming First Amendment rights to do so.

New York Times v. Sullivan, 376 U.S. 254 (1964), is often regarded as the zenith of constitutional protection of the press. The U.S. Supreme Court ruled that the First Amendment protects criticism of public officials—even if the remarks are false and defamatory—unless "actual malice" is proven. This is the *New York Times* rule—a public libel plaintiff having to prove that the press acted with knowledge of falsity or with reckless disregard for the truth. This ruling and its progeny heralded a new era of First Amendment press freedom.

I would assume then, that that was part of the attractiveness of representing Mr. Cohen in the first place.

ELLIOT ROTHENBERG: Yes, yes. There are a number of things that made it attractive—the fascination of the case, the fact that the guy really got screwed and was treated very, very shabbily, especially by the *Star Tribune*—little guy versus the big corporation. You've got that there. Yeah, yeah, all those things. And we got along fine. We had certain disagreements along the way, but I think the thing about Dan is he's extremely smart. He's one of the smartest people you'd ever want to come across. He was a graduate of Harvard Law School, went to Stanford. It was very interesting working with him during this thing. It turned out to be a full-time task for both of us, actually. His obsession with it didn't cause any problems at all. He had good ideas as the case went on. It was good working with somebody who was so smart.

Cohen says that at the time that he was looking for a new attorney to represent him, that he needed to find a lawyer who, like him, harbored a deep-seated hatred of the newspapers. Did he find one?

ELLIOT ROTHENBERG: (laughs)(laughs)(laughs) I wouldn't say I have a deep-seated hatred of the newspapers. Although I certainly resented what they did to him, and I didn't like their treatment of me during the attorney general race. But you have to keep in mind that when you're going into a case like this, you can't be governed by emotions. Although I didn't particularly like the *Star Tribune*, especially—I didn't have any problems with the *Pioneer Press*—I didn't particularly like the *Star Tribune* more in the nature that I think there was a grave injustice done to Dan in this situation. I tried not to let any personal views against the *Star Tribune* have any role in how I handled the case. It was hard enough to handle it without letting that enter into it. I think Dan's on the right track, but I think my feelings —my emotions—weren't as strong as his were.

PREPARATIONS

ELLIOT ROTHENBERG: Besides the legal research—the conventional sorts of legal research—the heart of the case, the heart of the trial, especially, was my collection of newspaper articles, editorials, and things of that sort. I had accumulated over 500 articles regarding a bunch of things—the use of confidential sources, focusing among other things, on confidential sources, criticizing candidates late in political campaigns, articles and editorials dealing with the seriousness of shoplifting, articles dealing with cases where confidential sources revealed that politicians had been arrested or convicted of shoplifting. Of course, there were hundreds and hundreds of articles, mainly from the *Star Tribune* and *Pioneer Press*, but some of them from other newspapers where they would be relevant to the case—those newspapers being *The New York Times*, *Washington Post*, *Wall Street Journal*, there were a few from the *Des Moines Register*. We had a few articles from, I think it was the *New York Daily News* dealing with Bess Myerson, the former Miss America's conviction of shoplifting several years before they finally disclosed it. Now, why was all of this necessary? Well, it was necessary because of the newspapers' strategy. There was no question that the reporters had made an agreement with Cohen for confidentiality and the editors decided to dishonor the agreement. That was undisputed. But their whole strategy in the trial was to claim that this was such a horrible, dirty trick that they just had to disclose his name to serve the public interest and to inform the public, and that we were so shocked by Cohen's conduct. Well, what I was trying to do with these articles—and that's one of the reasons that the trial went on so long, was because of that strategy—was to show that this was rank hypocrisy on the newspapers' part, that they have regularly made and honored these promises, especially where politicians were involved—involving criticism of politicians. They had regularly taken the position that shoplifting was a very serious offense and deserved the widest possible public disclosure. And that the ethics of the newspapers and the whole journalistic profession was that once you made a promise of confidentiality, you don't break that promise, you don't burn that source. That's a cardinal rule of the journalistic profession.

You were Mr. Cohen's sole legal counsel versus quite an array of attorneys opposing you.

ELLIOT ROTHENBERG: Right. Once that one firm was out of there and I was in, I was his only attorney throughout the rest of the thing. Now that caused the most difficulties, as you can imagine, during the trial when they have literally an army of lawyers right there. It was, oh, 18-to-20 hours a day on the trial just keeping everything organized and having the cross-examination, preparing for the next day, making sure everybody showed up for the next day, never having time for lunch or anything like that. The trial went on for 3 weeks. In a way, this may have been helpful because you have the jury there seeing all these corporate lawyers taking up the table and a few rows behind their conference table on the one hand, and one sole person on the other. I think this helped in a way with the jury. I wouldn't recommend it (laughs) to tell you the truth, but in a way I think to a certain extent it helped with the jury at least maybe giving me a little bit more trust or support—something of that sort. Now the "one against the many" applied all the way through the case, too, on the appellate level as well. I think the most discomfort for this was really at the trial level. On the appellate level I could prepare the briefs and the petition and what not. It would have been nice to have help, but it wasn't as an extreme deprivation for that as it was on the trial level.

Could tell me a little bit about some of the strategies that you were trying to execute at trial, some of the primary points you were trying to establish there?

ELLIOT ROTHENBERG: The strategy was this: They had made the promise, they had broken the promise, they had caused him damage, and they had no excuse for doing so. You use their own practices against them whether through expert witnesses, other witnesses, or cross-examination on the basis of these newspaper articles. This is the only time that they had broken a promise like this. They had made numerous promises of this sort, especially during political campaigns—hundreds, thousands, millions, who knows how many. They had never, ever broken a promise of confidentiality on the grounds of a so-called dirty trick or any other grounds. Further, the grounds were that this was for a trivial offense for shoplifting. They themselves had taken the position that that was a very serious offense. And I brought all of those articles. So we were able to try to show the hypocrisy of their own positions here that it was a dirty trick, or that shoplifting was a trivial offense, or that these promises may need to be broken in certain circumstances. For any argument they had, I had scores of their own articles and editorials to use against them.

For the uninitiated who are unfamiliar with the Twin Cities, describe for me if you would the challenge of taking on this powerful institution of the local press there.

DAN COHEN: I had no choice. I would take it on or die. This is the hotbed of Fifties conformity here. These institutions have grown accustomed to their own faces as being the moral arbiters of everything that happens here. They're not reluctant to use their power in that regard. *The New York Times* described the Minneapolis papers as "perhaps the most widely ridiculed newspapers in the country." They're just simply the monolithic moral arbiters of this community. They are not reluctant to use that power. This isn't like New York where you've got the *Times*, but you've got the *Post* and you've got a bunch of opinions bouncing around. You want everything here, but we're too small to have two of anything. So we've got one of everything, and they're the one, and they're not reluctant to stomp on people that they don't approve of. The people they hire don't write well, they don't think things through. They just tend to be rather stupid people who are down-the-line left-wing ideologues. That's what you get there.

ELLIOT ROTHENBERG: When I took on the case, I was no longer in politics. If I were still running for some office, if I were still in the legislature at the time, well, one, I wouldn't have had the time to do the case, and secondly, the political retaliation that you could expect—you could not do this case and expect to be in politics at the same time. A number of reasons: First, the power of these institutions, particularly the *Star Tribune*, and then keep in mind throughout the case, that the odds appeared to be hopeless against us. So you have the worst of all possible worlds. You take on a very, very, long shot against probably the most powerful political institution in Minnesota. When you have the *Star Tribune*, especially, you have a history of vindictiveness on their part towards people who would offend them for one reason or another. It was a concern. It was a big concern.

Were you ever a recipient of that vindictiveness?

ELLIOT ROTHENBERG: The *Star Tribune*, especially, is very passionate about the positions they take, and one of them was the death penalty. The death penalty issue to them is kind of on the level of abortion—the type of thing that you don't have rational disagreements about. I did take a position favoring capital punishment in certain extreme cases. They had the nasty editorial, they also had the editorial cartoon. I thought that was an example of vindictiveness on their part. Interestingly enough, I don't think it's been as much since the case has been over with.

THE TRIAL

ELLIOT ROTHENBERG: I had never done a jury trial before this. The trial work I had done was mainly on the administrative law level. Well, it really wasn't jury trial work. It was before judges or administrative hearing officers. But this is the first case I had before a jury.

To me, what I found to be an interesting element of this is that among the attorneys pitted opposite you was your ex-wife.

ELLIOT ROTHENBERG: Yeah! (laughs) That was a very interesting part of the case.

At a real personal level, how was it to deal with that?

ELLIOT ROTHENBERG: Very, very difficult. Of course Pat and I had been divorced before the case started. One of the things I had to do right off the bat was to call her and let her know that—this is in '86 after Dan had asked me to become his attorney—to call her and let her know that I was going to be doing this unless it would really hurt her position with the *Star Tribune*. I was hoping that she would say it would not hurt her position, and she was very gracious about that. So that was good. It became evident as the case proceeded that she was not at all happy about me being involved in the case. And the first time we had a motion, we actually opposed each other in the courtroom. It wasn't on the summary judgment motion. And at that time she was the chief counsel of the *Star Tribune* in the trial. Now when the actual trial came, they brought in the firm of Faegre & Benson and Jim Fitzmaurice. But at that time she was the chief counsel of the *Star Tribune* and she argued the summary judgment motion. And it was very tense. It was very tense. I walked in there and it was not like arguing an ordinary case, even against a top notch lawyer: I did have butterflies in my stomach and all that sort of thing. It was a very uncomfortable experience the first time going against her.

Tell me a little bit about your testimony.

BILL SALISBURY: I reiterated the information about meeting Mr. Cohen, making the promise of anonymity in exchange for the information about Marlene Johnson. I testified as to the editor's initial decision to let me proceed with the story without naming Cohen and subsequently being ordered by Mr. Hall to put [Cohen's] name in my story.

It was pretty much straightforward. The attorneys did ask if I had objected and I said I certainly did and explained my reasoning.

Was there ever any pressure—either directly or indirectly, even implied— from the paper to testify in a particular way?

BILL SALISBURY: No.

Did you feel conflicted to any extent given the fact that what you were going to and did testify to incriminated the paper?

BILL SALISBURY: I was a little uncomfortable with that, yes. But I never had any doubts about what I should do just because my testimony would be damaging to my employer. That made me a little bit uncomfortable. I did the right thing. I told the truth. I explained my reasoning of why I felt we should keep our promises, why it was a bad decision to break that promise.

Did you ever feel any ramifications from that—from editors once you returned to work at the paper?

BILL SALISBURY: No, none whatsoever.

How important was the reporters' testimony?

ELLIOT ROTHENBERG: Very, very important. I think both of the reporters. They both were very strong in opposing the decisions of the editors to dishonor the promises. They were both absolutely candid and truthful. They didn't beat around the bush. They did not equivocate about what happened. They were forthright and direct in testifying that they had made these promises, that their editors violated them, and they were extremely angry that their editors had violated their promises. Of course, the *Star Tribune* reporter went so far as to say that she refused to allow her name to be used on the byline because she was so angry that her promise was dishonored. Now, I think Lori Studevant's testimony—the testimony of both reporters was very critical—but I think Lori Sturdevant's was especially critical for a couple of reasons. In the opening statement, Jim Fitzmaurice was setting up Cohen not only against

Marlene Johnson, but also against Lori Sturdevant. He made the argument that here was Dan Cohen, this hotshot who went to Harvard and Stanford and was this and that, and poor Lori Sturdevant grew up on a farm and all that sort of thing. And then it turned out that Lori Sturdevant comes and supports Dan Cohen in the testimony. I think that was very, very important because it just shot down part of their argument. I have no idea why they made that argument to begin with because they must have known—they had to have known—that she was going to come in and testify in support of Cohen. So I think that was important for that reason, too. The testimony of both reporters was very critical. And there was testimony of other reporters, too, who were not directly involved in the case, but were just testifying about the importance of promises of confidentiality and that you should not violate these promises and you have these supervisors of both reporters who came and testified that they were against breaking the promises, too. So there was a lot of support for Cohen among the reporters. One of the conflicts in this case and pretty much all the way through was not only between the newspapers and Cohen, but the editors of the newspapers versus the reporters who were virtually solid that once you make these promises you cannot violate these promises of confidentiality.

DAN COHEN: I think I was a minor part of that show, in terms of my testimony. I think that basically my exchange with Fitzmaurice was two guys parsing words. I don't think he got the best of me. I don't think I got the best of him.

BILL SALISBURY: I recall Dan Cohen's testimony. I was struck by the fact—he certainly made a case that we had damaged him professionally. He lost his job as a result of the stories being published with his name in them. I saw him both at the jury trial and subsequently I believe I saw him the day of the Supreme Court hearing as well. He thanked me for my honest testimony, which kind of surprised me.

DAN COHEN: I have no problem with [the reporters]. I communicated with Salisbury at the trial. I thanked him for his honest testimony. Lori—I don't know if I communicated directly with her or not. But I have no problem with either one of them. Lori took her name off the article. Her position was above reproach. She did what an honorable person would do. She disassociated herself from this.

ELLIOT ROTHENBERG: We had gone over the testimony. I think [Cohen] was real good in fending off the cross-examination of Fitzmaurice, who was an extraordinarily skilled lawyer. When we was parrying about the business of Watergate and all that—I don't think Dan did anything to—I think Dan, as a matter of fact, was relatively restrained in his testimony. If they tried to get him angry, he wouldn't get angry. He was very dignified on the stand. It was a real strain, you could tell, a real strain for him. He was very dignified. He did not perform the way they had tried to get him to perform. He was not outspoken on the stand, I don't think. They did try to embarrass him. He wouldn't take the bait. He would not take the bait on anything they tried to get him riled up on. I thought he was really good on the stand. He did very well. He understated things. He did not overstate things on the stand, which I thought was real good. He answered the questions. He responded properly to their questions. He did not let them make a fool of him.

Throughout the trial, your personal integrity and your character were attacked.

DAN COHEN: Oh, yeah, dirtytricks. Dirty tricks. He used it every opportunity he got. I wanted to kill the son of a bitch.

Inside, how do you deal with this?

DAN COHEN: I wanted to kill the son of a bitch. About 2 years afterward, he dropped dead in his driveway of lung cancer. I didn't shed many tears.

Would you say that in addition to Mr. Cohen and the newspapers, that the practice of journalism—or at least some of the practices of journalism— were on trial here?

ELLIOT ROTHENBERG: Oh yes, yes! It was—what I call a journalistic *mal*practice in this particular case. But the interesting thing here was there were no other examples—at least during that trial—of violations of promises of confidentiality. So certainly on trial was the journalistic malpractice of the *Star Tribune* especially, and also the *Pioneer Press*, when measured against the codes of ethics of the journalistic profession itself.

DAN COHEN: This wasn't about journalistic ethics. It was about a contractual arrangement. They tried to put it on an ethical plane because that was the only way they could escape their violating a contractual obligation and a solemn promise. They characterized it as having a higher standard than a mere keeping of promises. There are some promises that have to be broken because there are some things that are just so low and despicable that they just can't be tolerated. So that's where this so-called journalistic ethics came into it. Shit, they didn't even have any kind of a—I think St. Paul had some sort of handbook on this— these guys didn't even have any kind of handbook on it, or any kind of a written rule, or any of the rest of it. It's just bullshit. And it was totally self-contradictory. If there's such a thing as journalistic ethics, which is what *they* ascribed their actions to—a higher standard than keeping your promise, then journalistic ethics consists of lying when you feel it meets your needs to do so, when you're called upon to do so. I think you've got a good flavor of my opinion of journalistic ethics, which is like "jumbo shrimp." It's one of those nonsequiturs that we have in our language. There is no such thing in my opinion. There is no ethics in journalism. What motivated these people, other than the fact that they thought they could get away with it, was that both papers had this story, and they were pissed that I hadn't given it to one rather than the other exclusively. And so it was, in part, punishment for that.

Should a standard of journalistic ethics—some standard of conduct—be imposed by a court? Or should it be allowed to be self-imposed?

ELLIOT ROTHENBERG: The phrase rang hollow in this particular case. This is commented upon by the trial judge. Also, the court of appeals—the assurance that journalism can police their own ethics. Number one, the newspapers did not even properly apply journalistic ethics here because, as we know, it's a cardinal principle of journalism that you don't burn a source. Once you make a promise of confidentiality you honor that promise and don't betray the source. That was the violation even of the journalistic ethics. But then we get into the question of the law here, too, which goes beyond what is journalistic ethics. You don't give any other business or any other individual the right to say, "Well, we can police our own observance of the law—whether we're going to break contracts, or commit various other civil wrong or torts, or even go beyond that committing crimes." That's why we have courts. That's why we have the law—to make sure that everyone else has his or her rights observed. So, one, they didn't even police their own journalistic ethics and two, what they are saying is that they, in contrast to every other business and in contrast to every other individual in society, ought to be their sole determinant of what laws they're going to obey, what laws they're going to honor, and that no court ought to have the right to second guess or to hold them accountable.

You alluded to your political experience. Did that have any impact on your efforts with this case—either positively or negatively?

ELLIOT ROTHENBERG: Yeah, it did in a way. I think it was helpful in dealing with the jury. When I had my two successful legislative campaigns where I went door-to-door talking to ordinary people of various backgrounds and tried to make friends with them and all that sort of thing—that's the primary mode of campaigning for the state legislature or for local office in Minnesota is that you go door-knocking. You do this for 4 or 5 hours a day during the evening. I think that helped develop rapport with the jury—not having had experience with jury trials myself. This was a useful substitute. In that sense, I think the political experience was very helpful—just in the rapport with the jury.

BILL SALISBURY: I'm not a lawyer—I'm not that familiar with the law. But it seemed to me that I had made a contract with Dan Cohen and we broke that contract. I had no idea how the jury would react initially, but after their ruling I expected that Cohen would continue to win on appeal.

Under Minnesota law, its six-member juries can deliver binding verdicts with even one dissenter. By a five-to-one vote, the jury ruled for Cohen, and granted him $200,000 in compensatory damages (for lost income after losing his job) and $250,000 in punitive damages from each of the defendant newspapers—a total of $700,000. The size of the award prompted the defendants to negotiate a reduced settlement in exchange for an agreement not to appeal the ruling. Appeals court judges were less likely to be sympathetic to Cohen's case than was the jury. These negotiations produced no agreement.

In the appellate phase, the case first went to the Minnesota Court of Appeals. That court reversed in part and affirmed in part—affirming the misconduct of the newspapers, but reversing not only the verdict that there had been misrepresentation on the part of the papers, but also the $500,000 punitive damages award. In the words of one of the newspaper attorneys, the Court of Appeals provided "something for everyone." But it also provided reasons for both sides to appeal, this time to the Minnesota Supreme Court.

THE APPEALS

At the Minnesota Supreme Court—the first time around—you wrote a letter to the Chief Justice before the case was heard. What was that about?

ELLIOT ROTHENBERG: Yes. Chief Justice Peter Popovich, someone I had known for years before that—a delightful guy actually. He had been attorney for the *Pioneer Press*, and he had been a lobbyist for them, too, before the Minnesota legislature—as a matter of fact, at the same time I was at the legislature. And he was, generally speaking, very strong in promoting the interests of the newspapers. Well, I felt that we had to get him off of the case, justified by the fact that he had been the attorney for the *Pioneer Press* before that and the potential conflict of interest. It was how you do this without offending the guy—a very difficult thing to do. It was a very brief letter. I think it was about two or three lines. "We respectfully request that you recuse yourself because of your past representation of the *Pioneer Press*." The letter was just sent to him—no press releases, nothing made public to embarrass the guy. Just a private letter to him. If he had not taken himself out of the case, that may have been something to use in an appeal to the [U.S.] Supreme Court. Trying to get him to do this without publicly embarrassing him was the challenge. I didn't hear from him for several months, no response whatsoever until the time of the oral argument when he did come up to me and said that he was going to preside if it was okay, but he wouldn't take part in the consideration or the vote. He was laughing and joking. He was not offended at all—at least he didn't show any offense.

A majority of the Minnesota Supreme Court, however, did seem "offended" by Cohen's lawsuit. It ruled for the newspapers, wiping out all damages. The majority ruled that no contractual obligation had been created between Cohen and the newspapers. Moreover, the opinion was written without mention of the First Amendment or any U.S. Supreme Court decision as precedent. This was seen as an effort by the Minnesota Supreme Court majority to preclude any possibility of appeal to the U.S. Supreme Court.

ELLIOT ROTHENBERG: Up until the Minnesota Supreme Court decision, it had been a confrontation between Cohen's contract rights versus the First Amendment rights of the newspapers. That's the way the trial court saw it, that's the way the Minnesota Court of Appeals saw it. Going in, we thought that even if we lost at the Minnesota Supreme Court, we'd still have that confrontation between the First Amendment and contract rights in the case that could be used as a lever to get it up to the U.S. Supreme Court. But then they hit us with a fast one saying there's no contract here because the parties didn't intend a contract, or it's not a conventional contract. So we find there's no contract. Period. No mention of the First Amendment. The only way the First Amendment got in was kind of by the back door, in a very murky couple of sentences dealing with the issue of promissory estoppel which was just introduced. I think it was the intention of the majority to leave out any reference whatsoever to the First Amendment to block off any possible review to the [U.S.] Supreme Court. Because of the internal politics that they had [on the Minnesota Supreme Court], they had to give some lip service to it. But that was a shocker. It was an absolute shocker. I don't think anyone had expected that they would try to just eliminate the First Amendment from a case where everyone had agreed beforehand—the parties and all the judges—that this case presented fundamental First Amendment issues.

Promissory estoppel is a doctrine that requires that courts enforce a promise if breaking the promise creates an injustice that should be remedied by law.

The Minnesota Supreme Court's ruling took a particular toll on you.

ELLIOT ROTHENBERG: Yes. It did because there was the opportunity to settle the case for $200,000 plus a varying amount of interest, which seems to go up or down depending on who you talk to among the newspapers' lawyers. But at least we would have gotten something—all of the compensatory damages plus a substantial portion of the interest that we wanted, too. Of course, we wanted to get the punitive damages restored. There were *very* serious negotiations on that. We got very, very close to an agreement on a couple of occasions. So after the [Minnesota] Supreme Court decision—talk about having second thoughts. I was having those. I couldn't sleep for weeks really. Here you turn down this money. You could have declared victory, taken the money, and now you wind up with nothing for Cohen. And the way they wrote the decision, we had virtually no chance of getting U.S. Supreme Court review. It was just agony.

I would imagine that at the root of your feelings was that it seemed pretty clear that this was the end.

ELLIOT ROTHENBERG: That's what everybody thought. And that's what the contention was. Oh, yes, that was it. It was written in such a way that we wouldn't go any further. Yeah, we really got screwed this time around. Yeah, you hit the nail on the head there.

One of the dissenting opinions at the Minnesota Supreme Court, that by Justice Yetka, said, "The decision [by the majority] sends out a clear message that if you are wealthy and powerful enough, the law simply does not apply to you."

ELLIOT ROTHENBERG: Well, I think that's a general problem, especially applying to media organizations. I think it's very rare that you have a judge being so candid. Hey, I'm not going to disagree with him at all. Although I think he was saying it mainly within the context of media organizations. I think that this is one of the big problems in this whole area, up until the Supreme Court decision, that you have these very wealthy, very powerful media organizations—one newspaper like we have in Minneapolis and in St. Paul. There's such an enormous disparity in power between them and any individual they seek to damage, either through a breach of contract or through other torts. You combine that with their efforts to wrongfully use the First Amendment as a sword to attack individuals rather than as a means of protecting against government censorship—what it was really designed for. I think that's what he was referring to—that you have this enormous disparity to begin with, then giving them their claim of a First Amendment right to violate the rights of others—a privilege that not even any other businesses have, not even any rich businesses have—I think that justifies what Justice Yetka was saying. But I do think you have to keep in mind the context that he was talking about—media organizations against individuals. I'm sure that he was confining it to the facts of the case. I think it should be read that way.

After the Minnesota Supreme Court ruling you re-grouped and decided to submit a brief to the U.S. Supreme Court. Would to tell me about that "regrouping process?" And then more or less what your strategy was in that brief.

ELLIOT ROTHENBERG: You have, I think, 90 days to get the petition of certiorari into the Supreme Court. Cohen agreed that we had to try to get reviewed by the U.S. Supreme Court. And, of course, everyone—the experts—felt that it had zero chance. It's hard enough to get a case before the U.S. Supreme Court anyway, and in this case especially since the Minnesota Supreme Court, they thought, had successfully taken the First Amendment issue out. So there was not even a federal issue left to bring up to the Supreme Court. So the whole thing was hopeless. So I had to keep up my own optimism in preparing this petition. That was the toughest thing I think I've ever had to write in law. The thing is, brevity is critical. The limit may be 25 pages now, but you really have to keep it within 15 pages. Every word and every punctuation mark is important. And you've gotta catch their interest.

They've got a couple hundred coming in every week. So you've gotta get their attention. I tried to focus on the importance of the issue, on the importance of confidential sources to the media and that this case had received national attention—to show that this was an interesting case, too. They've got total discretion. Among other things on this, along with the virtual absence of the First Amendment issue—there was just a sliver there, a couple of sentences—you had the problem that this was a case of first impression which adds to its interest, but at least within the U.S. Supreme Court context, it seems that the majority of the cases they take—or a large percentage, anyway—involve conflicts between circuit courts or conflicts with a state supreme court where they have to resolve this. So we had that problem against us, too. I don't know what the odds were against getting them to take the case. It was, I would say, considerably less than one out of a thousand to do this. These are the kinds of things. I tried to make the petition readable. I tried to make it interesting so it would grab their attention, and show that the conduct was of an egregious nature, although that supposedly isn't supposed to be one of the criteria for taking a case. But still, the criteria is whatever they want to take, they take. So these are the things I tried to focus on. I tried to make the absolute maximum of what I could on the First Amendment issue, to establish that the decision was, in fact, based on the First Amendment—to try to convince the Court of that—and that getting over that hurdle—a very, very, difficult hurdle—to show that they should exercise their discretion to take the case because it involves a very, very important issue in the journalistic profession, in the dissemination of information to the public, and also it involves particularly outrageous conduct that ought not to have the backing of the First Amendment to deliberately violate people's right to contract or other rights. So these are some of the things I tried to say in the petition.

Is it for those reasons and the Court's acceptance of them that you believe that cert. was granted?

ELLIOT ROTHENBERG: Yes. Of course, it's hard to say. Even in the Marshall papers, we don't get the reasons. We don't have any of the reasons in favor of granting certiorari. We have a memo or two from clerks saying that—oh, they did agree that the case was interesting. The clerk agreed that the case was very interesting, but that they shouldn't take it. And the clerk also agreed that there was a First Amendment issue, but that this is a case of first impression and that how many times would this happen in the future? And that there was no conflict between the circuits. So some of the stuff did get through. Some of it did get through. It would be nice if we had something from other Justices as to why they voted to take the case. But that's not in the Marshall papers.

THE U.S. SUPREME COURT

Can you tell me a little bit about your preparations for your oral arguments before the Supreme Court?

ELLIOT ROTHENBERG: Yeah. Of course, we had the briefs. We had more briefs to the Supreme Court. I had an initial brief on the merits [of the case], then also a reply brief. Plus the newspapers had their briefs, plus there was an amicus brief—from a variety of media organizations combined on one amicus brief. So I tried to read up what I could on oral arguments before the Supreme Court. And I did have one practice oral argument a couple of days before the Supreme Court—some guys in Washington, and I had that practice. The thing is, you never know what they're going to be asking there. You try to be ready for everything. Some of these questions I'm still baffled by, to tell you the truth. It's difficult. The question then arises—and something I can't answer—how important is the oral argument as opposed to other things in the process? It's great theater, no question about it. It's very dramatic and it's wonderful going up there and arguing. But how many votes does it affect? I assume different Justices would say different things. I tend to look at the most important part of the process being the petition. Now it's about one percent of the petitions that actually result in review. In a case like this, I think the chances were considerably less than one in a hundred. I think everyone would agree to that. But once you get the petition accepted by the Supreme Court and they agree to hear the case, then you have a better than 50–50 chance of winning—just statistically speaking. So that's possibly the most important part, although not very dramatic—not as dramatic as the oral argument.

If you could just tell me a bit about the personal experience and reaction to being at the United States Supreme Court.

DAN COHEN: Well, it's in a bad part of town, it's not a very impressive building. I was not overwhelmed by the experience because I kind of knew the lay of the land. These are nine politicians up there, and knew that it was going to be a fairly close vote. But I also knew that they don't call up cases from the dumb-ass Minnesota Supreme Court in order to put their imprimatur on it—put their seal of approval. They call up cases from the Minnesota Supreme Court to reverse them because the Minnesota Supreme Court is what it is—a mirror image of that newspaper, for the most part. I knew by the time that once we beat the odds and got it up to the United States Supreme Court, I thought we were going to win the thing. But so far as being overwhelmed by the grandeur of the place and all the rest of that, no. So I wasn't overwhelmed with the place.

ELLIOT ROTHENBERG: It's almost a religious experience. You're going into a temple, you're not just going into another courtroom. It is a different universe when you go to the U.S. Supreme Court—all the history there and the power that's arrayed before you, and the tradition, and the size of the room and the height of the ceilings, and the columns, and the clock behind the Chief Justice. It makes you appear so insignificant in comparison. It's awe-inspiring. It's a religious experience. That's what it is. It really is a religious experience. No matter what the relative importance of the oral argument versus the briefs or the petition is, there's nothing like it in the practice of law to go before the U.S. Supreme Court.

BILL SALISBURY: The courtroom was packed, but it usually is. The case seemed to draw an unusual amount of interest. I do recall upon leaving the court, getting out on the steps, being (laughs) surrounded by my colleagues in the press, and peppered with questions. What was most memorable about it was that Justice Scalia and the attorney for the *Star Tribune*, John French, had been law school classmates. And there was a series of exchanges between the two of them in which Scalia challenged French. I didn't realize until later that that was the case—the law school competitiveness that flared up. If I recall, my impression from the tone of the questions was that the Court had very serious reservations about what the newspapers had done. They questioned the papers' reliance on the First Amendment in that situation.

ELLIOT ROTHENBERG: Well, it's extraordinarily intimidating. It's terrifying, in fact. But then you get up there and you have these nine judges. You can almost reach out and touch them, you're so close. They're arranged in a sort of half hexagon or semicircle kind of a winged thing where you're close. Then you're hammered immediately by questions. And actually I found that once the questions start coming, you relax. You tend to get over the initial nervousness by just having to deal with the questions.

Do you think that that's part of their strategy—to put the attorneys at ease?

ELLIOT ROTHENBERG: Well (laughs), I (laughs), uh, some are more humane than others.

Would you care to name names?

ELLIOT ROTHENBERG: Well, for example, I think that Scalia is a real jovial guy. And he's joking and I think he generally likes the give and take of these things. Now I think some of these other Justices are not so nice about it, possibly even— well ... Well, you talk to some of the guys on the other side, they were carrying on about White. Byron White didn't ask me any questions. Of course, he was on my side. I remember [*Pioneer Press* attorney] Paul Hannah's comment on the way out about White: "What a mean guy that is"—an opinion that I didn't share. But it's extraordinarily intimidating. But I think the good part is, is that by getting their questions, it shows interest on the case—that they're involving themselves.

I think that's a real good sign. I didn't feel that I got any—I got a lot of tough questions—but I don't think I got any questions of the nasty or mean sort. I don't think that was the case. I think many were very, very difficult questions, but I don't think they had any motive to try to hurt the lawyer.

Wasn't there even what we might call an unplanned moment of levity?

ELLIOT ROTHENBERG: (laughs) Right. It was unplanned, yeah. In the rebuttal, there was a question about why Cohen he felt he actually had to meet with the reporters, why he didn't just in the dead of night slip a plain manila envelope under the door of their office so that no one would know that he was the guy, so he wouldn't have to have had personal confrontation. And my response was that he thought he could trust the promise of the reporters. O'Connor asked a question, I believe, then Scalia started to get into an argument with her about this. The thing I've read is that Scalia and O'Connor don't like each other. At the end of their discussion, I said, "Thank you Justice O'Connor. Thank you Justice Scalia on that one." It was just totally spontaneous and the room erupted. Scalia was fine, I don't know about O'Connor. I couldn't resist it, I just couldn't resist it, although you're told not to do that sort of thing at the Supreme Court. Actually I didn't mean to make fun. It was kind of an aside that turned out to be a real laugher there.

DAN COHEN: Thurgood Marshall opened up that case when it was being argued. That was the moment when I knew I had won. That was the only emotional moment in this whole thing for me in terms of feelings. The pompous ass they had arguing for the newspapers, a fella by the name of John French—who was a three-piece suit, bow-tie prick—was up there bloviating about how the honesty and the integrity of the newspaper—and this was the supreme moment for me in the whole 10 years of this thing from the standpoint of the judicial part of it—and Marshall interrupts and says, "Just a minute. You're talking about honesty. You weren't honest with Mr. Cohen, were you?" "Well, (blah, blah)." "You weren't honest with Mr. Cohen, were you?" "Well, (blah, blah)." "You didn't tell Mr. Cohen the truth, did you?" "Well, (blah, blah)." "That's enough. Thank you."

ELLIOT ROTHENBERG: One of the things that struck me was when Marshall was skewering the newspapers' lawyer, John French, about them not disclosing that they had made the promise. He was just skewering him. And you wondered at the time if Marshall was going to support the newspapers. Well, of course, he was solid for the newspapers all the way through. But he helped to embarrass the guy with a question.

DAN COHEN: That was the end of the case. I knew I'd won the case.

And yet he voted against you.

DAN COHEN: Yeah, but that didn't matter. He had to vote against me. He's been voting with the press for 8 zillion years, and he was in his last year of life, and he wasn't going to change that record any. But he laid it out for the rest of them. And that was what it was all about: They don't have a higher privilege to lie than you and I have. They're human. They've got the same kinds of obligations you and I have in their business dealings. And their business is the news business—to tell the truth to the people they deal with or pay the consequences.

When you concluded your presentation there, what goes through your mind at that moment?

ELLIOT ROTHENBERG: Actually I was numb at that point. I have to tell you. Usually when you're finished with an argument you always think, at whatever level—every other time I've been involved—"Gosh, I should have raised that issue" or "I should have asked the question this way" or "I should have emphasized this point" invariably in any other case. Here, I was just numb, I have to tell you. And even now I find it—I haven't had the second-guessing—"Well, should I have answered this way?"—because some of these questions were so tough that even now you can't think of what they were possibly looking for—the correct answer. So it's part of a feeling of relief, too, that the oral argument was over—that sort of thing.

And what did you feel at that time with regard to the outcome?

ELLIOT ROTHENBERG: Some other people there—kind of friends—they told me they felt we had won. Some of these guys felt we had won a unanimous decision. I didn't think it was going to be unanimous, by any means. But I was cautiously optimistic that it had gone well.

Of course, there is a lag time between this and hearing the result. What is that experience like, of waiting for that?

ELLIOT ROTHENBERG: Oh, well. This was in March. March 27th [1991] was the oral argument. On these controversial cases, invariably they take until the last couple of weeks in June before they come up with the decision. So I thought that we wouldn't be getting a decision anytime soon. I thought it would be sometime in that late June period when we would get the decision. It was three months, which was pretty much expected. I was very, very pleased with the ruling on the principle established. I was concerned, though, that they had sent the decision back to the Minnesota Supreme Court for further consideration there. You had the danger that you had established a wonderful principle at the U.S. Supreme Court but that Cohen would wind up with no money out of the deal. There was that problem. But, of course, very, very happy that the Supreme Court had ruled the right way on the principle. And, again, you've got the nail-biter, the five-to-four decision, too.

By that one-vote margin, the U.S. Supreme Court ruled for Cohen, relying on the concept of promissory estoppel that was first raised by the Minnesota Supreme Court (see Court opinion excerpts at chapter's conclusion). The Court ruled that the First Amendment freedom of press does not immunize a news media organization from its obligation to keep a promise—or from obeying any other generally applicable law. But rather than render a final judgment, the Court remanded the case to the Minnesota Supreme Court to rule in a way that would not be inconsistent with its ruling.

DAN COHEN: It wasn't until the United States Supreme Court decision came down that I said what I wanted to say, and I can remember *that* after 20 years, and that went as follows, because I honed it for years. I practiced it for

10 years. I wanted to get as many insults as I could into a single sentence. "Thanks to their arrogance and stupidity, the *Minneapolis Star Tribune* and the *St. Paul Pioneer Press* are now nationally certified as liars." I saved up for that one for 10 years. And by God, that was it word for word. I'll go to my grave remembering that.

ONE LAST STEP

So you went back to the Minnesota Supreme Court. Wasn't there a difference in its make-up this second time around?

ELLIOT ROTHENBERG: Yes. There were some different judges there. One of the good judges from the last time around, Kelly, was off the court. The Chief Justice, Popovich, was off the court. So there were two different judges at that point. Of course, all the experts had predicted that the [Minnesota] Supreme Court, even with the two different judges, would rule against Cohen, that they would just find a state law excuse to do so. They wouldn't make the same mistake again by allowing the sliver of the First Amendment [into the ruling]. They'd do it right this time. So there was unanimous shock that this time the Minnesota Supreme Court unanimously voted—it was the most decisive decision of the case—to the surprise of just about everyone.

Including yourself?

ELLIOT ROTHENBERG: Yeah, Cohen and I had feared—well, the one possibility was that they would try to definitively rule against him. The other one—and a likely one—is that they'd say, "Well, we're going to have to send this down for another trial"—a ghastly thought to have to go through the whole process a second time. So this was a shocker, especially the newspaper lawyers thought. They were convinced—or they convinced themselves, anyway—that at the very least they'd have a new trial. They never thought that the court would rule in favor of Cohen this time around.

When they did rule as they did, did you feel vindicated?

ELLIOT ROTHENBERG: Oh, yes. Yes. Absolutely. Absolutely. That we'd been right all along there. That's right. That's right.

The Minnesota Supreme Court's second ruling was in favor of Cohen (see court opinion excerpts at chapter's conclusion). It restored the award of $200,000 in compensatory damages, concluding that the verdict was sustainable on the theory of promissory estoppel. The newspapers and Cohen negotiated an additional interest payment, and eventually agreed to a total payment of $339,830.24.

AFTERMATH & LEGACY

DAN COHEN: People ask me, "Dan, how could you have endured a 10-year trial, gone through all this business, to exact your payback to the *Minneapolis Star Tribune* and the *St. Paul Pioneer Press*?" My answer is, I wish it had lasted 20 years, and not 10. I had absolutely no problem with what I did. I have no problem because every day those two criminal newspapers accept material from anonymous sources and observe promises of anonymity. There's nothing *at all* unusual in what I did. This is the way political information of a negative nature is most usually disseminated. It isn't passed out by the mothers and fathers of the candidates. It's passed out by their opponents. Absolutely no secret about that. That these newspapers should attempt to get away with something like that is outrageous.

Media organizations use the First Amendment in a variety of ways—sometimes as sword, sometimes as shield. Sometimes, though, that shield is used improperly, in some peoples' view at least, to cloak what might be deemed as otherwise inappropriate actions. Was this case an example of that?

ELLIOT ROTHENBERG: Yes, yes. It was used as a cloak for inappropriate actions—illegal actions. And it's an example of deliberate misconduct. Not merely accidental, not merely negligent, not even merely reckless misconduct, but deliberate. The deliberate violation would be, with any other business or any other individual, an enforceable legal contract. This used to be clearly a case like this. This is how the trial judge saw it particularly and, of course, other judges along the way, too—that the First Amendment ought not to be an excuse or a sanction to engage in conduct which anyone else would be held at least civilly liable for.

The circumstances here seem to present an interesting parallel—or an ironic twist or flip-flop—with reporter's privilege. How do you see that?

ELLIOT ROTHENBERG: With the privilege, the media take the position that they have an absolute right to keep sources secret once they make the promise. We had fun with that during the case, too. They, on the one hand claimed an unlimited right to keep their sources confidential when they want to, and on the other hand—this case—they're claiming an equally unlimited right to violate the promises when they want to. Some of the judges—one of the Minnesota Supreme Court justices—commented on that, too. That was something I used throughout the case and even at the Supreme Court level, that there's a lot of hypocrisy here. They wanted it both ways. Their position was that they have a First Amendment right to honor these promises because if they violate these promises and expose the sources, even under court order, then the sources of information will dry up and the public will be denied important information. Therefore, they should not be required to disclose their sources. But what is it when they say that they ought to have the right to dishonor these promises and expose our sources when we want to? I was making the point that the First Amendment requires that these sources be kept secret. Their response was that it wouldn't have that effect whatsoever. I referred to that in my Supreme Court briefs. Well, totally going against their own previous positions in the case. It was hypocrisy. That was an issue that I tried to exploit throughout the case.

There are some other cases and their rulings that come to mind in examining this case. One is Miami Herald v. Tornillo. *How can this ruling be squared with* Tornillo?

ELLIOT ROTHENBERG: As a matter of fact, I did refer to that very case in the Supreme Court brief. I had it a couple of places. One of the cases relied upon in the Minnesota Supreme Court was this *Tornillo* case which struck down a requirement that newspapers publish replies to charges against candidates. And here's what it says in the petition of certiorari: "However, the present case involves no governmental compulsion over editorial judgment, but rather the exercise of that judgment through a voluntary promise of confidentiality in return for desired information. Indeed, *Miami Herald v. Tornillo* distinguished between consensual conduct and governmental coercion and stressed that it is the latter which implicates the First Amendment." Then I referred to another case, *Herbert v. Lando* held that *Miami Herald v. Tornillo* "neither expressly or impliedly suggests that the editorial process is immune from any inquiry whatsoever." So you see, I think there is a fundamental difference between the government compulsion on the one hand in the *Tornillo* case, and here the voluntary agreement for that promise of confidentiality.

In *Miami Herald v. Tornillo*, 418 U.S. 241 (1974), a unanimous U.S. Supreme Court ruled that a Florida right of reply law was unconstitutional. That law required that newspapers publish the responses of candidates who had been editorialized against. Ruling that judgments regarding what to publish and what not to publish are internal decisions, the Court said that compelling publication interferes with the free functioning of editors that is guaranteed by the First Amendment. In *Herbert v. Lando*, 441 U.S. 153 (1979), the Supreme Court held that the First Amendment does not bar inquiry into the editorial decision-making process.

Throughout the process, there was a lot written, much of it negative ...

ELLIOT ROTHENBERG: Yes.

... in reaction to the various rulings. How did you personally deal with all of that?

ELLIOT ROTHENBERG: Well, it was part of the process of being beleaguered throughout the case. That only reinforced it, and what it did, I found, all it did was encourage me to work harder and to try to be more innovative in winning the case. They had all these guys against us—nothing new really. But in a perverse way it sort of helped.

Does this ruling become a strong statement for media accountability?

ELLIOT ROTHENBERG: It is, it is. It has become, I think a decision that has been referred to and cited in many other decisions at the federal and state levels—federal courts, federal courts of appeal, state supreme courts, all the way up and down the line. Media organizations are accountable, they are subject to the same law as everyone else, that they are not above the law, but that they are indeed accountable. This case has been the lone star in that area.

BILL SALISBURY: In retrospect, I think it is something that had been brewing and I think it was important for us in journalism to learn the lesson from this case.

Would you concur with the characterization that this case was a watershed event?

ELLIOT ROTHENBERG: Oh, absolutely. It was. It was a watershed event, and I think it's the most important media decision since *New York Times v. Sullivan*. Of course, time will tell, but I'd like to look at it as the *New York Times v. Sullivan* of the 21st Century. But who knows? There might be a decision next year that totally changes everything.

DAN COHEN: This case has now—as a result of my efforts and those of my attorney, Mr. Rothenberg—all but supplanted *New York Times v. Sullivan* as the single most important First Amendment newspaper case of the last 35 years. It is cited by everyone who has been harmed by the media. It is *the* landmark media case of the times. No better proof of that exists than the fact that the *Minneapolis Star Tribune* and the *St. Paul Pioneer Press*—they are criminal newspapers that cannot bear to admit they were wrong, and who have suppressed to the best of their ability news about this case, except when they thought things were going their way. Then they publicized it. They publicized it during the trial. They publicized it up to the United States Supreme Court. They got very quiet after the United State Supreme Court because they got their asses kicked all over the United States of America.

Bottom line, what was really at issue here?

DAN COHEN: What happened was the two of them got pissed at me because they thought they'd been snookered. I gave them both the story and they both made separate promises. And Dave Hall over at the *St. Paul Pioneer*

Press decided "Fuck Cohen." And then the Minneapolis paper decided to try to top them. Instead of just "Fuck Cohen" in the 13th paragraph, it was "Fuck Cohen" with a picture. That's what happened. What motivated them, what really was at stake here so far as I was concerned, was my life. I was not going to let these arrogant bastards get away with that. Had they handled it differently—I still could have gotten canned, the public still would have known my identity, but it would have been handled obliquely. And I wouldn't have had any recourse. But they had to stomp on it with both feet. It wasn't enough that the sons of bitches had to lie, they had to humiliate me on top of it. And they did it because they thought I was a coward, that I was too weak to stick up for myself, that I was—as a Republican Jew—I had very little leverage, I would be an unpopular plaintiff if I chose to go up against them, that they were holding all the cards, and that they could do whatever they wanted to do to me with impunity. What was at stake here was my life. And I wasn't going to let them do it. I would have blown the place up if I had to (laughs)—if I had to. I was and am—and you can tell by talking to me 18 years afterwards—that mad at them. And I still am. And I will always be. I do not take unanswered blows. I do not take my reputation lightly. I'm just sorry it still isn't going on. That's one of the reasons why I'm hoping to promote Elliot's book. I tried to get mine published. I was unsuccessful. Of course, I'm a little jealous that he was able to, but at the same time, I'm pleased. If it wasn't going to be me, let it be him. So anything that's said about this case causes them pain and causes me pleasure, and that's what I want to see happen.

ELLIOT ROTHENBERG: Bottom line, the issue, I think, was the rights of media organizations—or the *claimed* rights of media organizations—to harm individuals with impunity for the purpose of gathering news. I think [the central questions are] what powers are media organizations going to have to harm others without being subject to the same laws as everyone else? Do they have special privileges under the First Amendment to harm others? I think the answer is No.

BILL SALISBURY: Bottom line for us was that our credibility was really at stake in this case. I think the bottom line is that

we've learned that we can't burn our sources. We
have to keep our promises. If we don't, we're liable.

*What sort of signal do you think this case has sent, not just to the Minnesota
newspapers, but to all media?*

DAN COHEN: That they cannot lie, cheat, and steal with impunity.
That they have to at least observe some minimal
standards of decency in their dealing with other people and their adherence to the same rules of conduct
and law that other people have to adhere to, or they'll
get their pants pulled down. They got pulled down a
peg. They deserved to be pulled down a peg. They're
pricks. They're bastards. They're criminals. They're
terrible people. I don't like the media.

BILL SALISBURY: I think perhaps the most important ramification is
that our sources are aware of it and typically the peo-
ple that I deal with in politics and government are
somewhat familiar with our workings. I think they feel
more confident about dealing with us—that if we do
make a promise, for example to go off the record, that
we will keep that promise. I think the decision has
helped us in the practice of journalism. I think sources
trust us more knowing that we have to keep our
promises or we risk being sued.

ELLIOT ROTHENBERG: I think there are certain responsibilities on the part of
the media, and I think this case has restored some of
the balance that I think was skewed by cases like *New
York Times v. Sullivan*. I think we can all agree that
where there's censorship involved, where there's government interference with the press—that sort of
thing—the press ought to have freedom—the classic
cases of the First Amendment. But I think newspapers and media organizations are so overwhelmingly
powerful that they have a certain amount of responsibility to honor the rights of others as well.

Do you feel that the media have too much First Amendment protection?

DAN COHEN: Not anymore. Thanks to me they don't.

*In many ways, this case really seemed to pit reporter versus editor, or the re-
portorial function of a newspaper versus more of its corporate aspects.*

BILL SALISBURY: Well, your analysis is right. I think reporters in the subsequent suit felt that our paper was wrong. No matter whether we broke the law or not, they thought that morally it was wrong for us to break our promise. It was a bad practice because it raised suspicion about the newspaper by our sources. By burning a source we made a lot of potential sources worried about coming to us and giving us information. We may have lost some of our subsequent stories because of our actions. Most people in media agreed with the ruling and thought it was appropriate. I can't speak for editors. By the time the Supreme Court ruled, Mr. Hall had left, and I think the editors who had replaced him agreed that we would no longer break promises to sources—that we would keep our promises of confidentiality. And it did change our policy. I think that was generally applauded by journalists in Minnesota.

Do you at your paper have a written policy manual, or is this something that is communicated verbally?

BILL SALISBURY: We do now have a policy manual. It first of all discourages us from granting anonymity. It requires us whenever possible to get permission from an editor before we do. In cases where we do make a promise of confidentiality, it says the editors will not break it.

Particularly given that these rulings were so close, what if the final outcome had gone the other way? What kind of signal do you think that sends?

ELLIOT ROTHENBERG: It would have revolutionized the law in this area. The signal that the newspapers can deliberately and intentionally commit misconduct of this sort, would have been a terrible thing in many ways, just on the level of sources. I think it would have had a bad effect for the journalistic profession in terms of the trust that we've just been talking about. But also in some of these other areas of the law of newsgathering that have developed since the *Cohen* case. Literally, the media would have had the right to do anything to get factual information. Well, not killing somebody and things of that sort, but certainly civil torts. Now why I think this would have been so critical is that when you look at some of these other decisions—well, even *New*

York Times v. Sullivan and things of that sort—the defamation area—it didn't involve deliberate lies. It involved situations where the newspaper didn't know. I think there was a significant difference between this type of situation and the *New York Times v. Sullivan* situation where there were no deliberate lies. It may have involved negligence or gross negligence, but not deliberate. If the Supreme Court had sanctioned this type of conduct, and had given its approval, you would have said that newspapers and other media have the right to commit *deliberate* violations of a contract. As trial judge Knoll said, they deliberately sat around making a corporate decision to violate this contract. So I think this would have carried what I like to call the abuse of the First Amendment to new heights, if that decision had gone five-to-four the other way.

BILL SALISBURY: I suspect that had the ruling gone the other way, editors would have been more likely to break promises of confidentiality and reveal the names of sources to whom promises had been made. I think that would have damaged us with a lot of potential sources who would no longer trust us to keep their names confidential.

For you personally, what is the lasting memory of your work on this case?

ELLIOT ROTHENBERG: Hmmm. Wow. I think it's a sense of accomplishment that this is the high point of my professional career—no question about that—that you're able to leave a legacy behind in doing this case. Not to brag, or anything like that ...

But please do.

ELLIOT ROTHENBERG: (laughs) ... the feeling that you're able to accomplish something very important against great odds.

Personally, what's been the effect on you through all these years?

DAN COHEN: Nothing, really. I landed on my feet. I made more money as a freelancer than I ever made as anybody's employee. I'm probably not well-suited to be anybody's employee. I'm probably better off having been a freelancer.

ELLIOT ROTHENBERG: I've had other media cases. I was able to write a book about it [*The Taming of the Press*]. I think it's affected me in that way with the law practice and the book, and that sort of thing. It's certainly been helpful in that regard. The sense of having done something that will make some sort of historical mark. Personally ... What other personal things? Uhhh ... Hey, I'd like to think that I'm the same old guy that I always was (laughs).

Has anyone from these newspapers ever issued anything resembling an apology to you?

DAN COHEN: No, absolutely not. Absolutely not (laughs). They'll never do that. They're incapable of it. They're incapable of human error, because they're not human. They are the moral paragons of our community. They're above making human error. They can't do that. They're incapable of it. But they've had to pay every dime of the eventual judgment, and the interest, and the interest on the interest. They've paid every goddamn nickel of it.

When this began, going back to the campaign meeting and then the meeting with each of the reporters, did you have any idea—could you have imagined—that events would have unfolded as they did?

DAN COHEN: No, I didn't have any idea how it would unfold. I just knew what I had to do—that I had to put the bit in my mouth and pursue this thing for however long it took and for however far I had to go with it. I did not know. Obviously no one can predict that they're going to the United States Supreme Court.

If I asked you to pick out one thing or one memory that surprised you most about this entire process, what would that be?

DAN COHEN: That I finally won.

That surprised you?

DAN COHEN: Sure. You live in this state where these newspapers control the flow of information here, shape public opinion here, terrorize everybody in this seven-county metropolitan area into obedience—who'd ever think you could take them on and beat them? I had to do it. Was I confident that I was going to win? No, I wasn't confident that I was going to win. But I just knew what I had to do. I just had to do it. I couldn't survive with that goddam fucking garbage can cartoon dancing in my head. I had to shove it up their asses, which I did.

How often do you think of these events? Is there a day that goes by that they don't occur to you?

DAN COHEN: A day? Well, no, I don't have a *day* without it occurring to me. I occasionally probably have an hour or two. You know, we can all probably write our own obituaries to an extent. I can write mine. It won't appear in this newspaper because they ain't gonna give much play to my passing or to this case. But this is my 15 minutes. It's perfectly clear that's what it is.

And to that end, let me ask you this: How does it feel to know that your name is forever in the title of the case that has come to be regarded as one of the landmark cases in this area?

DAN COHEN: I'll tell you what, you're asking the wrong guy. What you should ask is how those pricks at Cowles Media at the *Minneapolis Star Tribune* feel to have their names linked as loser to it. That's the fun part. Having my own name on it—that's okay. I really don't care that much about immortality. But having *their* names linked to it—is what's fun. Seeing them in the toilet is what's fun.

With several years now—it's been almost 10 years since the Supreme Court ruling—with those years now to reflect on these events …

DAN COHEN: You notice how I've mellowed? How could I have been any angrier then than I am now? I'm just as angry at them.

When you reflect, have your views on anything changed in any way over the years?

DAN COHEN: Yeah, I'm angrier. I like them even less. I look at that newspaper and I look at these people in their editorial boardrooms and lording it over everybody around here and I'm just as angry as I always was. I've done my part. And I know when they see me, they ain't happy to see me. And that gives me a great deal of pleasure because I always insult them to their faces. That's part of the fun.

So was it all worth it?

DAN COHEN: Yes! Oh, yes. Oh, yes. It's worth it. It's just like one of those things where you just never quite get enough. Every contact I have with them—when I see one of these people—makes me feel pleasure at their pain in my contact with them. But there isn't enough if it. They travel in different circles than I do. They are still riding the crest of the wave, and they always will. They're isolated from common people. They're isolated from people like me. So they don't have to think about it, they don't have to worry about it. But I like just passing through their lives occasionally as a reminder. I've sent a couple of letters to the editor on innocuous subjects, you know. Probably in the past 8 to 10 years, I've probably sent two or three. They're nothing. They never publish them. They never publish them (laughs). I'm a nonperson until they see me. Until they see me. And then I ain't a nonperson any more. But you should see the expressions on their faces when they see me. It's like a whore seeing Jack the Ripper in the alley. And they're the whores.

In your book you wrote, " … the law stated in the abstract was bloodless. It told nothing about the consequences to real people in real cases."

ELLIOT ROTHENBERG: Yes! Oh, yes! Yes! We talk about these concepts like freedom of the press and the media, which sound really wonderful—publishing the truth and doing this and that. But when you get down to the issue of whether one person's freedom of the press means that somebody else has his or her rights violated and loses his or her job and suffers all sorts of financial and emotional consequences as a result or wrongs committed against him or her, then it becomes quite a different story from the lofty concepts that we've been talking about. All the way through, you had this one individual who had been harmed by the conduct of the newspapers, by conduct which was excused by a lawfully generalized concept of freedom of the press. But what it amounted to, really, was whether this involved a freedom to harm others by deliberate conduct. So we have the individual here—and in some of these other cases we've been talking about, too—who took years to reestablish his professional reputation and his professional standing. I think it took at least up to the trial that he was able to do this. So you've got flesh and blood people here. It's not just ivory tower general legal principles. People are actually getting hurt.

***Cohen v. Cowles Media Co.,
DBA Minneapolis Star
& Tribune Co., et al.***

**SUPREME COURT OF
THE UNITED STATES**

501 U.S. 663
Argued: March 27, 1991
Decided: June 24, 1991

COUNSEL: Elliot C. Rothenberg argued the cause and filed briefs for petitioner.

John D. French argued the cause for respondents. With him on the brief for respondent Cowles Media Co. were John Borger and Randy M. Lebedoff. Stephen M. Shapiro, Andrew L. Frey, Kenneth S. Geller, Mark I. Levy, Michael W. McConnell, Paul R. Hannah, Laurie A. Zenner, John C. Fontaine, and Cristina L. Mendoza filed a brief for respondent Northwest Publications, Inc.

JUSTICE WHITE delivered the opinion of the Court.

The question before us is whether the First Amendment prohibits a plaintiff from recovering damages, under state promissory estoppel law, for a newspaper's breach of a promise of confidentiality given to the plaintiff in exchange for information. We hold that it does not.

…

Respondents rely on the proposition that "if a newspaper lawfully obtains truthful information about a matter of public significance then state officials may not constitutionally punish publication of the information, absent a need to further a state interest of the highest order."

…

That proposition is unexceptionable, and it has been applied in various cases that have found insufficient the asserted state interests in preventing publication of truthful, lawfully obtained information.

…

This case, however, is not controlled by this line of cases but, rather, by the equally well-established line of decisions holding that generally applicable laws do not offend the First Amendment simply because their enforcement against the press has incidental effects on its ability to gather and report the news.

…

It is, therefore, beyond dispute that "the publisher of a newspaper has no special immunity from the application of general laws. He has no special privilege to invade the rights and liberties of others."

...

There can be little doubt that the Minnesota doctrine of promissory estoppel is a law of general applicability. It does not target or single out the press. Rather, insofar as we are advised, the doctrine is generally applicable to the daily transactions of all the citizens of Minnesota. The First Amendment does not forbid its application to the press.

...

Minnesota law simply requires those making promises to keep them. The parties themselves, as in this case, determine the scope of their legal obligations, and any restrictions that may be placed on the publication of truthful information are self-imposed.

...

The dissenting opinions suggest that the press should not be subject to any law, including copyright law for example, which in any fashion or to any degree limits or restricts the press' right to report truthful information. The First Amendment does not grant the press such limitless protection.

...

Respondents and amici argue that permitting Cohen to maintain a cause of action for promissory estoppel will inhibit truthful reporting because news organizations will have legal incentives not to disclose a confidential source's identity even when that person's identity is itself newsworthy. JUSTICE SOUTER makes a similar argument. But if this is the case, it is no more than the incidental, and constitutionally insignificant, consequence of applying to the press a generally applicable law that requires those who make certain kinds of promises to keep them.

...

Accordingly, the judgment of the Minnesota Supreme Court is reversed, and the case is remanded for further proceedings not inconsistent with this opinion.

So ordered.

*Dan Cohen, petitioner,
Respondent, v. Cowles Media
Company*

**SUPREME COURT
OF MINNESOTA**

---

479 N.W.2d 387
January 24, 1992, Filed

COUNSEL: John P. Borger, John D. French (for Cowles Media Co.); Paul R. Hannah (for Northwest Publications, Inc.) for appellant.

Elliot C. Rothenberg for respondent.

JUDGES: En banc.

OPINION BY: SIMONETT

OPINION: Heard, considered, and decided by the court en banc.

SIMONETT, Justice.

This case comes to us on remand from the United States Supreme Court. We previously held that plaintiff's verdict of $200,000 could not be sustained on a theory of breach of contract. On remand, we now conclude the verdict is sustainable on the theory of promissory estoppel and affirm the jury's award of damages.

...

I.

Generally, litigants are bound on appeal by the theory or theories upon which the case was tried.... Here, promissory estoppel was neither pled nor presented at the trial, and this court first raised the applicability of that theory during oral argument in Cohen I.... Nevertheless, this court considered promissory estoppel and held that the First Amendment barred recovery under that theory.

The defendant newspapers argue it is too late for Cohen to proceed now under promissory estoppel, and this case should be at an end. We have, however, on rare occasions exercised our discretion to allow a party to proceed on a theory not raised at trial.

...

We conclude it would be unfair not to allow Cohen to proceed under promissory estoppel. Throughout the litigation, the issue has been the legal enforceability of a promise of anonymity. Promissory estoppel is essentially a variation of contract theory, a theory on which plaintiff prevailed through the court of appeals.

II.

The defendant newspapers next argue that in this case our own state constitution should be interpreted to provide broader free press protection than does the First Amendment.

...

We may, of course, construe our free speech provision to afford broader protection than the federal clause; however, we decline to do so in this case.

...

The newspapers also contend that enforcing the promises of confidentiality would contravene public policy because enforcement would limit the free flow of important information. Courts should not invalidate enforceable promises except in the clearest of cases.... We are not prepared to say here that the newsworthiness of Cohen's identity had achieved a level of such grave importance as to require invalidation of the anonymity promise on grounds of public policy.

III.

...

Under promissory estoppel, a promise which is expected to induce definite action by the promisee, and does induce the action, is binding if injustice can be avoided only by enforcing the promise.

...

Secondly, the promisor must have intended to induce reliance on the part of the promisee, and such reliance must have occurred to the promisee's detriment.

...

This leads to the third step in a promissory estoppel analysis: Must the promise be enforced to prevent an injustice?

...

The newspapers argue it is unjust to be penalized for publishing the whole truth, but it is not clear this would result in an injustice in this case. For example, it would seem veiling Cohen's identity by publishing the source as someone close to the opposing gubernatorial ticket would have sufficed as a sufficient reporting of the "whole truth."

Cohen, on the other hand, argues that it would be unjust for the law to countenance, at least in this instance, the breaking of a promise. We agree that denying Cohen any recourse would be unjust. What is significant in this case is that the record shows the defendant newspapers themselves believed that they generally must keep promises of confidentiality given a news source. The reporters who actually gave the promises adamantly testified that their promises should have been honored. The editors who countermanded the promises conceded that never before or since have they reneged on a promise of confidentiality. A former Minneapolis Star managing editor testified that the newspapers had "hung Mr. Cohen out to dry because they didn't regard him very highly as a source." The Pioneer Press Dispatch editor stated nothing like this had happened in her 27 years in journalism. The Star Tribune's editor testified that protection of sources was "extremely important."

Other experts, too, stressed the ethical importance, except on rare occasions, of keeping promises of confidentiality. It was this long-standing journalistic tradition that Cohen, who has worked in journalism, relied upon in asking for and receiving a promise of anonymity.

Neither side in this case clearly holds the higher moral ground, but in view of the defendants' concurrence in the importance of honoring promises of confidentiality, and absent the showing of any compelling need in this case to break that promise, we conclude that the resultant harm to Cohen requires a remedy here to avoid an injustice. In short, defendants are liable in damages to plaintiff for their broken promise.

...

Our prior reversal of the verdict having been vacated, we now affirm the court of appeals' decision, but on promissory estoppel grounds. We affirm, therefore, plaintiff's verdict and judgment for $200,000 compensatory damages.

Affirmed on remand on different grounds.

7 Nebraska Press Association, et al. v. Stuart, Judge, et al.

"[I]t should not be government that is determining what is newsworthy and when [information] should be published. That should be in the hands of the press. If you don't believe that, then I don't think you really believe in the First Amendment because that's the guts of the First Amendment as far as the press is concerned."

—E. Barrett Prettyman, Jr., co-counsel, Nebraska Press Association

"[O]ur concern was less reporting about trials, which was specifically at issue in this case, and more about being free to report about *anything* free of prior restraints."

—Floyd Abrams, co-counsel in *Nebraska Press Association v. Stuart*

"[W]e weren't going to let the lawyers edit the newspaper."

—Keith Blackledge, editor emeritus, *North Platte Telegraph*

"If we didn't fight this—win or lose—we were done."

—Alan Peterson, co-counsel, Nebraska Press Association

"Do I think [the ruling] is right? No. I think there should be more effective means of giving the citizenry a fair trial and not allow the press to make a mockery of the justice system which they can possibly do under some of the tests that have been set forth."

—Hon. Hugh Stuart, respondent in *Nebraska Press Association v. Stuart*

They were all killed. All six of them. Henry Kellie. His wife. His son. And three grandchildren. Murdered (and worse) in their home in Sutherland,

Nebraska—population about 850 on that Saturday night in '75. October 18th, it was. Sutherland. That's on Highway 30, about halfway between Ogallala and North Platte.

It was Simants. Erwin Simants, their next door neighbor. Police got him the next day. And he confessed. When he was arraigned in county court, the details of the crime were mentioned. The press was there. TV, too. Lots of them, from all over. And they wanted to report what they heard. And what they knew. It was news, after all. But the county judge said, "No." He didn't want the pool of potential jurors in the small community knowing that information. Something about a fair trial. So he issued a restrictive order. Some people call it a "gag" order. Then another judge—Judge Hugh Stuart, who presided over Simants' murder trial in district court—reissued what he calls a more "liberalized" order. He gagged the press until a jury could be empanelled and sequestered. And the press wasn't happy.

That's how the ultimate clash between these two constitutional values began. Freedom of the press versus a criminal defendant's right to a fair trial. First Amendment versus Sixth Amendment. *Nebraska Press Association v. Stuart.*

Led by an organization called Media of Nebraska, several media outlets and the Nebraska Press Association took it from there. Judge Stuart's restrictive order had prohibited them from reporting the existence or contents of Simants' confession, the nature of any statements made by Simants, the contents of a note he had written the night of the crime, certain aspects of the medical testimony at the preliminary hearing, and the identity of the alleged sexual assault victims and the nature of the assault. Like the County Court's order, this order incorporated the Nebraska Bar-Press Guidelines (see Appendix to U.S. Supreme Court ruling at chapter's conclusion). The order also set out a plan for attendance, seating, and courthouse traffic control during the trial. All of this was in an effort to assure the defendant a fair trial.

Four days later, the Nebraska Press Association asked the District Court to stay its order, and at the same time, applied to the Nebraska Supreme Court for an expedited appeal from the order. The Nebraska Press Association had also applied to U.S. Supreme Court Justice Harry A. Blackmun, in his role as Circuit Justice, for a stay of the District Court's order. Justice Blackmun initially postponed any decision in deference to the Nebraska Supreme Court. When he issued his decision, he declined to impose a prohibition on the Nebraska courts from placing restrictions on what the media may report prior to trial. The Nebraska Supreme Court then modified the District Court's order, but like Justice Blackmun, upheld the lower court's authority to prohibit the reporting of any confession by Simants.

The Nebraska Press Association then appealed to the U.S. Supreme Court. Representing it there was E. Barrett Prettyman, Jr. This was one of 19 presentations he has made to the Supreme Court. He remains a partner

for the Washington, D.C. firm of Hogan & Harston. Alan Peterson represented the interests of the *Lincoln Star Journal* and other Nebraska media.
He was and is with the Lincoln law firm Cline, Williams, Johnson &
Oldfather. Noted First Amendment expert Floyd Abrams joined that side,
representing a group of media organizations. He has argued before the Supreme Court 13 times; *Nebraska Press Association* was his first. Today he
is a partner with Cahill Gordon & Reindel of New York.

Hugh Stuart, judge for the 13th Judicial District of Nebraska from 1965
until 1986, was the respondent. He is now retired and living in Omaha.
Leonard Vyhnalek was the public defender who represented Simants, and
who initially filed the motion asking that the press be restricted in its ability
to report details of the crime and his client's confession. He is still practicing law in North Platte. Keith Blackledge was the editor of the *North Platte
Telegraph*, one of the first newspapers impacted by Judge Stuart's order,
and was at the forefront in seeking its dismissal. He is now editor-emeritus
of the *Telegraph*. G. Woodson Howe was vice-president and editor of the
Omaha World-Herald and chairman of the Media of Nebraska, a lobbying
organization of which the Nebraska Press Association was a member. He is
now retired. Jack Pollock was publisher of the *Sutherland-Paxton Courier
Times* at the time of the crime and president of the Nebraska Press Association when much of the legal battle over the restrictive order was being
waged. Today he is publisher emeritus of the *Keith County News* in
Ogallala.

THE CRIME, THE PRESS, & THE ORDER

HUGH STUART:

Parts of Lincoln County, Nebraska are sparsely settled. The general nature of the county is that most of
the people live along the highway. There are two high-
ways. Highway 30 is a highway from Boston to San
Francisco. And then there's Highway 80. And they
generally run parallel to each other. Along this same
route in the Platte Valley is the Union Pacific Railroad
and, of course, the Platte River. The valley is fertile
farmland and when you get out of the valley, it's
sparsely settled. Most of the people live along the valley. It's generally a typical American community, I
would say, of law-abiding citizens.

JACK POLLOCK: In October, 1975, 40-to-50 Nebraskans, all members
of the Nebraska Press Association, were attending a
National Newspaper Association convention in Las Vegas. One morning I picked up a newspaper and the
headline said, "Six in Family Slain." And my first
thought was, "What do you expect in Los Angeles or

Las Vegas?" Then I looked at the Associated Press dateline and it said, "Sutherland, Nebraska." I owned the paper [there] at the time. That was my introduction to what became *Nebraska Press Association v. Stuart.*

LEONARD VYHNALEK: The basics of the offense—and this is based on the evidence as it was introduced at the time of trial—was that Simants had been doing a little drinking in Sutherland, Nebraska on the Saturday. He was with his sister and brother-in-law at one of the beer joints, went home, took a .22 rifle and went over next door to where the young Kellie girl was—and she was a very young girl, 10 or 12 years old—got her in the house, apparently initiated sexual contact with her, sexual intercourse, shot and killed her, may have had intercourse with her afterward. Then the members of the Kellie family started coming home, and he shot each one of them as they came in the house. Later when he was asked why he did that, he said, "Because I had to." And no one was really able to figure out why he said that, except that it might have been for the purpose of covering the offense up. And then he left the house and hid out under a bridge that was on a county road just back of the Kellie residence perhaps 200-to-300 yards, if that. And then in the morning when the bodies were discovered and all the law enforcement officers were out there, he just simply came out and went up to the local sheriff and said, "I did it."

KEITH BLACKLEDGE: I think I heard about it, maybe the first time, was when my associate editor came by and told me about it. He was going out to cover it. That was the night. They found these bodies and the sheriff's department almost immediately got on the radio. They originally said that they thought there was a sniper loose in the area and that people should lock their doors. The whole region was in kind of a panic situation.

LEONARD VYHLANEK: When I first learned of the circumstances of the crime was on the Saturday night that it happened when they ran a special news release on KNOP-TV—I think it was around 8:00 or 9:00 o'clock in the evening, maybe earlier. It was during the showing of a movie, "The Texas Tower Assassination" or something like that. And that was the way I learned about it first.

KEITH BLACKLEDGE: There was considerable shock. You always think that things like this don't happen in small towns. Are you aware that Simants shot this girl as he was trying to sexually assault her? And that he apparently, after he shot her, continued the sexual assault? He apparently did the same thing with the grandmother and maybe with another child. It was pretty horrible. That was the thing that I think had Judge Stuart really on edge. He didn't want that to come out.

HUGH STUART: This crime was shocking to the citizenry. There was a lot of interest in it. Some of the citizens, including me, were shocked with the depravity of the crime. To me, a person having intercourse with a dead person is repulsive. But it was doubly repulsive for a male to kill a female and have intercourse with her as she was dying. I found that doubly repulsive, triply repulsive. I felt that if the particulars, some of the gorier details of the crime were publicized, that it would impair my ability first to get a jury and secondly to conduct a fair trial.

JACK POLLOCK: The community, of course, was stunned. Six members in one family. It was a very brutal crime. The suspect had raped two girls and one woman after he had shot them. It started when he attempted to rape one of the girls and she protested so he shot her and then raped her. And then as members of the family returned home he shot each of them and raped another woman in her 50s and then another young girl.

LEONARD VYHLANEK:  The next morning I learned about it when someone called from the courthouse—I can't remember who, maybe the bailiff—and asked that we come to court—that was on Sunday morning—to have a hearing on Mr. Simants, what I guess could be called a bond hearing, arraignment, whatever. Then we were appointed to defend him. Actually, the situation was I was public defender here, and had resigned in April of that year—April of 1975—and there was a new public defender who came on board in August of '75. And he was just getting his feet on the ground. This Simants incident occurred in October. So the court appointment was by the court to the public defender's office. Since I was there and I had agreed to stay on until the new public defender had got acclimated, that's how I got involved in the case.

HUGH STUART: There were two judges. The district where this happened, there are eight counties. And the judge travels from county to county. Each county has a courthouse. Both judges lived in North Platte. With my fellow judge, who was relatively new to the bench, we divided the cases according to lottery. But when this case happened, he objected to that assignment on the grounds that it was going to be a hard case to try. He thought that I, as the more experienced judge ought to do it.

KEITH BLACKLEDGE:  The truth was, I was deeply involved in another project. This was October 19th. We had a $10 million school bond issue coming up on October 21st, the next Tuesday, that I'd been pretty involved in. And I was working on a news editorial presentation for the Monday paper. I'd spent a lot of time on it. As far as I was concerned, this was an unneeded distraction (laughs).

LEONARD VYHLANEK: [Simants] gave the highway patrol a recorded confession that would be considered to be a true confession touching on all elements of the offenses. It was before we were into the case. He was jailed, and that was when the highway patrol talked to him.

KEITH BLACKLEDGE: There are really a lot of ironies in this. [Simants] was a neighbor and well acquainted with the family, and had, in fact, helped them. There was one other daughter of Henry Kellie's who was grown and married and who moved away just before this happened. Henry Kellie had bailed out Simants. Simants had been picked up on an intoxication charge not very long before this happened. Henry had bailed him out. He was supposed to do some work for Henry to pay back the $60. Part of the work that he did was to help this daughter and her husband pack up and move.

JACK POLLOCK: The circumstances were that the crime was so brutal that the judge was trying to do everything he could to ensure a fair trial for the suspect. Of course, information around the community was pretty common knowledge what had happened.

LEONARD VYHLANEK: There was a lot of local media interest. Of course, once you get in the *Omaha World-Herald* and the [*Lin-*

coln] Journal Star and so forth, it gets onto the wire and because we anticipated that there would be a lot of press coverage, we filed this motion to close off all the hearings. That was first done by both the prosecution and defense. The prosecution kind of lost interest in it, and the defense had to carry the ball on trying to keep that order in place. There was an incredible amount of conversation about it. Community reaction was one of being appalled at what occurred. The Kellie family was fairly well-known in the Sutherland community which is a very, very small community. The reaction, of course, was to do something to Simants.

Was all this conversation the reasoning behind wanting the press gagged?

LEONARD VYHLANEK: Yes, so that the facts wouldn't get out to the general public and contaminate the jury pool. Lincoln County is a small county in a sparsely settled area. I think that in 1975 the population was around 25,000 and that would include North Platte. And it's a fairly large county. The population of North Platte at that time was around 20,000. So 5000 were out in the county. In a county such as this, which would be just like a large neighborhood, you'd have a lot of word of mouth and conversation, plus the county was pretty well saturated with the local media, certainly. So, to keep the jury pool clean.

But wasn't much of this information already in the public consciousness anyway?

LEONARD VYHLANEK: Yes.

And given the nature of the crime, people were already talking about it?

LEONARD VYHLANEK: Yes.

Then what was the value of preventing the press from reporting on the issues?

LEONARD VYHLANEK: Even though the community had already been talking about it and there had already been a dispersal of some of the facts prior to that time, from the defense standpoint—from our standpoint—it was necessary to file the motion to avoid a situation whereby you raise everything that you can if there's the possibility of a death sentence. The one thing that, as far as the press is concerned, if we hadn't raised it, somebody could come along later if there was more of a splash in the press, and said, "Look, you guys didn't take whatever steps were necessary in order to shut that off, and now look what you did. You got the jury pool contaminated and there wasn't any question that he wasn't going to get a fair trial in the county."

So that could have raised the issue of inadequate defense, if you hadn't filed the motion in the first place?

LEONARD VYHLANEK: Yes, inadequate assistance from counsel. [We had to] file the motion in the first place and then continue to try to keep it in play.

KEITH BLACKLEDGE: They had the confession introduced at the preliminary hearing but it was submitted to the judge and immediately sealed. So the contents of that did not actually come out at the preliminary hearing. But that was also one of the big issues. We made some reference to that in the story, but I don't think we called it a confession.

LEONARD VYHLANEK: The order was first issued in the county court by [Lincoln County] Judge [Ronald] Ruff and then later was modified to some degree by Judge Stuart. Of course, then when the Nebraska Press Association, primarily, got itself involved in an effort to upset the order, that required countering every action that they took.

KEITH BLACKLEDGE: So then things escalated from there. I don't remember how or when I heard of the first meeting with Judge Ruff when the gag order was issued that Monday morning, I think it was.

HUGH STUART: I do remember I was out on the road when the preliminary hearing was held. I don't remember when that was. I think October the 18th was a Saturday. I think the preliminary hearing was held the next week. I was out on the road. I had a trial in another county. When I got back to North Platte, there had been a filing by the Nebraska Press Association. The fat was in the fire. Because of the pressures involved, when I got back to North Platte that night, I had a hearing after supper. So the first hearing in the case was after supper, I think on the same day as the preliminary hearing.

KEITH BLACKLEDGE: The county judge was the one who issued the gag order first. I had thought that Judge Stuart would overturn it, but everybody was really on edge about the nature of the crimes and they perceived that if there was full disclosure there it would be almost impossible to get a trial. But I had thought Judge Stuart would just close the thing down, and he didn't. So I had a lot of respect for his judgment. He was pretty tense on this issue, too.

JACK POLLOCK: The judge was trying to keep the media from publicizing information about the confession and some of the other information in an effort to not inflame any potential jurors, to give the defendant the best possible protection for a fair trial that he could.

HUGH STUART: So far as the Bar-Press Guidelines were concerned, as soon as I got the jury impaneled, I said to the press they could print anything that they wanted to. I had my jury and I had them sequestered and I wasn't going to let the jury read what the press said either about me or about the order I had entered or about the crime that they were trying.

Obviously among your concerns was the press and the information that they were able to able to disseminate to the public there.

HUGH STUART: That's right. That was the reason for this hearing after supper was that the press was objecting strenuously to the order. I was the in-between guy on this. The restrictive order—the prior restraint as it's sometimes called—was entered by the county judge at the preliminary hearing. That was appealed to me, and I modified it. And it was appealed from me to the Nebraska Supreme Court. So three courts acted on it—the county judge, the district judge, and the Nebraska Supreme Court. And I felt I was kind of the fall guy because three guys acted on it. We all had to deal with it and I was the one that picked up the black hat when the Nebraska Press Association sued.

How and why did that happen?

HUGH STUART: I tried the case. They could have sued the Nebraska Supreme Court instead of Hugh Stuart. The actual case was filed by the Nebraska Press Association after the conclusion of the murder trial. Obviously they're not going to sue the county judge because he lost jurisdiction when it was appealed to me. But when it was appealed from me to the Nebraska Supreme Court I also lost jurisdiction.

ALAN PETERSON: The issue of jurisdiction was huge. [We asked ourselves,] "What do we do if they tell us we're not properly intervenors?" We intervened in a criminal case, which was novel and, I thought, daring and, as it turned out, a darned good strategy. Strategically, we backed up our bet when we went to the Nebraska Supreme Court by giving them the option of acknowledging our valid status as an intervenor in a criminal case or taking our case as an original action against Judge Stuart. You know, they knew what we were doing. We had them one way or the other. So they went ahead and decided the issues. It didn't go up as the intervention. That's why it's *Nebraska Press Association v. Stuart.* It's not *State v. Simants and Nebraska Press Association* as intervenor. So that's the option which was chosen.

An intervenor is an individual, not originally a party to the suit but claiming an interest in the matter, who comes into a case in order to protect his or her rights as they relate to the contested matter.

JACK POLLOCK: The thing was what he was restricting were things that came out in court. It's pretty difficult to restrict something in this country that takes place in a public courtroom. Hopefully our courts will always be open to the public. I don't believe in gag orders of any type. I believe in open courts, and most members of the press do. Not necessarily for the press, but for the public. It's a public freedom, it's not a press freedom.

When the gag order was issued, as the editor of a newspaper in that area, how did it make doing your job more difficult?

KEITH BLACKLEDGE: It just seemed like it made no sense. Sutherland is a real small town. There were all kinds of rumors and word of mouth items going around Sutherland and

North Platte as well. To have a preliminary hearing at which the public and the press could attend, and the public could go out and repeat anything that they heard at the preliminary hearing, but the press wasn't supposed to print what they heard at the preliminary hearing—it seemed unbelievably self-defeating and kind of crazy. I guess we were trying to ride the fine line between reporting what we thought ought to be reported, and we were trying to be careful not to prejudice the trial. So everything was read with considerable care, but we tried to make it clear that we weren't going to let the lawyers edit the newspaper. We had all sorts of outside news media coming in— the larger Nebraska newspapers, and newspapers from Colorado and Washington, D.C. and the Associated Press. It wasn't just what we were doing. The national media were involved. It was an interesting time.

HUGH STUART: I wanted to get the trial out of the way in a reasonable time. As I remember it was in January of '76. I remember that it was awfully cold at the time. The prosecuting attorney and the defense counsel—we had a public defender then—were both loath to come to trial at that time. I think it started about the middle of January, or maybe the latter part of January so that they had about three months to get ready. Particularly for the defense counsel, it's always part of a defense counsel's strategy to delay the thing. Maybe it'll just go away in the meantime. So the defendant was glad to have a delay. And the prosecutor had a lot of work to do including some of the more exotic examinations of the evidence including DNA work and work on fluids found around, and examination of the weapon and the method of death. All of these things meant he had quite a lot of work to do. He wasn't very eager to do all this work in 3 months. This is not atypical, but this was a time that the courts were busy, as were the attorneys for both sides. They couldn't just lay everything down and do this case alone. I had other work that I had to do, also.

Tell me about the challenge of trying to defend someone under these circumstances.

LEONARD VYHLANEK: It was a substantial challenge from the standpoint that there was a lot of animosity from the community. We were pushed to trial rather fast on it. Really the only defense that we had was to try to get together an insanity defense which meant getting experts to look at him. Also in an insanity defense case, the important part of one of those defenses is to get a lot of fact witnesses who can corroborate the fact that the guy had some problems mentally—erratic behavior and so forth. We had a real problem in getting that kind of evidence together. People wouldn't talk to us when they found out that we were defending Simants.

HUGH STUART: As I look back on it, I was concerned with a lot of things besides the conflict between the First and Sixth Amendments. I was concerned with the safety of the defendant. I guess I wouldn't say fearful, but I was concerned. I remember that normally the defendants will move from the jail to the courthouse. This is across a principal street in North Platte, and this highway goes by the courthouse—Highway 30. Normally the way that the sheriff would bring a defendant to trial would be to get him out of his cell and walk him across the street. That was not done in this case. The courthouse has doors facing all four directions, the principal doors being on the east and west sides. But after discussing it with the sheriff, he would take the prisoner out of the cell and put him in a car in which there was some darkening, possibly camouflage, and drive around to the north side of the courthouse where he'd laid a plank across the curb. He'd drive across the curb and up the sidewalk where he was immediately next to the door of the courthouse. He'd get him out of the car and bring him up to the third floor where the trial was.

LEONARD VYHLANEK: [There was] tremendous media coverage. At the outset, the media coverage was just the local print and broadcast media. We had one TV station in the county—KNOP-TV, which was and is an NBC affiliate. At time I think there were just three radio stations. One newspaper of general circulation in the county, and there's a statewide paper, the *Omaha World-Herald* that comes in there. The media coverage was just confined to that, but it was rather intensive, of course. It did get out on the wire services. It was intensive. It set out all the facts of the case but it didn't include the sexual things or his confession.

KEITH BLACKLEDGE: From an editor's point of view, it was kind of a nightmare. The general sympathy in the community was with the courts and not with the newspaper and the media. Everybody wanted a conviction and they didn't want anything to get in the way. The free press arguments aren't real appealing to a lot of people. So I spent quite a bit of editorial time trying to frame what the issue was for the community, and try to help people understand why we were pursuing this.

And how were you framing this at the time?

KEITH BLACKLEDGE: That one constitutional right wasn't subservient to another. That we had an obligation to defend the First Amendment, not just for ourselves, but for the public at large. I tried to explain that several different ways. We, of course, were caught up in all of the processes. We had 2- or 3-night hearings in which the media intervened relating to this gag order.

When did the effort to contest the restrictive order begin?

JACK POLLOCK: Immediately.

ALAN PETERSON: When the gag order came up, issued first by the county judge, Ron Ruff, I was called by [the late] Joe R. Seacrest, the editor [of the *Lincoln Journal Star*]. Joe asked me to get involved, although at that point when I first received the call I had a fairly deadly case of the flu, as I remember. I said, "Look, I can't quite get out there right now, but I'll work on it on the phone. Why don't you check with the *World-Herald's* counsel, see if they've got somebody that might be able to run out and fill in for me until I can get on my feet."

KEITH BLACKLEDGE: The battle happened in less than a week after the killings. The Media of Nebraska was involved, we were involved, and the issue almost from the start looked like it was headed to the U.S. Supreme Court.

The Media of Nebraska was an organization that was established in 1972, largely in response to what media leaders perceived to be a hostile environment in the state legislature toward the press. Media of Nebraska was, thus, a lobbying organization. Its membership included the state's largest newspapers, the *Omaha World-Herald* and the *Lincoln Journal Star*, the out-state dailies and the weekly papers—all represented by the Nebraska Press Association—and the Nebraska Broadcaster's Association, which represented more than 100 television and radio stations. One goal of the organization was to present a unified front. When media interests were threatened with the restrictive order in 1975, leadership believed that the same unified approach was required. That leadership included Media of Nebraska's chairman that year, G. Woodson (Woody) Howe.

G. WOODSON HOWE:

We didn't want to convert this lobbying organization into a litigation organization. Those are two different things. But we used the same guys that were active in Media of Nebraska. They just dropped that name and continued to function as a loose-knit group. I was chairman of Media of Nebraska in '75 and so I wound up being the guy who called the meetings and coordinated telephone conversations and acted as kind of a treasurer. All the money came through me. I just kind of fell into it. But there is a mistaken impression out there that this was a Media of Nebraska lawsuit. That's not true in the sense that we didn't act under the Media of Nebraska umbrella. Nebraska Press Association was one of the members of Media of Nebraska.

ALAN PETERSON: The reason for the use of Nebraska Press was to get some oomph. You know, part of my game as a litigator is to get what you want with a bully pulpit. Here we could say, "Hey, this is the entire media standing together saying, 'You're violating the rights of one of our little brothers.'" So it was certainly to have the strongest entity, not just one paper and certainly not one reporter, going up against the entire judiciary. I don't recall the conversation, but I bet our thinking was, "We want our strongest entity face-to-face against the judiciary." That whole judiciary got behind Judge Stuart, I assure you of that.

HUGH STUART: I was concerned about the length of the trial. There had been a murder trial in California shortly before this where the case had gone on for an extended period of time. The jury was sequestered, and as a result of this sequestration, at least one marriage had broken up. The spouse that wasn't sequestered couldn't wait for the one that was. By the time the trial was over, he or she had picked another partner. I was concerned about the length of the trial. I wanted first to have it in a reasonable length of time after the crime. I wanted to run it as fast as deliberate haste would allow. I wanted to keep the jury sequestered for a reasonable time. I felt that I had to sequester the jury—and I had never done this—this was a problem that I was meeting, as to how to physically go about sequestering the jury. One of the local motels—I think this was a Howard Johnson's—had closed one of its wings because their traffic had dropped off, and in order to save money they had closed one of their wings. I went up there and hired this closed wing, and then I put the jury on the second floor of this closed wing so that they were number one, by themselves and number two, although they weren't imprisoned, they were in such a place that I could put a bailiff down at the end of the hall so that once the jurors retired to their rooms, if they were to leave—which they were told not to—the bailiff would see them. With sequestering the jury, I had to get more bailiffs. This was an economic problem. I didn't have any money in my budget to do that. Finding people who were willing to do it was a problem. It was in January, and as I remember it, I had some college students that were home for the holidays—part of the time, anyway. There was a man who had worked as a radio broadcaster in North Platte—kind of the head bailiff. As I look back on it, one mistake that I made was not spending more money to hire a little higher type of bailiff and more of them. I think that generally describes the circumstances.

You say that you modified the restrictive order?

HUGH STUART: Yeah, [Judge Ruff's] order was *very* restrictive and I liberalized it considerably. The order that I entered, it did have to do with the publication of the news, but it also had to do with a lot of the nuts and bolts of how to run the trial. For instance, I remember a part of the order had to do with the defendant's safety. The trial was held on the third floor of the courthouse and there are only two ways to get from the ground floor to the third floor. One was by the main stairway and the other is by an elevator. There was only one stairway. Part of the order was that the deputy sheriff would clear out the third floor hallway prior to bringing the prisoner over there. No one was allowed in that hallway. And then the prisoner would be brought from the outside door into the elevator, then conveyed to the third floor in the elevator, and then walked from the elevator into the courtroom. And part of this had to do with how we were going to do that. There was lots going on besides worries about the bar and press.

You say you liberalized the restrictive order. Do you have any regrets about not changing it further than you did?

HUGH STUART: Not particularly. The Bar-Press Guidelines played a very important role. Prior to this time I had gone to meetings where these Bar-Press Guidelines were discussed and described so that I was familiar with them. Prior to making an order here, I studied the Guidelines and I would tell you that I was not particularly concerned with the press ruining my opportunity to have a fair trial. I was concerned about the television station locally that I was afraid was going to ruin it. The person that was the central figure over there—the anchorman, if you will—he was a college graduate, but I think his subject in college was theater. He conducted his news program in a somewhat theatrical fashion. He was the guy that I was really worried about. I didn't think the *North Platte Telegraph* was going to do anything that would prevent me from giving Mr. Simants a fair trial. They never considered not following the order. In fact, all of the media did follow the order. In discussing it with both the *North Platte Telegraph* people and the *Omaha World-Herald* people, there was never any thought that they weren't going to follow the order.

It was the Association, then, that had the problems with it?

HUGH STUART: Well, all of them. They didn't like the order. One of the things that I found interesting was—to me it was a little inconsistent—I patterned my prior restraint order along the Bar-Press Guidelines. One of the things that they were vehement about objecting to was that I—this was a voluntary agreement between the bar and the press—that I had had the "audacity" to adopt it as a part of my order and make it an order. They were willing just as good citizens to follow these things, but they sure as hell objected to a judge putting it into an order and saying this is what they *had* to do. That was one of the things they were screaming about the worst—not what the order said, but the fact that there was an order.

G. WOODSON HOWE: The order tried to take the Bar-Press Guidelines and incorporate them into the order. That really infuriated us. That was a betrayal. I had been working on these Guidelines for 10 years and I knew the background on them. I knew that we had to negotiate them sort of at gunpoint to get anything at all out of the courts. I didn't like the provisions of the Guidelines. But I knew they were voluntary and I knew they were guidelines.

ALAN PETERSON: [There] was a feeling of betrayal by the news media in that Judge Ruff and then Judge Stuart had incorporated large parts of what had been adamantly claimed to be expressly voluntary guidelines for fair trial/free press, and ignored the voluntary language disclaimer that existed in the guidelines. We thought that was terrible and I suppose we felt stupid for having been had in regard to having ever agreed to such guidelines.

To what extent did Sheppard v. Maxwell *influence your decision making on the restrictive order?*

The circumstances surrounding *Sheppard v. Maxwell*, 384 U.S. 333 (1966), are the quintessential examples of pretrial publicity and courtroom behavior run amok. The murder of an Ohio doctor's wife and the sensational media coverage that followed provided the backdrop. In overturning Dr. Sheppard's conviction, the U.S. Supreme Court largely blamed the trial court for not taking the necessary precautions. These included change of venue, delaying the trial until the publicity subsides, sequestering the jury, and "voir dire"—careful questioning of potential jurors to determine whether they are qualified, that is, impartial. In the wake of *Sheppard*, many trial judges interpreted the ruling to mean they were required to strongly exercise their authority when they believed that circumstances warranted.

HUGH STUART: I was reading books on this thing. I studied it. I was staying up late at night studying. Obviously I was affected by all of the decisions. I was trying to make the proper decision under the law as I saw it. My philosophy on this is that a trial judge should not attempt to make law; a trial judge's job is to study and to discover what the law is, and then follow the law. This case was a change in the law. Should I have anticipated the change? No. By all means, no. I should attempt to find out what the law was at that time and follow that law, which I think I did.

JACK POLLOCK: I think that [*Sheppard*] had a direct impact on this. I think that was in the back of everyone's mind, including the judge's.

KEITH BLACKLEDGE: I know that he felt he had no choice and that he was trying to be sure that he got a trial. I think in light of the *Sheppard* decision and the way the courts generally were holding at that time, the pretrial publicity was a big concern in his mind. I guess I felt at the time that the issue was manufactured by the bar without justification, but then I was from a press perspective. I think I would hold that it was more a mental attitude of the bar, in general, than Judge Stuart.

G. WOODSON HOWE: Lawyers were all the time trying to interpret [the Bar-Press Guidelines], and they would always interpret them in the most extreme manner. The defense bar really became our adversary because they were always trying to put these broad interpretations on these Guidelines and then yell and scream if we reported the mere arrest of somebody, or the details of the crime scene.

So this case was by no means the one and only time you ever ran into some difficulty vis-a-vis these Bar-Press Guidelines?

G. WOODSON HOWE: Oh, no. No, no. Throughout the late '60s and early '70s, there were continual efforts by courts and defense attorneys—and sometimes joined by the prosecutors—to close courtrooms or allow us to be admitted to courtrooms only if our reporters would sign an agreement with the judge that they wouldn't report certain things. We found that pretty burdensome.

In the wake of *Sheppard*, the American Bar Association established the Advisory Committee of Fair Trial and Free Press. The Committee was chaired by Paul Reardon, Massachusetts Supreme Judicial Court associate justice. In 1968, the Committee finalized a set of standards commonly known as the Reardon Report. These standards became the basis of the voluntary Bar-Press Guidelines that were adopted in many states, including Nebraska.

Do you have any reason to believe that some of that behavior by the courts and attorneys was stemming from the Sheppard *case?*

G. WOODSON HOWE: Oh, yeah. The *Sheppard* ruling led to the creation of a bar committee headed by a judge named Reardon. You may have come across the Reardon Commission.
From the late 60s on, were we on the defensive fighting the recommendations of the Reardon Commission. And trying to be reasonable and reach an accommodation of what the lawyers felt was the Sixth Amendment right to a fair trial by agreeing. In 22 states, at one time, the press was party to these agreements with the local bar association.

Do you feel that the ultimate outcome of this case was in some ways a response to the ramifications of Sheppard, *and with this case we saw the pendulum swinging back?*

G. WOODSON HOWE: Yeah, I think the ruling and even the concurring opinions certainly brought some sense back to what the *Sheppard* ruling threw out of balance.

Do you know Judge Stuart personally? What kind of fellow would you describe him to be?

KEITH BLACKLEDGE: I liked him generally. We were friends before, and we were friends after. I think everybody thought he was a good judge and had respect for him. He had a sense of humor, but he could also be pretty stiff. He was determined to get that case tried, and he succeeded. The irony is that in spite of the publicity, the constitutional issue generated even more publicity than would have been generated otherwise. But in spite of that, he got a conviction that was upheld.

G. WOODSON HOWE: I think he's a good man who wants to do the right thing. Very earnest. I think he's a very, very decent guy. I have no hostility toward Judge Stuart at all.

JACK POLLOCK: He is very dignified, stately, and known for his decorum. He was known as a fair judge. He's not what you'd call a prude, but he's not really known for his jokes in the courtroom. He's known more for his judicial demeanor.

ALAN PETERSON: While I tend to like Judge Stuart, I'm aware that he then, and I think now, regards the courtroom in some really important way to be his. And other judges have the same attitude once they have the black robe on. This [case] was always, in part, a turf war—whether it would be the people or individual judges who would be able to most appropriately say, "This is my courtroom."

LEONARD VYHLANEK: When the Nebraska Press Association got itself involved in an effort to upset [his] order, that required countering every action that they took. They came in to dissolve the order, and we wound up going to the Supreme Court of Nebraska. We were also confronted with the situation whereby they had applied to the Supreme Court of the United States to have the order stayed or dissolved. And that was handled by Justice Blackmun, the judge of the Supreme Court of the United States who was in charge of this area. And we had to fight that issue.

KEITH BLACKLEDGE: It all came together right away as the Media of Nebraska, which included the Nebraska Press Association, Nebraska broadcasters, Sigma Delta Chi—a lot of organizations. There had been a Media of Nebraska —it was kind of an informal organization, but it had been in existence for some time. The *World-Herald* was right on top of it. Woody Howe was also active in the Media of Nebraska. So we had the two largest newspapers in the state and we were just a part of the whole thing. I don't know what would have happened if we'd just been by ourselves. There wasn't money in our budget for that (laughs). We got quite a bit of support from around the country.

JACK POLLOCK: As an officer of the Press Association, my role was in raising funds to fight the battle to cover the legal costs. It was just coincidental that I was serving as

the president of the Nebraska Press Association
when the ruling came out. Our press association
raised about $100,000 for the cause. That was our
principal function. The Media of Nebraska actually
fought the battle.

The fight for their First Amendment rights was one that some in the Nebraska media entered somewhat reluctantly. Their efforts were seen by many in the community as interfering with the need to convict Simants. An October 23, 1975, *North Platte Telegraph* editorial undoubtedly spoke for many in the media: "The free press-fair trial controversy ... has visited itself upon North Platte and Lincoln County. We did not ask for it. We do not enjoy it. We just as soon it would go away. But it won't."

What was your reaction to the effort to contest the motion and the order?

LEONARD VYHLANEK: (laughs) We hadn't anticipated that the press would be as cranked up about it as they were. So our reaction was, "Oh, my god." I mean, we had to protect the issue. That was the only reason we took an aggressive stance toward the thing.

KEITH BLACKLEDGE: Media of Nebraska was prepared to go all the way from the beginning. I think some of the people involved there thought that probably it would go to the Supreme Court, and they were going to have to raise money. But they were prepared to fight it all the way.

HUGH STUART: As soon as the case was tried, and as soon as I pronounced sentence, I felt it my principal duty as a roving judge to resume my obligations. After that, the defense filed a motion for a new trial. I heard that and overruled it. To illustrate my point, the trial was in January.

So once the state attorney general's office picked up the ball on this, that was the end of any involvement that you had?

HUGH STUART: That's right. I didn't attend any hearings, I didn't participate in any brief writing, I was never consulted. I had a few conversations with the Lincoln County attorney about it, but—he wasn't interested in hearing my thoughts on it.

The Nebraska Supreme Court balanced the "heavy presumption against constitutional validity" associated with an order restraining publication against the importance of the defendant's right to a trial by an impartial jury. The court determined that because of the publicity surrounding the crime, Simants' right to a fair trial was jeopardized. Barring the adoption of an absolutist First Amendment position, the court said, the District Court acted properly. The Nebraska Supreme Court, however, slightly modified Judge Stuart's order, prohibiting the reporting of information in three categories—confessions made to law enforcement officers, confessions made to third parties, and other facts "strongly implicative of the accused"—rather than the five categories of information previously restricted.

FROM NEBRASKA TO WASHINGTON

G. WOODSON HOWE: There was an element within the [Media of Nebraska] that didn't want to appeal [to the U.S. Supreme Court]. They thought there was a chance we would lose. They argued that, after all, we had gotten most of what we wanted, especially when the Nebraska Supreme Court, under Blackmun's urging, came down with a modified ruling. Some people didn't want to proceed, didn't want to pick it up, for fear of getting an unfavorable ruling. It wasn't ironclad at all. Even though it [turned out to be] a nine-to-nothing decision, we all think, "Well, that was a piece of cake. Nine to nothing! That just proves what an open-and-shut case it was. They didn't have any fear of failure." Well, we did. That was a crossroads. There were some people with cold feet who had to be urged to hang in there. "Let's take some risks. There's a lot at stake. We've got good attorneys. They say our case is fairly strong."

KEITH BLACKLEDGE: I'm not sure that I saw it going to the U.S. Supreme Court (laughs). I think my feeling was more, "How could this be happening to a little small-town editor (laughs)?"

HUGH STUART: I received a telephone call from one of the assistant clerks in the United States Supreme Court saying that I had been sued by the Nebraska Press Association, and that I had a certain time to answer. I said to this person, "What if I don't answer?" And she said, "Oh, you've got to answer, Judge. Everyone answers." And I said, "Why do I have to answer? What is it to me? I don't care what the United States Supreme Court says with reference to my order. This case is moot." She said, "Oh, no. The Supreme Court has accepted jurisdiction on it, and you must answer." And I said,

"Well, I'm not at all sure I'm going to," and I left it at that. After that I telephoned the Nebraska attorney general and described to him, and repeated, "Why should I bother to answer? Let them do whatever they want to down there in Washington. I'm busy being the District Judge for the 13th Judicial District, and I've got a lot of work to do here. Why don't they just run their own little show?" And the attorney general said, "Judge, you can't do that. You're a respondent in the United States Supreme Court and we've got to represent you." And I said, "Okay, go ahead and represent me. But don't bother me with it. I'm doing other things."

G. WOODSON HOWE: We in Nebraska had two good law firms advising the Lincoln paper and the Omaha paper on freedom of the press issues. They were pretty good First Amendment law firms. But as good as they were, we felt we needed outside help once it got past the state level.

ALAN PETERSON: We got a lot of financial support from the [television] networks and major national newspapers. I think that part of the condition of their large financial contributions was that they would get to choose absolute top-notch, experienced Supreme Court counsel.

BARRETT PRETTYMAN:  I, for some years, had represented The Reporter's Committee for Freedom of the Press, mostly on a pro bono basis. I had been in on the early stages of that because I had a friend who was energizing it. And he would send me various cases from time to time, some of which I would file amicus briefs in, some of which I actually argued. It is my recollection that my representation of the press people in *Nebraska Press* was an outgrowth of that—that is, the press people up in Nebraska were seeking advice from the Reporter's Committee, and the Reporter's Committee recommended me. I believe that happened in November of '75—when I first became aware of the case and became involved.

The phrase *amicus curiae* literally means "friend of the court." It is a person or group that is not specifically a party to the case, but who is allowed to provide information on behalf of one of the parties in the form of a brief and/or argument.

FLOYD ABRAMS:

I first read about it in some very small articles in the newspaper. I may not have been aware of it until the first stay motion came to the U.S. Supreme Court. But I do remember being disturbed that the ruling of Justice Blackmun—which did stay the implementation of significant parts of the court order, did not stay the entirety of the order. So we were left with a prior restraint on a reportage on certain matters. I believe not too long after that I had a discussion with James Goodale who was then general counsel to *The New York Times*. And then with various attorneys in Lincoln, Nebraska who were either involved in the case or who had a relationship with the Nebraska Press Association.

ALAN PETERSON:

Floyd pretty instantly spotted it as having procedural cleanness that made it a terrific opportunity to get a possible victory for the First Amendment and for newspapers all over the country. I think he saw it as a case that he thought we could get cert. or get reviewed.

FLOYD ABRAMS:

The subject came up of whether I would be willing to become involved in the case. It was unclear for a considerable time what the involvement would be. But at the end of a number of discussions, it was agreed that Barrett Prettyman would represent the Nebraska Press Association, that I would represent a large group of national press entities including, but not limited to, *The New York Times*, that were very interested and concerned about the case. Both of us would argue the case in the U.S. Supreme Court if they agreed to hear it, and if they agreed to hear both of us.

As you began to become involved and, in fact, assumed the representation of Nebraska Press, were you envisioning it immediately as potential landmark level?

BARRETT PRETTYMAN: Yes, I think so. Of course, it's awfully hard to know because these cases, in my experience—I've argued 19 cases in the Supreme Court and I've been involved in literally hundreds of them in one form or another. It's always hard to tell because some cases that look very big at the start then end up getting narrowed down to some jurisdictional or standing question and amount to very little or nothing. Then other cases sneak up on you and take on great significance. It's just not always easy to foresee, but certainly by the time of Blackmun's interim order, it was apparent that this was going to be a difficult and important First Amendment case. The breadth of the order, also, was indicative of the seriousness with which everybody was and should have been viewing it.

In *New York Times v. U.S.*, 403 U.S. 713 (1971), also known as the "Pentagon Papers" case, the United States government sought an injunction against the publication by *The New York Times* of the contents of a classified study entitled "History of U.S. Decision-Making Process on Viet Nam Policy." In a per curiam opinion expressing the view of six members of the Court, it was held that the government did not meet its burden of showing justification for the imposition of a prior restraint of expression.

Did you sense from the beginning that this case had landmark potential?

FLOYD ABRAMS:　　Yes, I really did. I remember that this was 5 years—and it turned out to be literally 5 years to the day—from the Pentagon Papers case in terms of its decision. The Pentagon Papers case was decided June 30, 1971 and this was June 30, 1976. When I began to work on this in February, certainly the Pentagon Papers and other press cases involving prior restraints were very fresh in my mind. The case was always a matter of concern because it was not always clear to me that the Court would provide enough protection to really permit all the speech involved to be freely engaged in. Remember that speech like this is a contempt of court in England. Speech like this is a crime in Canada. Most democratic countries bar newspapers from publishing information of the very sort involved in this case. Confessions of defendants, prior criminal records of defendants prior to the resolution of a trial and after someone's arrest. So here we had newspapers that had indeed published information of a sort which many people consider very sensitive in nature. We were coming in front of a Supreme Court that was not terribly pro-criminal defendant, but increasingly less pro-press. It was difficult to assess our chances. One of the fears we always had was that one thing that judges really do know about—more than almost any other subject that they have before them—is about trials because they're lawyers. They may hear cases, and in the case of the Supreme Court—appeals on a wide range of matters—involving medicine and physics and foreign policy. But the one thing they think they know about is courts and about providing a fair trial and about providing free speech, or assuring that free speech is protected. So this is not the sort of a case where the Supreme Court tends to be self-doubting about its own institutional capacity. From the start we were concerned that they would simply say, "These are two very important rights and certainly First Amendment rights shouldn't *easily* be overcome, but there are the rights of a defendant at stake here, we will not deprive state court judges of the leeway they think they need to assure that defendants have fair trials." And that sort of approach was one which was always a matter of great concern to us. It just wasn't very clear, notwithstanding the magnitude of the victory in the Pentagon Papers case 5 years before, which direction the Court would ideologically lean toward.

At what point along the way did you sense that this case had landmark potential?

G. WOODSON HOWE: I guess when Floyd Abrams and the lawyer for the ACLU and the Reporter's Committee and some of these other organizations came out to Nebraska to talk to us. I could sense that they were pretty excited about it. Fred Friendly, formerly of CBS, who was involved in public television in New York at the time, was very interested. He came out and had dinner with us. I spent a lot of time with Fred and his wife. He sort of convinced me that this was a big deal. And so did Floyd. I think they saw the opportunity for correcting the problems that had been created for us by the *Sheppard* case.

FLOYD ABRAMS: At the beginning [my role] wasn't clear. I finally appeared as representing a group of amicie curiae. And that was my final role. My only point is that when this began, it was less than clear who I would represent and specifically it wasn't clear—to me, at least— whether Barrett Prettyman or I would be representing the Nebraska Press Association. It was, I guess determined by them—they had spoken to him before me—he would indeed represent them and that I would represent a large group of amicie curiae, including NBC and *The New York Times* and newspapers and broadcasters and magazines from around the country.

It sounds as if there was a desire to have you involved in some way first, and then folks figured out how to do that second.

FLOYD ABRAMS: Well, I think that's so. Yes. I don't know if I knew then—and I certainly don't remember now—the precise order in terms of when Barrett became involved and when I became involved. I certainly do remember very early on getting on a plane and flying to Nebraska through Dayton, Ohio. I remember that. I was delighted that there was only one stop en route. It was an American flight from New York to Dayton to Lincoln on a very cold February day. And talking with people from various newspapers and who represented various newspapers in Nebraska.

G. WOODSON HOWE: Floyd Abrams got involved fairly early. He came out and we had lunch with him, and we talked with him, and he attended a couple of meetings. There was some concern. Floyd wanted to present the oral argument before the Supreme Court. And Floyd had never argued before the Supreme Court. This was, as it turned out, his maiden oral argument. And we felt we needed somebody who had been there before, and that was the decision that led to Barrett Prettyman. The decision to have both Floyd and Barrett argue before the Supreme Court was kind of a compromise. Abrams had given us a great deal of help and we wanted to help him live his dream. But we were worried about him having the burden of the whole argument.

ALAN PETERSON: I had one particular concern that I kept pressing which was that this was a great case, we might well win it on the gag order, but there was a terrible risk of a backlash in the form of closed courts. It's not real helpful to be able to report everything that occurs in open court if you don't have one. I had already had one or two experiences with motions to close courts and simply knew that that would be the reaction of the Nebraska judges and probably judges nationwide if our win in the gag order situation did not somehow also close off that seemingly obvious remedy for judges who didn't like what we did to them (laughs). I think Floyd Abrams felt it was a legitimate concern, but [said] let's win one battle and then we'll go on and take on the next battle after that. Nationally, that's exactly what happened. We had a terrible backlash for about 5 to 7 years, with many, many court-closing motions. Usually we would win on those, usually on the ground that there were other remedies less drastic than closing the court. It was becoming a rather nasty war between the media and the judges.

CONSTITUTIONAL ISSUES & HISTORICAL CONTEXT

Why do you think this fair trial-free press issue generates such intense debate?

BARRETT PRETTYMAN: Because it's a clear clash of two very strong constitutional guarantees. You want to make sure that the defendant does, indeed, receive a fair trial in every respect that it's humanly possible to give him or her. And it is totally clear that when you publish in advance of even selecting your jury an alleged confession where the defendant not only admits killing six people but having sex with dead bodies and the rest of it, what in the world could prejudice that defendant's case more than that? So on the one hand you have the concept that you are destroying any possibility that that defendant has of a fair trial which he's constitutionally guaranteed. On the other hand, you have all of the factors that we've just been talking about that are in favor of a free press and you do not want, in an effort to give a fair trial, to destroy the freedom of the press that's so valuable to us. I don't see anything unusual that when those two concepts clash, it becomes very, difficult to put one over the other. You say you're not doing that, but in truth that's what it amounts to.

LEONARD VYHLANEK: I don't know whether the people don't like the justice system or whether they don't like the press. I know there was a certain amount of animosity generated toward the press during this whole episode. And, of course, there's always a lot of criticism of the justice system, especially when you raise an insanity defense. People don't like that. It's unpopular. It's not acceptable.

HUGH STUART: I do think that the amendments to the Constitution set off rights that are well known and well established but that tend to infringe upon each other. It's a natural contest.

G. WOODSON HOWE: On the press side, it's censorship, pure and simple. It would severely limit our ability to report on government. The judiciary is part of government. I've been taught for my whole career, and I believe it strongly, that we need to have total freedom to be able to report on what our elected and sometimes unelected officials are doing. When they close the doors, or they tell us, "You can come in, but we can tell you what you can report once you get in," we bow our necks when people say things like that.

KEITH BLACKLEDGE: The public wants the bad guys convicted, and they don't want anybody standing in the way. Of course, the prosecution wants the bad guys convicted, and they don't want to run the risk of having it overturned because of pretrial publicity. That's the material for continuing arguments. The outgrowth of the *Sheppard* case was that the lawyers and the courts, in my opinion, over-reacted to that and tended to be very self-protective to try to avoid falling within that decision. The mindset at that time was very restrictive and growing more and more restrictive. You can make the case that the way things were going, it was only going to get worse. This worked to turn things around in favor of the press.

As you know, in the Supreme Court and elsewhere, the question was raised whether contesting your order was somewhat of a moot point given that the restrictive order had expired by the time this case was heard.

HUGH STUART: Not somewhat. It was flat out moot. What they have done—and I think Burger touched on this in the first part of his decision—is that these things happen so fast they don't have time to decide them. Therefore, they were taking jurisdiction here. The way they took jurisdiction was for the Nebraska Supreme Court to file a petition with them and for them to notify me that I had so much time to answer.

Do you agree with the idea that a gag order is a prior restraint on the press?

KEITH BLACKLEDGE: Oh, yeah! It's intolerable if you have any respect for the First Amendment guarantee of freedom of the press. You can't let any government agency, including the courts, do that.

ALAN PETERSON: [A gag order is] closing off a subject, so it's content-specific in that regard, which is a no-no in the First Amendment area. It is hiding from the general public the workings of their government, one of the three very powerful branches of government, and in situations where frequently somebody's life or lifetime may be at stake. It's a classic prior restraint.

You've alluded to the fact that sometimes the restrictive order is sometimes referred to as a prior restraint. Do you agree with the assessment that it is a prior restraint of some kind?

HUGH STUART: (laughs) You never heard that word from the press, did you? They constantly referred to it as a gag order.

And you'll notice that I've been careful not to refer to it as that with you.

HUGH STUART: (laughs)(laughs) I think that's a descriptive term—a prior restraint. I was restraining the press before the trial.

Why is it that prior restraint is regarded as being so antithetical to the First Amendment and a free press?

BARRETT PRETTYMAN: I'm not sure I can express it any better than Burger and Brennan did in their opinions. Basically it puts in the hands of government an *extraordinarily* important power. If, in fact, government can stop the publication of otherwise printable news for even a short time, the place where the effect is most apparent would be in an election situation, for example, where somebody makes a charge at the last moment that a candidate has been pilfering funds or whatever, and you prevent the press from publishing that. The election is held, the opponent is re-elected, and then it turns out that that information was true, and if it had been published that candidate would have been defeated. That's just

one example. There are myriad examples of the concept that it should not be government that is determining what is newsworthy and when [information]
should be published. That should be in the hands of
the press. If you don't believe that, then I don't think
you really believe in the First Amendment because
that's the guts of the First Amendment as far as the
press is concerned. The press is not in the hands of
the government. The basic decisions as to what is going to be published and when it's going to be published
is not in the hands of government. There is a natural
antipathy between the press and the government in
the sense that the press is expected to print whatever it finds—good or bad—about government. The decision that the press cannot print is essentially a
totalitarian decision that you find in ranging from the
old Germany to some South American or Asian countries even today. It's directly antithetic to our own
concept of a free press.

FLOYD ABRAMS: One of the most dangerous qualities of a prior restraint is that it stops the speech in its tracks. Alex-
ander Bickel, a great professor from Yale who
represented *The New York Times* in the Pentagon Papers case—I had been his student and was co-counsel
on the case, but he did the argument—had written a
beautiful line in our brief in that case which has since
been quoted and adopted by the Supreme Court. The
line was, "If subsequent punishment chills speech,
prior restraint freezes it." What he meant by that
was if you write something and you fear that you
might be prosecuted for saying it, you might be
chilled. You might not say it. But a prior restraint
strikes down speech in the very course of speaking. It
prevents you from engaging in the speech at all. It
prevents you from taking a chance, for example, and
saying, "Well, I know it's sort of risky, but I'm going to
do it anyway." Because it is a court order and as a
general matter court orders have to be obeyed even if
they're wrong. We were indeed very concerned about
a rule of law which would establish a sort of balancing
test which was essentially subjective in nature and
which allowed judges to simply flip a coin, as it were,
and say, "Well, I think this is the sort of case where
it's better to have less said." So we were quite concerned about that.

PREPARATIONS

BARRETT PRETTYMAN: This was an extraordinarily busy time for me. I was right in the middle of a trial with [former Beatle] John Lennon. We had had hearings back in January of '76. We had a trial date on March 18th and March 30th , April 8th and April 21st. I had argued another Supreme Court case, *Nader v. Allegheny Airlines*, on March 24th. I had argued a case in the D.C. Circuit, *TelePrompTer Cable Systems v. FCC*, on April 2nd. And I was representing people like Howard Hughes and Katherine Anne Porter rather vigorously during this period along with some other cases. So the months of March and April (laughs) were very, very busy ones for me. While I hope it didn't adversely affect in any way my presentation, I think it's interesting that it's the kind of schedule I could not as easily do today at my advanced age (laughs) as I could then.

FLOYD ABRAMS· I began a practice then that I've followed since. I went down to Washington a few days in advance, checked into the Watergate Hotel. I spent a few days practicing with colleagues and clients. I remember walking with my associate with whom I worked on this from the Watergate, across the Potomac, all the way up to Arlington. All that time—and really every minute of every day—talking about "What do I say if they say this? What's the worst question they could ask? Suppose that a judge was absolutely sure that a defendant couldn't get a fair trial. Was I saying that there should *never* be a prior restraint in circumstances like that? And if I wasn't saying that, just *what* was I saying?"

BARRETT PRETTYMAN: I always do at least one moot court and usually two or three. I believe that when I had this one, that in addition to people in the office, I also had Floyd Abrams there and [others]. The moot court that I would have done in those days was not quite as sophisticated as the ones that I do now. Today I would argue for 30 minutes, or in this case 20 minutes, without interruption and then get critiqued. And then I would argue for 20 minutes with a lot of questions, and then get critiqued. And then just go with questions for as long as we can last. In those days, I think we just did the latter. I would start to argue and they would break in with questions. It's quite unnerving because no matter how well prepared you think you are, you always get questions that you had not anticipated at those moot courts. You shouldn't get questions about the record that you haven't anticipated because you should know that thoroughly. And you certainly shouldn't get questions about cases that you hadn't expected. You certainly ought to know those. But the ones that really hurt—the ones that are so difficult to plan for and get the best of—are the hypothetical questions.

FLOYD ABRAMS: The law was in still quite a formative stage, at least in this area. Everything was up for grabs. The Court could have gone all the way to essentially what Justice Brennan was urging, which is no prior restraint in this area at all. Or it could have gone in a far more restrictive mode, simply giving trial judges broad authority to limit speech in the service of protecting fair trials. That's what I spent all my time practicing. I remember Barrett Prettyman and I had worked on a hypothetical which he wound up using in his argument with great effect. He asked a hypothetical about a minister or a priest saying something to his congregation about the facts of an ongoing criminal case. He asked if it was even conceivable that that person could be jailed for that.

BARRETT PRETTYMAN: Normally, of course, the hypothetical comes from the Justices. It is up to you to have foreseen, if not the exact question, you at least should have had a theory of the case that embraces the question so that you can quickly work the question inside or outside of the ambit that you've drawn around your case and therefore answer it with ease. Normally the Justices ask the hypotheticals, and you don't pose hypotheticals to them. It's very dangerous. I did do that in *Nebraska Press* because it just seemed to me that it was basically unanswerable. It occurred to me that if these judges who entered the two gag orders had learned that the following Saturday and Sunday that in their pulpits the rabbis and priests and preachers were all going to announce this confession—maybe even read from it—and denounce the man and say this is the kind of inhuman person we don't want here and there must be vengeance against him—something of that sort. It was inconceivable to me that a judge would issue a prior restraint against the clergy and forbid

them from using that as a religious text. And yet, I
didn't see any real difference between that and the
press unless you make religion a first among equals
and say that the press does not enjoy First Amendment rights and privileges that religion does. So it
seemed to me that that was a telling point. In fact,
Floyd Abrams was nice enough to cite it as a successful gimmick. But it's dangerous, it is. There's no
question about it. That's the only time that I can think
of in my arguments that I have done it.

FLOYD ABRAMS: We talked a lot about gossip, too. If there could be a
prior restraint on the press, surely there could be
prior restraints on everyone else. But everyone else—
you know, in a small town in Nebraska—means real
people, not just well placed journalists. It means that
neighbors and friends and other people couldn't talk
about something that they knew about or thought
they knew about or were worried about. We thought
that was a very good line for our side—a very good direction—to try to steer the argument.

To what extent was Sheppard v. Maxwell *casting a shadow over this case?*

BARRETT PRETTYMAN: Oh, I think that that was something that had to be
dealt with. The *Sheppard* case was a problem, as I re-
call, simply because it was an example of how the
press can go haywire and can dramatically impact a
result unless you use some measures to prevent the
trial from becoming a circus. But our answer to that
was that those means are readily at hand. You have
ways of keeping even the publication of a horrible confession—and I say that because as I remember this
one, it dealt with necrophilia and so forth; it was a
very, very, serious confession. There are ways that
you can deal with that. Now, it is true—and this is
one of the things that was worrying me as an advocate—that when you get into each one of those ways
that you normally think of to deal with those kinds of
problems, they really didn't work too well in this case.
Changing venue—you'd have to change it a hell of a
long way (laughs) before you'd ever get a community
that really wasn't aware of this case in Nebraska. I
don't know that postponing the trial—well, you
couldn't postpone it for too long or you'd be denying
the defendant his rights, and postponing it for a short

time, I think, would have done nothing to take away the impact of the confession. Voir dire—my guess is that you'd just keep throwing people off. And instructions—that works for some people and not for others. So it worried me a lot that the things we were saying you could do to protect the defendant don't work where you have a small, isolated community where it's virtually impossible to find anybody not only who hasn't just heard about it or read about it, but who doesn't have a very strong feeling about what the results should be. So that was difficult. That was the difficult aspect of the case. And we just had to argue as we did that when you put all those together you can, indeed, come up with perhaps not the perfect trial, but with enough of a fair trial to be guaranteed by the Constitution.

Branzburg v. Hayes, 408 U.S. 665 (1972), held that the First Amendment does not free journalists from the obligation of appearing and testifying before grand juries when called upon to do so. Justice Byron White's opinion for the Supreme Court stated that First Amendment interests are outweighed by the responsibility of all citizens to cooperate with grand jury investigations.

FLOYD ABRAMS: My recollection is that this was by no means the only court that had issued a prior restraint in the five year period for the ostensible purpose of protecting the right of fair trial. We also had another concern, and that concern was that there was language in two Supreme Court cases which had been relied upon by the Nebraska Supreme Court. One was the Sam Sheppard case, which had gone to the Supreme Court. There was language there which the Nebraska Supreme Court viewed as permitting a prior restraint to be entered. I didn't think that was a very strong argument because that argument was more about the desirability of a responsible press rather than any particular language allowing prior restraints to be entered on the press. But even worse was some language in the 1972 case of *Branzburg v. Hayes* which was the case involving confidential sources of journalists. There was a line in the majority opinion that had said that journalists "may be prohibited from attending or publishing information about trials if such restrictions are necessary to assure a defendant a fair trial before and impartial tribunal." The Nebraska Supreme Court said, "Look, it said that there can be a limitation on publishing information about trials, and that's what we are doing." So we had to make a very serious tactical decision about just what to say about that case. Obviously, one doesn't like to tell the Supreme Court that it got something wrong in the past. We thought long and hard and finally argued that the *Branzburg* case had not even referred to the prior restraint doctrine which essentially all but bars injunctions against speech, and therefore couldn't really be taken as authorizing a prior restraint on speech. Then we just bit the bullet and finally said that to the extent the *Branzburg* language was so understood, "we believe it is inconsistent with the First Amendment and should on reflection be rejected." And that was certainly something that we gave a lot of thinking to. So that was our concern. I would say more broadly, though, our concern was less reporting about trials, which was specifically at issue in this case, and more about being free to report about *anything* free of prior restraints. Reporting about trials is only one example of a wide range of reporting that journalists engage in. If a prior restraint were authorized here, we thought and I still think, it could well have been authorized in other cases, too. The government rarely lacks arguments in favor of restraining speech. There are always competing interests. There are always other values that are assessed against freedom of the press. We really did view this case very broadly in terms of its potential for harm. That was why so many news organizations joined this brief that I worked on.

Was there a specific Justice who you felt might be particularly key in trying to win over to your side of the argument?

BARRETT PRETTYMAN: As I remember, White bothered me a lot because he was not always terribly friendly to the press. *Branzburg* was in '72. I had argued *Branzburg*, and that was a case I thought I should have won. His attitude there that the press was no different from anybody else— that's overstated, but that's sort of where he's from—and that kind of an attitude made me feel that he was going to be a very tough nut to crack. And

Burger—although very good in a lot of press cases—you just never knew where he was going to fall. As I recall, I thought of those two particularly as important for me to get to. I don't know exactly what I thought of to do in order to get to them, but I do recall that I thought they were going to be a problem.

THE U.S. SUPREME COURT

FLOYD ABRAMS: I remember going to the Court that day, getting there early. The argument was in the afternoon, at 1 p.m. Since we represented the side that had lost below, we argued first. This was my first argument before the Court, so I was not familiar with them. I had appeared with Professor Bickel in the Pentagon Papers case and written amicus curiae briefs in some other cases in that 5-year period, but this was my debut argument in front of the Court.

Given that you have argued at the U.S. Supreme Court 19 times, what kind of dynamic unfolds with that?

BARRETT PRETTYMAN: First of all, it gets easier. It never gets boring. It is always exciting. I'm sure that if I were arguing my 200th case there it would be just as exciting. But the first time is just absolutely terrifying, at least for me. It's not for everybody, but for me it was. And the second time it was easier, and by the third time I was really getting to like it. By the fourth time I would think to myself—literally think to myself in the middle of the argument—"My God, this is fun!" So it's a wonderful, wonderful experience. It's mentally challenging. The by-play of the Justices off each other as well as off you is just fascinating. The trickiness of trying to foresee all those hypothetical questions—you know, you think you've got them all and Justice Stevens will come up with one that just never occurred to you. It's a very exciting experience. I don't think that changes.

Do you feel that over time in any way the Justices get to know you at all and, if so, how does that play out?

BARRETT PRETTYMAN: Well, certainly all the Justices know me. I know them both on the bench and off the bench. I see them all the time at different functions and they come to things that I've been involved in. I received an award from one of them. You know, you see them around, you get to know them, you get to know their wives and things like that. I was born in Washington and lived here all my life except for times away at war and special assignments, so, yes, you get to know them. One of the things where that's extremely helpful is that they get to know that if you say something, it's true. They don't have to go look it up. They don't start with a reservation about what you're saying. They tend to believe that if you say something is in the record, for example, they know they'll find it there, which is good. It makes them more at ease with you. Now, one thing it doesn't do is make them easier on you in argument. In fact, if anything, if they know you are capable and can handle questions, they may be twice as rough with you as with somebody who either doesn't appear to know the record or doesn't even appear to understand what the game is, what the purpose of the argument is. So in that sense, it makes it harder for you, but it also produces a much more effective interchange.

G. WOODSON HOWE: I'm kind of in awe of great institutions. It was an emotional thing just to be there and watch the nine Justices in their robes walk in. The seriousness with which these men approach their jobs was pretty impressive. The repartée back and forth between the lawyers trying to give a speech and the Justices who keep interrupting them is really pretty interesting. The lawyers really have to be quick on their feet because they never get to say what they intended to say. They're just sort of in the docks and the questions are coming at them from right, left, and center, fast and furious.

FLOYD ABRAMS: Barrett Prettyman and I split the time. He argued first on behalf of the Nebraska Press Association. Then I rose and, probably a little too grandiloquently, spoke. I was a bit nervous but more about the possibility of losing the case and all it meant than about being thought to have done a poor performance or anything. I was reasonably confident that I'd be at home once they started questioning me, and I was. But I did say in the second sentence of the argument to the Court that I was asking them to make a ruling,

I said, which would be unthinkable in any nation in the world except ours, and unlikely in the rest. I'm not sure I would (laughs)—that's a little more literary than I would be today. Looking back on it, it's not the way I argue now. One tends to argue with a little less rhetorical flourish and generally on a more practical level with examples which one offers to the Court immediately. I don't think I hurt us at all. I'm looking at the transcript now, and I see I said that, "What we would ask of you is nothing less than a renunciation of power. The conclusion by this Court that the judiciary should not and indeed may not tell the press in advance what news it may print ... " Again looking back on that, I sort of like that line, but I think today when there is a lot less sympathy for the press within the public and certainly within the Court, I wouldn't phrase it as a renunciation of power by the Court. That is the way I viewed it, and indeed that is *still* the way I view it. It asks a lot of a court to essentially strip it of certain powers. What had happened in Nebraska, after all, was that a judge was doing his best to give a defendant a fair trial. He may have been wrong. I think he was. But he was using the weapons he thought he had. I was saying to the Court, in effect, "Take this particular weapon away. Just put the potential weapons of a prior restraint out of reach of trial judges." But it's easy to forget after all these years that it was by no means a sure thing walking in, whether we would eventually walk out with a victory.

I notice that throughout your oral argument, you refer to the restrictive order as a prior restraint. Was that part of a strategy to convince the Court that such an order is, in fact, a prior restraint?

BARRETT PRETTYMAN: Yeah, I think so. It is true that the orders were not permanently restrictive—that they did not suppress the reporting permanently. All they did was to delay the reporting and, in fact, as you know from the opinion, the cases were almost mooted because by the time they got up to the Supreme Court the trial had been had, the orders had become inoperative and the press was free to print anything it pleased. The Court fell back on the by-then time-honored theory that a question which is capable of repetition and which may well occur again keeps the case from being moot. Our position had to be—and the press' position has consistently been both before and since this case—that any delay is a gag order, a prior restraint, a suppression. If you prevent the press as in Pentagon Papers and all the others from printing even for a very short time the public may be harmed to a very high degree because you don't know what the public would have done with that information during the meantime. It's a slippery slope if you start saying, "Well, you can delay for a little while, but not too long." Doesn't that vary from case to case? What's too long in a murder case? What's too short in a case involving the Pentagon Papers, for example? So, yes, my position was flat out that it was a prior restraint because it did come in advance of publication and it was a restraint. It was to my advantage to paint it in that fashion.

FLOYD ABRAMS: I was sure it was a prior restraint. The question was whether it was a constitutional prior restraint. A prior restraint isn't a judicial curse word. There was no doubt that a restrictive order, by its nature, is a prior restraint. The question was just how hard would it be to get a prior restraint in a situation like this. That's what we were arguing about.

I noted in the oral arguments that you briefly mentioned Watergate, obviously based on the fact that this case virtually came on the heels of that. Is there something that you can share with me in this regard in terms of better understanding the case and what we need to keep in mind with regard to that period?

In an effort to illustrate the problematic nature of prior restraints, Mr. Prettyman said to the Court, "If one of those Watergate people had broken in and immediately confessed that he had broken into the Democratic Headquarters at the direction of the White House, could we restrain for 6 months from trial time the fact that that happened? That is what you are going to get into."

BARRETT PRETTYMAN: I guess that was very much on everybody's mind, obviously, and I think I figured that their internal reaction to that point would be, "No, for God's sake, we couldn't have restrained that at all." That's an example of the importance of having something come out right away instead of being put off for awhile.

FLOYD ABRAMS: In 1976 we were still at a point when the press was rather popular and tended to be viewed as fulfilling the function set forth by the Framers in the First Amendment. The press was viewed as performing functions that were essential to living in a democratic society. I've commented in a few speeches that I've given that in the early 1970s we were at a point after the Pentagon Papers case, after the war in Vietnam, there really was an image of the journalist as the romantic hero. So 1976 wasn't a bad year to have this case in front of the Court. One of my concerns if this had not been there before is that there is a lot less regard right now for the press and how it plays its function than there was back then.

In reading through the oral arguments, I was struck by what I perceived to be far less give-and-take between the Justices and you. Were the mid-Seventies a different era in that regard than the 1990s up to the present?

BARRETT PRETTYMAN: Yes. I think today's Court would have been much more active. I think part of what you detected was the fact that the Court really didn't like the case. I think they were disturbed by the case. I think it was one of those cases that they wished hadn't happened (laughs) and were serious about it. It was a bothersome case, and I think that part of it was that they knew where they had to go. That wasn't as clear to me, but I think it turned out to be clear with them that they knew where they were going to go in the case [but] maybe not too happy about how they were going to get there.

Can you tell more about that—about their apparent discomfort with this issue?

BARRETT PRETTYMAN: In order to rule for the press, they had to take a chance on making a fair trial difficult or even impossible. That's just not the kind of choice you want in most cases. Despite the fact that Brennan's opinion was quite strong, I think it was difficult for him, too. Although he believes very, very strongly in the press and would have been unalterably opposed, obviously, to a government order telling the press that they couldn't publish, the other side of his liberalism, if you will, surely was hanging by the prospect that this guy might be deprived of a fair trial because of strong

	prejudice as a result of his confession, which at that stage hadn't even proved to be admissible.
FLOYD ABRAMS:	I think there are more questions [from the Court] now as a generality. And I also think, looking back on the case, that we were going to win the case and the only question was how they were going to write it. There was no need for them to go too much into the facts if they didn't care about the facts in that they weren't easily going to sustain a prior restraint in any event. They just may not have needed very extensive questioning here, and what really divided them in the legal standard was something that, like a lot of things in law, reads better and writes better than it speaks. For things like that, oral argument is less relevant. As to whether there are more questions generally asked now, I think so. I hadn't thought of that question. I think that there is some greater tendency to have more questions, yes.
HUGH STUART:	You asked how much I followed this. I want to emphasize to you that I had eight counties in which I was working. It may be a landmark case to you as we talk about it 25 years later, but I was busy with trying to be a fair and hard working judge. How closely did I follow it? I didn't follow it closely at all. I thought that this was a moot case.
FLOYD ABRAMS:	I thought that Barrett seemed to have done well in terms of connecting with the Court. I thought that my argument had been reasonably effective, although I was asked a difficult question by Justice Stevens. And then I started to relax a little bit after I sat down and the Justices started asking questions of the Assistant Attorney General from Nebraska who they gave a difficult time to. So walking in, I think we both felt pretty good.

Was the question from Stevens where he asked you if this is just something that we have to live with?

FLOYD ABRAMS:	Yeah. Yes.

In responding in the affirmative, was that saying, in effect, that, yes, this is a difficult issue but nonetheless this is the best way to handle it?

FLOYD ABRAMS:	Yes. Again, looking back on it, one can try to answer it a little less directly (laughs), but generally I have be-

lieved that one does better with the Court by being *very* responsive. There are judges that one can sort of change the subject with (laughs), but they don't tend to be on the Supreme Court (laughs). So I think even if there's a really hard question, one of the first things you really want to do is answer it directly and then defend yourself because they get irritated and they think that you're afraid of the conclusion [if you don't].

The exchange between Justice Stevens and Mr. Abrams was as follows:

Justice Stevens: *Mr. Abrams, let me just ask a specific question. What do you do about the problem of the inadmissible confession? Say for some reason a confession is very dramatic, but yet it would be rather clear that it would not be admissible to trial. Is that just something we have to live with? There is no way of curtailing the publication of that kind of information?*

Mr. Abrams: *Well, I think you have to live with it, Mr. Justice Stevens, and one of the ways that you live with it is by giving jury instructions, by appropriate* voir dires, *by all of the* Sheppard *methods. But to take your question at its narrowest, yes, it is our view that there are such things as we do have to live with, if it finally comes to that, be it confessions or something else.*

As you wrapped up your oral arguments and then as the wait began for the ruling, were you optimistic?

BARRETT PRETTYMAN: First of all, you have to understand that two things are going on inside you when you get through with one of these arguments. Number one is, "How did I do?" And number two, "Are we going to win?" And they can be two completely opposite things. You can feel that you did a terrible, terrible job but are probably going to win. And you can feel that you really did well, but you're very worried about the result. And it's almost impossible, really, even for an old-timer and for people who have done it for years, to guess how these things are going to turn out. I remember one case I argued and as we were leaving the courtroom my client who was there said, "Well, what do you think?" And I said, "The only thing I'm absolutely certain of is that Justice O'Connor is going to rule against us." And she wrote the opinion in our favor. So it's difficult. I felt that I had done a credible job. I had not fallen down or failed to answer anything critical. At the same time, I

had hope about the result, but I certainly did not foresee that it would effectively be unanimous.

*When you found out about the ruling and the specifics of it, please share with
me what that experience is like.*

BARRETT PRETTYMAN: Oh, well, that's—(laughs)—that's just great. When
you win (laughs).

G. WOODSON HOWE: We thought we would win. We were stunned that it
was nine to nothing. I was elated. It came close to
July 4th. I thought that was just a wonderful gift to
the American people, and certainly vindicated us. I
didn't so much feel vindicated as just pleased for the
country that it came down as it did. It was kind of
nice that it happened close to Independence Day.

Just days before the nation celebrated its bicentennial, the United States
Supreme Court unanimously reversed the decision by the Nebraska Supreme Court. Chief Justice Burger's opinion held that even though the restrictive order had expired, the case was not moot, that the order violated
the First Amendment, that alternatives to a prior restraint on the press were
not presented, and that it was not shown that the order would achieve its intended purpose.

AFTERMATH & LEGACY

G. WOODSON HOWE: I think people tend to say, "It can't be a landmark case
because it was so open and shut. Nine to nothing. The
law was easy. It was a clear-cut case. The judge was
wrong. Let's not make a big deal about it." It wasn't
that easy. We were gambling a little bit. It took some
courage. We could have screwed it up. We could have
appealed at the wrong time, or failed to appeal at the
right time.

HUGH STUART: Did I regret [issuing the order]? Not really. I got quite
well acquainted with a fella by the name of Fred
Friendly. After this was over, we were talking about it.
He had gone down to the [Supreme Court] argument
on April 19th. He told me that at a later social hour—
I think it was actually a cocktail hour, but I'm not
sure—that he saw Chief Justice Burger. And Chief
Justice Burger said to him, "I saw that you were
down for the Bar-Press Guidelines case." And Fred
said, "Yes, I wanted to hear it." And Burger com-

mented, "You know, that trial judge out there in Nebraska—" And Friendly said, "You mean Stuart?" And
Burger said, "Whatever his name was. That trial judge
out there in Nebraska did the only thing that a responsible judge could do in the circumstances." And
Fred asked, "Why didn't you put that in your decision?" And Burger said, "Well, I thought I did." And
Fred said he'd only read the decision maybe a dozen
times. So he went back and read it again, and what
Burger actually wrote—and I can't quote you his exact
words, but you can find them in his decision—was,
"The trial judge acted responsibly in the circumstances." Well, that's a far cry from Burger's comment that I did the only thing that a responsible judge
could do. So do I regret it? No. I was endorsed in my
action by the decision writer in a landmark case.

Chief Justice Warren Burger's exact words in his majority opinion pertain-
ing to Judge Stuart's actions: "The state trial judge in the case before us
acted responsibly, out of a legitimate concern, in an effort to protect the
defendant's right to a fair trial. What we must decide is not simply whether
the Nebraska courts erred in seeing the possibility of real danger to the defendant's rights, but whether in the circumstances of this case the means
employed were foreclosed by another provision of the Constitution" 427
U.S. 539, 555–56 (footnote omitted)(1976).

*Did you anywhere throughout this process feel that you and your judgment
and your integrity as a judge were questioned in any way?*

HUGH STUART: No. No, the way I see it from my standpoint is that the
law has an ebb and flow to it. This case came along not
too long after the press made heroes of themselves
with regard to the Richard Nixon resignation. They
were riding high. If there was ever a favorable time to
approach the Supreme Court and ask the law to be
changed with regard to the parameters of respective
actions on the bar-press [issue], this was it.

*How did the U.S. Supreme Court ruling change the balance between First
and Sixth Amendment rights?*

HUGH STUART: Oh, it changed it remarkably. The law after this case
was much different than it was before. It's a landmark
case.

LEONARD VYHLANEK: It tipped it toward the press, I'm sure. Things are totally different now.

What is your opinion of the test that the U.S. Supreme Court fashioned out of this case?

LEONARD VYHLANEK: I thought probably the way in which the Court ruled was a correct ruling. Being a lawyer, what you do is look at those cases, decide that's the law, and you follow it.

HUGH STUART: I think it's the law of the land. It was adopted unanimously by the Supreme Court. Do I think it's right? No. I think there should be more effective means of giving the citizenry a fair trial and not allow the press to make a mockery of the justice system which they can possibly do under some of the tests that have been set forth.

Would it be fair, then, to characterize your opinion as one that when we try to balance these First and Sixth Amendment rights, that it should be weighted a bit more heavily on the Sixth Amendment side?

HUGH STUART: Sure. Sure. I see it from the standpoint of an attorney and a judge. At the same time I want to emphasize to you that I don't have any antagonism toward the press. At the time of this trial, my only brother was the editor of a newspaper. My brother, John, was over in St. Paul, Nebraska which is a little town north of Grand Island. He was the owner and publisher and editor of the *St. Paul Phonograph*. He was a graduate of the University of Nebraska with a degree in journalism. The work that journalists do and the work that attorneys do is to to use similar skills. They're a related effort.

Given your perspective on this now, how do you think this tension between First Amendment rights of the press and the Sixth Amendment rights of a criminal defendant ought to be balanced?

LEONARD VYHLANEK: We have the Nebraska Bar Association-Press Association Guidelines. I guess as an old defense counsel, my attitude is kind of like the English approach, and that is to say that the guy is charged and let it go at that, and not disseminate all that fact basis for the charges. I think that the press has to recognize its responsibility.

Judging the phrase "landmark case" is certainly subjective, but by any measure this one was. But what was it about it that made it landmark, and in general what makes for a landmark case, especially in the First Amendment area?

LEONARD VYHLANEK: One that seriously defines a constitutional provision that has not previously been defined. In this case, the First Amendment.

> *Near v. Minnesota*, 283 U.S. 697 (1931), is a seminal ruling in which the U.S. Supreme Court ruled that except in rare circumstances—for example, when national security is at stake, or when the material in question is legally obscene—prior restraints on the media violate the First Amendment. In the ruling, Chief Justice Charles Evans Hughes made it clear that hostility to prior restraint is at the very core of the First Amendment.

BARRETT PRETTYMAN: Several things. First of all, how serious are the interests involved? I mean, I've argued a case in the Supreme Court involving whether on the docks is a "seaman" or a "longshoreman" or something when he steps on an intervening board. That is going to effect a certain small group of people, but it's just not going to be terribly important in terms of the overall values of the Constitution. Here, you have two overriding issues in the Constitution—two that could hardly be more important: Number one, to make sure that all of those who we accuse of crime do, in fact, receive justice and a fair trial. And secondly, the fact that we maintain in this country forever a free and vigorous press, uncontrolled by the government. To have those issues in a case conflict with each other, I think anybody would say that has to be a case of great importance. Also, it had not come up that many times. I think the *Near* case—*Near v. Minnesota*—was about the closest. It had not been firmly established, particularly within the contours of these two principles that hadn't been so firmly established. And it could have gone the other way. Even though it was unanimous, I don't think that should mislead people. I wonder, for example, if that case had come up today with nothing in between from *Near v. Minnesota* until today—no intervening cases, and if that came up today—I'm not very sanguine about it being unanimous. And I'm not even certain about the result with this Court. That would be a *really* interesting case.

Is your uncertainty based on the fact that the Court is so different?

BARRETT PRETTYMAN: Yes.

FLOYD ABRAMS: I think we'd still win it [today]. But the lack of sympathy with which the press is often viewed cannot be forgotten.

LEONARD VYHLANEK: In retrospect, as far as the gag order is concerned, it *is* a landmark decision. It served a purpose in defining the law as far as the press is concerned in the coverage of high profile, or even low profile, cases.

FLOYD ABRAMS: I think a case is a landmark case because of its impact on history. There are lots of cases that the Supreme Court hears that simply need resolution. You simply need to know one way or the other what the law is. And you can live with the law either way, as long as you know what it is. *Nebraska Press* was not that sort of case. *Nebraska Press* was a case in which, as I observed earlier, we would live in a different country if we lost. It would still be in its way a free country, as England certainly is a free country. But it would be a country in which less was said freely and in which the judiciary had far more power to interpose itself into the editorial process. So I think it was a landmark case. While you can't prove a negative—you can't prove what would have happened had we lost—there certainly is every reason to think that if that had happened, that we would certainly have a lot less information than we do now.

Given time to reflect, how does it feel to know that your actions and your name are forever linked to this landmark case?

HUGH STUART: I don't have any control over that. I'm not sure that it makes any difference to me one way or the other.

Do you wish in any way that you had had the Nebraska Press Association test at your disposal?

HUGH STUART: I did what Chief Justice Burger said only a responsible judge would do. My philosophy as a trial judge was to find out what the law is and follow the law. Were I to try this same horrible crime again, I would follow the law.

If somehow this ruling had gone the other way, what kind of signal do you think that would have sent?

JACK POLLOCK: It would have sent a signal that freedom of speech in this country was in jeopardy.

BARRETT PRETTYMAN: It would have sent a signal to courts that they had a great deal of discretion in dealing with the press in making sure that the press did not print things which the courts would have deemed adverse to a whole lot of people. For example, right now, you can prevent the press from being present during a very limited number of situations—for example, involving sex crimes and youngsters. But there are very few restrictions that you can put on the press now. You can put restrictions in terms of not filming the trial, you can put restrictions in terms of limiting the number of pool reporters present, you can place those kinds of restrictions. But if this case had gone the other way, you would have seen a great variety of orders attempting to either keep the press from printing things that the judges thought shouldn't be printed or other restrictions on them that are not advocable today. You would have had a whole new—oh, my God—you would have had a whole new set of rulings from the Supreme Court on down as to what was permissible and what wasn't and all kinds of degrees. Whereas the rule now is almost across the board. They have carved out the exception—you know, the famous one of the date of the troops sailing—but I'm sure that there are other things that will come up eventually. But basically the bottom line rule is you can't stop the press from printing what they see and hear. I think that's very good for all of us.

What do you think of the notion that for trials to truly be fair, the press has to be free to cover them?

HUGH STUART: I think that part of our legal system is that it be open. When it's open, obviously the press can cover it. I think it's broader than that. It isn't just that the press be given a right to cover it. I think the theory of fairness is that it be an open trial, not a Star Chamber proceeding. But it's not the press that does that. The press certainly has a role there, but it isn't an exclusive role. If we were to close the case and allow the press to come in and report it, that would be wrong. The secret to the foundation is to have it open and above board.

What value do you see there being to allowing press coverage of the judicial process?

HUGH STUART: That's part of the openness. It's very important.

It seems as if in reading through your oral argument, much of it was based in history. When you are involved with a case like this and issues of this nature that permeate it, does it ever strike you that in some ways you're carrying on the same tradition and following through on the same principles that began with the likes of Madison and Jefferson and the other Framers?

FLOYD ABRAMS: Yes! In a case like this, it has a profound effect on the sort of country we live in.

BARRETT PRETTYMAN: Yes. Absolutely. I feel very proud in whatever hand that I've had in that—not only in the Supreme Court, but in lower courts.

FLOYD ABRAMS: It's hard not to keep that in mind as one does the argument. Looking at what I said, and thinking about how I would say it today, I would think that I might have been even more specific from a historical point of view, focusing on the Framers and what they said, focusing on the English common law history with regard to prior restraints and the like. Particularly in the circumstances in which we had gone so long as a nation without any prior restraint being affirmed by the Court. It seemed to me that it was very important to treat this as a matter of great historical moment. I remembered then the circumstances that Professor Bickel and I had seen develop before us in the Pentagon Papers case five years before. I remember his argument that there had never been a case in which the Supreme Court had ever affirmed a limitation by prior restraint on the publication of news. In the five years after the Pentagon Papers case, they hadn't done it either. Here I was, and here was Barrett Prettyman getting up, and our side still had a no-hitter going. Things like that certainly do make you think historically and think about the role that you're playing. Hopefully the consistency of that role with what the Framers might have wanted.

BARRETT PRETTYMAN: I feel the same way when I represent, usually pro bono, people accused of crime who otherwise either would have no representation or would have such poor representation that they are effectively railroaded. Yes, I feel like I am taking part in the process that was put together by the Framers to make as sure as they could that the system would operate correctly and that we would do no harm and assure justice.

If I were to ask you one, maybe two, really lasting memories from your work on this case, what would those be?

G. WOODSON HOWE: Hard work and quite a thrill when I read the opinions, including the concurring opinions. I had to say, "Right on! That's what we've been saying." It's finally sunk in, what we've been trying to say for years. Somebody has heard us. They agreed with us. There's a certain satisfaction in the resounding language that was used in this 9-to-nothing ruling and in the concurring opinions.

ALAN PETERSON: A recognition of the very high priority of the freedom of the press as compared to the normal assumption that trials are a judge's turf. It was kind of an awakening, I suspect, to the judiciary that we would yell so loud and long that not only access, but the right to report freely what occurs in open court is so fundamental that we'll never let it go, that they're going to have to bury it with us if they're not going to give it to us. I think that's what was at issue for us, and I think we gained some animosity but also a great deal of respect as fighters in the state. If we didn't fight this—win or lose—we were done. That's what was really at stake. We were done as far as court trial reporting because this precedent would have been followed a lot on the turf basis.

FLOYD ABRAMS: One [memory] was leaving Lincoln [Nebraska] knowing that I'd get to work on my first Supreme Court argument. And the other was getting up for the first time in the Court on my own and looking the Chief Justice in the eye and doing my thing. The memories are good ones.

JACK POLLOCK: The thing that will never be forgotten is that six members of a family were slain. That's something that you don't forget. The [legal] effort was exceedingly well coordinated. It was a magnificent effort headed by Woody Howe and Joe R. Seacrest. And I think all members of the press—not only in Nebraska, but throughout the country—owe them a debt of thanks. This was a very important ruling in regard to freedom of the press.

KEITH BLACKLEDGE: That we were involved in a very serious constitutional issue that you don't often expect to be. When you're a small-town newspaper you don't really expect to be the center of a major constitutional issue that goes this far and has this impact. In some respects that's a pain in the butt, and in some respects it's a privilege. It's kind of an honor.

ALAN PETERSON: This case started with a very inexperienced county judge who was a dear friend of mine in law school—Ron Ruff. If I had been on the ball and [was] not ill and able to get out there, I think I probably could have short-circuited this thing, but [I would have] ruined the chance of getting this precedent. I think I could have talked Ron out of it. But it didn't happen that way, and we have a precedent that at least a lot of lawyers in my business think is terrific.

BARRETT PRETTYMAN: I thoroughly enjoyed working with Floyd Abrams who's a real pro and who since then has become an even better lawyer than he was then—and he was awfully good then. I think anytime that you work with people who are really intelligent and who are imaginative and who work well with you, it really gives you a surge. It's great fun. But then I would also have to say that simply arguing this kind of a case before the Supreme Court is—it's just—it's the kind of experience that's very difficult to explain to people because until you're there with all the juices going and the excitement and the exchange of views and the tough questions from somebody who may be against you or at least is giving you a hard time, if you haven't done it, there's no way that anybody can quite make you feel what it's like.

FLOYD ABRAMS: I'll tell you, it's rare to work with someone on an argument, and to do so in a continuing, constructive—not to say friendly—fashion. And [with Barrett] it always was that. We really were case oriented and we really did our best and didn't let egos get involved and didn't let any conflict develop. Lawyers always have different ways of doing something, and that's the norm. We worked very well together and I was very pleased with that.

What do you think the legacy of this case and ruling has been and will continue to be?

BARRETT PRETTYMAN: I think it has been and, God knows, I hope it will continue to be that government, in the form of the courts, cannot prevent a free press from publishing what occurs not only in open court but I would say openly period. If a reporter sees something in the street, he doesn't have to worry about a court order that tells him, "Even though you saw it with your own eyes, you cannot print it because it would not be good for the country, or for the President, or for some defendant, or for whatever other reason." The courts have no business making those judgments. Those judgements as to whether to print are to be made by the press. Now the press itself can make those decisions. Those are the kinds of decisions that a free press can make on its own. But government is not going to step in and make that decision for them. In the same way, it can't tell them to print an editorial on a certain subject or to publish or not publish a letter on a certain subject—unless it is the most extraordinary situation, where lives are at stake and so forth.

LEONARD VYHLANEK: Because of the incredibly unique situation, I think the press probably puts a great deal of emphasis on this primarily because prior to the time that this case was decided by the United States Supreme Court, there weren't any real guidelines that could be followed from a legal sense as to what could or couldn't be shut down. I guess from that standpoint, it was a landmark case. It defined the law.

G. WOODSON HOWE: I do know that in the '80s and the '90s following this ruling, we didn't have nearly the running battles that we had until 1976. I don't think that newspapers ran amok with this freedom. They continued to abide by the spirit of the Guidelines. We didn't have any repeats of the Cleveland newspapers' performance [as in *Sheppard*]. I haven't seen that happening at major national trials. In the run-of-the-mill, capital cases in Nebraska, the coverage is pretty restrained, judges are no longer entertaining motions to close trials or slap gag orders on reporters who might be there. I think it's had a very beneficial effect on the press. We have the freedom now to go about our main business, which is to report the news instead of sitting in conferences with lawyers all the time.

LEONARD VYHLANEK: You know, this was just a once in a lifetime deal. Gee whiz, you don't in most instances even think about a gag order any more. There wasn't anything that's come down the pike since then that I've been involved in—a good number of murder cases that just don't generate the kind of publicity that this thing did, mainly because of the bizarre fact situation that you had in the Simants case coupled with the gag order. What we were really successful in doing was getting the case more press than we intended for it to get (laughs). We had every major newspaper in the country in here, reporters from every major newspaper in the country, the magazines—*Time* and *Newsweek*. But that wasn't until the ruckus from the gag order.

JACK POLLOCK: I think sometimes people have a tendency to forget what Judge Stuart was attempting to do. And that's to protect the rights of a suspect to a fair trial. Sometimes people in the press feel that their right is absolute, which it is not. We carry responsibilities.

Bottom line, what was this case about?

FLOYD ABRAMS: Would the press be able to decide for itself what's fit to print?

G. WOODSON HOWE: News delayed is news denied.

HUGH STUART: I thought the case was about trying a man for murder.

Erwin Simants was found guilty of murder and sentenced to death. Before his execution, however, it was discovered that despite the efforts to keep jury members unbiased, they had been contaminated. Ironically, it was not the media, but the county sheriff, acting as court bailiff, who was responsible. He had visited members of the jury and socialized with them during their sequestration. The conversation included statements by him regarding Simants' criminal activity. A new trial was granted. More than three years after the U.S. Supreme Court's ruling in *Nebraska Press Association v. Stuart*, the trial began. This time, rather than issuing any sort of restrictive order in an effort to insulate jurors from another round of pretrial publicity, the court granted a change of venue. One day prior to the fourth anniversary of the murders he committed, Simants was acquitted by reason of insanity. He was committed to the Lincoln Regional Mental Health Center. A review hearing takes place annually to determine whether he should be released.

*Nebraska Press Assn. et al. v.
Stuart, Judge, et al.*

SUPREME COURT
OF THE UNITED STATES

427 U.S. 539
Argued: April 19, 1976
Decided: June 30, 1976

PRIOR HISTORY: CERTIORARI
TO THE SUPREME COURT OF
NEBRASKA

COUNSEL: E. Barrett Prettyman,
Jr., argued the cause for petitioners.
With him on the briefs were James L.
Koley and Stephen T. McGill.

Harold Mosher, Assistant Attorney
General of Nebraska, argued the
cause for respondent Stuart. With
him on the brief was Paul L.
Douglas, Attorney General. Milton
R. Larson argued the cause for respondent State of Nebraska. With
him on the brief was Erwin N.
Griswold. Leonard P. Vyhnalek
filed a brief for respondent Simants.

Floyd Abrams argued the cause for
the National Broadcasting Co. et al.
as amici curiae urging reversal. With
him on the brief were Eugene R.
Scheiman, Corydon B. Dunham,
David H. Marion, Harold E. Kohn,
Robert Sack, John B. Summers,
William Barnabas McHenry, David

Otis Fuller, Jr., Richard M. Schmidt,
Jr., Ian Volner, and J. Laurent
Scharff.

JUDGES: Burger, White, Blackmun,
Powell, Rehnquist, White, Powell,
Brennan, Stewart, Marshall, Stevens.

MR. CHIEF JUSTICE BURGER delivered the opinion of the Court.

…

The problems presented by this
case are almost as old as the Republic. Neither in the Constitution nor in
contemporaneous writings do we
find that the conflict between these
two important rights was anticipated,
yet it is inconceivable that the authors
of the Constitution were unaware of
the potential conflicts between the
right to an unbiased jury and the
guarantee of freedom of the press.

[E]ven the most ideal guidelines
are subjected to powerful strains
when a case such as Simants' arises,
with reporters from many parts of
the country on the scene. Reporters
from distant places are unlikely to
consider themselves bound by local
standards. They report to editors
outside the area covered by the
guidelines, and their editors are
likely to be guided only by their own
standards.

[P]retrial publicity—even pervasive, adverse publicity—does not in-

evitably lead to an unfair trial....
[T]he measures a judge takes or fails
to take to mitigate the effects of
pre-trial publicity—the measures described in Sheppard—may well determine whether the defendant
receives a trial consistent with the requirements of due process.

...

The state trial judge in the case before us acted responsibly, out of a legitimate concern, in an effort to
protect the defendant's right to a fair
trial. What we must decide is not simply whether the Nebraska courts
erred in seeing the possibility of real
danger to the defendant's rights, but
whether in the circumstances of this
case the means employed were foreclosed by another provision of the
Constitution.

The First Amendment provides
that "Congress shall make no law ...
abridging the freedom ... of the
press." ... The Court has interpreted
these guarantees to afford special
protection against orders that prohibit the publication or broadcast of
particular information or commentary—orders that impose a "previous" or "prior" restraint on speech.

...

"Any prior restraint on expression
comes to this Court with a 'heavy
presumption' against its constitu-

tional validity (citations omitted).
Respondent thus carries a heavy burden of showing justification for the
imposition of such a restraint. He has
not met that burden."

...

[P]rior restraints on speech and
publication are the most serious and
the least tolerable infringement on
First Amendment rights.

...

If it can be said that a threat of
criminal or civil sanctions after publication "chills" speech, prior restraint "freezes" it at least for the
time. The damage can be particularly great when the prior restraint
falls upon the communication of
news and commentary on current
events. Truthful reports of public judicial proceedings have been afforded special protection against
subsequent punishment (citations
omitted). For the same reasons the
protection against prior restraint
should have particular force as applied to reporting of criminal proceedings.

...

The extraordinary protections afforded by the First Amendment carry
with them something in the nature of
a fiduciary duty to exercise the protected rights responsibly—a duty

widely acknowledged but not always observed by editors and publishers. It is not asking too much to suggest that those who exercise First Amendment rights in newspapers or broadcasting enterprises direct some effort to protect the rights of an accused to a fair trial by unbiased jurors.

…

As a practical matter, moreover, the element of time is not unimportant if press coverage is to fulfill its traditional function of bringing news to the public promptly.

The authors of the Bill of Rights did not undertake to assign priorities as between First Amendment and Sixth Amendment rights, ranking one as superior to the other. In this case, the petitioners would have us declare the right of an accused subordinate to their right to publish in all circumstances. But if the authors of these guarantees, fully aware of the potential conflicts between them, were unwilling or unable to resolve the issue by assigning to one priority over the other, it is not for us to rewrite the Constitution by undertaking what they declined to do…. [T]he barriers to prior restraint remain high unless we are to abandon what the Court has said for nearly a quarter of our national existence and implied throughout all of it.

…

[W]e must examine the evidence before the trial judge when the order was entered to determine (a) the nature and extent of pre-trial news coverage; (b) whether other measures would be likely to mitigate the effects of unrestrained pre-trial publicity; and (c) how effectively a restraining order would operate to prevent the threatened danger. The precise terms of the restraining order are also important. We must then consider whether the record supports the entry of a prior restraint on publication, one of the most extraordinary remedies known to our jurisprudence.

…

Our review of the pre-trial record persuades us that the trial judge was justified in concluding that there would be intense and pervasive pre-trial publicity concerning this case. He could also reasonably conclude, based on common human experience, that publicity might impair the defendant's right to a fair trial. He did not purport to say more, for he found only "a clear and present danger that pre-trial publicity could impinge upon the defendant's right to a fair trial" (emphasis added). His conclusion as to the impact of such publicity on prospective jurors was of necessity speculative, dealing as he was with factors unknown and unknowable.

We find little in the record that goes to another aspect of our task, determining whether measures short of an order restraining all publication would have insured the defendant a fair trial. Although the entry of the order might be read as a judicial determination that other measures would not suffice, the trial court made no express findings to that effect; the Nebraska Supreme Court referred to the issue only by implication (citations omitted),

Most of the alternatives to prior restraint of publication in these circumstances were discussed with obvious approval in *Sheppard v. Maxwell.*

...

This Court has outlined other measures short of prior restraints on publication tending to blunt the impact of pre-trial publicity. See *Sheppard v. Maxwell.*

...

We have noted earlier that pre-trial publicity, even if pervasive and concentrated, cannot be regarded as leading automatically and in every kind of criminal case to an unfair trial. The de-

cided cases "cannot be made to stand for the proposition that juror exposure to information about a state defendant's prior convictions or to news accounts of the crime with which he is charged alone presumptively deprives the defendant of due process."

...

There is no finding that alternative measures would not have protected Simants' rights, and the Nebraska Supreme Court did no more than imply that such measures might not be adequate.

...

The Nebraska Supreme Court narrowed the scope of the restrictive order, and its opinion reflects awareness of the tensions between the need to protect the accused as fully as possible and the need to restrict publication as little as possible. The dilemma posed underscores how difficult it is for trial judges to predict what information will in fact undermine the impartiality of jurors, and the difficulty of drafting an order that will effectively keep prejudicial information from prospective jurors.

...

Finally, we note that the events disclosed by the record took place in a community of 850 people. It is reasonable to assume that, without any news accounts being printed or broadcast, rumors would travel swiftly by word of mouth. One can only speculate on the accuracy of such reports, given the generative propensities of rumors; they could well be more damaging than reasonably accurate news accounts. But plainly a whole community cannot be restrained from discussing a subject intimately affecting life within it.

...

To the extent that this order prohibited the reporting of evidence adduced at the open preliminary hearing, it plainly violated settled principles: "[T]here is nothing that proscribes the press from reporting events that transpire in the courtroom."

...

The record demonstrates, as the Nebraska courts held, that there was indeed a risk that pretrial news accounts, true or false, would have some adverse impact on the attitudes of those who might be called as jurors. But on the record now before us it is not clear that further publicity, unchecked, would so distort the views of potential jurors that 12 could not be found who would, under proper instructions, fulfill their

sworn duty to render a just verdict exclusively on the evidence presented in open court.

...

We reaffirm that the guarantees of freedom of expression are not an absolute prohibition under all circumstances, but the barriers to prior restraint remain high and the presumption against its use continues intact. We hold that, with respect to the order entered in this case prohibiting reporting or commentary on judicial proceedings held in public, the barriers have not been overcome; to the extent that this order restrained publication of such material, it is clearly invalid. To the extent that it prohibited publication based on information gained from other sources, we conclude that the heavy burden imposed as a condition to securing a prior restraint was not met and the judgment of the Nebraska Supreme Court is therefore

Reversed.

...

MR. JUSTICE POWELL, concurring.

...

In my judgment a prior restraint properly may issue only when it is shown to be necessary to prevent the dissemination of prejudicial publicity that otherwise poses a high likelihood of preventing, directly and irreparably, the impaneling of a jury meeting the Sixth Amendment requirement of impartiality. This requires a showing that (i) there is a clear threat to the fairness of trial, (ii) such a threat is posed by the actual publicity to be restrained, and (iii) no less restrictive alternatives are available. Notwithstanding such a showing, a restraint may not issue unless it also is shown that previous publicity or publicity from unrestrained sources will not Render the restraint inefficacious....

APPENDIX TO OPINION OF
BRENNAN, J., CONCURRING IN
JUDGMENT NEBRASKA BAR-
PRESS GUIDELINES FOR DIS-
CLOSURE AND REPORTING OF
INFORMATION RELATING TO
IMMINENT OR PENDING CRIMI-
NAL LITIGATION

These voluntary guidelines reflect
standards which bar and news media
representatives believe are a reasonable means of accommodating, on a
voluntary basis, the correlative constitutional rights of free speech and
free press with the right of an accused to a fair trial. They are not intended to prevent the news media
from inquiring into and reporting on
the integrity, fairness, efficiency and
effectiveness of law enforcement,
the administration of justice, or political or governmental questions
whenever involved in the judicial
process.

As a voluntary code, these guidelines do not necessarily reflect in all
respects what the members of the
bar or the news media believe would
be permitted or required by law.

Information Generally Appropriate for Disclosure, Reporting

Generally, it is appropriate to disclose and report the following information:

1. The arrested person's name,
   age, residence, employment,
   marital status and similar biographical information.

2. The charge, its text, any amendments thereto, and, if applicable, the identity of the
   complainant.

3. The amount or conditions of
   bail.

4. The identity of and biographical information concerning the
   complaining party and victim,
   and, if a death is involved, the
   apparent cause of death unless
   it appears that the cause of
   death may be a contested issue.

5. The identity of the investigating
   and arresting agencies and the
   length of the investigation.

6. The circumstances of arrest, including time, place, resistance,
   pursuit, possession of and all
   weapons used, and a description of the items seized at the
   time of arrest. It is appropriate
   to disclose and report at the
   time of seizure the description
   of physical evidence subsequently seized other than a confession, admission or statement.
   It is appropriate to disclose and
   report the subsequent finding of
   weapons, bodies, contraband,

stolen property and similar physical items if, in view of the time and other circumstances, such disclosure and reporting are not likely to interfere with a fair trial.

7. Information disclosed by the public records, including all testimony and other evidence adduced at the trial.

Information Generally Not Appropriate for Disclosure, Reporting

Generally, it is not appropriate to disclose or report the following information because of the risk of prejudice to the right of an accused to a fair trial:

1. The existence or contents of any confession, admission or statement given by the accuse, except it may be stated that the accused denies the charges made against him. This paragraph is not intended to apply to statements made by the accused to representatives of the news media or to the public.

2. Opinions concerning the guilt, the innocence or the character of the accused.

3. Statements predicting or influencing the outcome of the trial.

4. Results of any examination or tests or the accused's refusal or failure to submit to an examination or test.

5. Statements or opinions concerning the credibility or anticipated testimony of prospective witnesses.

6. Statements made in the judicial proceedings outside the presence of the jury relating to confessions or other matters which, if reported, would likely interfere with a fair trial.

Prior Criminal Records

Lawyers and law enforcement personnel should not volunteer the prior criminal records of an accused except to aid in his apprehension or to warn the public of any dangers he presents. The news media can obtain prior criminal records form the public records of the courts, police agencies and other governmental agencies and from their own files. The news media acknowledge, however, that publication or broadcast of an individual's criminal record can be prejudicial, and its publication or broadcast should be considered very carefully, particularly after the filing of formal charges and as the time of the trial approaches, and such publication or broadcast should generally be avoided because readers, viewers and listeners are potential jurors and an accused is presumed innocent until proven guilty.

Photographs

1. Generally, it is not appropriate for law enforcement personnel to deliberately pose a person in custody for photographing or televising by representatives of the news media.

2. Unposed photographing and televising of an accused outside the courtroom is generally appropriate, and law enforcement personnel should not interfere with such photographing or televising except in compliance with an order of the court or unless such photographing or televising would interfere with their official duties.

3. It is appropriate for law enforcement personnel to release to representatives of the news media photographs of a suspect or an accused. Before publication of any such photographs, the news media should eliminate any portions of the photographs that would indicate a prior criminal offense or police record.

Continuing Committee for Cooperation

The members of the bar and the news media recognize the desirability of continued joint efforts in attempting to resolve any areas of differences that may arise in their mutual objective of assuring to all Americans both the correlative constitutional rights to freedom of speech and press and to a fair trial. The bar and the news media, through their respective associations, have determined to establish a permanent committee to revise these guidelines whenever this appears necessary or appropriate, to issue opinions as to their application to specific situations, to receive, evaluate and make recommendations with respect to complaints and to seek to effect through educational and other voluntary means a proper accommodation of the constitutional correlative rights of free speech, free press, and fair trial.

June, 1970

8   44 Liquormart, Inc. and Peoples Super Liquor Stores, Inc. v. Rhode Island and Rhode Island Liquor Stores Association

"It was just a matter of wanting to say, 'We have X bottle of wine available at Y price.' And so this [law] was purely stifling information. I think that that was a key point. It's really core commercial speech."

—Evan Lawson, counsel for *44 Liquormart*

Advertising, or commercial speech, was not always considered a First Amendment value. Only in the last quarter of the 20th Century did the U.S. Supreme Court begin to view truthful, nondeceptive advertising as a kind of information dissemination and therefore subject to First Amendment protection. But what happens when such advertisements promote a value that a state government believes it has an obligation to curb? In an effort to promote temperance, a Rhode Island law made it illegal to include product prices in advertisements of alcoholic beverages. The rationale was rooted in the belief that when informed of low prices, consumers increase consumption.

When one liquor store owner, John Haronian, was fined for violating this law, he decided to take the state to court. He hired Boston attorney Evan Lawson to represent him. Today, Haronian is the president of Douglas Wine and Spirits, the umbrella organization under which 44 Liquormart resides. Lawson is senior partner of the Boston law firm Lawson & Weitzen.

EVAN LAWSON: The principal of *44 Liquormart* was someone who had been very successful in other aspects of retail selling,

313

principally in the drugstore business. He sold his drugstore business, didn't like being idle, so thought he would get into the liquor business. When he got into the liquor business, he tried to apply his marketing principles that he had used for his various businesses to liquor and discovered, much to his amazement, that he couldn't price advertise. I guess price advertising, he felt, was a big component of his marketing strategy in the drugstore business.

JOHN HARONIAN: What happened is that we were looking for a creative way to tell our customers and the public about our products and our services and all about our new company that we were building.

EVAN LAWSON: He went to a variety of lawyers in Rhode Island who told him, "Well, that's just the way it is." So he decided that he would market by sort of hinting at price advertising.

JOHN HARONIAN: We spent a lot of time brainstorming, and we came up with this idea of putting—because here in Rhode Island, you understand, we could not advertise the price of our product—so we came up with this idea that we would put the product name and a description of the product that we were trying to promote with some kind of a slick picture of it and so on and so forth. And under it, we'd just put the word, "Wow."

EVAN LAWSON: He felt that that would be a sufficient tie-in so that a consumer would understand that his prices were good.

JOHN HARONIAN: Now we did it several times and there was no one complaining. So we got a little bit more bold with the size of our ads and the items that we were putting in them. And the customers started to recognize that that was the item that was on sale, and we enticed them to our store. Of course, in big, bold print we'd always say that Rhode Island does not allow us to advertise price.

So you acknowledged that in the ad?

JOHN HARONIAN: In the ad. And [in] every ad we'd make sure they understood that—that Rhode Island does not allow us to advertise price. "Here are the items. Wow."

EVAN LAWSON: That led to an enforcement action by the Rhode Island liquor administrator. They found that his "Wow" ad was in violation and penalized him. That really got him agitated.

JOHN HARONIAN:  In comes the state inspector, they sent us a letter stating that we were in violation of the state law, and that we must cease and desist. But we couldn't understand why. I called her up and she cited me to come to a hearing. And I said, "That's fine." I went down there with my attorney and he tried to explain to her. After the hearing, she fined us $400 for using the word "Wow" in our advertising. I said "Fine." I accepted the fine. Off the record, after the meeting, we were having a conversation, and I told her that that $400 that I was going to pay to the state was going to cost the state an awful lot of money because I'm appealing her decision to federal court regarding advertising. That's all I said, and I didn't even know what the hell I was getting into. I didn't know where I was going to go from there, I was just aggravated that she had the nerve to fine us $400 for something like that.

Were these advertisements in the local newspaper there?

JOHN HARONIAN: Yes. There were two ways. I did it two ways. I wanted to make sure that we had them dead wrong. One was in the newspaper. I also went to a local radio station here in Rhode Island, representing our stores in Massachusetts, and asked them if they would take a People's Liquor ad because their station is heard in an area wide enough to get our Massachusetts stores and Rhode Island would hear these prices also. I asked them to take my advertisement for my Massachusetts stores only. And they called up the liquor administrator and she said, "That's forbidden. You cannot accept it. We understand that we have no control over the stores in Massachusetts, but we do have control of the radio station [in Rhode Island] and you would be in violation for advertising price."

EVAN LAWSON: He went back to lawyers in Rhode Island and they explained to him that the Rhode Island Supreme Court had decided in two cases that this price ban was constitutional. The lawyers there told him that there wasn't a case to be made. He just kept asking people, and he asked someone in the liquor industry who referred him to me, and said that I was someone who was interested in this kind of thing and might take a fresh look at it. So he came to see me with his case. That's how he got to me, after having been turned down by other lawyers—not turned down, but told by other lawyers that it would just be a waste of time.

JOHN HARONIAN: I did some research and I found Evan Lawson. His name came up several times—several different people telling me if there's anything about liquor laws and liability and so on and so forth, he was the guy to see. And that's what I did—called him up, made an appointment, and we sat down and I explained to him what had happened and why I was aggravated about it. He said, "I think we've got a pretty good case. I can't guarantee it, but I think we've got a pretty good case."

In *Queensgate Investment Co. v. Liquor Control Commission*, 433 N.E.2d 138 (1982), a Cincinnati establishment was cited for advertising drink prices off premises. At an administrative hearing, the Commission suspended the club's liquor license for 7 days. On appeal, the court of common pleas reversed, but an Ohio court of appeals reinstated the Commission's decision. The Supreme Court of Ohio affirmed and held that the regulation did not violate the First Amendment. It also concluded that the state's asserted interest in discouraging the evils associated with "excessive consumption" of alcoholic beverages was substantial and valid. The court reinforced the latter finding with the Twenty-first Amendment, reasoning that the amendment allows states to confine liquor traffic to minimize its attendant evils. Queensgate appealed to the U.S. Supreme Court, but the Court dismissed the appeal for "want of a substantial federal question."

When he first came to you, did you initially see this as, in fact, a First Amendment-related case?

EVAN LAWSON: I definitely did. What happened was he called me and told me what the problem was. So I did some initial research, saw the Rhode Island cases, and felt that they were vulnerable based on the dissent in one of them. Then there was the *Queensgate* case, which was sort of a similar case where the Supreme Court did something that arguably was a stand in favor of the validity of controlling price advertising, but also, arguably, wasn't really a clear statement. So I saw that those cases were negative, but I kind of reflected on the basic *Central Hudson* test which I felt at least was supposed to be fact specific. I felt that there was room to make a factual record that would support a

Central Hudson v. Public Service Commission, 447 U.S. 557 (1980), is generally considered the starting place for any evaluation of an advertisement and whether it qualifies for First Amendment protection. In *Central Hudson*, the U.S. Supreme Court outlined a four-part test to make that determination: 1) Is the ad false and/or misleading? 2) Is there a substantial state interest in regulating the ad? 3) Does the regulation in question advance the state interest? 4) Is the regulation sufficiently narrow? Is there a "reasonable fit" between the state interest and the regulation?

Central Hudson challenge. Then there was a second problem with this case, which was something that had been of great interest to me for many years. And that is there was a statement in *California v. LaRue*, written by Chief Justice Rehnquist, about whether you can ban nude dancing in places that sell alcoholic beverages. There was this sort of throwaway statement that said that the Twenty-first Amendment of the Constitution gave an added presumption of validity to state regulation of alcoholic beverages. That language had been picked up by many courts and used to fend off constitutional challenges to state liquor regulations in general. Since this is an area in which I do a lot of work, it always was an annoyance to me because I took the view, as Justice Stevens did, that the Twenty-first Amendment did nothing more than remove the so-called dormant commerce clause problem. Because there is a commerce clause, there was developed a body of law that said just by its very existence, the commerce clause inhibits states' ability to regulate commerce when it has to do with interstate commerce. And so, in fact, before Prohibition, states were not able to prevent alcoholic beverages from coming into the state based on this dormant com-

Chief Justice Rehnquist's statement included the following: "Given the added presumption in favor of the validity of the state regulation in this area that the Twenty-first Amendment requires, we cannot hold that the regulations [at issue in this case] on their face violate the Federal Constitution." *California v. La Rue*, 409 U.S. 109, 118 (1972), holding that in the context of licensing bars and nightclubs to sell liquor by the drink, the states have broad latitude under the Twenty-first Amendment to control the manner and circumstances under which liquor may be dispensed.

The Twenty-first Amendment, in addition to repealing the Eighteenth Amendment, provides: "The transportation or importation into any State, Territory, or possession of the United States for delivery or use therein of intoxicating liquors, in violation of the laws thereof, is hereby prohibited." This provision was interpreted as empowering states to regulate alcohol and its consumption.

merce clause. But then we had Prohibition which was a constitutional amendment so that was fine. Then when Prohibition was repealed, the repeal recognized that they'd be back to the dormant commerce clause problem and they wanted to give individual states the right to remain dry. So they passed, as part of the Twenty-first Amendment, they said that the importation of alcoholic beverages into any state contrary to the laws thereof was prohibited. And that was for the purpose of simply wiping out the dormant commerce clause problem, but had been used to give states a great deal more constitutional leeway—as opposed to practical or other leeway—in regulating alcoholic beverages. That had become quite an issue because there were a variety of Supreme Court decisions that applied other constitutional provisions to alcoholic beverages regulation—for example, when the states would allow women to drink at a younger age than men and where there was a state law that required posting of the names of alcoholics (laughs) so they couldn't buy liquor. Finally it got down to the actual commerce clause itself in the cases that dealt with price fixing and price maintenance on alcoholic beverages. Notwithstanding that, the Court had frequently applied other constitutional provisions to alcoholic beverages regulation. This language from *California v. LaRue* was still creating problems in my view for me, as someone who was dealing with those issues. I knew that that would be used to try to justify this price advertising ban, and to try to apply a less stringent standard than *Central Hudson* would suggest. Then, of course, at the time, the whole application of *Central Hudson* in a lot of contexts was being revisited and you had a lot of inconsistent results. You had the *Posadas* case involving regulation of advertising of gambling. You had *Edge Broadcasting*, which involved cross-border advertising of gambling. So you had this kind of murky area. I felt that while it was by no means a sure thing that one would win, at least you could try to mount a very specific factual attack on the statute. That is, the government could not show that the regulation of advertising really had any effect on its espoused concern, which was promoting temperance. Even though under *Central Hudson* the burden is on the government, I felt that I would have to put together a case to state the contrary.

In *Posadas de Puerto Rico Associates v. Tourism Company of Puerto Rico*, 478 U.S. 328 (1986), the U. S. Supreme Court applied the *Central Hudson* test and concluded that restrictions on casino gambling advertising by Puerto Rican casinos to citizens of Puerto Rico were constitutional and did not violate the First Amendment. The ruling was seen as supporting the view that if a government can ban an activity, then it can also ban the advertising of it—even if it chooses not to ban the activity itself. In *FCC v. Edge Broadcasting*, 509 U.S. 418 (1993), the Fourth Circuit Court of Appeals had also utilized *Central Hudson* in ruling that regulations limiting broadcast advertisements for a state lottery did not directly advance an asserted government interest. The U.S. Supreme Court reversed.

Am I hearing you accurately in saying that at this time the application and interpretation of **Central Hudson** *was in flux, and that that was a window of opportunity for you?*

EVAN LAWSON: Well, it was definitely in flux. *Central Hudson* is difficult to apply. [But] I didn't feel I had a window of opportunity because it was in flux. I felt that I had a window of opportunity because I thought that I could show that there was no real evidence that regulating price advertising would have any effect on temperance and that I could bring the case within the confines of what wasn't in flux. In other words, I wasn't gambling on getting an outcome because the law wasn't clear because, quite frankly, the *Posadas* case and *Edge Broadcasting* gave me a lot of pause in terms of the leeway that was given. And also the *Queensgate* case was something that I saw as a problem. But my position was that these other cases had not done what the Court seemed to want people to do, which was to deal with the evidence for or against the efficacy of the regulations. The flux nature of it, I think, was more in my ability to say there's really no clearcut case that's against me.

Why is it that price advertising is important?

JOHN HARONIAN: That's the only way that you're able to entice your customer into your store. This industry is a very price-sensitive industry. In fact, you know something? Most industries are becoming very competitive today. You have to make some way that your stores are different than all others, and price is one of the ways of doing it, along with the cleanliness, the service, and the selection and so on.

So you would say it's an important ingredient in your success as a businessman?

JOHN HARONIAN: That's absolutely right.

This law that was on the books in Rhode Island, I presume that you thought it was unfair.

JOHN HARONIAN: Absolutely.

Would you tell me why you had that opinion of it?

JOHN HARONIAN: Because we couldn't understand why they would not allow us to advertise price. They told us that it was an enticement or an inducement to drink. And I said, "You know, you tell me the difference—if that's so, then take every single sign—whether it be a Budweiser or a Jack Daniels advertisement—down, and I'll abide by it. You're telling me seeing the word 'Bud' is not an inducement, and yet '$1.77' is an inducement for the Bud? If you can prove that that's so, then I'll be glad to take it down." But neither one, whether it's just advertising Bud or adding a price—it's been proven and we did that in court—is an inducement nor will it increase consumption. It doesn't. What happens is, there's a shift of market share. And that's okay. But that's not an increase in consumption. It shifts market share. To us, that's competition. That's just good business practice.

In other words, people are going to buy the product anyway, it's just a matter of from whom?

JOHN HARONIAN: Right. It's not that I'm going to drink more because it's $1.77 when it used to be $1.99. That's ridiculous.

Could you comment on this Rhode Island statute itself, especially in the context of this paternalistic approach that it had in singling out speech about a particular product?

EVAN LAWSON: I think that I believe that—and this was not really part of the case other than as a subtext—I believe that the statute was never really passed to be paternalistic or to regulate temperance. I believe the law was passed because a consortium of small retailers had more influence with the legislature than anyone else. I think it was passed to protect retailers from competition rather than for any other purpose. But, of course, they couldn't overtly say that, so they talk about promoting temperance instead.

Did you ever, throughout the process, experience what might be referred to as a public relations problem? By that I mean you were fighting a law which, at least on its surface, promoted temperance. Many people would regard that as a good thing. And so therefore that's why I ask about this "public relations problem."

EVAN LAWSON: I didn't see a public relations problem. I certainly didn't detect any public sentiment against me or, for that matter, any public sentiment for me. No, I didn't detect that problem, nor did we—at least from my perspective—we didn't take any action to deal with that. Now whether my client did on his own is a different story.

Throughout this process, how was your relationship with the public? Were people supportive of your cause?

JOHN HARONIAN: Definitely. More and more people could not understand why we couldn't advertise price. When you talk to the average consumer out there—the public—they can't understand why these laws are put into place. They can't understand why we couldn't advertise price. I couldn't even use the word "sail," and [the state liquor administrator] would cite me—call me up and tell me I can't do it. I'd say, "Okay. The next ad we'll make sure we don't have it in." We'd change. But when she fined me the $400, that went up my buttocks.

How would you respond if someone were to ask you either during the process or now, "How can it be that fighting a regulation that promotes temperance with regard to alcohol consumption is a good thing?"

EVAN LAWSON: First of all, in my view, the regulation didn't promote temperance at all. Second of all, I was promoting a value of consumer access to information which I think is very important. And also the effect of the law was to maintain artificially high prices in Rhode Island, which is one of the things that we showed. Therefore artificially high prices, of course, have a negative impact on the less affluent, more disproportionately. So in my view we were fighting for the right of all consumers to have meaningful information about prices before they make a purchase. And secondly, we were fighting so that people who are going to buy a product are going to get a fair price that reflects a competitive environment.

THE U.S. DISTRICT COURT TRIAL

JOHN HARONIAN: It's a thrill to go into a federal court. They're tough, they ask really serious questions. If you don't know what the hell you're talking about, they'll eat you up alive.

EVAN LAWSON: I think we were fortunate to have drawn Judge [Raymond] Pettine who was someone with a long history of respecting the Constitution, shall we say, and he wasn't giving deference to the state the way other judges might. I thought his opinion was very good. There really weren't any interesting stories to tell. We just sort of slugged it out in the District Court, presenting our various experts and he made a decision.

In the fact-finding, did information come out that put into question the kind of impact that advertising, in general, has on the consumer?

EVAN LAWSON: Yeah, I presented two expert witnesses on advertising. Our focus was on price advertising—the effect that price advertising has on consumption. In other words, does the ability to buy a product at a lower price mean you're going to buy more of it? The evidence, I felt, was pretty clear that that wasn't the case, that what you were really doing is you were giving people a choice of prices, but that their consumption patterns weren't going to change. Of course, one of the interesting things is if you look at per capita consumption per state, Rhode Island is in the top third of the states. And yet it bans price advertising whereas states that have vigorous price advertising have lower consumption. So you could at least reasonably conclude from that that there isn't that much of a correlation. Also, when you're dealing with alcoholic beverages, there are very interesting issues. Half the people don't consume any alcoholic beverages. Of the remaining roughly half who do, about 35% of them are what you'd call occasional drinkers. So the hard-core drinking population is roughly 15%. They are the people who you would think would be most influenced, but in fact they drink as much as they can anyway, and will drink really bad products. If you really look at the reality of it, it's just nonsense to think that that was the case. The ultimate theory that the government came up with—which wasn't their original theory was that, "We're not saying that the advertising of the prices stimulates consumption. What we're saying is that banning price advertising keeps prices artificially high, and artificially high prices lower consumption." Within bounds, my experts had to agree with that. They just said there was a narrower effect than the state's experts said. But that, of course, gets us to the problem that that's an indirect, as opposed to a direct, effect—and one which the state could carry out without limiting price advertising. They could increase the taxes, they could set minimum prices—there's millions of things they could do. Of course, they can't do that because of the political issue. So what it really boils down to is you've got 15% of the population that have a drinking problem. Some percentage of them are sensitive to prices and might drink less if prices were higher. So to address this relatively minor aspect of a problem, you're taking away the First Amendment rights of businessmen. Of course, if I say taking away the First Amendment rights, I'm begging the question. I'm phrasing it in absolutist terms. Let me put it in a more neutral way. You're depriving consumers of significant consumer information in the interests of affecting some small percentage of a problem population which is itself a very small percentage of the population. Now, that creates some very interesting discussions that were never opened in this case— about the tail wagging the dog and so on. How much are we all to give up to solve a problem for a few people? That, of course, never surfaced as a direct issue in the case. But I think on some level it was there— the idea that nobody can find out what a bottle of wine costs because 300 people might drink an extra glass or two (laughs). I think that played into the outcome, although I have no way of demonstrating that.

In U.S. District Court, Judge Raymond J. Pettine utilized the *Central Hudson* test. He noted that under the test, "a state must justify restriction on truthful, nonmisleading commercial speech by demonstrating that its actions 'directly advance' a substantial state interest and are no more extensive than necessary to serve that interest." While acknowledging that Rhode Island had a legitimate interest in reducing overall consumption of alcohol, he concluded that the regulations in question did not directly advance that interest and were more extensive than necessary. Accordingly, the judge found that the statutes impermissibly restricted commercial speech and were unconstitutional.

On appeal, the U.S. Court of Appeals for the First Circuit reversed. It held that "the advertising ban directly advanced the governmental interest by increasing the cost of alcoholic beverages, thereby lowering the amount of alcohol consumption by residents of the State of Rhode Island." That court recognized precedents upholding 1) the "added presumption in favor of the validity of the state regulation in this area that the Twenty-first Amendment requires," and 2) states' authority under the Twenty-first Amendment to "curb the evils of alcoholic beverages."

THE U.S. COURT OF APPEALS

EVAN LAWSON: I thought the First Circuit used that Twenty-first Amendment argument to abdicate an independent analysis. Essentially what they said was, "Well, this is plausible. The state's position is plausible, and that's all it has to be, particularly under the Twenty-first Amendment." There is an issue under *Central Hudson* as to this fact-finding process. Essentially you've got a judge finding facts and overriding the judgment of the legislature. How many facts does he have to find, what level of evidence is necessary for the state to justify the statute? Those are thorny issues, which I think are still unresolved, really. I think the Court has not always been consistent in telling us what these things mean. They say, "Well, it's not the least restrictive alternative, but yet it's more than mere ordinary scrutiny." So who the hell knows what that means? I thought that really what you had here was Judge Pettine in the district court kind of adjudicating the thing, and then you had the First Circuit saying, "No, no. You shouldn't have adjudicated, you should have just looked to see if the government's position was plausible." The language they use is "it seems reasonable," or something like that. So that was the argument in the First Circuit, and its various opinions were essentially, "Well, this is an area that the state has so much power in we're not going to mess with it."

When you got word on the appeals court ruling that went against you, what was your reaction?

JOHN HARONIAN: I was disappointed. I thought for sure they would agree that it was a First Amendment violation because the [trial] judge that heard the case was truly focused on understanding. We took in expert witnesses who said that price does not increase consumption, therefore the state's reasons for not allowing price advertising was entirely wrong. It's a violation of the First Amendment and their decision is wrong. I thought it might be politically motivated when it went to the court of appeals. I just couldn't understand why, but who am I? I'm not a judge. [When] that court reversed the decision, we had to stop advertising at that particular time. We had only run one or two ads with price during this period. When I got that decision, naturally, if they told me I could no longer advertise, I said "That's fine." I had a conversation with Evan Lawson. Evan said, "Look, you've got a 50–50 chance that [the Supreme Court] will hear this case." He told me, "It's going to be costly. It would be a long road to hoe." I made my mind up that I went this far, and I wasn't going to allow the state to get the better of me. So I decided to go the full road.

You've mentioned the cost a couple of times. Would you be willing to share how much this particular case took out of your pocket?

JOHN HARONIAN: I know that [Evan] billed the state $368,000. I got
                                           tattooed.

So did that come out of your pocket?

JOHN HARONIAN: It must have been about $150,000.

Describe for me your relationship with your attorney, Mr. Lawson.

JOHN HARONIAN: He's a great guy. When you talk to him on the phone,
                                           he takes the time to explain why. When I talk to Evan to
                                           tell him what my problem is or ask his advice, he's just
                                           an easygoing guy who looks to solve my problems.

*Throughout this case, did you feel like you were able to voice your concerns
and have input on some of the decisionmaking?*

JOHN HARONIAN: Definitely. Definitely. He kept me well informed.

*How, throughout the process, would you describe your relationship with
your client?*

EVAN LAWSON: It was good. He's one of these sort of entrepreneurial
                                           businessmen who's motivated to make his business
                                           as successful as possible. It's the foundation of the
                                           capitalist system. I appreciated that. I think that win-
                                           ning at the district court level was good for our rela-
                                           tionship (laughs). I think if the district judge had gone
                                           against us, it would have been a harder sell to go to
                                           the next level and then to the Supreme Court. But to
                                           win in the district court, then have the First Circuit
                                           take it away, primed him to go to the Supreme Court.

*With something like the decision to go to the Supreme Court, was that some-
thing that was your decision, his, or a combination?*

JOHN HARONIAN: It was my decision. After the discussion with him—
                                           what the pros and cons were and the cost of it—
                                           I decided to go.

What went into deciding whether to appeal to the Supreme Court?

EVAN LAWSON: (laughs) The real answer to that is that I had a case in
                                           the Supreme Court in 1974. I had such a great time

that I always wanted to go back. When this opportunity came about, I saw that this case had the potential to go to the Supreme Court. That was one thing. Another thing was having won in the district court and have the First Circuit take it away was pretty stinging to my client. He really wanted to go for it. So he wanted to go for it and I certainly was anxious to do it myself. And that's what played into it, plus I felt that the First Circuit was wrong, obviously. And I saw the Twenty-first Amendment issue, really, as the hook to get certiorari.

THE U.S. SUPREME COURT

Why do you think the Supreme Court granted certiorari?

EVAN LAWSON: I think the Twenty-first Amendment issue was an issue that once it was brought to their attention, they were interested in. I also thought that they were interested in the advertising issue because at around the same time they had the *Coors* case which dealt with the federal government's power to regulate advertising and how that would be examined. So they would then have two cases—one with the federal government and one with a state government. Essentially the strategy was to show the Court what we felt was the lower court going astray from what the Court had intended with *Central Hudson* and also showing how the Twenty-first Amendment phraseology was really inconsistent with what the Court was really doing in applying constitutional principles to alcoholic beverages regulation generally.

In *Rubin v. Coors Brewing Co.*, 514 U.S. 476 (1995), the U.S. Supreme Court held that a provision of the Federal Alcohol Administration Act that prohibited beer labels from displaying alcohol content violated the commercial speech protections of the First Amendment.

Were you surprised that the Supreme Court agreed to hear the case?

JOHN HARONIAN: Not surprised. Wishful in my thinking.

Was part of your strategy to show the Court where it went wrong with Posadas?

EVAN LAWSON: No, that wasn't part of the strategy. *Posadas* was the case that worried me the most. What I really wanted to do is to say, "This isn't *Posadas*. This is different. We have a factual record." So I didn't try to box in *Posadas*, although actually that's what happened in the decision. The Court actually stepped back from *Posadas*, which was very gratifying since the Court was unanimous.

JOHN HARONIAN: When we went into the United States Supreme Court, it was the biggest thrill of my life. I told my wife if there's anything that can surpass seeing my children born and married life, or close to it, was being in that courtroom and listening to that case. Just getting into the courtroom, there are three tiers. It's unbelievable. You go through one section, then another section, then a third section. They really scrutinize the person and making sure you don't have any firearms—guns or knives. It's a thrill. When I saw the [2000 Presidential election contest], I could visualize what these people were going through, having a flashback to when I was there.

Did anything surprise you about the way it unfolded?

JOHN HARONIAN: The performance of the attorneys is such that these judges, before the attorney finishes answering one question, they whack 'em with another, and another. You've really got to know what the hell you're talking about. The attorney for the state—[Rebecca Partington]—she did a superb job in presenting her case, just like Evan did with our case. I came out of that wondering how it was going to go because she did such a superb job of answering questions that the judges were throwing at her.

EVAN LAWSON: I'll tell you a quick aside. She's a very attractive woman. And so when we showed up to argue—and, of course, we're all dressed up—she just looked stunning. And I said to myself, "If this is a beauty contest, I'm in a lot of trouble." And I was tempted to say that to her, but I felt that it might have been inappropriate at the time, so I never said it.

Wasn't one thing that came up at the Supreme Court that several of the Justices asked how alcohol can be singled out as a product whose consumption the state has a right to curb? Don't we step on a slippery slope? Where are we going to stop? Are we going to start regulating other products because temperance of those would be a good thing?

EVAN LAWSON: Right. It did come up in a couple of ways. It was raised in the argument and also we argued it in our brief. The whole "liquor is special" argument, which played into the Twenty-first Amendment piece, was an important aspect of it.

Could you talk a little bit about the personal dynamics, the feelings and emotions of arguing a case in the U.S. Supreme Court, what the atmosphere is like?

EVAN LAWSON: Well, I'm essentially—even though I might concentrate my practice in certain areas—I regard myself as a trial lawyer. And so I've always considered arguing in the Supreme Court to be the very epitome or the apex of that aspect of practicing law. So I was extremely psyched to be doing it. I've also handled in my career a large number of appeals, so I've argued well over a hundred appellate cases in the Supreme Court of Massachusetts, the appeals courts of Massachusetts, the circuit courts, and so on. So I'm an experienced appellate lawyer. And I had argued before [at the Supreme Court]. I had a lot of enthusiasm with very little anxiety about it. It was more like being up for the big game when you feel you have a good team. To me it was just a great thing. I was just very, very excited about it. To get ready for it, I did essentially study every Justice's opinion on the subject so that I felt that I understood—at least the ones that you could derive where they were coming from—I understood where they were coming from. We had the *Coors* opinion come out, which was a great comfort. Once that came out, I thought, "Wow, we're in very good shape." And also I had a read that I thought some of the Justices, particularly Clarence Thomas—who I might have been concerned about—I thought they would be on board where we were.

Am I reading you correctly that you were not in awe of the environment?

EVAN LAWSON: One the one hand, having been a lawyer for 30 years and getting there twice, that's pretty inspiring to know that's as high as you can go. So, yeah, there was a whole sense of "This is great!" But it wasn't an intimidating thing. It was a very positive, upbeat thing. But certainly I was very fired up and at the same time I appreciated that this is sort of my moment to be at the pinnacle. So I won't say I wasn't in awe, but it was more of really wanting to get in there and mix it up with them. I wanted to have them ask me questions and answer them. It's hard for me to really put into words the exact feeling because it was sort of a mixture of being very grateful and respectful and appreciative of where I was and at the same time feeling that I really wanted to get into it.

Was there one or two points that you felt were particularly key to winning the Justices over to your side?

EVAN LAWSON: I thought that this was a very good case for this issue because it was really pure price advertising. It was just a matter of wanting to say, "We have X bottle of wine available at Y price." And so this was purely stifling information. I think that that was a key point. It's really core commercial speech. And then the other point was the idea that the Twenty-first Amendment did anything more than it said it did was sort of contrary to the conservatives' philosophy, and at the same time it was contrary to the liberals' philosophy. So I thought that those two key points were the main points. The strategy in writing the brief was to write the main brief in such a way that I would force the state to commit itself to exactly what its point was before I had to take a position on it, so that I could then come back in the reply brief and take them apart. Whereas if I had tried to anticipate what their point was and then argue against it, I was giving them an opportunity to deal with my argument much more effectively. The first brief I wrote was sort of generalized. I referred to drawing them out into the open—made the state come out in the open with what was, I thought, an easy-to-attack position. I was able to do that. The other thing that I did that I thought was effective was you've got a limitation on the size of the briefs. There are various aspects of every case that you'd like to argue more, but you can't because of the limitation and also because it makes for a cumbersome brief. So what I did was I coordinated with various groups that wanted to submit amicus briefs. We kind of pushed them into emphasizing different things so that in one brief—I forget who it was now—sort of focused on the history of advertising and advertising regulation, and another brief focused on other issues. So the various groups that wanted to file amicus briefs helped me out by fleshing out arguments and I didn't have to write it, and I also didn't have to own it if the Court decided they didn't like it (laughs). So I thought that was something that I was pleased with—making use of amicus briefs to fill things out.

JOHN HARONIAN: Evan did an outstanding job. We won the case. Ever since, we've been advertising price. It's done a lot of things for the state. People don't realize how much we've accomplished by getting this law thrown out. One of the things that was happening in the state of Rhode Island—we're small compared to the other states. The amount of alcoholic beverages that are used in this state as opposed to other states is not that great. So therefore, people in Rhode Island and the wholesalers were not given the best possible prices for their goods at the wholesale level. And neither was the wholesaler giving the best possible prices to the retailer because they didn't have to. There was no need for a supplier to give a wholesaler the best price because there was no way to tell the public that you had the best price until a person came into the liquor store and wanted to buy something. At that time it was either too late, or what difference does it make? When we were able to start advertising, it showed how far inflated our prices were compared to those in Massachusetts because people were now comparing what our prices in Rhode Island were to the prices they could pay in Massachusetts. This caused an awful lot of pressure on retailers and in turn, we put the pressure on the wholesalers and in turn put the pressure on the suppliers. They are now—not that they're there yet because we haven't finished our job—but our pricing is becoming more and more in line with Massachusetts. Now why is Rhode Island different than Massachusetts? In Massachusetts—we have stores in Massachusetts, so we do know the difference—we have stores in Massachusetts and Rhode Island. The stores in Massachusetts

are able to buy a particular product from many wholesalers, so they don't have a franchise rule in Massachusetts. In Rhode Island, we have a franchise rule
that says if you're a distributor of Absolut [for exam-
ple], you are the only one to distribute that product. I
cannot go any other place to buy it. So therefore I
have to go to that particular wholesaler who can uphold his prices to where he feels he wants them. But
because right now we're able to advertise and show
the difference between Rhode Island and Massachusetts prices, you put them under tremendous pressure. So that's what it's done.

The U.S. Supreme Court reversed the First Circuit's decision and ruled
unanimously in favor of 44 Liquormart. Justice Stevens' opinion for the
Court (see Court opinion excerpts at chapter's conclusion) held that the
Rhode Island statutes banning the inclusion of prices in advertisements for
alcoholic beverages were an abridgement of the First Amendment and are
not shielded from constitutional scrutiny by the Twenty-first Amendment.
In turn, the Court admitted that *Posadas* had been incorrectly decided.

THE RULING

*Can you describe for me a bit the feelings and any emotions that you had
when you heard about the ruling?*

EVAN LAWSON: Well, yeah, I was very happy (laughs). It sounds trite
but let me put it on a scale. I used to say that the
really happiest—an undiluted happiness—of my life
was the day that I learned that I passed the bar
exam. Then I said next to that was the day that my
ex-wife got remarried (laughs)(laughs). I was very
happy when my children were born, too. But that
kind of happiness is different. So if you're talking
about this kind of discreet event-oriented, rather
than the sort of cosmic life event kind of thing—I
can't put having a child in the same emotional category as winning a case in the Supreme Court or
passing the bar or having your ex-wife get remarried. So it was that kind of happiness—that sort of
unmitigated and uncomplicated happiness. So the
first thing I heard was we had won. Then, when I got
the opinion and started reading it and saw that the
Court had essentially adopted or accepted the essence of the arguments that I had made, and that

it was—even though fractured as to its reasoning—
a unanimous decision. I guess the feeling is a sort
of very—it wasn't an elation, but it was this kind of
feeling of calm satisfaction. You know, now you can
stop (laughs). Not that I stopped, but it was a feeling of having really accomplished something—even
though all I really accomplished is that liquor retailers get to advertise their prices. In that sense, not
much of an accomplishment, really. But in the sense
of sort of getting the system to work the way I
thought it should work, it was just this kind of
"Wow!" Because remember, having taken this from
conception, not often do you get to do that. Often
you get brought in later, or just handle the appeal,
but in this case to have the person come with the
problem, to work out the solution, and years later it
just turned out the way I thought it should. It was
very satisfying—not sort of jumping up and down
and running around satisfying, but that kind of good
feeling satisfying. I wasn't about to throw a noisy
party or anything. It's not like winning a sporting
event where usually there's a lot of pouring cham-
pagne on everybody's heads. That may have to do
more with the fact that I'm in my 50s as opposed
to in my teens or 20s. It's still to this day very satisfying. I've had a number of satisfying moments in
the law, but this was certainly a big one.

JOHN HARONIAN: Just to know that you won what you set out to do.
Evan called me. I think that next week we put out the
first full-page ad of item and price.

So it was within a week that you price advertised?

JOHN HARONIAN: Within a week, and from then on we've been doing it.
And I don't think consumption has increased in the
state of Rhode Island. Maybe sales have increased because they're not going across the state line to buy
their goods. I think the state has received more sales
tax money. But I doubt very much if consumption has
increased.

AFTERMATH & LEGACY

Given the outcome, what sort of signal or message does this ruling send?

JOHN HARONIAN: A person has a right to know. That's all it is. A person has a right to know.

EVAN LAWSON: Well, I think it sends the message that the current makeup of the Supreme Court—and I would say for the foreseeable future—is very favorably disposed toward protecting informational advertising. I think it also sends a message by way of illustration that very often casual pronouncements from the Supreme Court will get distorted and misapplied, and you need to be careful about that and you need to always be thinking about, "Do we need to go back to the Supreme Court so they can say, 'Wait a minute, that's not what we meant?'" I think that's the message. I think the message is that the current Supreme Court understands the importance of communication and wants to protect it and in its various incarnations.

If somehow the ruling by the Supreme Court had gone against you, what kind of signal would that have sent to businessmen, to the public, and so on?

JOHN HARONIAN: I think they may have believed that advertising price of alcoholic beverages increased consumption. They may have bought that argument. But it's bullshit.

EVAN LAWSON: Certainly it would have emboldened the forces of speech repression and, of course, there are other areas besides alcoholic beverages. There are environmental areas. There may be other health areas where the handy solution to the problem is to prevent people from talking about something. If it had gone the other way, it would have set a precedent that would have emboldened people who want to prevent the public from having information—in other words, people who would control peoples' choices by depriving them of the information that would enable them to make a meaningful choice.

Is at the heart of that a trust that the government arguably ought to have for the citizenry?

EVAN LAWSON: Yes! Yes. If you think about the philosophy of our government is that the government's power comes from the people—it comes through the peoples' elections of representatives and it comes from the peoples' acceptance of the Constitution and the laws that are enacted under it. If you really believe that, then you have to trust the people.

What do you think the legacy of this case and this ruling will be?

EVAN LAWSON: I think the legacy is to enable businesses that are subject to advertising restrictions to at least try to prove that the restrictions are not effective or not designed to do what the restrictors say they will. Remember, a lot of regulation happens by regulation rather than by legislation. There's a lot more at stake. I think that if you want to use your thought, it does reaffirm trust in the peoples' ability to make their own choices.

When this all began, way back when you were first contacted by the state board, could you have imagined that events would have unfolded as they did?

JOHN HARONIAN: No. You know, you always have hopes and dreams. And we hope.

For you personally, what would you say is the lasting memory of your work on this case?

EVAN LAWSON: Well, (laughs) the most important memory to me is the experience of doing it, being there, being *the* person who actually moved the law in one direction or another. That's the most enduring part of it. There's also the satisfaction of having wiped out a rule that I despised, or at least—it really wasn't a rule, but the effects of the Twenty-first Amendment. Having had to listen to so many judges tell me, "Well, the Twenty-first Amendment gives an added presumption of validity." So now to be able to say, "No, it doesn't" (laughs)—that's an ongoing source of satisfaction, as well. You know, a long time ago I came to the conclusion that if you get too caught up in winning and losing, you're going to burn out or be unhappy because there are so many things that go into winning and losing that you have no control over. So really what you have to do is feel that you've done the best job you can. I know this sounds somewhat trite, but that's the way I deal with the vagaries of outcomes. So this was one that I really felt that I had done my best and had I lost, at least I would have felt that I did the best I could, but having won it's so much better (laughs).

JOHN HARONIAN:　　My lasting memory? I'm proud that we were able to do what we've accomplished. You know, I don't work for money. I enjoy what I'm doing. I probably could have retired many, many years ago. Thank God I've been very successful and not in any need for anything. But I work because I enjoy what I'm doing. I love to see people grow, especially my people. I love putting it all together like a chess game—anticipating, moving, going in the right direction, and always little steps of accomplishment. That's what I get out of life. I go home tired, I get up real early, I work hard. But it's an enjoyable situation.

How often do you think of these events? Is there a day that goes by that they don't occur to you in some way?

JOHN HARONIAN:　　During the court proceedings of the 2000 election, that was the flashback. I talked about it more then than ever. It's something that happened in the past and I put it aside. It wasn't until the election problems developed that I talked about it.

Are you aware of the fact that this case has now found its way into virtually every textbook in this area? How does it feel to know that forever in textbooks, in college and university classrooms across the country that the name 44 Liquormart will always come up in discussions when this area of law is discussed?

JOHN HARONIAN:　　(laughs) I wasn't aware. Is that right? Because of the First Amendment? Unbelievable!

If I were to ask you bottom line, what was really at issue in this case, what would you say?

JOHN HARONIAN:　　It was so the public would know before they enter the store, of what they were paying for goods. That's all it meant. And all I wanted the consumer to understand was to make a decision where you're going to spend your money, not being forced to spend your money where you don't want to. In other words, have all the tools and have all the information in front of you so you can make a proper decision. That's all it is. Is that a hard thing? We go on the Internet now, where before we used to take out the newspaper and compare ads. There are services that will do all the ranking for you if you're looking for a particular product. They'll rank it so you know where to go. That's the only thing I wanted to do with alcoholic beverages is to say, "Here are all the prices." It's another tool to make a decision where you want to spend your money, not where you're forced into spending it. And knowing that we made a difference. And you know, I often think the people of Rhode Island, I don't know if they know—if they really are aware—of what we've done for the state and the consumer and bringing the prices for alcoholic beverages in line with competition of other states, and how they'd gotten screwed before. Yeah, we're making money and we've grown a nice, nice company, but the bottom line of the whole thing is what we've accomplished.

EVAN LAWSON: Hmmm. The bottom line of what was at issue in this case ... I think what was at issue in this case was how important the Court was going to see informational advertising. As you know, there are various kinds of advertising. Informational advertising—where you're providing the consumer with information about the product so that they can make a reasoned choice, so to speak—that has always had a very high value, I think, in the Court's mind, at least since it held that advertising was protected [by the First Amendment]. And it has a high value in a capitalist society, and a high value in a democratic system. And, in fact, I wanted to make the argument, but didn't, that informational advertising should get full First Amendment protection, which, of course, is the Clarence Thomas position. So what was really at stake here was how much protection is going to be given to purely informational advertising. I think that the Court came out with "high" protection, but did so by applying *Central Hudson*. So what they did—if *Central Hudson* had been drifting towards a permissive end of the spectrum—permissive towards the legislatures—this case pulled it back, if not to the restrictive side, at least back to the center.

One law review article author has the opinion that this ruling undermines Central Hudson. *How would you comment on that?*

EVAN LAWSON: Well, you know, that's very interesting because I've actually been doing a fair amount of thinking about that, particularly because I'm interested now in regulation of lifestyle and subliminal advertising. I've been thinking about how you would come up with a coherent theory that would accommodate First Amendment values and also accommodate some of society's legitimate interests. This is a long answer to a short question, but to give you an example, the *Central Hudson* test says that commercial speech that's not misleading and about a lawful product, that's commercial speech. Well, if you just applied the First Amendment rule, you could argue that misleading speech could not be regulated. Even though we've always penalized fraud, we've penalized it by way of its effect. In other words, we've haven't said you can't say fraudulent things. We've said that if people rely on them and are harmed, they can sue you. But we haven't said if you say something fraudulent per se, it has consequences. I think that I would disagree with the statement even though I recognize that Justice Thomas, supported by I forget who, is of the opinion that really *Central Hudson* should be abandoned. But I think the majority of the Court sees the need to keep *Central Hudson*. I started out disliking *Central Hudson*, but the more I think about how you can accommodate the competing interests, the more I think that *Central Hudson* at least provides a workable framework. So I think that this case does *not* undermine *Central Hudson*, it actually cuts back on judicial trends that were undermining *Central Hudson*. I think it undermined *Central Hudson* for the test to drift towards a totally permissive—permissive in terms of the states' approach. *Posadas* undercut *Central Hudson* a lot more than this case does by making it essentially a meaningless test.

Did being involved with this case—especially given the various steps and that it took awhile to resolve it—did it take any kind of personal toll on you or family members?

JOHN HARONIAN: No, I don't think so. It's exciting. Is it exciting to the average person out there? I really don't think that he realized when you're in the environment of the United States Supreme Court what it's like. There's talk about it being political. I think that's bullshit. I look at that as pure. Yes, they're sworn in. Could they be swayed if there's a gray area? Yeah, they probably could—in an interpretation. But I still look at it as one of the purest forms of our government. They can say what they want. I've been there and done it.

So was it all worth it?

JOHN HARONIAN: Oh, absolutely! Absolutely! I loved it.

Any regrets about being involved in the whole process?

JOHN HARONIAN: None. Not one bit. You know, the things we're accomplishing in this industry, just like we did with the other two—it's untravelled paths, and anytime you travel a road that's never been traveled, you're going to get your nose pushed in every so often. You're going to have some losses, but you keep going forward with what you believe in.

*44 Liquormart, Inc. and Peoples
Super Liquor Stores, Inc.,
Petitioners v. Rhode Island and
Rhode Island Liquor Stores
Association*

SUPREME COURT
OF THE UNITED STATES

517 U.S. 484
Argued: November 1, 1995
Decided: May 13, 1996

COUNSEL: Evan T. Lawson argued the cause and filed briefs for petitioners.

Rebecca Tedford Partington, Special Assistant Attorney General, argued the cause and filed a brief for respondent State of Rhode Island.

STEVENS, J., announced the judgment of the Court.

OPINION:

…

We now hold that Rhode Island's statutory prohibition against advertisements that provide the public with accurate information about retail prices of alcoholic beverages is also invalid. Our holding rests on the conclusion that such an advertising ban is an abridgment of speech protected by the First Amendment and that it is not shielded from constitutional scrutiny by the Twenty-first Amendment.

…

Complaints from competitors about an advertisement placed by *44 Liquormart* in a Rhode Island newspaper in 1991 generated enforcement proceedings that in turn led to the initiation of this litigation. The advertisement did not state the price of any alcoholic beverages. Indeed, it noted that "State law prohibits advertising liquor prices." The ad did, however, state the low prices at which peanuts, potato chips, and Schweppes mixers were being offered, identify various brands of packaged liquor, and include the word "WOW" in large letters next to pictures of vodka and rum bottles. Based on the conclusion that the implied reference to bargain prices for liquor violated the statutory ban on price advertising, the Rhode Island Liquor Control Administrator assessed a $400 fine.

In his findings of fact, the District Judge first noted that there was a pronounced lack of unanimity among researchers who have studied the impact of advertising on the level of consumption of alcoholic beverages.… After summarizing the testimony of the expert witnesses for both parties, he found "as a fact that

Rhode Island's off-premises liquor price advertising ban has no significant impact on levels of alcohol consumption in Rhode Island."

As a matter of law, he concluded that the price advertising ban was unconstitutional because it did not "directly advance" the State's interest in reducing alcohol consumption and was "more extensive than necessary to serve that interest." ... He reasoned that the party seeking to uphold a restriction on commercial speech carries the burden of justifying it and that the Twenty-first Amendment did not shift or diminish that burden.

...

The Court of Appeals reversed.... It found "inherent merit" in the State's submission that competitive price advertising would lower prices and that lower prices would produce more sales.

...

Advertising has been a part of our culture throughout our history. Even in colonial days, the public relied on "commercial speech" for vital information about the market.

...

In accord with the role that commercial messages have long played,

the law has developed to ensure that advertising provides consumers with accurate information about the availability of goods and services.

...

[O]ur early cases uniformly struck down several broadly based bans on truthful, nonmisleading commercial speech, each of which served ends unrelated to consumer protection.

...

At the same time, our early cases recognized that the State may regulate some types of commercial advertising more freely than other forms of protected speech. Specifically, we explained that the State may require commercial messages to "appear in such a form, or include such additional information, warnings, and disclaimers, as are necessary to prevent its being deceptive," *Virginia Bd. of Pharmacy*, 425 U.S. at 772, n. 24.

...

In *Central Hudson Gas & Elec. Corp. v. Public Serv. Comm'n of N.Y.*, 447 U.S. 557, 65 L. Ed. 2d 341, 100 S. Ct. 2343 (1980), we took stock of our developing commercial speech jurisprudence.

...

"In commercial speech cases, then, a four-part analysis has developed. At the outset, we must determine whether the expression is protected by the First Amendment. For commercial speech to come within that provision, it at least must concern lawful activity and not be misleading. Next, we ask whether the asserted governmental interest is substantial. If both inquiries yield positive answers, we must determine whether the regulation directly advances the governmental interest asserted, and whether it is not more extensive than is necessary to serve that interest." *Central Hudson*, 447 U.S. at 566.

...

[W]hen a State entirely prohibits the dissemination of truthful, nonmisleading commercial messages for reasons unrelated to the preservation of a fair bargaining process, there is far less reason to depart from the rigorous review that the First Amendment generally demands.

...

Our commercial speech cases have recognized the dangers that attend governmental attempts to single out certain messages for suppression.

...

It is the State's interest in protecting consumers from "commercial harms" that provides "the typical reason why commercial speech can be subject to greater governmental regulation than noncommercial speech."

...

Yet bans that target truthful, nonmisleading commercial messages rarely protect consumers from such harms. Instead, such bans often serve only to obscure an "underlying governmental policy" that could be implemented without regulating speech.

...

In this way, these commercial speech bans not only hinder consumer choice, but also impede debate over central issues of public policy.

...

Precisely because bans against truthful, nonmisleading commercial speech rarely seek to protect consumers from either deception or overreaching, they usually rest solely on the offensive assumption that the public will respond "irrationally" to the truth. The First Amendment directs us to be especially skeptical of regulations that seek to keep people in the dark for what the government perceives to be their own good.

...

In this case, there is no question that Rhode Island's price advertising ban constitutes a blanket prohibition against truthful, nonmisleading speech about a lawful product. There is also no question that the ban serves an end unrelated to consumer protection.

...

The State argues that the price advertising prohibition should nevertheless be upheld because it directly advances the State's substantial interest in promoting temperance.

...

[A] commercial speech regulation "may not be sustained if it provides only ineffective or remote support for the government's purpose."

...

[W]e cannot agree with the assertion that the price advertising ban will significantly advance the State's interest in promoting temperance.

...

[T]he State has presented no evidence to suggest that its speech prohibition will significantly reduce marketwide consumption.

...

The State also cannot satisfy the requirement that its restriction on speech be no more extensive than necessary. It is perfectly obvious that alternative forms of regulation that would not involve any restriction on speech would be more likely to achieve the State's goal of promoting temperance.

...

[T]he State has failed to establish a "reasonable fit" between its abridgment of speech and its temperance goal.

...

[A] state legislature does not have the broad discretion to suppress truthful, nonmisleading information for paternalistic purposes.... "[I]t is precisely this kind of choice, between the dangers of suppressing information, and the dangers of its misuse if it is freely available, that the First Amendment makes for us."

...

[W]e think it quite clear that banning speech may sometimes prove far more intrusive than banning conduct.

...

[I]t is no answer that commercial speech concerns products and services that the government may freely regulate.... [A] State's regulation of the sale of goods differs in kind from a State's regulation of accurate information about those goods. The distinction that our cases have consistently drawn between these two types of governmental action is fundamentally incompatible with the absolutist view that the State may ban commercial speech simply because it may constitutionally prohibit the underlying conduct.

...

[W]e find unpersuasive the State's contention that ... the price advertising ban should be upheld because it targets commercial speech that pertains to a "vice" activity.

...

[T]he scope of any "vice" exception to the protection afforded by the First Amendment would be difficult, if not impossible, to define. Almost any product that poses some threat to public health or public morals might reasonably be characterized by a state legislature as relating to "vice activity."

...

Section 1 of the Twenty-first Amendment repealed that prohibition, and Section 2 delegated to the several States the power to prohibit commerce in, or the use of, alcoholic beverages.

...

Rhode Island argues, and the Court of Appeals agreed, that in this case the Twenty-first Amendment tilts the First Amendment analysis in the State's favor.

...

[W]e now hold that the Twenty-first Amendment does not qualify the constitutional prohibition against laws abridging the freedom of speech embodied in the First Amendment. The Twenty-first Amendment, therefore, cannot save Rhode Island's ban on liquor price advertising.

...

Because Rhode Island has failed to carry its heavy burden of justifying its complete ban on price advertising, we conclude that R. I. Gen. Laws sections 3-8-7 and 3-8–8.1 (1987), as well as Regulation 32 of the Rhode Island Liquor Control Administration, abridge speech in violation of the First Amendment as made applicable to the States by the Due Process Clause of the Fourteenth Amendment. The judgment of the Court of Appeals is therefore reversed.

It is so ordered.

9 Turner Broadcasting System, Inc., et al. v. Federal Communications Commission, et al.

"What would the broadcasting industry look like [without must carry]? I think it's absolutely fair to assume that it would be a lot more shriveled up than it is now. Would the network affiliates be there? Sure they would. Would they be as strong as they are now? Probably not quite. Would the UPN network and WB have emerged the way they did? No chance."

—Donald B. Verrilli, Jr., defense co-counsel, *Turner Broadcasting v. FCC*

"If you want to control the flow of information or programming to an individual's television set, there is a valid public policy question as to whether you should have an effective monopoly—total control. Traditionally in a monopoly situation, there is a public policy justification for government involvement."

—James Popham, defense co-counsel, *Turner Broadcasting v. FCC*

"[O]ne of the tougher arguments the other side made is to say, 'Cable capacity is so constrained that valuable cable programming will not be carried if we devote eight or nine of our slots to local broadcast stations.' My reaction to that is this: Go to the bottom of the cable dial and look at the quality of the cable programming that's on. How many versions of 'Gilligan's Island' do you need to see?"

—Kit A. Pierson, defense co-counsel, *Turner Broadcasting v. FCC*

The authority of Congress and the Federal Communications Commission (FCC) to regulate broadcasting has been affirmed by the U.S. Supreme Court. The Court has acknowledged that because of the unique nature of broadcasting—for example, the scarcity of spectrum—the First Amendment standard that applies to broadcasters is a different one than what is applicable to other media. With the advent of cable television—a medium that does not transmit its programming by utilizing the public airwaves—a question arose whether it was subject to the same kind of regulatory authority. While by no means free from regulatory measures, the cable industry was the beneficiary of a deregulatory mindset in its infancy, particularly relative to broadcasting. One result was tremendous growth of the cable television industry. As it grew, so did sentiments in Congress and the FCC to preserve a balance between, and the existence of, broadcast and cable television.

One method of doing so was the "must carry" provisions of the Cable Television Consumer Protection and Competition Act of 1992. They required cable television systems to dedicate some of their channels to accommodate all of the local broadcast television stations in a given market. The cable industry did not exactly embrace the new regulations. In fact, a group of cable interests led by Turner Broadcasting Systems challenged must carry in U.S. District Court. It claimed the provisions violated its members' First Amendment rights by inhibiting their editorial discretion in determining what programming messages they could send. The government and broadcast interests countered by arguing, in part, that must carry furthers the government interest of ensuring the survival of new and developing local broadcast stations, that the provision enhanced the diversity of programming options for noncable households, and did so in a content-neutral way.

To determine the constitutionality of must carry, the courts had to determine whether the provision was content-based and, in turn, what level of First Amendment scrutiny to apply to the requirement. Under an intermediate level of scrutiny, a content-neutral regulation will survive a First Amendment challenge if it furthers an important or substantial governmental interest; if the interest is unrelated to the suppression of free expression; and if the incidental restriction on alleged First Amendment freedoms is not greater than is necessary to further the interest.

The case was heard twice by both the U.S. District Court in the D.C. Circuit and the U.S. Supreme Court. In *Turner I*, by a 2-to-1 margin, a three- judge district court panel denied the cable industry's motion for summary judgment, granted the government's motion for summary judgment, and ruled that the must carry provisions were not unconstitutional. On appeal, the U.S. Supreme Court upheld the decision that the provisions are content-neutral and should be subjected to the intermediate level of scrutiny under the First Amendment, but vacated the district court's judgment and remanded the case to allow both sides to better develop a thorough factual record.

In *Turner II*, the same three-judge panel reached conclusions similar to those it had arrived at 18 months previously. Again by a 2-to-1 margin, the court ruled that the must carry provisions were not unconstitutional, denied the plaintiff's motion for summary judgment, and granted the summary judgment by the defendants. The Supreme Court that heard the appeal was slightly different that the *Turner I* Court. Justice Breyer had replaced Justice Blackmun. Displaying an exceedingly deferential attitude toward Congress and the record it had developed when the Cable Act of 1992 and the must carry provisions were being debated, the Court affirmed the district court's judgment by a 5-to-4 margin.

Many different organizations and interests intervened on both sides of the case, each represented by their own counsel. Along with the government, the National Association of Broadcasters (NAB) led the fight to defend the must carry provision. NAB senior vice-president and general counsel Jack Goodman directed that effort. When NAB opted for outside counsel, it hired the Washington, D.C. firm of Jenner & Block. The late Bruce Ennis led that team, which also included Donald B. Verrilli, Jr. and Nory Miller—both still with that firm—and Kit A. Pierson—now with Heller, Ehrman, White & McAuliffe in Washington. Mr. Ennis argued *Turner II* before the U.S. Supreme Court. (See chap. 10 for more on Mr. Ennis).

Also defending the must carry provision was James Popham, general counsel of the Association of Local Television Stations, which previously had been the Association of Independent Television Stations. He is now vice-president and statutory license counsel for the Motion Picture Association of America. Mark Lynch was and is with the Washington law firm Covington & Burling and represented the Association of Public Television Stations, the Corporation for Public Broadcasting, and the Public Broadcasting Service.

MUST CARRY: THE CASE BACKGROUND

DON VERRILLI:

Must carry is part of the 1992 Cable Act, and it was a requirement that Congress imposed on all cable operators in the country, except for the very smallest ones that they had to make up to one-third of the channel capacity available for the carriage of local broadcast stations. [Under the law] they had no right to refuse broadcast stations carriage. Essentially, it was a right of access to cable systems for broadcasters. The reason that was important to our clients—the broadcasters—is that broadcasting is free. You don't pay to get it. It's supported by advertising revenues. Advertisers pay depending on audience size, so the larger the audience the larger the advertising revenues. Conversely, the smaller the audience size, the smaller advertising revenues. If advertising revenues shrink, the quality and diversity of what a broadcaster can provide will diminish, which will further reduce your audience size, which will further diminish your ability to achieve quality and diversity in programming. It's really a vicious downward spiral. The reason that must carry was so important—and it's been fairly well documented—that once a household gets cable, it no longer views television signals over the air. Everything comes through the cable. So if you're not on the cable [system], effectively you don't have an audience of cable households. Since at the time cable households were about 60% of all households, it meant that broadcasters who weren't carried would lose 60% of their potential audience, which would dramatically shrink their ability to earn advertising revenue, which would trigger that downward spiral.

KIT PIERSON: What must carry did—the statute required cable companies to carry a certain number of channels, up to a cap, they had to use a certain amount of cable capacity to carry local broadcast stations.

JIM POPHAM:  [The lobbying effort] was over several Congresses. And must carry was always part of the bill. So most of what we were doing in the course of the lobbying was working on the details—not so much the concept of must carry. Congress then, and I think even until now, has always favored must carry very strongly. At the time, with the Cable Act, there was such an antagonism toward the cable industry that the basic concept of must carry and doing something that the cable industry didn't want was not that much of a trick (laughs). There was trickiness in the details in a few places, but basically the concept of must carry and the politics of it were right.

JACK GOODMAN: I've been doing must carry for what seems to be all of my adult life. Before I came to the NAB, I was in a law firm that at one point represented NAB and what was then called INTV—now ALTV—involved in must carry cases. When I came to the NAB in 1990, I was brought in at that point primarily to work on cable issues as NAB was gearing up to try to get passage of what became the 1992 Cable Act. So I was the principal legal counsel for NAB internally in the development of the '92 Cable Act—in helping to draft sections which we submitted to Congress, testimony for Congress, etc., etc., including some drafts of what became the ultimate committee report.

DON VERRILLI: In the Fall of '92 then-President Bush vetoed [the Cable Act], and Congress overrode the veto.

JIM POPHAM: At that time, we were in the final year or so of the Bush Administration which had been antagonistic toward must carry. There was a serious question in our mind whether Bush's lame duck Justice Department at that point would even be willing to defend the rule. [Our side] played a very significant role in assuring that the Department of Justice did come in to defend the rules and that that could be carried forward, then, after Clinton was elected and his Justice Department was in place. Had the Justice Department not defended the rules, it may have been a tougher case.

JACK GOODMAN: Once the Act passed in the fall of 1992, NAB took the lead for the industry along with the government in defending the statute in court, which were the cases that ultimately become the *Turner* cases. Again, there, I was the principal [counsel] at NAB working with our outside counsel, Bruce Ennis, on our defense of the must carry statute. We actually conducted a "beauty contest" between law firms in the fall of '92 and selected Jenner & Block with Bruce Ennis and his team as among the most experienced. We knew this case was going to the Supreme Court. They are among the best Supreme Court litigators and First Amendment experts in the country.

With regard to the origins of must carry itself, it seems that early in its development, cable was afforded a lot of freedom and a lot of opportunity to grow. It seems that it was a victim of its own good fortune in that Congress, at some point along the way, said, "Enough."

JACK GOODMAN: I think a considerable amount of that is true, particularly since must carry was not the only part of the legislation. The rate regulation, which was certainly a key part of the political equation in passing the bill, was *certainly* a response to a belief that cable was an unregulated monopoly and was abusing that privilege. There were other parts—the program access provision related to the feeling that cable had taken incredible advantage of its position in disadvantaging potential competitors. In other words, people who wanted to overbuild cable systems or satellite carriers by denying the ability to get programming. Almost every provision of the '92 Act responds to at least somebody in Congress who perceived an abuse of monopoly position by cable. So that is absolutely correct. That is the political basis of the '92 Act.

KIT PIERSON:

Cable, without a doubt, was a tremendous beneficiary of certain regulatory regimes. Cable had not been operating in a free market context. I think that's right that cable had grown to a point where there was concern on Congress' part that it was creating problems for some of the competing interests. In some ways, this was not an over-reaching statute. The percentage of cable capacity that's actually devoted to these stations is relatively small. I don't know whether Congress was trying to rein in cable, or just make sure that a reasonable balance was maintained. But cable was in a funny position to be arguing that this should be completely governed by the free market.

JIM POPHAM:

I think what happened is—and my personal experience is illustrative of this—I worked for NAB in the '70s. We were constantly fighting a losing battle against cable, because cable was the darling of everybody at that point. It was going to be millions of channels for everybody—pie in the sky and all that. I would not for a minute denigrate the value of cable service. It has provided an enormous diversity of programming that people didn't have before. But the politic of it was all pro-cable and "Broadcasting is going to die and cable is going to take over, and we have to pave the way for cable." I left D.C. for about 7 years, came back in '89. The winds were blowing entirely the other way because the cable industry, I think, had exploited its monopoly position in a number of ways, the most visible of which was raising rates and aggravating consumers, thereby aggravating their representatives in Congress. The cable industry had lost all favor and, in fact, had become very much disfavored. And they were very arrogant. I think in large part their arrogance did not help them in the *Turner* case.

NORY MILLER:

The cable industry wouldn't exist if it had not received all kinds of help from local and federal government. Cable operators were permitted to dig up the streets to lay their cable wires and use public rights of way.

They were given a special and virtual exemption called a compulsory copyright license which gives them free access to television programming. In contrast, they pay for cable network programming; they pay billions and billions of dollars for that. But they get broadcast programming for free without even the cost of negotiating. So immense amounts of government help have been given, especially to cable, but to many, if not all, the communications industries. Thus, to claim that by enacting must carry rules, the government had suddenly walked into an otherwise free market situation is ludicrous.

MARK LYNCH:

[My law firm], Covington & Burling, has represented what we could call the public television group for quite some time. In fact, there are three different clients—the Association of Public Television Stations, the Corporation for Public Broadcasting, and the Public Broadcasting Service. We frequently do projects on behalf of all three together. The *Turner* litigation—and there were a number of cases there—was one example of this. We represented all three as intervenors in the cases brought to have the must carry legislation declared unconstitutional. We have quite an active communications practice, and the lawyers in the practice are the people who deal principally with these clients and in this particular instance I was asked to come in and litigate it. I'm a general litigator here, although for 9 years before I came to Covington I was a staff attorney for the American Civil Liberties Union. So I know a little bit about First Amendment litigation and I frequently get involved in these cases for the firm's clients when these kinds of issues come up.

MUST CARRY: DEFINITIONS AND JUSTIFICATIONS

JIM POPHAM:

[Must carry] aimed to do a couple of things. I think the first thing it aimed to do, and the primary thing that it aimed to do, was to assure that all local television stations had the ability to reach their audiences. The emphasis would have to be on "all," because that became a critical element of the case, as well. We knew, and the cable industry knew, that most cable systems were carrying most of the local stations most of the time. So the issue was really with the marginal stations—the stations that were not being carried and would not be carried in the absence of the rules. Our association at that time represented the interests of stations not affiliated with ABC, CBS, and NBC. So at that point, we were representing the independent stations, the FOX affiliates, the independent stations that would become affiliates of UPN and WB, and also, I guess, a number of specialty sorts of stations—religious stations, foreign language stations, and what have you. Basically, these were the sorts of stations most vulnerable to not being carried. The second aim was to maintain broadcasting as a competitor to cable and maintain a parity of competition among broadcast stations in any given market.

MARK LYNCH: Must carry, in layman's terms, was a statutory requirement that cable systems carry the commercial and non-commercial broadcast stations. There were certain limits imposed on the number of stations they had to carry. There were two sections—one that dealt with commercial broadcasters and another that dealt with noncommercial broadcasters. The limitations for duplicative service and the number of stations that had to be carried were different between the commercial and noncommercial broadcasters. So while our positions were very, very close, there were some differences in the statute that were worth pointing out.

NORY MILLER: Must carry was the government's response to a situation that developed as the cable industry developed. Initially, cable operators carried the local broadcast stations in their communities because it was a source of programming. Cable operators, unlike broadcasters, did not produce their own programming; they just delivered programming created by others. At first, there weren't any cable programming networks like ESPN or HBO. But as these programming networks developed, often with investments from the cable operators themselves, cable providers would increasingly pick and choose among the broadcast stations in a market. They'd take some stations, but they wouldn't carry everything. And that created real problems within a broadcast market in terms of the stations that were not carried—which were also often the smaller, more vulnerable stations—because they could no longer reach all the homes in the market they were licensed to serve. They were cut off from the homes that subscribed to cable.

JACK GOODMAN: Must carry is a rule that provides that local cable systems must carry the broadcast stations in their market to their viewers. The reason is that cable stands as a gatekeeper between those viewers' access to stations or to signals. Once people are connected to cable, they typically will watch only what's on the cable system. If a local broadcast station is not on the cable system, its audience diminishes from the TVs hooked up to cable to zero, or very close to zero. Given the fact that in '92 you had almost 60% of TV households' primary TV set hooked up to cable, and now you have well over two thirds, if you lose access to two thirds of your potential market, as a matter of economics it becomes nonviable. Largely, the interest of NAB and its members was to ensure access to their audience.

Would you comment then on the notion that must carry has, in fact, enhanced the multiplicity of voices and the marketplace of ideas?

JIM POPHAM: I don't think there's any question about that if you work from the premise that one more broadcast station is one more voice and one more outlet for expression.

The Eighth Circuit Court of Appeals has defined vertical integration as "the inclusion within a single firm of two or more stages in the production or distribution of an end product" (*Paschall v. Kansas City Star Co.*, 727 F.2d 692, 696 n.3 (8th Cir. 1984) (quoting *Paschall v. Kansas City Star Co.*, 695 F.2d 322, 327 n.6 8th Cir. 1982)). As it relates to the media, a vertically integrated company is one that owns the means to produce and distribute (and sometimes exhibit) content. For example, a single conglomerate that owns the company that makes a television program, owns the company that delivers that program to cable and/or broadcast networks, and owns one or more of those networks is vertically integrated.

Why should the government, in this case Congress, be inserting itself into this issue and dictating how it should play out? Since these are private businesses, why shouldn't the market be allowed to sort this out?

KIT PIERSON: I guess part of the answer would be that if you say there's an interest in protecting the noncable households which presumably are going to tend to be lower income households, then I think part of Congress' determination was that the market is not necessarily the best way to sort that out. The market was creating a situation in which the programming available to those households was jeopardized. That was Congress' conclusion—the quality of the programming available to them was going to be jeopardized because of increasing concentration and vertical integration in the cable industry that gave them certain incentive not to carry local broadcast stations—at least not to carry the non-network local broadcast stations. That was a phenomenon that was playing out in the marketplace. That had implications for the availability of free TV to noncable households. And since the market basically votes with dollars, it's not necessarily always the best mechanism for dealing with questions of distributional justice. That's what Congress was trying to address. One can debate whether empirically they did or didn't get it right. The issue was very vigorously debated. But I don't think it's unreasonable for Congress to ask the question, "Is the market solving this problem, or are there certain tendencies in the market such as increasing concentration of the cable industry, the shift of television watching to cable households and away from broadcast stations?" It was not unreasonable for Congress to say that the market isn't necessarily the best mechanism for dealing with those distributional questions.

JACK GOODMAN: It's not really an open marketplace. Typically what we have—particularly up to 1992—you had largely monopoly cable operators often who were granted that monopoly through government franchise. Cable gets television signals, especially local ones, essentially for free under the cable compulsory copyright license. But there was no reciprocal obligation imposed on cable to carry all of them or to even pay anything for them to the broadcasters who created it. In many cases, they are the engine on which cable built their systems. They were and remain the most-watched signals on cable systems. So there really isn't a marketplace. What you have is what the antitrust experts call a gatekeeper—somebody who stands in between a provider of services, i.e., us, and the consumer. In this particular case, the gatekeeper not only has the interest of beating the system, but as Congress found, cable operators have an interest in disadvantaging non-owned competitors. In other words, people like broadcasters against whom they sell advertising, against whom they compete for viewers. So there is a strong incentive for cable to discriminate, particularly against less-watched TV stations because there they can essentially override consumer complaints easier and thereby diminish the level of competition in their market.

NORY MILLER: Marketplace discipline cannot solve this problem. It won't even do a very good job of ensuring that cable subscribers receive the programming they want to see because there is little or no competition. It's not a real marketplace. Each cable company was the monopoly provider to anyone in the area it served, in virtually every community. So subscribers didn't really have a choice. This is an entirely different situation from a truly competitive marketplace. For example, you can go to an office supply store and look at all kinds of pens and choose exactly which one you want with the characteristics you want. You don't have that kind of market for cable services. So people interested in what cable can provide generally are stuck with the choices their cable company has made. This simply isn't the kind of market where subscribers can vote effectively with their pocketbooks to get what they want.

Analyses of this case have included the idea that cable operators create a bottleneck in the flow of information and that they verge on being monopolistic gatekeepers. Are they?

JIM POPHAM: I don't think there's any question. As a practical matter, when someone subscribes to cable, that's how they get their television. There may be a set with rabbit ears somewhere else in the house. While cable has always argued, "Well, you can still get it off the air," as a practical matter, when you subscribe to cable, you get rid of your outdoor antenna. You hook up to cable and that's what comes in to your set, and that's it. So yeah, I think it is a bottleneck. I think by its nature it always will be a bottleneck. I don't think people are going to go for putting an antenna on the roof and having an A/B switch necessarily. To most of us, it's not a practical or certainly not a convenient sort of solution.

On a practical level, how can the government tell a private businessperson—a cable operator—what they can and can't do?

JIM POPHAM: The heart of the answer to that goes back to the bottleneck theory. If you want to control the flow of information or programming to an individual's television set, there is a valid public policy question as to whether you should have an effective monopoly—total control. Traditionally in a monopoly situation, there is a public policy justification for government involvement. You can go back to the old St. Louis Railroad terminal case where you had one railroad that owned the bridge that got trains into St. Louis. If they didn't let the competitors in, there was no way a competing railroad was going to get across and into St. Louis. That's probably the original bottleneck case. If you own the only bridge into St. Louis, you have to make it available to other people.

NORY MILLER: In terms of a philosophy of a how-government-ought-to-work question, I think that it is simply incorrect to claim that but for the must carry rule, the context in which these industries operated was a pure marketplace. I don't think any of these industries have ever been pure marketplace industries. Broadcasting has been regulated from day one because it was believed that if broadcasters simply used any spectrum they chose, there would be so much signal interference that the result would be a cacophony and broadcasting wouldn't work. Therefore, the government stepped in and undertook to divide up the spectrum and to license it to broadcasters to make sure that the spectrum was efficiently and fully used and also that every community would be served.

DON VERRILLI: The point was, the cable companies said they would carry the network stations, but they wouldn't carry anybody else. If they made good on that, they would inflict harms.

KIT PIERSON: I think one of the tougher arguments the other side made is to say, "Cable capacity is so constrained that valuable cable programming will not be carried if we devote eight or nine of our slots to local broadcast stations." My reaction to that is this: Go to the bottom of the cable dial and look at the quality of the cable programming that's on. How many versions of "Gilligan's Island" do you need to see?

DON VERRILLI: An important fact here is that there's a mismatch between what's in the economic interests of the cable operator and the demands of its subscribers. A cable company doesn't maximize its income by having an overall programming lineup that is in maximum accord with what its subscribers want. That's true for a couple of reasons. The first one is advertising. Cable companies compete with broadcasters for advertising. So they have an interest in having a cable service on rather than a broadcaster because they can sell the advertising and earn advertising revenues that they wouldn't get if they were carrying the broadcaster. And that would be true even if the broadcaster was more popular than the cable service that replaced it. Second is vertical integration. Most cable companies that distribute programming to your home are vertically integrated with companies that produce cable programming, Time Warner being the most obvious example of that. So cable companies have incentives therefore to carry cable programming that they produce rather than broadcasting because they'll earn more revenues from it even if the broadcasting is more popular than the cable programming that replaces it. The fact that most vividly confirms this—and the Supreme Court mentions it somewhat in the *Turner* decisions, and it's remained true—is that as a general matter in any given locality, the least-watched broadcast station usually achieves significantly higher ratings than the most-watched cable station. That's pretty good evidence that Congress was right about that—that there is a mismatch between the economic interests of cable operators and programmers and the desires of their subscribers.

KIT PIERSON: My perspective as a layman—and this was a significant argument in the case, given the enormous expansion in cable channel capacity, the amount of carriage that the statute required for local broadcast stations to achieve, and to make sure that local broadcasting remained a high-quality alternative for all households, including noncable households—that the corresponding interest on the cable industry side that significant and important cable programming was going to get displaced, I do not think was supported by the facts. My personal opinion as someone who subscribed to cable is that the eight or nine slots that are devoted to local broadcast stations is

a very small price to pay to achieve the goals that
Congress had.

MARK LYNCH: You get to another prong of the argument which is
that the television industry has been subject to much
more extensive regulation throughout its history than
the print media. And that has to do with the limited
amount of television spectrum that's available. Historically, a much greater role for government regulation has been accepted in broadcasting than it ever
has been in the print media. Although, there certainly
were examples of government imposing rules and regulations for structural reasons in the print world—not
that many, but there have been. For example, the application of the antitrust laws and the Newspaper
Preservation Act. Even with respect to the print media, when Congress has acted to deal with the economics and structure of the industry rather than the
content of what anybody is publishing, then those regulations are more likely to be sustained.

> By upholding the constitutionality of the FCC's personal attack rule in
> *Red Lion Broadcasting Co. v. FCC,* 395 U.S. 367 (1969), the U.S. Su-
> preme Court reinforced the idea that because of phenomena such as spec-
> trum scarcity, a lower First Amendment standard applies to broadcasters
> than to the print media, thus justifying a greater role for government regu-
> lation of broadcast licensees.

*With regard to the history of broadcast regulation, to what extent there was
an effort to distinguish these circumstances from those in* Red Lion?

MARK LYNCH: That was about the only point on which the public
television stations and the commercial television stations diverged at all. The National Association of
Broadcasters has been at the forefront of the battle
against the regulation of broadcasting and the *Red
Lion* case, which stands for a greater role for the government in the regulation of broadcasting, is something that the commercial broadcasters have been
vehemently opposed to. The public television industry
has been less concerned about that. That enabled us
to argue more aggressively than the commercial
broadcasters were able to argue that the history of
the regulation of broadcasting was applicable here,

and these regulations were certainly no more intrusive than the regulations that were sustained in the *Red Lion* case.

To what extent were you trying to distinguish between these circumstances and something like Red Lion?

JIM POPHAM: That's a tricky question because there was early on in the litigation an argument that we made that a lesser standard should apply. The broadcasting industry by and large has no love for *Red Lion* and I think we generally made an effort to avoid it as much as possible because we didn't want to embrace it. We were trying to stay away from any content basis for the rule. I think, actually, that the Department of Justice did go forward with arguments on that basis, more so than we might have liked. It's not an argument that we would have pressed. *Red Lion* has always been held up for the proposition that broadcasting has a lesser amount of First Amendment protection than other media. It's not something that's ever sat well with broadcasters.

DON VERRILLI: The other thing, too, there has been in the last decade such an explosion in cable capacity that the requirement of carrying these broadcast stations really isn't putting any kind of a major crimp on their ability to carry all the cable programming that they want. There's not a lot of displacement going on because there's so much capacity.

Was there, in fact, a real and legitimate concern that cable systems would not carry public broadcast stations?

MARK LYNCH: Oh, absolutely! There was no doubt. I'm not sure that there was ever any doubt that ABC, NBC, and CBS were going to be carried, but there was a great deal of doubt about a number of independent and certainly public television stations that were definitely at risk. And the factual record demonstrated that during the periods before the legislation, there were various times when the FCC promulgated must carry rules. Then they were struck down by the D.C. Circuit. And we were able to show that during the periods when must carry was not in effect, public television stations were dropped. And that was all the more remarkable, we argued, because we also had pretty good evidence that the cable industry was on instruction from its association to be on their best behavior whenever they won one of these cases striking down the [FCC] administrative rules because they didn't want to provoke a congressional reaction. There were some interesting statements by association officials saying, in effect, "We need to be on our best behavior. We shouldn't take full advantage of the victories won in these early cases because that will provoke Congress into enacting legislation to do exactly what the FCC rules had done." Well, Congress ended up doing that anyway, and the legislation was sustained.

JIM POPHAM: Most stations were being carried [by cable operators before must carry]. But if a station was not carried, it effectively lost access to 60% of its audience, on the average. If you can't reach 60% of your market, you're not going to survive. And there were stations that were not being carried that were not surviving or had not survived. Was that most of the stations in the industry? No. Was it half the stations in the industry? No. But it was a significant enough piece that Congress was legitimately concerned. And I think on a theoretical basis—and I think this ultimately became important to the Court—the notion that Congress had given the FCC long ago the directive to establish a system of local broadcasting. And the Commission back in the '50s and '60s a system of allocating channels to communities all over the country. There were more channels in larger markets, but they also wanted smaller cities and communities to have service as well. So there were also stations placed in those markets. Our theory was that whole system should be protected, not just the strongest stations in the largest markets, but all the stations—including the ones in the smaller markets, including the stations that were perhaps less popular in the larger markets—should also be entitled to compete and should not have the rug pulled out from under them by not being carried on cable.

Were broadcast stations really being threatened?

DON VERRILLI: We certainly heard a lot of that. There was a lot of evidence of what happens when broadcasters don't get carried on cable systems, particularly as cable systems get bigger and bigger. There was a lot of evidence about it and the Supreme Court found that we had proved our case sufficiently to uphold the statute. Broadcasting certainly isn't a license to print money any more. It's a heck of a lot more competitive than it used to be. To the extent that broadcasters have been successful in the last decade, you have to remember that the must carry requirement has been in place. Since 1992, they had access to their full audience since they've been on cable. The relevant question, it seems to me, is "What would the broadcasting industry look like if they hadn't been carried?" I think it's absolutely fair to assume that it would be a lot more shriveled up than it is now. Would the network affiliates be there? Sure they would. Would they be as strong as they are now? Probably not quite. Would the UPN network and WB have emerged the way they did? No chance. Because what happened there was that because of must carry, stations that were not network affiliates and were independent stations were able to retain sufficiently large audience size that they could prosper. And that created the fertile ground for new networks to arise by linking up all those stations. That's really what happened. There's a heck of a lot more broadcast diversity in that sense. FOX emerged that way, and after FOX, UPN and WB and PAX and Univision for Latino populations. That's been a very salutary development for the public. And that's because must carry has been in place.

JIM POPHAM: I think the reality was—and the reality has been since then—that with must carry, it basically breathes life into a number of stations which I don't think would exist today without must carry. Again, is it most of the stations in the country? No. But it's the stations that have formed the basis for UPN and the WB network. Those stations were dead or dying or struggling in the absence of must carry. And because must carry came in and because it has been upheld, they have been able to gain a foothold, and because they were able to gain a foothold, there were enough potential affiliates out there to form three new networks— UPN, WB, and the PAX network. I'm not sure those networks would have been able to get a foothold in the absence of must carry. There were a lot of stations that were hanging onto shopping stations, they were not hanging on at all, they were just doing a minimal amount of programming and just trying to hang on in the hope that must carry would be reenacted and upheld. Once it was, those stations literally came to life or had a new vitality to them, and that bore out what exactly must carry was supposed to do, and that is to assure that not only the strong, but also the fledglings and the new stations would have an opportunity to compete as well.

THE LEGAL ARGUMENTS: PREPARATIONS & STRATEGIES

KIT PIERSON: Our argument was that the statute says, for example, "You carry eight local broadcast stations, and all of the rest of your slots can be used for whatever cable stations you want." And it does that without reference to the content. It didn't matter what the underlying content of the cable programming was or the local broadcasting was. It was just allocating a certain percentage of your capacity to one form. That was our argument—that it was completely content-neutral.

JIM POPHAM: We always believed that the rules would be evaluated under the [intermediate] standard as not content-related rules, but under a more generally applicable First Amendment standard.

KIT PIERSON: There was a debate about once a home gets cable, it is not likely to get local broadcast stations unless the cable company chooses to carry them. There are ways you can do it, but the best empirical evidence was that very, very few homes that once they get cable are going to use any of the alternatives to watch anything that isn't carried by the cable carrier itself. I think that one important way to understand the must carry cases is that ultimately, it wasn't a fight about carrying the major networks. Nor was it a fight about carrying the major cable programs, like ESPN. Those programs, in general, were going to get carried. It was much more a fight about non-network broadcasting programs, which could have smaller audiences, and less popular cable programming. The most popular shows were going to be carried in either event.

DON VERRILLI: Most of my work on the case was principally to handle the legal issues, as opposed to the factual development. And so my work was trying to figure out what our position ought to be on the standard of review, what our best arguments were for achieving something less than strict scrutiny, which we were quite concerned would have been fatal to our prospects on the case.

Why is that?

DON VERRILLI: There is an adage in constitutional law that strict scrutiny is strict in theory and fatal in fact. And while that's not universally true, it's almost always true. The key in the First Amendment context is whether a law is content-based or content-neutral. If it's content-based then it's subject to strict scrutiny except in the broadcast context. If it's content-neutral, it's subject to lesser scrutiny, either intermediate scrutiny or sometimes even a very deferential rational basis scrutiny. There was a fork in the road for us very early on in conceptualizing the case. It was whether we would accept that the proposition was content-based, but then argue that it should nevertheless be subject to reduced scrutiny on the ground that it was analogous to a regulation in broadcasting, which is subject to less rigorous review. That was one path we could have taken. The other path was to contend that the statute was content-neutral, and thus subject to intermediate scrutiny. We had to make an evaluation of what we thought our prospects would be going down either road. We didn't think going down the former road had a significant prospect of success because even in the broadcast context, arguments that content-based laws should receive relaxed scrutiny were being met with more and more hostility by the courts, and certainly the commentators were almost uniform in their rejection of that way of thinking at the time. So we felt that our best prospect of prevailing was to make the argument that this was a content-neutral purpose. The difference between content-based and content-neutral statutes is that the former are generally efforts by government to regulate expression on the basis of the content of the expression. That can either be an effort by the government to express its hostility to the expression and restrict it in some form, or an effort by government conversely to prefer and advance particular messages of view. So either to prefer or suppress particular messages of view. Content-neutral laws, in contrast, are generally laws that serve objectives that are unrelated to the speech at issue. So what we sought to do was conceptualize the statute as one that would principally serve interests unrelated to the content of the speech.

When strict scrutiny is applied, exactly what does that mean?

DON VERRILLI: If the Court decides strict scrutiny applies, then the burden is on the proponents of the statute—usually the government, although here it was the government *and* the broadcasters who had intervened on the government's side—to show that the statute serves a compelling interest. That requires you to not only identify an interest that's compelling in nature, but to prove that the statute is really necessary to serve that interest. Then to show that the statute is the least restrictive means of achieving the government's interest, which means, in English, that there can't be any other method by which the government could have achieved its goal while suppressing or restricting less speech than the statute being challenged does. It's a very, very hard standard to meet. Had that been applied, it would have been very, very hard to sustain the statute. Intermediate scrutiny is much more relaxed. For a content-neutral law, intermediate scrutiny requires that the interest be important and that you make an evidentiary showing that it was reasonable of Congress to think that the legislative remedy was needed to serve the interest and that there is a pretty good fit between the statute and the interest—in other words, that it doesn't gratuitously suppress a lot of expression on the way to serving the government's interest. So as you can see, the latter test is a lot easier to meet than the former.

MARK LYNCH: One of the big issues here on whether you adopted strict scrutiny was the role of the *Tornillo* case. The *Tornillo* case struck down a Florida statute that required newspapers to carry replies by political figures who were attacked editorially. That was struck down in a 9-to-nothing decision by the Supreme Court saying that it obviously violated the First Amendment to require newspapers to carry anything that they didn't want to carry. The cable people thought that that applied to their situation. We had a lot of arguments why it didn't. Fortunately for us, those arguments prevailed.

In *Miami Herald v. Tornillo,* 418 U.S. 241 (1974), a unanimous U.S. Supreme Court ruled that a Florida right of reply law was unconstitutional. That law required that newspapers publish the responses of candidates who had been editorialized against. Ruling that judgments regarding what to publish—and what not to publish—are internal decisions, the Court said that compelling publication interferes with the free functioning of editors that is guaranteed by the First Amendment.

Given some of the circumstantial similarities, this case is somewhat reminiscent of Miami Herald v. Tornillo. *How do you square this ruling with that case?*

JACK GOODMAN: I think it's relatively easy to do. *Tornillo* is a direct content-based regulation. In other words, the obligation of *Tornillo* was triggered if the newspaper ran a story that said something adverse about candidate X. Then candidate X had a right of reply. It punished the newspaper for what its content was. There's nothing about must carry that does that at all. *Turner I* is primarily about this issue. Cable's argument was that in some fashion, must carry was content-based. They failed in that, and they failed because it isn't. It doesn't matter what's on the local broadcast station. It's not a preference for broadcast programming because of its content, it's a preference for broadcast programming because it's local and it is broadcast. But it has nothing to do with the content of it. That is the distinction between [*Turner*] and *Tornillo*.

DON VERRILLI: That was a big, big issue in our early conceptualizing of the case. That was the big thing we needed to deal with, was *Miami Herald v. Tornillo*. I think that the answer is that *Tornillo*, when you read it carefully, was not as broad of an opinion as it seems. What *Tornillo* essentially said was that a right of reply statute was essentially a content-based penalty. If you made the choice, as a newspaper, to criticize a public official, then you were subjected to this right of reply which required you to print something that you absolutely would not have printed [otherwise]. The government's purpose there was to change the debate. In other words, government was trying to intervene for a content-based reason there which was to counterbalance the debate—to make sure the public heard both sides of the debate. It also could have the effect of deterring you as a newspaper from running the criticism in the first place because you'd be forced to publish this thing you didn't want to publish. And there was some risk of misidentification. There was some risk you might be perceived as a newspaper as endorsing the message of the reply, and it would muck up the message that you were trying to get out. When you get to something like cable must carry, those arguments just don't apply. It wouldn't make any sense to think about this that way. First of all, it's not a content-based penalty, it's mandatory obligation. No matter what you have on your cable system, you've got to put the broadcasters on. There's no content-based trigger. It certainly wasn't an effort by government to change the public debate—to make sure both sides of a political issue were heard or anything like that. Cable is fundamentally different from a newspaper. Cable is essentially a conduit and certainly cable operators exercise editorial discretion in choosing what programmers to enter into affiliation agreements with and transmit, but that's really a different thing than what a newspaper does. That was a big issue in the case, but especially in the first of the *Turner* opinions there's a long discussion why *Tornillo* is different, and that was the product of the arguments we made in our briefs about why *Tornillo* was different.

MARK LYNCH: The main [difference] was that the right of reply in *Tornillo* was clearly triggered by the content of what the newspaper wrote. If I attack a politician and say he's a crook or I say he's got no business being elected—I'm the editor of the newspaper—the content of what I say triggers the right of the person I've attacked to reply. The cable rules, on the other hand, are not content-based. They're structural. The requirements are not in any way triggered by what the cable system is carrying, nor are they in any way triggered by what the broadcast station is carrying. It's strictly a functional/structural device meant to ensure the viability of a system of free over-the-air television. Perhaps the most important point there from our side was the evidence—and it was almost self-evident—if cable companies stopped carrying stations, there will be fewer people viewing those stations. And if there are fewer viewers in the case of commercial stations they will get less advertising revenue. And if there are fewer viewers of public television stations they will attract fewer contributions, both directly from their members and underwritings from corporations and foundations and so forth. And they will wither on the vine. It's self-evident that if a television station doesn't have viewers, it's not going to thrive economically, whether it's a public television station or a commercial television station.

NORY MILLER: There really isn't any contradiction between *Tornillo* and the *Turner* decisions. This is discussed extensively both in the briefs and in *Turner I.* Basically what the cable companies attempted to argue was that *Tornillo* said you can never require any speech to be carried under any circumstances. And what the Court made clear is that *Tornillo* said nothing of the kind and was not such a broad holding. What *Tornillo* was concerned about was the government saying, "We don't want people to hear one point of view without hearing another point of view. Therefore, if a newspaper publishes one point of view, it has to give space to other points of view." So in *Tornillo* you have the government having a very specific interest in what information is presented to the public and what points of view are expressed, and it is placing a burden on newspapers that is very likely to deter them from including controversial points of view because then they're going to have to give up their pages to responses. That really raises a First Amendment concern. You don't want government forcing newspapers not to take controversial positions. You don't want government forcing anybody not to take controversial positions. And you don't want government enacting regulations in order to control the impact of speech on those who hear or read it, and you don't want government trying to control the debate and determine what is said and heard. The must carry rules are nothing like that. The government had no interest in what any cable operator decides to say or what the programming it chooses says, or what broadcasters choose to say. That has no effect on whether or how the must carry rules apply.

JIM POPHAM: *Tornillo* was clearly content-based. I would not say that must carry was content-based. It wasn't assuring that any station or any programming would succeed. It was simply assuring that the pipeline wouldn't be closed to them, regardless of what their programming was or would be or wanted to be. It was just a matter of getting that electronic signal from Point A to Point B, and if you could interdict that signal—regardless of its content—you had a monopoly power. I don't think it's unusual for the government to be able to step in in that case and regulate that monopoly.

KIT PIERSON: There was a considerable amount of evidence before Congress that many local broadcast stations were having trouble getting onto cable systems, and that cable had a variety of interests which led them to favor cable programming rather than these lesser-watched broadcast stations. One of those interests between cable operators and cable programming was that there was an increasingly vertical relationship between them so that a cable operator might have an incentive to carry a cable program where it had an equity interest in cable programming. Cable programmers would sell some of their advertising time to the local cable operator to provide an incentive to carry the program in a way that the local broadcast stations just weren't in a position to do because they were entirely dependent on their advertising revenue. These issues were debated in a very, very heated way. There was empirical evidence on both sides.

NORY MILLER: The question in any First Amendment challenge is to distinguish between the types of regulations that are permissible and those that are not. The First Amendment concern is to protect people from the government when it is trying to control what they may say and believe. The idea is that the country will work best if there is a marketplace of ideas—lots of ideas of all kinds being heard, being debated, being sorted through by a population free to determine what is true and what is right. The cure for speech that might be deemed wrong or dangerous or offensive is more speech, expressing alternate points of view. So the question, when a statute is challenged on First Amendment grounds, is "What's going on in this statute? Is the government trying to control what people know and what they believe?" The must carry provisions, of course, are not an attempt to exert this type of interference. Cable operators are free to produce any programming they want, say whatever they want. The government has no interest in what subjects they address or what points of view they take on those subjects. The government has no interest in silencing them or in making them toe some government propaganda line. The government's motivation here is therefore not one that raises First Amendment suspicions. This is economic regulation. The government realized that there was a situation that was developing that messed up normal marketplace behavior. Normally, the way broadcasting works is that you're in your home, you turn on your TV, and you have the choice of whatever is there. If some choices aren't getting into your television, you don't have those choices. That was the concern. People who had cable generally did not have antennas, and even those who did, did not switch between cable and over-the-air reception from their antenna. Congress had very good evidence on that. The cable operator really determined the range of television choices the subscriber was going to choose among. Noncarried broadcasters lost the ability to attract the cable subscribers in their markets to any of their programming. Of course, no broadcaster is going to survive if no one watches its programming. But Congress found that cable distorted the broadcast market because cable subscribership resulted in noncarried stations losing viewers who would have watched them, and therefore threatened to leave those who relied on over-the-air free television with fewer and less diverse choices.

JIM POPHAM: The First Amendment standard, of course—whether [must carry] was content-based or not content-based—was a critical issue. The test for content-based would have been harder for us to make. You have to go back to what happened in Congress. We were very conscious that there would be a challenge. We went to extraordinary lengths to assure that the legislative history was *very* extensive, and was very complete in terms of all the arguments that would be raised in a challenge, and also address the question of whether it was content-based. We were anticipating this from the time we began lobbying on this until the time the bill passed. And, indeed, there were very specific findings that Congress made to buttress the must carry provision, and that was further supported by a very extensive legislative history including testimony and what have you. Again, I think that was an unprecedented amount of legislative history in support of the statute.

You say you were anticipating the challenge. What was it about this measure in particular that accounts for that?

JIM POPHAM: There had been two court challenges previously—both of which we had lost. The parties on the other side—Turner, in particular—were the same people. We knew that they would continue to be antagonistic. We knew that they thought they would win going away. So the challenge was inevitable. Indeed, the provision in the bill was written anticipating the challenge, directing it immediately to a three-judge court with direct appeal to the Supreme Court. We knew it was coming and everybody wanted to get it resolved as expeditiously as possible, one way or the other.

KIT PIERSON: A major part of our argument and a major part of my responsibility in the case was to assemble this tremendous congressional record. It was literally tens of thousands of pages of material that had been put in front of Congress. There had been a series of hearings over the years. To indicate to the Court that one can debate how substantial the government interest was here in carrying these additional stations, but there was an enormous evidentiary basis for Congress to conclude that making sure that a certain number of local broadcast stations got carried was important to those stations, it was important to the diversity of options that would be available. The major part of our argument was that while reasonable people might disagree about these things, Congress had an unusually large volume—both quantitatively and qualitatively—of evidence on the competing economic and policy arguments, and made a reasonable decision that it was necessary to protect in particular noncable households.

MARK LYNCH: Our argument in the first instance was that these requirements that were placed on the cable operators were of a kind that warranted only rational basis scrutiny. We argued that these were economic regulations rather than regulations that really impinged on First Amendment rights and were therefore limited to a rational basis scrutiny. The cable operators and the programmers—and that's an important point, that there were two distinct groups of parties seeking to have this statute declared unconstitutional. On the one hand, you have the cablecasters, and on the other hand, you have the people who produced the programming. And they had different perspectives on it. They argued that the statute should be subjected to the most rigorous level of First Amendment scrutiny. They claimed that it was content-based and viewpoint-based and they marshaled every argument that they could to get strict scrutiny. In the first phase of the litigation, in *Turner I*, the Supreme Court rejected both of those arguments and said that intermediate scrutiny was appropriate. The Supreme Court in a somewhat unusual opinion, said that there had to be a factual inquiry under the intermediate level of scrutiny to see if there was justification for Congress' predictive findings. That always struck me as rather odd that you could have a trial over congressional findings. In any event, we went back and there was an enormous amount of discovery taken.

In a general sense, "discovery" is the ascertainment of that which was previously unknown, or the disclosure or coming to light of what was previously hidden. Within the context of a trial, it is the pre-trial devices that can be used by one party to obtain facts and information about the case from the other party in order to assist in the preparation for trial.

KIT PIERSON: There's one other argument I should mention. This was important. For a significant percentage of the television audience still—it's a minority, but a significant percentage—the only way they get TV is through local broadcast stations because they don't have cable, particularly lower income people. And part of Congress' concern was if local broadcast stations were shut out of all cable households, the remaining audience available to them wouldn't be enough to sustain them. If you were only able to get into the noncable households, that base would not support the stations. One of the conclusions that Congress made was that you've got to give the local stations reasonable entrée into cable households or it's going to jeopardize the television options that are available to homes that can't afford cable. Those were the competing arguments.

DON VERRILLI: More of a personal memory about this case was the ferment of the first couple of months where it was Bruce [Ennis] and me and another fellow named David Ogden, who's since moved on to work in the government. The three of us were working together to come up with the theory of the case. In retrospect once the case is over and the Supreme Court has rendered its decision, everything seems clear. "Well, yes, this was our best argument. It was an intermediate scrutiny case, and this was the best way to get intermediate scrutiny." But when we got the case it was sort of an unformed mass. It was that first month or two of incredible effort and ferment where the three of us were together talking all the time about how we were going to approach this case, what the best arguments were, and really zeroing in on this claim that what this statute was all about was protecting the interests of the then-40% of Americans that didn't have cable. The goal here was to show that what this was about was not trying to alter the content on cable, but to protect the interests of the people who didn't have cable by insuring that broadcast remained vigorous by virtue of having access to its full audience. That kind of emerged in our minds after a month or six weeks of real frantic and intense effort as the key to the whole case. And I still think over my 15 or 20 years of practicing law that that process and that moment of settling on that particular defense of the statute was one of the things that I'm most proud of and one of the fondest memories I have of working with Bruce. It was the kind of experience that you had working with him—that intense intellectual engagement and intense thinking. There were times when out of that would pop a truly powerful idea I think that was one—a truly powerful defense of that statute that wasn't at all clear from the get-go. Once we latched onto it, we organized our whole case around that idea. The thing really fell into place, first in the district court and then at the Supreme Court.

KIT PIERSON: Their argument in a nutshell was that basically both the cable operators and the programmers had a First Amendment right to essentially [decide] what programming they wanted. They argued that there was a scarcity of cable channels and they shouldn't be forced to use a limited platform of speech to carry speech they didn't want to carry. Their other primary argument was that if local broadcast stations were popular, they were going to get carried, and if they weren't popular they probably shouldn't be carried. So there's a market argument.

JIM POPHAM: It's hard to compare or contrast this with other cases because in so many ways it was unique being, in a sense, a facial challenge to the statute. The record, as such, was the record in Congress. And then the district court had opened that up to look at subsequent evidence to confirm what Congress had found. There was a great element of fact-finding that went on. There was a great deal of discovery and document production and review, all of which ended up in massive motions for summary judgment on both sides. And ultimately in the district court in both cases, it was decided on summary judgment without trials, which just would have been a nightmare. I think it's a fairly unique case in that there was a tremendous amount of gathering of facts that had already been gathered by Congress. There was one lawyer who was a partner at Jenner & Block whose job it was to pull together and organize everything that had been before Congress.

DON VERRILLI: As the case evolved, one of my partners, Kit Pierson, who's now a lawyer over at Heller Ehrman, handled the factual development. He came in after the first Supreme Court decision in *Turner I*, when we went back to the district court for that massive factual proceeding. Prior to that, that case had been done on an expedited basis. There were factual submissions and affidavits and what not, but we all thought of it as principally a legal case the first time around. It was only after the first of the two Supreme Court decisions that the need for large-scale factual development was required.

KIT PIERSON: My job on the case was to deal with two aspects of it. First, we've got this congressional record. Does it provide reasonable support for the conclusions Congress reached? And secondly, because there was this *massive* discovery undertaken after *Turner I*—really roll-out-the-tanks discovery—principally by the cable industry to try to prove that this statute was unjustified. My job in this case was to focus on those factual aspects of it.

JIM POPHAM: It was a *huge* undertaking because you're trying to file a brief citing boxes and boxes of records that were before Congress plus all the other additional depositions and the document production that had developed subsequent to that at the district court level. I think it was very different from an appeal of an FCC rule where you have an administrative record and that's about it. The thing that stood out in this was that there was so much gathering and organizing of a factual record, which was critical to our case.

MARK LYNCH: The case got a lot more difficult to handle later on. An enormous record was mustered to demonstrate that there was a sound basis for Congress' findings. In fact, there were dangers to the viability to a public broadcast system if cable operators were free to exclude broadcast stations.

IN THE COURTS

DON VERRILLI: In the first of the two *Turner* arguments, [the broadcast intervenors] did not get argument time. The government argued it exclusively. That first time around, we thought the more liberal Justices would favor our position because it was one where it seemed like a valid and attractive public policy. Property rights conservatives would be more hostile to it. So the goal there was to figure out how to appeal to the middle of the Court—Justice O'Connor and Justice Kennedy, in particular. We weren't clear exactly how we were going to do that, but we relied a great deal on O'Connor and Kennedy opinions about standard of review to try to show them that we were engaged with their jurisprudence, took it very seriously, and thought based on the way they thought that intermediate scrutiny ought to apply here. Now we had to feed all of that through the Solicitor General who argued the case the first time around. The second time around, the key thing was that Justice Breyer had replaced Justice Blackmun, who had voted with us. In *Turner I* they didn't give us the whole thing. They gave us the standard of review but said, "You've got to prove your case now."

NORY MILLER: [In *Turner I*, the government argued a theory based on the *Red Lion* decision that said the government has more leeway for regulating broadcasting because there is only a limited amount of spectrum available for broadcast, and tried to argue that the government had extra leeway here as well—an argument with which we did not agree and which we did not argue. That argument was just destroyed by some of the Justices. It was actually painful to watch. There were minutes of dead silence. Our view, and our clients' view, was that *Red Lion* itself is likely to be overturned the next time the doctrine is reviewed by the Court. And that it should apply in this context made no sense to us.

JIM POPHAM: Breyer was the new Justice on the Court. He was obviously going to be critical to this decision. I don't recall coming out of the courthouse with any feel one way of the other with as to how he was going to go on it.

KIT PIERSON: [Breyer], of course, was key, a real wild card. It was very unclear how he was going to vote. He was the key Justice. He was new on the Court and he was politically ambiguous.

JIM POPHAM: Our concern was very basic. We always believed that broadcasting is embued with public interest obligations and does serve the public in unique ways, and all stations deserved the chance. That was the other aspect of it which I don't think Breyer bought into, and that was the anti-competitive aspect of it. Cable systems, by virtue of their vertical integration and other economic incentives, were excluding stations.

MARK LYNCH: I certainly recall that everyone thought that there are Justices that on any close case are going to be key. O'Connor is going to be key, and Kennedy is going to be key. And Ginsburg would be key.

DON VERRILLI: We knew there were some doubts, but we thought we had done a good enough evidentiary job that we could prevail on the evidence with the four Justices who were there before. But we didn't know what Justice Breyer would do because he wasn't there before. So the whole case turned on trying to make sure we could get his vote. With respect to that, we studied his First Amendment and constitutional law jurisprudence from his Court of Appeals days and his tenure up to that point on the Supreme Court. We did so very, very vigorously and we recognized something that has now emerged more clearly. He is a person who weighs interests. It was important, we thought, to make him see that there were constitutional values on both sides of the equation—in other words, that this statute promoted First Amendment rights because it preserved the diversity of media options and viewpoints for households that didn't have cable. At the same time, we were less optimistic about our ability to convince him that the Cable Act was a valid piece of industry-specific antitrust legislation, as opposed to legislation that enhanced the diversity of viewpoints. Of all the members of the Court, Justice Breyer has perhaps the strongest engagement historically on antitrust law. He has a powerful mind on these subjects. He's something of a skeptic about aggressive antitrust enforcement. So we thought we weren't going to get very far if we pushed this statute as an antitrust statute. So we really focused on a statute that preserved the multiplicity of programming options for noncable households. Justice Breyer is also very, very sensitive to the specifics of the record and to context. So we were very well prepared on that. As oral argument turned out, it didn't go that way. The petitioners realized that the way to make their argument most attractive to Justice Breyer was to hammer on the fact that this didn't make any sense as a piece of antitrust legislation. The government argued effectively and we had 10 minutes, and moved decisively away from this point about it being antitrust legislation and hammered our theme about it being a statute to preserve options for noncable households. Toward the end of the argument, Justice Breyer leaned in and asked questions that were evidence-focused—"What's your proof of A, B, and C?"—and Ennis was very well prepared and rattled off several key points, and Breyer seemed satisfied.

JIM POPHAM: By the time we had reached *Turner II*—and, indeed, part of the way through *Turner I*—we knew that Bruce [Ennis] would do a really fine job. We were confident that he could explain what was going on as well as we could, and that's a very rare statement for me to make (laughs). Most of the time I've sat in arguments and hearings in the past and I've thought, "I can answer that better than that." This was a case where I was confident that would not be the case. He had an enormous grasp of a substantial record and understood the nuances and understood how to deal with the arguments that had superficial appeal on the cable side—which, when all is said and done, really didn't have much appeal.

KIT PIERSON: [Bruce Ennis] had a strikingly deep voice—a baritone voice. And that was relevant to his lawyering because when he would start speaking in a courtroom—and I remember this from the *Turner* case—when he would start speaking, his voice had an ability to fill up a room. It was unlike any voice I had ever heard. It was really striking. It was striking in the *Turner* case in the D.C. Circuit that he would just silence an audience with the first five or ten words that he uttered. He had this rich, deep, unusual voice and a lot of brilliance behind it. It was a silencer. He did a brilliant job in front of the D.C. Circuit. I actually have a clearer recollection of the D.C. Circuit argument than the Supreme Court argument. In the D.C. Circuit argument, the government's lawyer had really been very aggressively questioned by Judge Williams who was skeptical of our position and ultimately dissented. When Bruce got up to speak after this very tough cross-examination of the government's lawyer, Bruce really took the issues head on and was extremely effective. I don't know ultimately how much difference it made because we lost Judge Williams. But that is one thing that I'll always remember about Bruce is that after this very difficult exchange right before he got up, just taking the issues head on and doing a superb job.

DON VERRILLI: I worked with Bruce for many, many years—from the mid-1980s until his death—and on many of his most important cases in the Supreme Court. He was one of the absolute premier Supreme Court advocates of this past generation. His loss is enormous. *Turner* was one case in which I thought Bruce's oral advocacy skills, which were his particular strength—his courtroom arguments were of enormous importance. I recall one in particular—not in the Supreme Court, but in front of the three-judge trial court that heard the case on remand after the first Supreme Court decision. The panel consisted of Judges Jackson and Sporkin from the district court and Judge Williams. On remand there was basically the better part of the day set aside for oral arguments. There were a lot of real legal heavyweights in the case. Judge Williams was extremely hostile to our position, and in the remand argument in particular became extremely aggressive in attacking our position and in attacking every one of its suppositions and attacking our views about the evidence. The other side had fared very, very well and got a very sympathetic ear from Judge Williams. The government lawyer got up and did a very fine job, but Judge Williams was just absolutely relentless and devastating with his questions. Bruce had the amazing ability which was a combination of his physical traits—his stature and posture and the deep tone of his voice—and his extraordinarily quick and incisive mind. The momentum was running so strongly against us, and he just stood up and stopped it dead. It was just a remarkable thing. He was up there for about 40 minutes. He stood up to Judge Williams, he backed him down, and I really think that the whole thing turned right at that moment. The force of Bruce's advocacy, the force of his personality, the force of his mind turned the thing right at that point. Of course, we didn't get Judge Williams' vote, but I think it was Bruce's ability to have the courage of his convictions and show the strength of his case and to be able to answer every brutally tough question that Judge Williams asked that I'm quite confident had a strong effect on Judges Sporkin and Jackson in helping us get their votes. I did think that was the key moment.

KIT PIERSON: Everyone at the Supreme Court level did a very good job. It was several skilled and experienced Supreme Court advocates. What I remember of the Supreme Court argument is that it was very unclear how it had gone after the argument. In fact, I know from talking to the other side that they thought they were going to win. We felt that we had the better side of the argument and felt that we should win, but we were quite uncertain afterward. The Court was clearly struggling with it. The cable industry was quite confident after the argument, and I think that the view on our side was that they were overconfident and that the Court was really grappling with the issues and it was very unclear which way it was going to come out.

DON VERRILLI: There's a dynamic sometimes in oral argument that you can't pick up on paper where it's not just the questions, it's the emotional flow back and forth between the judge and the advocate. That was one where there was force coming from Breyer—not hostility, because I think Breyer is really superb on the bench of not being aggressive or hostile to any point of view. He asks tough questions and he can be insistent about getting answers, but without engaging in advocacy himself. He was doing that, and he was being quite forceful about it. And Ennis was quite forceful and precise and had specific record cites, and you could see Breyer nodding his head, sitting back in his chair and writing down the record cites that Ennis was giving him. We actually took some encouragement from that that our message had gotten through and he was going to go look at what we had claimed about the record and we were confident that when he did we could back up what we were saying.

Did you perceive that this was a tough case for the Court?

MARK LYNCH: Oh, yeah! I don't think anybody doubted that this was a tough case that could have gone in any number of directions. First of all, the Court's First Amendment jurisprudence is sufficiently diffused so you're never quite sure how anything is going to come out. Certainly the argument that this was a *Tornillo*-type restriction on the press was not without some force. There were good counterarguments. It was an argument that had to be reckoned with.

JIM POPHAM: I think [the attorneys on the other side] were so sure they were going to win all the time, because they were so sure they were right and they'd won before. They could just not conceive the possibility of losing and they never quite appreciated what broadcasters were saying. There was one lawyer, Joe Klein, who became the head of the antitrust division later in the Clinton Administration, who was in the firm that was representing NCTA [National Cable Television Association] in the early phases of the *Turner* litigation. I thought he was one of the few lawyers who had an objective grasp of the arguments and was probably their most effective advocate. I told him that once. And he said, "I didn't care one way or the other about must carry. I didn't have an ax to grind one way or the other. I was just looking at the case and trying to represent my client." I thought he was very effective because of that. When he left to go to the Justice Department, they lost that and the arrogance that had characterized their prosecution of the case just took over again completely. I think it hurt them. The cable industry was considered arrogant by Congress, and that's why Congress slapped them down. It was incredible that that was one of the few vetoes that Congress overrode in passing that legislation. But that bill—because the world had turned so against cable—took on a life of its own. It made lobbying on our side a lot easier. Our tensest moments were seeing whether the veto would be sustained. It was close. And then hanging on for two 5-to-4 victories in the Court.

KIT PIERSON: I don't know if it was arrogance. It was something I've seen before. I think they felt that the argument went well for them. Supreme Court arguments are interesting and one of comments that I remember Bruce telling me on more than one occasion was that you've got to be very careful into reading too much into what happens at the argument. The nature of the questioning made the cable industry quite confident. They thought questioning really favored them. I think on our side there was some nervousness that we were being pushed on some issues. But I remember thinking at the time that the case—I really felt, and I know the cable industry felt the opposite way—I felt that we should win the case, that we were right on the law and the facts. And I felt that as the Court dug into the record, that while there had been some tough questioning, ultimately we were right and that the Court was likely to decide it that way. But it was very close and could go either way. I would not have described them as arrogant. I would describe them as confident and, given the way the questioning went—I've seen that in other cases where people get confident because of the tenor of the argument and end up losing.

MARK LYNCH: I don't know whether [our adversaries] were overconfident. They certainly had grounds for some confidence because there had been two D.C. Circuit opinions that overturned the FCC rules, and had done so on the basis of strict scrutiny. It always seemed to me that it would be a much more difficult case for them to get an act of Congress struck down than an FCC rule. They certainly had some grounds for optimism or confidence. I'm not sure I can say they were overconfident. But they had a couple of decisions that were in their favor.

JIM POPHAM: The attorneys who had been so caught up in this, particularly on the cable side, and had embraced and had been enthusiastic about the cause, lost their objectivity. I think the cable industry thought, "Look, we're carrying most of the stations most of the time. Nobody is really going to care about these little stations out on the fringe." I think we were able to fashion an argument that said, "No, what's at stake here is not just most of broadcasting, but what Congress wanted to do was to assure that all of broadcasting had the opportunity to provide service and to compete." I think that was a great part of the case. It was a part of the decision where the Court was saying that Congress was not just trying to preserve a group of stations. It was trying to preserve the whole system of allocation that the Commission had adopted. I think attorneys have to believe in their clients' cause, but I think you have to be very objective about the merits of the arguments on the other side so you can deal with them most effectively. If you're arrogant and just try to dismiss them out of hand, eventually it can come back to hurt you.

What is it like waiting for the ruling, and then hearing about the ruling.

MARK LYNCH: I've been at this business for about 25 years. I've been involved in some cases at the Supreme Court, and I've gotten to the point where I've just got too many other things to do than to let yourself be consumed by waiting for a decision. *Turner I* was probably the one we were most surprised about. Once that framework had been established, there was probably less concern over *Turner II*—not to say that anybody thought that *Turner II* was a slam dunk. As I recall, the argument went better in *Turner II*. The framework had been set and made it more favorable for us. But *Turner I* was the one that was very close, could have gone either way, and we were quite happily surprised. Whenever you get into June and you're still waiting for an opinion, you know it's probably got the Court divided and they're probably going back and forth. The sense of anticipation does mount once you get on into June.

JACK GOODMAN: The day the second decision came out, and we had won, it was an incredible, exhilarating moment—particularly given the fact that I had been working on must carry off and on for 17 years, and we had been working consistently at that point for more than seven years on must carry issues and defending this. So it was a great moment.

KIT PIERSON: The ultimate ruling was fact-based. Five Justices rejected the notion that this was content-based regulation. I guess it's fair to say that they said this is a permissible form of regulation if there's an adequate factual predicate for it, or that a substantial basis for Congress to reach the conclusion that it did. The message of that is to marshal your facts, and if there's an adequate factual basis and the burdens imposed by the statute are not completely disproportionate to the benefit that Congress was trying to achieve, the *Turner* case provided a reasonable legal framework for upholding regulation of that kind. If you had a weaker factual record, obviously you'd get a very different argument from the cable industry.

NORY MILLER: The dissenters had a number of concerns, but I thought the concern that had the most resonance was based on the fact that broadcast regulations had been subjected to a different scrutiny so that there is a little more leeway for the government to do content-based regulation of broadcast programming that it cannot do with the programming produced by cable networks. There was some concern that this situation indicated some actual preference for broadcast programming over cable network programming based on the content of the programming. But the majority decided that there really was not a basis to suspect that this was Congress' motive. The majority also noted that there weren't ostensible differences between broadcast and cable programming as categories in terms of subject matter or point of view. Which is why the majority decided that the must carry rules were not the type of government interference that the First Amendment was intended to prevent.

DON VERRILLI: I will say that all of us came out of oral argument very glum about our prospects for winning. The other side seemed to do much better than we did. We got beat up pretty badly. There was a fair amount of skepticism, a little coming even from Justice Breyer. And that happened even in *Turner I*. It happened both times that we got beat up in oral argument and thought things went poorly, and ended up prevailing. So it is a good object lesson in not over-reading the signals you get from oral argument.

MARK LYNCH: We were surprised to win either one of them (laughs). We didn't think that the arguments went that well. I can't remember how everybody was counting the votes. I think we were very happily surprised both times around.

Citing 18 months of factual development that yielded a record of "tens of thousands of pages," Justice Anthony Kennedy's opinion for the Supreme Court affirmed the district court's finding for the government and broadcast interests. That court had held must carry is narrowly tailored to promote the government's legitimate interests, and that must carry's effects on cable operators are minimal. The Supreme Court accepted not only the arguments that the must carry provisions are content-neutral, but also the claim that they serve three important government interests: (a) preserving the benefits of free, over-the-air local broadcast television, (b) promoting the widespread dissemination of information from a multiplicity of sources, and (c) promoting fair competition in the market for television programming. Moreover, the Court said it owed Congress' findings deference in part because that institution "is far better equipped than the judiciary to amass and evaluate the vast amounts of data bearing upon legislative questions" (see Court opinion excerpts at chapter's conclusion).

AFTERMATH & LEGACY

KIT PIERSON: I thought it was a *really* important case, and for a lot of reasons. I do think this question about the First

Amendment and letting free markets operate versus Congress intervening to try to protect the interests of noncable households was a really significant issue, and a really hard issue. The fact that the case went up to the Supreme Court twice and they were both 5-to-4 decisions is a reflection of how hard that issue is.

NORY MILLER: There is a major effort on the part of some businesses and some prominent conservatives to use the First Amendment for economic gain, to protect against economic regulation rather than to protect against government censorship, which is a real perversion of the First Amendment. I think *Turner* was probably the first big case where we saw that happen. But we've seen a lot more. I think this was an important moment. I think it was important that the Court turned it back and that the majority of the Justices kept their eyes focused on what the First Amendment is *really* there to prevent, what the real concerns are. To me, that's the significance of this case. I think it's very important when dealing with the First Amendment, or any of the Bill of Rights or any constitutional provision, to ask, "What is the point of it? What is the worry that made people adopt it?" and to stay very focused on that. If you just apply little doctrinal phrases that were attempts to provide lines in the sand in other contexts, the results get very twisted. I thought it was really a shining moment for the Court to keep its eye very firmly on what threatens First Amendment values and what doesn't.

JACK GOODMAN: Within the field of the First Amendment and communications regulation, yes, this is a landmark case. Certainly for the role of government regulation of media interests, yes, *Turner* is very significant.

DON VERRILLI: I think some cases you know at the moment they're occurring that they're landmark cases. Some cases you only know afterwards. This was more in the latter category. In *Turner*, we knew it was a very, very serious case. It was of great importance to very important industries in the economy. It was a very important case about the government's power and how it would be reviewed. And there were a bunch of really great lawyers working on it, so it was a very big, important case. It wasn't clear that it would be a landmark case at the time. I think it has emerged as a case of extreme importance.

KIT PIERSON: One of the interesting questions posed by the case was, "When you've got this massive record that was developed in front of Congress, to what extent can that record be displaced or supplemented by discovery between the economic powers that are involved, and to some extent the government which also brought resources to the discovery table?" Our position in the case was if the record before Congress was sufficient to justify what it did—the fact that several years later the cable industry could marshal its resources and develop a lot of facts that, for whatever reason it chose not to present to Congress when the matter was before Congress—that the statute can be sustained based on the record that was in front of Congress. That's an issue that I don't think the Court really resolved.

DON VERRILLI: It is probably the most important case the Court has rendered on the question of First Amendment standard of review in a long time. Virtually every First Amendment case that I do now, we're talking about *Turner* in one way or another. That's a sign of its importance. Lots and lots of First Amendment cases are that way. I think it's had a great deal of importance, and the importance it's had is in directing the standard of review that courts should apply in First Amendment cases. What's interesting and in some respects gratifying to me as a lawyer is when we first parachuted into the case in the Fall of 1992, that's what we thought it was all about and we spent all of our energy and efforts in those first couple of months trying to get that standard of review question figured out.

KIT PIERSON: I do think the distributional aspect that was at issue and how Congress intervened to protect it is quite interesting. What the cable industry argued was that there were more [broadcast] networks than there were 20 years ago. We now have four or five. UPN had become a network in the course of the case. The cable industry argued, "All these noncable households that you're worrying about are better off now than they were 20 years ago." In some ways the way to view it, and what was happening in the television marketplace, was that you have a curve of cable households which is exponentially rising in terms of the number of viewing options. For noncable households, you've got a curve that was, at best, slowly rising.

The gap between those two curves was growing larger and larger. Part of what Congress was trying to deal with was to make sure that balance didn't get too completely out of whack.

JIM POPHAM: Certainly from where I was sitting at the time, it was the landmark of landmarks (laughs). I think stepping back a little bit and looking at it in the greater scheme of First Amendment jurisprudence, I think that may be a stretch. The facts are unique in a number of ways. I don't know that it has enormous precedential value or might be considered a landmark in a broader perspective. I guess the one thing that may stand out in the case is the issue of how much deference does the Court owe to Congress? I think that if you look at the breadth and depth of the record that was before Congress, and that was later corroborated and substantiated by the subsequent evidence, I think in that sense the case was truly unprecedented. I don't think that a record that strong in support of the statute and evidence that broad and deep subsequent to the statute to confirm what Congress had found—I'm not familiar with any case that has had that depth of factual inquiry. If that case could be read to suggest that in order to prevail, for Congress to convince the Court that it has made a rational decision on substantial evidence, that's an awfully high bar. I'm not sure you can read it to say that. It's pretty clear, though, that if this case wasn't going to clear the bar, no case was going to clear the bar. Again, the amount of the record generated in Congress and the trial court record were all just so incredibly substantial that if that record had not been adequate, I don't know how you could ever have a record that would be adequate.

KIT PIERSON: The other aspect of the case that really did interest me is the aspect of, in the First Amendment context, where Congress has taken a really hard look at a problem and ultimately the constitutionality—at least in the eyes of five Justices—turns on certain factual questions: What degree of deference do you or don't you afford to that congressional record? I thought that was really significant.

Throughout the Supreme Court opinion in Turner, *you see expressed a deference toward Congress and its findings. That seems as being a little out of*

the ordinary, particularly when you look at some other cases such as Reno
v. ACLU *where the Court picked apart a measure that Congress had passed.
Yet here, the Court seemed reluctant to do so.*

In *Reno v. ACLU,* 521 U.S. 844 (1997), the U.S. Supreme Court upheld
a ruling that critically examined a Congressional act—the
Communcations Decency Act—and ruled it to be in violation of the First
Amendment in part because it was a "content-based blanket restriction on
speech." See chapter 10 for a more thorough analysis of *Reno v. ACLU.*

JACK GOODMAN: You're absolutely right. The Court is not 100% consistent here. There are cases where a congressional en-
actment essentially got treated as trash by the
Supreme Court. That was an enactment that was
made virtually without hearings, virtually without consideration, and where there were significant constitutional issues raised that were simply brushed aside. In
ACLU v. Reno, involving the online Internet regulation,
again Congress brushed aside constitutional objections
and basically said, "We don't care. We want this."
When Congress acts that way, it gets very little deference. In this case, the consideration that Congress
gave [the measure] stands in remarkable difference to
that. Several observers have said that for the '92
Cable Act, this may be the best legislative record of
any act that Congress has ever passed. In terms of
the volume of material and the careful analysis that
went into the committee reports, it is absolutely unusual if not unique. When Congress does that—in other
words, when Congress says, "We're going to look very
carefully at this, we're *very* concerned about these
constitutional questions, we've assembled a record
which gives us a strong reason to believe in these determinations, and we've carefully weighed these constitutional concerns, and this is our judgment"—then I
think the Court is willing to give the Congress great
deference.

DON VERRILLI: I think it's fair to say the Court is not entirely consistent. But the standard of review issue and the defer-
ence issue are all bound up together. If the Court
decides to apply strict scrutiny, what it's saying is,
"We're really suspicious about this statute. You're directly trying to restrict speech because you don't like

it, and you better have a darn good reason for it, and
you're going to have to really prove it to us." If the
Court opts for intermediate scrutiny, it's saying
something different. It's saying, "We're not really
suspicious based on what we see on the face of this
statute. You're not trying to suppress speech or
change the public debate. But this statute is going to
have some significant effects on speech and speech
rights. And so we're going to give it a hard look. But
because we're in the realm where we're not as suspicious, we're going to do what we normally do as a
Court, which is extend a significant measure of deference to the superiority of the legislature as a
fact-finding and policymaking body." So that's the difference. I think your point is still a good one in that
even in intermediate scrutiny, the Court can vary in
the degree of vigor or deference it employs in looking
at legislative judgments.

KIT PIERSON: You look at a case like the *Reno* case, and my sense is
the record of hard facts that were behind congressio-
nal action was pretty thin compared to the massive
record developed in the must carry case over a period
of 7-to-10 years. I'm not saying that reasonable people can't look at that record and reach different conclusions. In fact, I think reasonable people *could* look
at that record and reach different conclusions. The
question becomes "What's the role for the Court in a
situation like that where you've got a massive amount
of evidence pointing in competing directions, and
where Congress looked at the same record and made
certain factual findings?" What a majority of the
Court ultimately decided was in those circumstances,
the record supporting the legislative judgments was
substantial enough that the Court was not going to
second-guess what Congress had decided.

NORY MILLER: *Reno v. ACLU* was very different than *Turner*. The regulation that *Reno v. ACLU* overturned restricted a lot
of speech when that restriction in no way furthered
what Congress was trying to do. Congress said, "This
is our one concern," and then restricted *enormous*
amounts of speech that weren't relevant to that concern. That is not the case here. Any station that
thinks the local cable company would like to carry it,
and would be willing to pay for the privilege, is going to
choose to follow the retransmission consent provi-

sions. The stations that are choosing must carry are literally the very ones that would not be carried if the statute had not been passed. So you have a very, very close relationship between the means chosen and the purposes that Congress was attempting to achieve. Whereas in *Reno v. ACLU*, you have a huge disparity, and it is a disparity that is restricting speech and restricting access to speech. When Congress uses a very broad bludgeon-like regulation to solve a narrow problem, you're going to have courts be very suspicious. And I think that's as it should be.

JIM POPHAM: I don't think the record in *Reno* was nearly as substantial or compelling as the record in the must carry case. I don't have the depth of familiarity with that case that I do with *Turner* obviously, but I just think the development of this record in Congress was so substantial and so significant, and then to have a district court develop a corroborative record essentially proving out what Congress had predicted and substantiated what Congress believed based on the record before—it's unique.

MARK LYNCH: One thing that was really quite extraordinary about this case was the mandate to have the lower courts assess whether there was a basis for Congress' factual findings. That struck me as a really extraordinary position that, if applied in other cases, could perhaps qualify this for landmark status on the doctrinal level. The idea that you could have cases coming along where courts are regularly, in effect, retrying whatever it is that Congress has found in a particular statute, that is just an incredible idea. There are a lot of cases that say Congress doesn't even need to make findings. All validly enacted legislation doesn't require findings. Scalia pounds that drum a lot. I'm not sure I would put this case in the category of those that represent excessive deference to Congress. The proceedings that the Court required on remand were really quite extraordinary. I had never been involved in anything like that before—having to go through and recreate a factual record to see whether Congress got it right.

KIT PIERSON: I think one of the interesting issues posed by the case is, "To what extent do you defer to Congress' factual determinations in a situation like this?" I don't remember how many sets of hearings had been held—

both by administrative agencies and by Congress—
but there were multiple investigations of this problem
both administratively and by Congress over what were
very empirical questions. This was the part of the
case that was near and dear to my heart. I essentially
had read the entire record before Congress, and it
was enormous. I think to some extent, the cable industry made a much greater empirical showing in the
courts than I think they did in front of Congress. They
marshaled a lot of evidence that they hadn't presented to Congress. But Congress had a tremendous
record on very complex factual decisions in which
there were really disputed views. A lot of these empirical questions are clearly areas where the administrative agency involved and Congress are in a better
position to make factual judgments than a court. The
question was, "What deference does the Court owe
to congressional factual determinations when they're
based on an enormous volume of testimony, and tens
of thousands of pages of material?" I suspect that's
an argument over which reasonable minds can disagree. Certainly, in the First Amendment context, the
Court has some obligation to take a look at those issues. And *Turner I* said, "Yeah, there was some need
to do that." On the other hand, by the time the case
got to the Court in *Turner II*, you had this enormous
record that had been in front of Congress, and then a
record of almost equal size that had been developed in
the course of litigation with two of the three judges
deciding that that record supported Congress', and
what was the Supreme Court to decide to do with
that? There are limits to the Supreme Court's ability—
or any court's ability—to parse a record like that and
second-guess the decisions which Congress made
which, I think, were certainly supported by the record
in front of them. People could look at that record and
reach different factual conclusions, but I think it would
be hard to argue that a reasonable person could not
reach the same conclusion that Congress reached.

NORY MILLER: The deference [the Supreme Court was] showing was
to Congress' ability to gather facts, and to its proper
legislative role in interpreting those facts and, especially, making predictions about the future. This is a
complicated industry; it's changing quickly; and courts
do not have the power or the ability to simply substi-

tute their own fact-gathering and predictions as if they were in charge of legislating. Courts have always shown a great deal of deference to legislatures and even to agencies whose power to adopt regulations is generally delegated by a legislature. The Supreme Court has long held that it must show deference to Congress' predictions and determinations. When the Court has been less deferential it is generally because it suspects a legislature of attempting to do something that is not legitimate, or because the legislature is trying to hit a nail with a sledgehammer, or because there's virtually no legislative record or other basis to understand what the legislature was thinking. Here Congress explained what it was trying to do and why and, although Congress doesn't have to make a record, there was a *huge* record; Congress studied these issues for years. Of course people are going to disagree about what is going to happen, and what should happen. But I don't think you'd find a lot of cases where the Court will second-guess those types of legislative judgments.

Do you agree with one analyst who wrote about Turner, *"This sets a dangerous precedent in granting Congress wide latitude in setting parameters in determining public discourse."*

JIM POPHAM: I think that's an overstatement. This involved competition between two competing media, and whether one of them could essentially put part of the other one out of business. We always looked at it more as an economic regulation matter than a freedom of expression matter, although obviously it had to be analyzed in constitutional terms. The practical side of it was basic economic regulation in an attempt to preserve competition and at the same time preserve a multitude of voices.

Bottom line, what was really at issue here?

JIM POPHAM: From a practical standpoint, what was at stake was the survival of some number of television stations. That's the very practical import, because had the rule been thrown out, there are stations that would have been dropped, and those stations would not have survived. You just can't do it without access to a majority of the local audience. From a legal perspective, I think it does show that the Court is still sensitive to the service that broadcasting provides. I think it will be interesting to see how influential the *Turner* precedent is and how much of a framework it has established for evaluating similar rules applicable to satellite carriers. I think the *Turner* case does establish a framework for that which, from the broadcasting perspective, has got to be good.

MARK LYNCH: There would have been a lot of public broadcasting stations dropped. There's no doubt there would have been a lot of injury to a lot of public television stations. Maybe not the biggest ones, maybe WGBH or WETA—some of the flagship stations. But a lot of public television stations would have been dropped. It was *very* crucial to them that we kept them on the air during the period of time that this legislation was being challenged in the courts. If, for example, the lower courts had invalidated the statute and we had not been able to get a stay, or if the broadcasters and programmers had gotten an injunction pending appeal and the public television stations had been kept off the air, no doubt in my mind that a number of them would have failed.

DON VERRILLI: Bottom line, I'm a big believer in the correctness of *Turner* and the correctness of the Supreme Court's judgment. As a litigator, it's impossible to separate yourself out from the positions you advocate. I understand that. Fundamentally, the Cable Act at issue in *Turner* was just not like a statute—like the Internet statute at issue in *ACLU v. Reno*—or other direct efforts to restrict speech or change the content of public debate. It wasn't that. It was something else. It does seem right to me that Congress really ought to have some leeway to engage in structural marketplace kind of regulation—even of industries that transmit expression—because if Congress doesn't have that power, then the interests of substantial segments of the population—in that case, households generally that weren't able to afford cable—can be sacrificed. The Court really got the balance right in *Turner*. It said this really isn't like a statute that aims to suppress speech, and we're not going to treat it like one. On the other hand, it is one that could have significant effects and we're not going to give it a free pass. We're going to give it a hard look. That seemed to me to be exactly the right way to approach this.

Would this case be decided similarly today given technological advancements such as digital compression and fiber optics?

JACK GOODMAN: To a large extent that makes our case easier. The burden of must carry, which was always low, has gone lower and lower and lower. We have figures that indicate that the average cable system in 1993 had to devote about 14.3% of its channel capacity to carrying local commercial television stations. That number now is a fraction of that because cable capacity has gone up and up and up, and while there are more broadcast stations, too, the growth curve is *vastly* smaller compared to the growth curve of cable capacity.

JIM POPHAM: I'm inclined to say no. I think the day may come when it will be. I think today the answer is no. If we're 10 years down the road from now and we have video on the Internet as commonplace, then I think the world is very different than it is now. But at this point we have a Court that is pretty much the same now as it was then. The more interesting question will be what will congressional attitudes be. [In late 2000] we were beginning to see some shift away from the continuing embrace of must carry. There was beginning in some quarters to be a view that the world has become so competitive now that we don't really need it—in particular, that satellite would be truly competitive with cable. The irony there may be that satellite would be competitive with cable if it was subject to must carry and had to do the same thing that cable did. Otherwise, I'm not sure satellite truly is directly competitive with cable. I think it's a little early to say that the world is that different, but it's going to be different at some point.

KIT PIERSON: I don't know the answer to that. It cuts both ways. Cable channel capacity continues to increase, and I think it continues to increase a lot faster than the quality of cable programming. On the other hand, you do have this phenomenon of DTV being more of an option. I remember the cable industry arguing at the time that that created an incentive for the cable industry to carry any quality local programming because that was one of the ways they differentiated themselves from DTV. I don't think the record at the time of the must carry case provided significant support for that. Satellite TV just wasn't that widespread of a phenomenon. It didn't have that big a part of the market.

NORY MILLER: Of the technological changes in these industries since *Turner II*, the main one that would be relevant would be the enormous expansion of channel capacity by virtually every cable company. But all that does is make the case for the side that won even stronger, because it shows that cable companies have the capacity to carry broadcasters and lots of other programming, so the statute doesn't impose a serious burden. The growth of the satellite companies since *Turner* doesn't change anything. In the *Turner* cases, the Court recognized that cable operators have a bottleneck or gateway monopoly over the programming their subscribers see. A consumer's ability to choose between one cable company and one or two satellite companies doesn't change that situation. Once people become cable subscribers, their cable operators have a bottleneck or gateway monopoly over what they see. They still would not watch noncarried stations and therefore any stations cable operators could choose not to carry would lose them as potential viewers. The emergence of satellite TV does not change the ability of the marketplace to preserve free television for those who can't cough up $40 a month [for cable television] or have better uses for that money. That's a lot of money for television that is otherwise free. Many people in this country don't have that kind of disposable income, or have other responsibilities. So even though people who are able to pay for television may now have slightly more choice than in 1992, it doesn't change the basic calculus here which is, "What happens to people relying on broadcast television?"

DON VERRILLI: I think it would make the case easier. There really were two arguments that the cable companies put forward. One is a displacement argument—that this is unfair because it displaces cable programmers that other speakers get denied the opportunity to get their messages out through cable systems because there's a preference here that Congress has created for broadcasters. The less the capacity and the fewer the outlets, the more powerful that argument is. So the advancements in technology makes that argument weaker and weaker. The other argument is one that is independent of technology. It's the editorial discretion argument. It's an argument that goes like this: "Look, the cable system is our property. We're the speaker here. There's a fundamental premise that we get to say what we want to say." That, seems to me, to be independent of technology. You either accept that or you don't. So I'm not sure that technological developments would have had that much effect one way or another on that latter argument.

What do you think the legacy of this case will be?

DON VERRILLI: It remains to be seen because it was such a close decision. If it has a legacy, it will be one of creating legitimate space for a kind of structural regulation by Congress.

JIM POPHAM: As a practical matter, I think the legacy will be probably two or three broadcast networks that didn't exist. Legally, I think it will set up a framework of analysis that will be beneficial to arguments in favor of satellite must carry and whether it's constitutional, and the same with digital must carry. And I think there's a lesson in it, too, in that if you have a statute that you want to preserve against constitutional attack, you need to have a substantial record.

MARK LYNCH: The message is that if Congress amasses an enormous factual record, the Court is going to give some deference to that. For example—not that the two cases are parallel in very many ways—but if you compare this factor where there were *years* of hearings. This bill went through numerous iterations. I remember doing a footnote once for all the hearings, and it went on for about two pages. There was an *enormous* factual record. Congress really did think hard about this. Contrast that to the flag-burning case which was some amendment offered on the floor of the House with about 20 minutes of deliberation. I don't think the Court ever comes right out and says this is a case that Congress thought hard about, or this is a law that Congress didn't think hard about. But I can't help think that at some level that's got to make a difference. The message that this case sends is that if Congress thinks very hard about a problem and comes up with a solution that reflects First Amendment sensitivity, the Court is less likely to take an unbending approach to that legislation. Slapdash legislation impinging on First Amendment rights is more likely to get the back of the hand from the Court.

JACK GOODMAN: I think the legacy of this case is an acceptance and affirmation of the notion that Congress can and should prevent the misuse of monopoly positions even in speech industries. The cable industry continues to argue that any regulation of them is subject to very strict scrutiny. I think *Turner* stands squarely in opposition to that point.

NORY MILLER: I think it's a very important case in that it presented the Court with a different kind of problem to solve, and the Court focused on the real principles and concerns underlying the First Amendment. You have to figure out *how* you decide which rule should apply and you don't do it by looking at the external characteristics of the case. You get to the real core. So I think it's a very important case and an excellent example of how to think about a new and difficult statute, how to figure out what's at stake here and whether it is something that really raises First Amendment concerns.

PERSONAL REFLECTIONS

KIT PIERSON: One recollection is that as we were finishing the Supreme Court brief—pulling three consecutive all-nighters, which I had never done before in my life—I remember on the third day as we were working on the brief falling asleep with my eyes open as I was literally trying to type out my portion of the brief. And repeatedly falling asleep with my eyes open. It was a good example of how the case really pushed the limits of endurance.

NORY MILLER: [At one point] the Department of Justice attorney and I took the deposition of the opposition's main economic expert. The Department of Justice lawyer went first and I was going to come in with my questions afterwards. I had terrible bronchitis and had these racking coughs. But I had been on antibiotics for a couple of days so not only was I not contagious, I was not feeling as bad as I looked and sounded. I looked like I was not going to make it through the day. The [opposition] lawyer insisted that we finish the deposition that day, however late, rather than continue it the next day as is usually done. We were on an expedited discovery schedule and basically just wanted to get the deposition done. So we went ahead. I think he must have been counting on the fact that I did not look like I would be alive by the time I would be asking questions. So we went until about 8:00 or 9:00 that night. No dinner. No nothing. This was a government building and there wasn't any food available. As it became clear I was going to survive and the deposition would go late, the lawyer called his wife and arranged for her to tape "ER."

MARK LYNCH: There were a lot of high-quality briefs produced in a short amount of time under a lot of pressure. That was one thing that stands out in my mind. The three-judge court was a very interesting one because you had three very, very different judges. It was interesting to watch them interact with each other. I think the Supreme Court argument was interesting in that it was one of the best examples of how things can look pretty grim at argument and you can still win. Because things did look grim at the argument in *Turner I*. In *Turner II*, by the time we got back on remand, Time Warner had this huge juggernaut that was grinding through these discovery proceedings at an incredible pace with seemingly unlimited manpower. We were holding our own and protecting our clients' interests.

JIM POPHAM: The rumor at one point was that [Turner Broadcasting owner] Time Warner was spending $1 million a month on this case. They were deposing people right and left, they had a huge team of lawyers working on it. They were sparing no effort in this litigation. There was a lot of hard work and a lot of brainstorming that went on on our side, too, to come up with an answer to all the questions that the cable industry had provided. The other thing that stands out was the cable industry made some claims that, when all was said and done, they could not substantiate—in particular, the degree to which they were being asked to do something they were not already doing, or to carry stations they were not already carrying, the impact on them on the margin was really pretty slight. For an individual station it's life or death, but for a cable system to allocate one more channel out of 50 or 70 or whatever, the margin is a little different there. I think the trial court discovery and factual record that was developed in the trial court really smoked out a lot of the huffing and puffing that had gone on on the cable side.

NORY MILLER: We were out-manned by [opposition law firm] Cravath, Swaine & Moore by about a gazillion to one—close to four or five to one. It was amazing how many lawyers they had and how few we had. So the David winning over Goliath was especially fun. There were these armies of lawyers and mounds of paper coming at us all the time (laughs).

DON VERRILLI: It wouldn't be a moment [that stands out]. There wasn't a "Eureka!" moment, or there wasn't any great turn in the courtroom. It would be that first month or 6 weeks. That is something that I'm extremely proud of. We put so much effort into figuring out the right way to think about this case, and it took 5 years for it to come to fruition and finally be vindicated by the Court. It was based on our theory about protecting noncable households and that's something Congress may do consistent with the First Amendment. And then convincing our clients, our co-counsel, the government, and then the courts that that was the right way to do it was something of which I'm very proud.

JACK GOODMAN: In many ways, this was great for a lawyer, particularly a lawyer who has an interest in this sort of thing. This is an exhilarating thing to do, to work at this level. There were many late nights working on briefs and writing different drafts and working with the people at Jenner & Block who I think are some of the finest lawyers in the country. They're treasured memories for me because they were very valuable and creative times, and you really feel you're accomplishing something.

NORY MILLER: I think really the best part of it was the analysis. There were a lot of parties and lawyers involved. The government, of course—and the Solicitor General changed in the middle so there were different decision-makers with different views; and the organizations of PBS and other public stations, and we were representing the commercial stations through their organizations. Everybody had very different legal theories. It was hard-fought—not in a mean sense, but in a really serious sense—all the way through. I think it

was really a lawyers' victory, where the legal reasoning made a huge difference—not just the presentation, but the really high level, careful, imaginative
conceptualizing. The quality of the legal argument
matters in any case, but the basic facts and prevailing law are going to determine the result most of the
time. In this one, I really think conceptualizing the issues the way we did made the difference. And that
was very exciting.

KIT PIERSON: I remember having an incredibly good relationship with
everyone. It was interesting. There are a lot of big
egos involved in the practice of law. I remember a tremendous sense of collegiality both with the attorneys
on our side at Covington & Burling and at the government. We had a wonderful relationship with them. And
we actually had an unusually good relationship with
the attorneys on the other side. This case was unusual in my experience. I've worked on a lot of big,
complex, tough cases like this that are very fact-in-
tensive. I think all the attorneys on the case really
went through an incredible push after *Turner I*. The
case was put on a very expedited schedule. There was
a massive amount of discovery. It was just an incredibly difficult experience for everyone involved.

DON VERRILLI: [That collegiality was] very true about this case. The
lawyers representing the NCTA are and have been for
a long time good friends and we have a lot of affection
for them and extraordinary respect. [They] were terrific as adversaries. We knew this was a big, important case. It was an incredible amount of fun, and I
think everyone was enjoying being in it. This case had a
terrific amount of that spirit to it. It was a big, important, great, fascinating case. We were really enjoying
being a part of it.

KIT PIERSON: There was an attorney on the other side of the case
[by the name of Peter Kimm, Jr.] who died in the
course of the case—a midlevel attorney who was a
superb attorney for the cable industry and had poured
his heart into the case. He was killed in an automobile
accident, and he was a friend of mine. So my reaction
to the case was I felt that we should win, and I was
glad that we won, but on the other hand, this is the
last case [Peter] had worked on. He poured his heart
into it, cared deeply about it, and I had mixed emo-

tions for that reason. Obviously, I was glad we won, but on a personal level this case for me—this case was a bit of his legacy. So I had complicated emotions.

MARK LYNCH: That was very tragic. He was a very nice guy. That was a terrible, terrible thing.

KIT PIERSON: There was a juxtaposition of all these Washington attorneys working incredibly hard on this case that everyone cared a lot about, going in different directions. Then you had this emotionally jarring, terrible experience. It created a sense of collegiality and affection in a lot of ways for a lot of attorneys involved in the case on opposite sides. He was a fabulous attorney and a fabulous human being. For any attorney who worked on the case, it was a tragic series of events. When I remember this case, that's what I'll always remember about it, and in a very, very sad way.

***Turner Broadcasting System, Inc.,
et al., appellants v.
Federal Communications
Commission et al.***

**SUPREME COURT
OF THE UNITED STATES**

520 U.S. 180
Argued: October 7, 1996
Decided: March 31, 1997

PRIOR HISTORY: ON APPEAL
FROM THE UNITED STATES DIS-
TRICT COURT FOR THE DIS-
TRICT OF COLUMBIA.

COUNSEL: H. Bartow Farr, III argued the cause for appellants.

Walter Dellinger argued the cause for
federal appellees.

Bruce J. Ennis, Jr. argued the cause
for private appellees.

JUDGES: KENNEDY, J., announced
the judgment of the Court and delivered the opinion of the Court, except
as to a portion of Part II-A-1.
REHNQUIST, C. J., and STEVENS
and SOUTER, JJ., joined that opinion in full, and BREYER, J., joined
except insofar as Part II-A-1 relied on
an anticompetitive rationale. STE-
VENS, J., filed a concurring opinion.
BREYER, J., filed an opinion concurring in part. O'CONNOR, J., filed

a dissenting opinion, in which
SCALIA, THOMAS, and
GINSBURG, JJ., joined.

OPINION: JUSTICE KENNEDY
delivered the opinion of the Court,
except as to a portion of Part II-A-1.

Sections 4 and 5 of the Cable Television Consumer Protection and
Competition Act of 1992 require
cable television systems to dedicate
some of their channels to local broadcast television stations. Earlier in this
case, we held the so-called "must-
carry" provisions to be content-neutral restrictions on speech, subject to
intermediate First Amendment scrutiny under *United States v. O'Brien*,
391 U.S. 367, 377, 20 L. Ed. 2d 672,
88 S. Ct. 1673 (1968). A plurality of
the Court considered the record as
then developed insufficient to determine whether the provisions were
narrowly tailored to further important governmental interests, and we
remanded the case to the District
Court for the District of Columbia for
additional factfinding.

On appeal from the District
Court's grant of summary judgment
for appellees, the case now presents
the two questions left open during the
first appeal: First, whether the record
as it now stands supports Congress'
predictive judgment that the must-
carry provisions further important
governmental interests; and second,

whether the provisions do not burden substantially more speech than necessary to further those interests. We answer both questions in the affirmative, and conclude the must-carry provisions are consistent with the First Amendment.

...

The three-judge District Court, in a divided opinion, granted summary judgment for the Government and intervenor-defendants. A majority of the court sustained the must-carry provisions under the intermediate standard of scrutiny set forth in *United States v. O'Brien*, supra, concluding the must-carry provisions were content-neutral "industry-specific antitrust and fair trade" legislation narrowly tailored to preserve local broadcasting beset by monopoly power in most cable systems, growing concentration in the cable industry, and concomitant risks of programming decisions driven by anticompetitive policies.

On appeal, we agreed with the District Court that must-carry does not "distinguish favored speech from disfavored speech on the basis of the ideas or views expressed."

...

[A] four-Justice plurality concluded genuine issues of material fact remained regarding whether "the economic health of local broadcasting is in genuine jeopardy and need of the protections afforded by must-carry," and whether must-carry "'burdens substantially more speech than is necessary to further the government's legitimate interests.'"

...

The District Court oversaw another 18 months of factual development on remand "yielding a record of tens of thousands of pages" of evidence.... The majority determined "Congress drew reasonable inferences" from substantial evidence before it to conclude that "in the absence of must-carry rules, 'significant' numbers of broadcast stations would be refused carriage." ... [T]he court decided the noncarriage problem would grow worse without must-carry because cable operators had refrained from dropping broadcast stations during Congress' investigation and the pendency of this litigation.

...

The court held must-carry to be narrowly tailored to promote the Government's legitimate interests. It found the effects of must-carry on cable operators to be minimal, noting evidence that: most cable systems had not been required to add any broadcast stations since the rules were adopted; only 1.2 percent of all cable channels had been devoted to broadcast stations added because of must-carry; and the burden was likely to diminish as channel capacity expanded in the future.

...

[W]e now affirm.

...

A content-neutral regulation will be sustained under the First Amendment if it advances important governmental interests unrelated to the suppression of free speech and does not burden substantially more speech than necessary to further those interests.... [M]ust-carry was designed to serve "three interrelated interests: (1) preserving the benefits of free, over-the-air local broadcast television, (2) promoting the widespread dissemination of information from a multiplicity of sources, and (3) promoting fair competition in the market for television programming." We decided then, and now reaffirm, that each of those is an important governmental interest.

...

Forty percent of American households continue to rely on over-the-air signals for television programming.

...

Congress predicted that "absent the reimposition of [must-carry], additional local broadcast signals will be deleted, repositioned, or not carried" with the end result that "the economic viability of free local broadcast television and its ability to originate quality local programming will be seriously jeopardized."

At the same time, Congress was under no illusion that there would be a complete disappearance of broadcast television nationwide in the absence of must-carry.

...

Congress was concerned not that broadcast television would disappear in its entirety without must-carry, but that without it, "significant numbers of broadcast stations will be refused carriage on cable systems," and those "broadcast stations denied carriage will either deteriorate to a substantial degree or fail altogether."

...

We have noted that "it has long been a basic tenet of national communications policy that 'the widest possible dissemination of information from diverse and antagonistic sources is essential to the welfare of the public.'" ... "Increasing the number of outlets for community self-expression" represents a "long-established regulatory goal in the field of television broadcasting."

...

The Government's assertion that "the economic health of local broadcasting is in genuine jeopardy and in need of the protections afforded by must-carry," rests on two component propositions: First, "significant numbers of broadcast stations will be refused carriage on cable systems" absent must-carry. Second, "the broadcast stations denied carriage will either deteriorate to a substantial degree or fail altogether."

...

We owe Congress' findings deference in part because the institution "is far better equipped than the judiciary to 'amass and evaluate the vast amounts of data' bearing upon" legislative questions.

...

We have no difficulty in finding a substantial basis to support Congress' conclusion that a real threat justified enactment of the must-carry provisions.

...

As to the evidence before Congress, there was specific support for its conclusion that cable operators had considerable and growing market power over local video programming markets.

...

Evidence indicated the structure of the cable industry would give cable operators increasing ability and incentive to drop local broadcast stations from their systems, or reposition them to a less-viewed channel.

...

Though the dissent criticizes our reliance on evidence provided to Congress by parties that are private appellees here, that argument displays a lack of regard for Congress' fact finding function. It is the nature of the legislative process to consider the submissions of the parties most affected by legislation.... After hearing years of testimony, and reviewing volumes of documentary evidence and studies offered by both sides, Congress concluded that the cable industry posed a threat to broadcast television. The Constitution gives to Congress the role of weighing conflicting evidence in the legislative process. Even when the resulting regulation touches on First Amendment concerns, we must give considerable deference, in examining the evidence, to Congress' findings and conclusions, including its findings and conclusions with respect to conflicting economic predictions.

...

Cable systems also have more systemic reasons for seeking to disadvantage broadcast stations: Simply stated, cable has little interest in assisting, through carriage, a competing medium of communication.

...

The dissent contends Congress could not reasonably conclude cable systems would engage in such predation because cable operators, whose primary source of revenue is subscriptions, would not risk dropping a widely viewed broadcast station in order to capture advertising revenues. However, if viewers are faced with the choice of sacrificing a handful of broadcast stations to gain access to dozens of cable channels (plus network affiliates), it is likely they would still subscribe to cable even if they would prefer the dropped television stations to the cable programming that replaced them.

...

It was more than a theoretical possibility in 1992 that cable operators would take actions adverse to local broadcasters; indeed, significant numbers of broadcasters had already been dropped. The record before Congress contained extensive anecdotal evidence about scores of adverse carriage decisions against broadcast stations.

...

Substantial evidence demonstrated that absent must-carry the already "serious," problem of noncarriage would grow worse because "additional local broadcast signals will be deleted, repositioned, or not carried."

...

The dissent cites evidence indicating that many dropped broadcasters were stations few viewers watch, and it suggests that must-carry thwarts noncable viewers' preferences.

...

The issue before us is whether, given conflicting views of the probable development of the television industry, Congress had substantial evidence for making the judgment that it did.

...

The harm Congress feared was that stations dropped or denied carriage would be at a "serious risk of financial difficulty," and would "deteriorate to a substantial degree or fail altogether."

...

[E]xpansion in the cable industry was causing harm to broadcasting.

...

We think it apparent must-carry serves the Government's interests "in a direct and effective way." Must-carry ensures that a number of local broadcasters retain cable carriage, with the concomitant audience access and advertising revenues needed to support a multiplicity of stations.

...

The second portion of the *O'Brien* inquiry concerns the fit between the asserted interests and the means chosen to advance them. Content-neutral regulations do not pose the same "inherent dangers to free expression," that content-based regulations do, and thus are subject to a less rigorous analysis, which affords the Government latitude in designing a regulatory solution.

...

The must-carry provisions have the potential to interfere with protected speech in two ways. First, the provisions restrain cable operators' editorial discretion in creating programming packages by "reducing the number of channels over which [they] exercise unfettered control." Second, the rules "render it more difficult for cable programmers to compete for carriage on the limited channels remaining."

...

Significant evidence indicates the vast majority of cable operators have not been affected in a significant manner by must-carry. Cable operators have been able to satisfy their must-carry obligations 87 percent of the time using previously unused channel capacity

...

Because the burden imposed by must-carry is congruent to the benefits it affords, we conclude must-carry is narrowly tailored to preserve a multiplicity of broadcast stations for the 40 percent of American households without cable.

...

Appellants say the must-carry provisions are overbroad because they require carriage in some instances when the Government's interests are not implicated: the must-carry rules prohibit a cable system operator from dropping a broadcaster "even if the operator has no anticompetitive motives, and even if the broadcaster that would have to be dropped ... would survive without cable access." We are not persuaded that either possibility is so prevalent that must-carry is substantially overbroad.

...

[A]fter careful examination of each of the alternatives suggested by appellants, we cannot conclude that any of them is an adequate alternative to must-carry for promoting the Government's legitimate interests.

...

Judgments about how competing economic interests are to be reconciled in the complex and fast-changing field of television are for Congress to make. Those judgments "cannot be ignored or undervalued simply because [appellants] cast [their] claims under the umbrella of the First Amendment." ... Appellants' challenges to must-carry reflect little more than disagreement over the level of protection broadcast stations are to be afforded and how protection is to be attained. We cannot displace Con-

gress' judgment respecting content-neutral regulations with our own, so long as its policy is grounded on reasonable factual findings supported by evidence that is substantial for a legislative determination. Those requirements were met in this case, and in these circumstances the First Amendment requires nothing more. The judgment of the District Court is affirmed.

It is so ordered.

...

DISSENT: JUSTICE O'CONNOR, with whom JUSTICE SCALIA, JUSTICE THOMAS, and JUSTICE GINSBURG join, dissenting.

[T]he Court errs in two crucial respects. First, the Court disregards one of the principal defenses of the statute urged by appellees on remand: that it serves a substantial interest in preserving "diverse," "quality" programming that is "responsive" to the needs of the local community ... Second, the Court misapplies the "intermediate scrutiny" framework it adopts. Although we owe deference to Congress' predictive judgments and its evaluation of complex economic questions, we have an independent duty to identify with care the Government interests supporting the scheme, to inquire into the reasonableness of congressional findings regarding its necessity, and to examine the fit between its goals and its consequences.

...

I fully agree that promoting fair competition is a legitimate and substantial Government goal. But the Court nowhere examines whether the breadth of the must-carry provisions comports with a goal of preventing anticompetitive harms. Instead, in the course of its inquiry into whether the must-carry provisions are "narrowly tailored," the principal opinion simply assumes that most adverse carriage decisions are anticompetitively motivated, and that must-carry is therefore a measured response to a problem of anticompetitive behavior.

...

[T]he must-carry provisions cannot be justified as a narrowly tailored means of addressing anti-competitive behavior.... Pressed to explain the importance of preserving noncable viewers' access to "vulnerable" broadcast stations, appellees emphasize that the must-carry rules are necessary to ensure that broadcast stations maintain "diverse," "quality" programming that is "responsive" to the needs of the local community.... Must-carry is thus justified as a way of preserving

viewers' access to a Spanish or Chinese language station or of preventing an independent station from adopting a home-shopping format.... [A]ppellees' characterization of must-carry as a means of protecting these stations, like the Court's explicit concern for promoting "community self-expression" and the "local origination of broadcast programming," reveals a content-based preference for broadcast programming.

...

[T]he larger problem with the Court's approach is that neither the FCC study nor the additional evidence on remand canvassed by the Court, says anything about the broadcast markets in which adverse carriage decisions take place. The Court accepts Congress' stated concern about preserving the availability of a "multiplicity" of broadcast stations, but apparently thinks it sufficient to evaluate that concern in the abstract, without considering how much local service is already available in a given broadcast market.

...

The principal opinion disavows a need to closely scrutinize the logic of the regulatory scheme at issue on the ground that it "need not put [its] imprimatur on Congress' economic theory in order to validate the reasonableness of its judgment." That approach trivializes the First Amendment issue at stake in this case. A highly dubious economic theory has been advanced as the "substantial interest" supporting a First Amendment burden on cable operators and cable programmers.

...

[T]he Court's leap to the conclusion that must-carry "is narrowly tailored to preserve a multiplicity of broadcast stations," is nothing short of astounding.

...

In my view, the statute is not narrowly tailored to serve a substantial interest in preventing anticompetitive conduct.

...

[B]ecause the undisputed facts demonstrate that the must-carry scheme is plainly not narrowly tailored to serving the only governmental interest the principal opinion fully explains and embraces—preventing anticompetitive behavior—appellants are entitled to summary judgment in their favor.

...

I therefore respectfully dissent, and would reverse the judgment below.

10 Reno v. American Civil Liberties Union, et al.

"[T]here weren't any hearings held. The congressmen, just like the courts, didn't know anything about the Internet. They didn't have a clue as to what this law would do."
—Ann Beeson, ACLU staff attorney, Co-counsel in *ACLU v. Reno*

"If I as an individual who believes in the American dream, and believes in free speech—and if I really think that our country has had a history of struggle to learn how to respect diverse viewpoints—then how can I live with myself if I allow this to be done to me? If I let it be done to me, what kind of signal does that send to other people? If they see a lot of us willing to eat dirt and bow our necks to the yoke, then that sends a terrible signal."
—Patricia Nell Warren, author, publisher, and plaintiff in *ACLU v. Reno*

"I think this decision will continue to be the starting point for 50 years—for a very long time it will be where courts start when they evaluate regulation of the Internet."
—John B. Morris, Jr., partner, Jenner & Block, Co-counsel in *ACLU v. Reno*

"[N]o issue is ever won, and no issue is ever lost."
—Chris Hansen, ACLU senior staff counsel, Co-counsel in *ACLU v. Reno*

"We changed the history of communication. It blows my mind."
—Judith Krug, director, Office of Intellectual Freedom, American Library Association

On February 8, 1996, the same day that President Clinton signed into law the Communications Decency Act (CDA), the American Civil Liberties

410

Union (ACLU) filed documents in a United States district court in Pennsylvania's Eastern District seeking a temporary restraining order against the statute. One week later, Judge Ronald Buckwalter granted the order, and a three-judge panel was convened to hear the case.

The CDA was part of the Telecommunications Act of 1996. In part, it subjected those who made, created, solicited, or initiated the communication of indecent or patently offensive material by means of a telecommunications device or an interactive computer service to criminal prosecution. Clearly, the CDA targeted "indecency" on the Internet. But at a deeper level, many believed that it also threatened the existence and development of this new communication medium.

As the measure was working its way through Congress, the American Civil Liberties Union and members of its national legal department took note. In the view of its staff, it was clear that the statute posed serious constitutional questions. An effort to challenge the law was organized, with several clients selected for representation. When the bill was signed, the ACLU struck immediately.

At the same time that the ACLU was monitoring the legislative progress of the CDA, a separate coalition of interests was assembled that had similar but slightly different concerns about the measure. Headlined by the American Library Association (ALA), this group ultimately selected the Washington, D.C., law firm of Jenner & Block for its legal representation. Several weeks after the ACLU challenged the CDA, the ALA coalition followed suit with its case. Because of their similarities, the court consolidated the cases and heard them simultaneously.

Trying the case largely became a mission to educate. The "teachers" were the lawyers who tried the case, many whose reflections are seen below. The "students" were three federal district court judges and later nine U.S. Supreme Court Justices. The "classrooms" were first a federal district courtroom in Philadelphia, then the United States Supreme Court in Washington, D.C. The "lesson" topic was the Internet. In the mid-1990s, this educational mission was no small task. Just what was this new communication tool? How did it work? And perhaps most importantly, what First Amendment standard should be applied to it? The result of these lessons is a ruling that is generally regarded as the first major decision in the age of "new media," and is likely to remain the starting point for any and all legal analyses of the Internet for decades.

While many people at the ACLU worked on the case, three attorneys in its national legal department led the effort: Chris Hansen, senior staff counsel, staff attorney Ann Beeson, and senior staff attorney Marjorie Heins, who was also director of the ACLU's Arts Censorship Project. Mr. Hansen and Ms. Beeson remain in those positions. Ms. Heins, whose books include *Sex, Sin, and Blasphemy: A Guide to America's Censorship Wars*, is no longer with the ACLU. Among the many plaintiffs that the ACLU represented was Wildcat Press. Its co-founder, Patricia Nell Warren—herself an author of many kinds of books available for sale through a Web site—was among the few people asked to provide live testimony at trial. The lead plaintiff in the other half of the consolidated case, the American Library Association, was led by Judith Krug, director of the ALA's Office of Intellectual Freedom and executive director of ALA's Freedom to Read Foundation. One member of the Jenner & Block team that represented the ALA coalition was John B. Morris, Jr., who now is with the Center for Democracy and Technology (CDT), a Washington-based policy organization. Prominent in bringing together this varied group was the executive director of the CDT, Jerry Berman. A former ACLU attorney himself, he is still executive director of the CDT.

ASSEMBLING THE CASE

MARJORIE HEINS: [W]e at the ACLU knew that this legislation was coming, at least a year before it finally was signed by the President. There was a lot of attention in Congress to what ultimately became part of the massive Telecommunications Act. I was there, I was a First Amendment expert in the legal department, and I was an obvious person to be involved in the case. I also had a special interest in this notion of "Do we need censorship? Are the rules different when the argument is 'We're protecting kids?'"

ANN BEESON: This, of course, was a challenge to a federal statute. And the ACLU, although known primarily for litigation—which is primarily what we do—also has a lobbying arm in Washington. So we are always on the lookout, of course, and constantly lobbying against various congressional bills that might restrict free speech. The Communications Decency Act was no different. The bill was passed in '95. So I spent the first several months at the ACLU lobbying against the bill, actually—doing various on-line kind of activism to encourage people to oppose the bill. This was sort of the very first wave of Net activism—you know, political activism. And then when it became clear that it was going to pass in some form or another, we all got together and we said, "Shouldn't we start to put together a lawsuit?" And unlike other lawyers, public interest lawyers are not constrained from soliciting clients directly. It's something that we routinely do. It tends to be sort of a two-way thing. At the same time that we are looking out for people who might want to be represented, people are also contacting us because, of course, they know the ACLU. And that was the case with the CDA.

MARJORIE HEINS: Ann was the primary person who was networking with people who had Web sites and people who were free speech activists, and youth arts activists, and people who would be concerned about this law.

ANN BEESON: Since the first job was to solicit a lot of clients, I decided that it would be a great use of the technology to get on line and send out notices to all sorts of various discussion groups having to do with the First Amendment and free speech, telling people that it was likely to pass and asking if they were worried about prosecution under the law and whether they wanted to be represented. It was a very exciting thing, because we were flooded with responses from hundreds and hundreds and hundreds of people and content providers on the Web who were worried about the law. Then we had to pick and choose because obviously we couldn't represent the world, really. We tried to put together a group of clients who represented both the broad spectrum of speech and content that was written into the law as well as the broad spectrum of on-line communication affected.

PATRICIA NELL WARREN: When the Internet came along and we became aware of it, we decided it would be very important to have a Web site and to try selling our books on the Internet. So we have a Web site. The ACLU first got interested in me when I published one of my new books. When they began moving towards [litigation], and there was all this talk of the first time that legislation that would limit content on the Internet in certain ways, they asked me if I would be interested in being a plaintiff. And I said, "Absolutely, I would." We went on that first lawsuit actually as Wildcat Press, the company, with my business partner's total support on this, knowing that we were sticking our necks out. We were selling books on the Internet. Inevitably we could be considered to be in violation of the law if it was determined that these gay books that we were selling online could be deemed [indecent]. That was how we got involved. From that point on, I said to the ACLU, "Consider me potentially on deck with any litigation that you want to do because I feel very, very strongly about this." I feel like authors themselves and small publishers as well as big publish-

ers really have to stick their necks out on these issues and fight for free speech.

ANN BEESON: [E]ven aside from our attempts to solicit clients, we were being flooded with requests from people who were just absolutely terrified of prosecution under the law that wanted to be represented. So there isn't any doubt in my mind that even if we hadn't affirmatively tried to solicit clients, they would have come to us. Ultimately, as a legal organization, we structured the case—which picked and chose which clients to represent—and said to all of the other people that whatever ruling we got on this facial challenge would protect them as well, but that it was just a matter of what the best evidence was to present to the judge.

CHRIS HANSEN:

We were looking for clients who had a credible argument that they would be at risk under the statute. But we were also looking for clients that everyone would consider to be respectable—to be *above* respectable, to be more than respectable. It's always been my view that our client selection was maybe the most important decision we made in the case. If the court believed that our clients were at risk under the statute, we were going to win. If the court believed that this statute was about the role of *Hustler* magazine on the Internet, we would have a much harder time winning.

PATRICIA NELL WARREN: What is the difference between preventing these things online and preventing them in the actual bookstores? Barnes and Noble carries my books. My books are carried by all the major wholesalers. So you see for me to impose this kind of thing on the Internet raises the larger questions of the larger book marketplace. Because all these big book companies—Barnes and Noble, Borders—not only do they have sales sites on the Internet, they have their physical bookstores. So if they can't sell the books on the Internet, then how can they continue to sell them in the bookstores?

ANN BEESON: Of course, at the time, the Web was still somewhat new, so we didn't want just worldwide Web providers [as clients]. We wanted people who ran Usenet news groups, people who ran list serves, etc. We ended up with a really very diverse group of plaintiffs. There were 20 clients in all, and those were all either organizational or Web site plaintiffs. And this tends to be the untold side of the story. We were distressed throughout the whole process that the press did not pay very much attention to who our clients really were. The case is only ever discussed as if the ACLU was the only client. And we were, of course, the main plaintiff in the case, but by no means the only client. I think, in fact, that it was ultimately the clients that won the case for us.

PATRICIA NELL WARREN: What's interesting to look at in the United States right now is where we're having situations where there is a gray area between government imposition of censorship and the political give and take of the marketplace and opinions where it can get very dangerous. That's a nexus where we're at right now. That's why I'm concerned about the Internet and some other things where people get confused about which is which. The feelings for me go very deep, they have very ancient roots. It certainly becomes something that's part of your life. Because I've been so deeply concerned about this for such a long time, this is an old, old issue with me. There's a sadness about knowing that it's there and that it's a constant in your life that you constantly have to fight against it. But it becomes like the little grit of sand that gets in the oyster. That's how a pearl begins in an oyster. The oyster begins dealing with that irritant by coating it with layers of nacre, until finally you have a beautiful pearl. So this irritant and this sadness and this challenge has actually inspired people to be creative, and to tell the stories about this and to fight against it.

JERRY BERMAN: We had a similar kind of line of plaintiffs, but what we did was expand it to bring together and give the courts a cross-section of the new Internet publishing arena. If you look at our papers, the main plaintiffs—the ISPs, AOL, Prodigy, CompuServe—they're there, plus the publishers and newspaper associations who are shifting from off line to on-line.

JOHN MORRIS: The Freedom to Read Foundation [of the American Library Association], run by Judy Krug, has been a long-term client of ours, probably for 10 or 12 years. So we've done a lot of First Amendment work. ALA and Judy Krug was one of the people very, very concerned about the Communications Decency Act as it was winding its way through Congress—or as these types of proposals were making their way through

Congress in 1995. Judy is very involved and connected to a network of First Amendment activists and advocates. Through Judy we had been asked to look at this thing and track it.

JUDITH KRUG:

What the CDA said is that, first of all, if you're a mere conduit to the Internet you have no liability, but if you provide content on the Internet and this content can be deemed to be "indecent" and is made available to anyone 17 years of age and under, you become liable. When we read the bill initially, we said, "We're not content providers." And then I got a telephone call from one of our colleagues who was putting her card catalog on the computer. And instead of having the card catalog, people would access the content of the collection through the computer. She said, "This is a great project and I put up almost every title but 40." I said, "Excuse me?" She said, "Well, 40 titles I was concerned with because of the language, because of the words used in the title." And so we went from having no concern to becoming extremely concerned. Our role as librarians is to make sure that people have the information they need when they need it or when they want it. My role has never been to keep people *from* information regardless of who thinks it might be detrimental. Because of that, we became very concerned when something as innocuous as a card catalog is deemed by some librarians to possibly put them at risk by virtue of a few of the titles contained in that card catalog.

ANN BEESON:

In the meantime, we had spent literally 6 months putting the case together both in terms of the clients and the drafting of all the legal papers which meant primarily writing a very lengthy complaint that described in very minute detail what the Internet was all about, since we knew the judges wouldn't know anything about it. We thought that it was very important because it was such an important bill having to do with this very important new medium of communication that we thought it was crucial that we go into court the day the bill was signed and file the suit. We had everything all ready to do that, and we filed. Of course, it was part of the much larger Telecommunications bill, and so it was a huge media event when the President signed the bill—the Telecommunications Act.

PATRICIA NELL WARREN: How is it that I would stick my neck out to get involved with this litigation? I am an author who has been publishing since 1954—so that's a long time—since I was 17 years old. I started publishing books in 1971. And I have published some books that have been considered controversial, notably my novel *The Front Runner*, which ran into some problems with libraries and communities when it first came out because it's a gay love story. There are people in the United States who consider that anything that has the word "gay" in it—whether it's a nonfiction book about gay rights, or whether it's a novel like the ones that I have written—these books are *ipso facto* objectionable by virtue of the very nature of their themes.

ANN BEESON: In general, we represented what I'll call the little guys that we felt were truly at risk of prosecution under the law. And the other case represented sort of the bigger media interests that theoretically could have been prosecuted under the law and certainly had an interest in seeing it overturned, but were probably less likely to actually be prosecuted. The exception to that in some ways was the lead plaintiff in the other case, the American Library Association.

JOHN MORRIS:  We were asked by the American Library Association to look at the bill and get an understanding of it. At the same time and unrelated to our office—we weren't directly involved in this—Judy was joining up with and becoming a key player in a coalition that was largely organized by Jerry Berman over at the Center for Democracy and Technology. Jerry was really the link between Judy Krug and the American Library Association and the kind of nonprofit association community including the American Booksellers Association, the Association of American Publishers, and other organizations in that category. Jerry Berman was the link between those groups and the computer industry—American Online, Microsoft, and others who ultimately got involved. And Berman was also well connected to other more generic advocacy groups like the People for the American Way. AOL made the decision that they wanted to go ahead and challenge the Communications Decency Act, and they made the decision that they did not want to be part of the ACLU's suit. Jerry Berman decided to try to get a coalition together that really was the computer industry and the mainstream public interest advocacy organizations like the ALA and others. They decided that it was an important thing to have one group of plaintiffs as opposed to two or three more suits beyond the ACLU suit. America Online very early on recognized that the American Library Association was a very important type of plaintiff because the Communications Decency Act would have totally incapacitated public libraries from being able to post their content online and being able to make content available in the library. The libraries were a key player. Judy Krug was probably, although I don't know, the one who first said, no, she wants Jenner & Block and Bruce Ennis to be involved. She was not going to sign on to an America Online run. The upshot of it was that this coalition decided to have a "beauty contest"—a law firm competition—where different law firms would come in and essentially pitch their services. In late January we were asked to participate in this beauty contest.

JUDITH KRUG: Jenner & Block, the Washington office and Bruce Ennis specifically, was legal counsel to the Freedom to Read Foundation. I was contacted by people who were concerned about the Communications Decency Act. I had been working with people like Jerry Berman and a variety of people. When it looked like the legislation was going to be passed, a request for proposal went out to several legal firms. It was when that was going on that Jerry called me and said, "We need you in here with us because we need the nonprofits." The negotiations went on and on and on. And the truth was in the end, I said that I would come in and bring ALA and the nonprofits on two conditions. The first condition was that the American Library Association was lead plaintiff, and the second condition was that Bruce Ennis was legal counsel. In my opinion Bruce Ennis was the best First Amendment lawyer in the United States of America for the last ten years. I had worked with him for 11 years. He was a brilliant man. He was wonderful.

ANN BEESON: A lot of the players that ended up being clients and lawyers in the two cases had been working together as a coalition, along with many other groups, to stop the bill. So it isn't the case that we were unaware of each other. We were. We were all working very closely together.

JOHN MORRIS: I was brought in. I had done a lot of First Amendment work before. But I was really brought in because of my technology background. I had been involved in computers for decades. I started programming computers in 1972, I think. I worked in the computer industry in the early '80s. I have a pretty long background with computers and I had been on the Internet since the pretty early days—the late 1980s. I was very, very familiar with both the technology and also with the First Amendment issues.

Why was it that it was the lawsuit was filed in the Eastern District of Pennsylvania?

CHRIS HANSEN: I think for two principle reasons. One, we have a very good and a very strong affiliate in Philadelphia. Whenever we do a case anywhere in the country, we have to do it with an affiliate office. And that's a particularly good one. And I think the second reason is after doing some research, we believed that the Third Circuit, which is the court that's headquartered in Philadelphia, was likely to be sympathetic to the issues in the case. We literally could have filed anywhere in the country. Once you have those kinds of options, the logical thing to do is to try to find a forum that will give serious consideration to your case.

ANN BEESON: We filed the case, and it was a couple of weeks before we even received a call that there was going to possibly be another lawsuit. What happened was we went in and asked for a temporary restraining order [TRO] the day the lawsuit was filed. We had a hearing that day, and got the TRO and it was only after the TRO that the other group decided that maybe there was a way to win this thing. We didn't get the call until after that, is my point—that there was possibly going to be another suit and that they had decided to file in the same place—the Eastern District of Pennsylvania—and that probably what would happen is that it would get consolidated with our suit. Even if they had filed somewhere else, it's very likely that the Justice Department would have asked that the cases be combined since they were both essentially the same case—facial challenges to the law.

JOHN MORRIS: I think there were some key fundamental concerns by some people who weren't part of the ACLU suit had about the ACLU suit. These were concerns that led them to not want to be a plaintiff in the ACLU suit, but also not necessarily to want to even allow the ACLU to be the final or only deciding, guiding factor for the litigation. And those factors were 1) some of the big companies that were very concerned about this, including America Online and Microsoft, had a little bit of hesitation in terms of becoming a plaintiff with the ACLU. AOL and these other companies were already sticking their neck out a lot by challenging a federal statute, especially a federal statute that was touted as protecting kids on the Internet and things like that. There already was a major public relations risk on their part. They then and now should be commended for taking that risk and taking the activist role that they and others in the computer industry have taken.

JUDITH KRUG: I could not imagine placing the future of my profession in any of the hands that were also being considered as chief legal counsel. I will go to my grave believing that we would never have gotten a 9-zero Supreme Court decision with any other lead plaintiff, and that includes ACLU. The baggage that they carry with them precludes a 9-zero Supreme Court decision. I believed that, and Bruce Ennis believed that.

What do you mean by the ACLU "baggage?"

JUDITH KRUG: Just because of who they are and what their reputation is and what they do. They bring a lot of baggage to court. The U.S. Supreme Court—the men and women on the Court—put on their underwear the same way you and I do. In other words, these are human beings. We're dealing with human beings. There's no way we would have gotten nine Justices to vote the way they did.

CHRIS HANSEN: I know that those plaintiffs were all skittish about being involved, and I know they were skittish about being represented by the ACLU. My guess would be—and I don't know this—that once it became clear that the case was going to be filed, that it became easier for them to say to themselves, "Given the fact that this litigation is going forward, we'd like to be a player rather than sit on the sidelines."

JOHN MORRIS: They were balancing a risk of taking action—and the element of being led by the ACLU was an added public relations concern. But I think much more fundamentally, the reason that the computer industry, especially, felt there needed to be another lawsuit—a lawsuit separate from the ACLU's—is the complaint in the initial documents that the ACLU filed in that case had a very distinct perspective. And without in any way criticizing those documents at all—the ACLU crafted what was a very well thought-out litigation plan and they very successfully convinced Judge Buckwalter, a fairly conservative member of the district court in Pennsylvania, to temporarily restrain the CDA. So the ACLU was very successful in their first days of litigation.

CHRIS HANSEN: I actually think that [the diversity of clients] was pretty impressive, although the truth is the clients that most people were impressed by were not our clients. We filed with 20 clients, including the ACLU and Human Rights Watch and EPIC, and so on. But most of the rest of our clients were relatively small folk. Even people who had huge Web sites, like Critical Path AIDS Project which was one of our key plaintiffs—it's not like he's Microsoft. It was basically a one-person shop. The second case, which was filed 2 or 3 weeks after ours, was filed by the American Library Association and then the industry—Microsoft and AOL and CompuServe and all of those.

JOHN MORRIS: The bottom line is that I think it was very, very powerful to be able to have sitting on the same side of the table in the same courtroom some of the very advanced and avant garde and "out there" organizations that the ACLU had as plaintiffs in terms of just being very cutting-edge stuff—talking to young kids about safe sex and things like that—to have those plaintiffs of theirs sitting at the adjoining table with America Online and the Association of American Publishers and Microsoft and the American Library Association. It was very, very effective to have them in a coordinated lawsuit.

MARJORIE HEINS: Certainly the variety of plaintiffs who joined in the case, I think, must have been impressive to the judges. We had, for the most part, smaller nonprofit entities unlike the case that was eventually joined with ours, the *American Library Association* case, the industry case. All of our clients were either nonprofits or small—not major corporate players. They were asserting, I think it's fair to say, an earlier vision of what the Internet was—participatory, decentralized, not dominated by large corporate interests. Our hope was that we'd be able to get the judges to appreciate the diversity of the Web and the extent to which small nonprofits and individuals and groups who represented the diversity of the American population including the interests of youth were concerned about this law.

ANN BEESON: Once [the cases] were consolidated, we from that point on worked together as an almost completely unified team. It was, of course, true that the lawyers were representing different clients, but we did everything together. We did all the depositions in the case, we did all the discovery together. The lawyer who was the lead counsel in that suit, who ultimately did the argument before the Supreme Court, Bruce Ennis, was the former legal director of the ACLU. So there was a longtime affiliation. We were all very friendly and, in fact, worked very well together. There really weren't many, if any at all, substantive differences in the strategy that we were both taking to the case.

The leader of the Jenner & Block team that represented the ALA coalition of plaintiffs was Bruce Ennis. A litigator known for his meticulous preparation, a forceful presence, and a wealth of experience with First Amendment cases, Ennis was ultimately selected to argue *Reno v. ACLU* before the U.S. Supreme Court. It was the 16th time he presented a case to the Supreme Court. His expertise there is summarized by John Morris:

"The Supreme Court provides a little booklet to people who are arguing a case. It gives rules and pointers about how to argue cases to the Supreme Court—how to address the Justices and what to say and where to stand. It's mundane stuff, but also substantive and helpful pointers about [for example] how you should assume the Justices have fully read your briefs, which is not something at a lower court you necessarily can assume—that the judges have fully understood your case, but at the Supreme Court you certainly can. That Supreme Court booklet includes a vignette, an example, of how one advocate before the Supreme Court had carried out what the Supreme Court wants. And although the Supreme Court does not identify the advocate in that case, the advocate was Bruce Ennis. This story typifies the reason Bruce was such a good litigator."

After a battle with leukemia, Bruce Ennis died in July 2000 at the age of 60.

JOHN MORRIS: I would say that the two trial teams worked *extremely* well together and coordinated very, very closely—still, having somewhat different agendas within the trial teams. There were a lot of substantive differences between the two trial teams, but throughout it all, we had an excellent relationship with the ACLU people. Bruce was the key person to start that relationship and to continue it, although I now work closely with Chris Hansen and Ann Beeson on a whole range of things and continue to have a good relationship with them, as the firm does. The ACLU was aware that we were going to proceed with this lawsuit, and I'm sure there was some element of ambivalence on their part because, of course, they had their lawsuit, it had been successful, and I'm sure on many levels they didn't feel they needed any other help or any other input into the process. But they also, I think, were very, very pleased that mainstream industry and the mainstream public organizations like the American Library Association and the Association of American Publishers were stepping up to join this battle. I think overall they were very happy to have us coming in.

MARJORIE HEINS: In terms of coordinating, of course, the more lawyers and the more plaintiffs you have, the more logistical problems you have with coordinating. But considering how many lawyers and plaintiffs were involved, we worked very well with Bruce Ennis and his team.

JOHN MORRIS: Obviously, just as a practical matter, when you have two separate groups of lawyers thinking about the same issues, you often have to spend additional time getting everybody onto the same page. But you also have the value of two separate groups of lawyers thinking about the same issues and the great value of having two sets of ideas come in to try to figure out what the best strategy is. Yes, it takes more time, but it's a luxury that you don't often get in lawsuits to have two groups of bright people trying to figure things out.

JUDITH KRUG: Contrary to killing each other, I think that the rivalry resulted in some of the best legal work that I have ever seen. It was almost a contest. Oh, God, did that team work. They worked like crazy. And, of course, we got the bills to prove it (laughs).

THE CASE

JOHN MORRIS: If you just compare the two complaints that we filed, the ACLU's suit was focusing on the speech. Our complaint was a very, very lengthy—an unusually long—document that really attempted to be an historical and technological primer on the Internet for the court. That complaint, which I was the primary drafter of—*The Washington Post* called it wonk-ish, but that was a great compliment. That's exactly what we were trying to do. We hoped to be somewhat wonk-ish, but also understandable. That complaint formed the basis of how we all—both the ACLU and us—together tried to educate the court and tried to get the court actually to understand how communication on the Internet worked. And also to understand its potential and its ability to empower people all over the world to speak fairly freely. That complaint ended up being the basis of the majority of the factual stipulations that parties entered into which themselves ended up being the basis of a great deal of the facts that the three-judge district court adopted and then themselves ended up being the basis of a great deal of what ended up in the factual discussions of the Supreme Court decision.

JERRY BERMAN: [One] point we were trying to make was that we were not just saying that this violates the First Amendment, go away. The point we wanted to make in addition to an overbreadth argument was that in this medium, there are less restrictive means. A good part of our case was devoted to saying that parents have options based on the user empowerment strategy.

Empowering Internet users includes the use of filtering software—an alternative to government-mandated measures that many people recommend. Once installed on a personal computer, the software allows for specific kinds of Internet content to be screened out. Proponents claim that the use of this software places the control of what Web sites and content are allowed onto a personal computer in the hands of the individual—particularly a parent—rather than allowing the decision to be in the hands of the government.

MARJORIE HEINS: I think there was a tension in the case. There was a tension in the case from the start. This is really a question of legal strategy. The whole argument that so-called voluntary filtering was a less restrictive alternative—you didn't need this Draconian law because you could protect children through these voluntary filters—that was something that made me uncomfortable from the beginning. That was an element of the ACLU's case. It became only more strongly an element when the industry case was joined with ours. But it was there from the start. It was a special concern of mine because, although lawyers very often argue in the alternative, the "voluntary filtering" argument really was in tension with our primary argument. That is, our number one argument was, this law is unconstitutional because it censors both adults and minors. Number two, even if it is appropriate to censor minors, there are less restrictive ways of doing this, i.e., filters. Those are alternative arguments that are legitimate to make, but on the other hand, there's no question that when you make the second argument you appear to be buying into the notion that indecency is harmful to minors. Since a big part of our case, and an important interest of our clients was speaking to minors in sexually explicit terms about things like safer sex, there was a tension built into that. Having the extra lawsuit I think probably added to the tension somewhat that was already there.

JERRY BERMAN:

There was also a strategy issue. The ACLU is a little wary about the user empowerment strategy—the technology issue. They have what I think is a misguided opinion. If you put a cyber-patrol on your computer to keep your kids from watching or dialing up pornography because it's blocked out by other software, some in the ACLU think that's censorship because it's keeping material out of your computer. But I believe censorship is a term that you apply to the government. If the government tells you that you have to use a filter, yeah, I agree [that's censorship]. That's my view. And we have argued about that in public since the case. It was muted in the case, but that was one of the tensions.

ANN BEESON:

[W]e have become very amused at the revisionist history that gets told about the case, and the sense that now after the fact, everybody goes on and on about what an easy case it was. In fact, it was not an easy case at all. Nobody during the process thought it was easy, including the three-judge court that heard the case. And the reason I say it wasn't easy is because it was a brand new communications medium, there had never been any case deciding what level of First Amendment scrutiny applied to it.

CHRIS HANSEN: Lots of people, when the statute was being considered and when the statute was passed, urged us not to bring the case because it couldn't be won. Lots of people urged us to concede that some of the statute was constitutional rather than challenge all of the statute because they thought we couldn't win the whole thing. It is only after the case that it has taken on this aura of, "Oh, gee, anybody could have won that case." That wasn't peoples' attitudes beforehand and I don't think it was true. I think the case was lose-able.

ANN BEESON: [W]e felt from the very beginning the most important thing for us to do was to convince the judges with a hands-on instruction basically what kind of a medium it was. We still feel very strongly that the way you win these kinds of cases is through putting on live testimony and having a hearing and having these great, wonderful clients of ours get up on the stand and tell the judges personally that they don't want to go to jail because they're sending out AIDS information over the Internet. A lot of lawyers, especially in First Amendment cases, try these cases on paper. We could have just as easily gone in and filed the preliminary injunction motion and submitted a bunch of affidavits and asked the court to rule. I feel very strongly that it's highly likely that we would have lost had we done that. Instead we pushed very hard to have a hearing.

In your view, how is it that these laws that seem to be unconstitutional on their face—or at least have serious questions about them—how can they be passed and signed into law in the first place?

JUDITH KRUG: That's easy. Congress doesn't care. I don't know of a legislature that does care about whether a law is constitutional or not. They're concerned about making sure that their constituents know that the constituents' best interests are at heart.

CHRIS HANSEN: (laughs) I don't do any lobbying, but I talk to our lobbyists all the time. I can't tell you how many times a lobbyist has said to me, "Well I told the congressman (or the Senator)"—and this is true of both federal and state legislators—"that it was unconstitutional, and the legislator said to me, 'Of course it's unconstitutional, but I'm going to vote for it anyway because I have to politically.'"

ANN BEESON: [T]here weren't any hearings held. The congressmen, just like the courts, didn't know anything about the Internet. They didn't have a clue as to what this law would do. They didn't understand that unlike the "real world," you can't verify age on the Internet, so they thought they could issue some kind of blanket ban on indecency to minors and that it wouldn't have any effect necessarily on adults. They just didn't understand at all.

JOHN MORRIS: We're seeing more and more instances of what I consider to be gross irresponsibility on the part of Congress to not actually grapple with whether something is constitutional or not, but to pass laws that sound good on the campaign trail, but are unconstitutional and require parties and courts to spend a huge amount of effort to get them to be declared unconstitutional.

CHRIS HANSEN: This was a bill pitched as a bill to protect children from hideously awful photographs. It's a little hard to vote against that if you're a politician and you're afraid that your opponent in the next election is going to run a TV ad claiming that you were in favor of giving pornography to small children.

ANN BEESON: [T]hey don't care whether it's unconstitutional. And you get congressmen literally admitting that, and passing laws because they get political points for passing them and being anti-porn. Then they know that the courts are going to strike them down as unconstitutional.

MARJORIE HEINS: There are people in Congress who are either more interested in advancing their own ideological agenda or in currying favor with their supporters or constituents or staking out a political position that they think is going to be to their political advantage. They're more interested in those kinds of things than in a close reading of Supreme Court precedent and making sure not to pass any laws that would appear to conflict with governing precedent. So there's a kind of cynicism and a kind of feeling that, "Well, we can gain some political capital from passing this and appear to be protecting the youth of America from pornography. If the courts want to strike it down, fine, but we've gotten the political advantage." I think there's, unfortunately, a lot of that kind of thinking.

ANN BEESON: Congress put a provision in the bill that said any constitutional challenge to the bill would be heard by a three-judge court. The funny thing is that when they do that, it's come to be a signal that they know there are constitutional problems with the law. They had some sense already that there was a challenge, and they want to get it over with as quickly as possible so that they can go back and try again and make it more constitutional next time. It's such a huge waste of taxpayers' dollars, it just kind of blows your mind.

CHRIS HANSEN: I don't think the sponsors thought it was unconstitutional. I think a lot of people who voted for it *knew* it was unconstitutional and figured the courts would just sort it all out. But I think the sponsors believed it to be constitutional. I *know* the author of it thought it was constitutional.

PATRICIA NELL WARREN: In the case of the Internet, I think that this has certainly become an issue that people who are running for office are using to get votes. They're out there screaming, "We have to protect children and get all the bad guys off the Internet." Well, it isn't that simple.

ANN BEESON: All of the attempts to pass these kinds of censorship laws all come from the same argument of some sort of need to protect minors. I think it will be interesting to see what happens as media continue to converge.

What would you tell a parent who comes to you and says, "I'm just trying to protect my child from indecent material. How is it that you can expend all this energy to get a law off the books that simply helps me in that effort?"

CHRIS HANSEN: A) This law doesn't help you. Instead this law overrides your opinions. This law takes material off of the Internet whether you think you want your kid to have access to it or not. B) It doesn't take all the material off the Internet that you want to protect your child from. All of the overseas sites material is still going to be available, so it doesn't protect your kids. C) We put on a lot of evidence about blocking software that is more effective in protecting your children if that's

your goal. Blocking software has its flaws and we recognized those even then, but it does reach overseas
sites and you can tailor it, if you're the parent, to
your own particular values.

JOHN MORRIS: I would respond to a parent by saying there are some
very, very effective tools out there to protect your
children. One of the simplest tools is America Online
itself, although I don't mean to be touting the services of a client of ours. They have very effective ways
that say your children can't go browse the Internet.
They can only have access to America Online content,
or can only browse the Internet in certain constrained
ways. I think there are a lot of ways that parents can
relatively easily, without a lot of sophistication on
their part, protect their children. Are those methods
100% effective? Probably not. But the reality is, I
cannot think of a congressional action that would be
more effective than parental-installed filtering—decisions that the parents make—in part because of the
intractable difficulty of the international nature of the
Internet.

MARJORIE HEINS: Different parents have different feelings about what
their kids should see and learn and at what ages.
Filters give them the ability to make those choices
whereas the government imposing its standard on
everybody through a criminal law is actually going to
be less effective. It won't, for example, do anything
about foreign Web sites. So one answer to the parent is that this law would just be symbolic. Relatively few people would get prosecuted, compared
to the amount of indecent speech that is out there.
In terms of actually assisting you in the upbringing
of your child, this law would not provide much assistance.

THE U.S. DISTRICT COURT TRIAL

CHRIS HANSEN: I loved the trial. It was one of my favorite trials. We
were in the ceremonial courtroom in Philadelphia, and
the very first day the court sent its own staff historian to take a picture of all of us. In a way that had
never occurred to me, it made vivid to me the notion
that everybody saw this as a really important case.
We thought it was important and we were really

pleased to be part of it, but in some ways it highlighted how important the rest of the world saw the
case, not just us.

JOHN MORRIS: From day one, the whole need to educate the court
and to make sure that the court fully appreciated the
unique nature of the Internet was *the* driving force in
the second lawsuit. We were very pleased at how
much, first, most intimately the three-judge panel in
Philadelphia got to know the Internet. And then also
later, although we had less direct contact with them,
the Supreme Court Justices also clearly understood
things. At the district court level, there were three
judges: Chief Judge Sloviter, Judge Buckwalter, and
Judge Dalzell. Judge Buckwalter is somewhat more
conservative than the other two judges and I think
prior to this lawsuit, he had the least personal direct
exposure to computers and things like e-mail. Judge
Sloviter, as I perceive it, prior to the lawsuit did use
e-mail and did have a laptop computer that she used,
so was personally a little bit aware of computers
and—I don't know one way or another whether any of
them had been on the Internet itself. Judge Dalzell,
though, really seized on this case as something that
fascinated him. I think he appreciated from day one
how important ultimately this litigation would be in
terms of being the starting point for legal analysis of
Internet-related issues.

JERRY BERMAN: [W]e thought we had an uphill fight going to the
courts to educate the court.... [W]hen we presented
the case to the court we wanted to make sure that
they got a full court press education in the new medium with no confusion.

ANN BEESON: [I]t was the first time that any court had been linked up to the Internet. The whole thing was all very exciting. We spent a lot of time on it. The way the courtroom was set up, there were terminals so that the press could stand behind where the lawyers were sitting and see a screen when we were putting on our testimony. We've actually done that many times since. It's finally getting to the point now where, we still in our Internet cases always make a point of asking the judges early on whether they're online and have been on the Internet before.

CHRIS HANSEN: We wired the courtroom, and took [the judges] on an in-court tour of the Internet, showing them some Web sites and some bulletin boards and e-mail—just so that they could see what it was all about. I think none of the three of them had been on the Net at the time we did all of that. I think they thought it was absolutely fascinating to watch this new medium begin to develop.

JOHN MORRIS: How important was the demonstration? I think it was vitally important to help the judges understand the Internet. The three judges had monitors on the bench so that they could directly look at the computer screen to see what was being demonstrated on the screen for the press and for the public and screens for the witness and for the different counsel tables. I felt that Dalzell really led the way in terms of fully understanding the Internet. I have a huge amount of respect for the amount of work he did. Having said that, I think the other two judges and also the Justices on the Supreme Court worked extremely hard. All three of the judges at the district court level fully understood what they were deciding and what the issues were.

CHRIS HANSEN: We had to explain to the court a) what the Internet was about, and b) who our clients were. That's essentially all the trial was.

ANN BEESON: I would almost say [the educational process] was *the* key, although up with that I would include the clients that we chose. And those things go together because the examples that we were using in the instructional part of the case were our own clients' sites, and included people like the Critical Path AIDS Project and a site called Stop Prisoner Rape which has all sorts of educational information about prison rape and very explicit letters from prisoners and all that kind of stuff. So they were seeing all that as part of the experience.

PATRICIA NELL WARREN: I was very impressed by the opening phase of the hearing which was to educate the judges about the Internet. There were all these displays that were set up. It made me realize—and I don't consider myself a techie by any means—but the little basic knowledge that I have about the Internet is not a thing that every American has even at this point. There are still people who are unfamiliar with the Internet, and they happen to occupy positions of power in the judicial system and the legislative system. They don't know! This is one of the problems that we have. These judges were very up front and honest about the fact that they wanted to know. There was this entire morning and afternoon that was spent educating the judges. At one point the system crashed so there was this great laugh in the courtroom that, "Well, this is one of the things that happens in real life." I was impressed by the judges' intelligent questions and curiosity about all of this, their complete lack of embarrassment that they needed to be educated. And they just bored straight into it. "This is what we've got to know in order to make this decision." That kind of honesty is refreshing. It was also a good sign that they really had an open mind about this, that they weren't coming into it with closed minds.

ANN BEESON: I think basically what happened is they fell in love with the Internet. They had never seen it before, they were wowed by it, and as a result wanted to do everything they could to protect it and ultimately they were able to issue a lot of fact findings that showed that they felt the Internet was *not* like broadcast television and shouldn't be subject to the weaker First Amendment standard, but rather the contrary—it should be entitled to the highest degree of First Amendment protection because it was such a speech-enhancing medium.

CHRIS HANSEN: [W]hat we were most concerned by [was that] it comes into your home on a screen. If you don't know what the Internet is, the first analogy that you would reach for would be television.

ANN BEESON: What we had to do was convince the judges that the broadcast analysis didn't apply. And that wasn't at all an easy task.

A recurring element in *ACLU v. Reno* was a case the U.S. Supreme Court ruled on in 1978, *FCC v. Pacifica*, 438 U.S. 726. The Court ruled then that because of broadcasting's unique properties—among them its limited spectrum space and its pervasive presence—the FCC was justified in the creation and enforcement of rules that banned the airing of indecent material by stations during periods when children are most likely to be in the audience. Given that protecting minors from indecent material was also at issue in *Reno*, the ACLU and ALA attorneys were concerned that the courts would determine that the Internet was most like broadcasting, and would therefore impose on it broadcasting's relatively weak First Amendment standard.

It seemed, to some extent, at least, that you felt you needed to distinguish these circumstances from those in a case like Pacifica.

CHRIS HANSEN: Oh! A huge amount of the case was designed to distinguish us from *Pacifica*. That's the whole fight. If we were television, then we were *Pacifica*. And if we were *Pacifica*, we lose.

ANN BEESON: [The courts had] upheld the ruling in *Pacifica* that allowed the FCC to censor stations that broadcast [indecent speech]. The CDA's language used the same kind of indecency language that had been upheld specifically with respect to broadcast. In the opinion itself, that's exactly the analysis that the Supreme Court went through—to distinguish very clearly the *Pacifica* decision from this one.

JERRY BERMAN: We had to make a case that the Internet is not scarce spectrum. It's unlimited. [Also], we had to make the case that this is not pervasive. You don't just turn your dial and not know what's coming in. You click and go to places that you want to go to. This is a technology that empowers the users to customize what their experience is. So with that distinction, there went radio, television, and to some extent cable.

CHRIS HANSEN: The government's argument was, "This is *Pacifica.*" The government's legal argument was, "This is *Pacifica*—that we have an interest in protecting children from bad stuff, and this statute is designed to get only bad stuff."

MARJORIE HEINS: What the Supreme Court had said in *Pacifica* was you can ban indecency during times when children may be listening, but there has to be a safe harbor period when you can't ban it absolutely. The Supreme Court's apparent approval of the indecency standard in *Pacifica* was a major problem for us. A lot of attention went into explaining how narrow *Pacifica* was, how distinguishable it was in terms of the medium that was being regulated, and *Pacifica* being an enforcement mechanism that didn't involve criminal prosecution and so forth.

JOHN MORRIS: [T]he government made very clear that the main part of their argument was the very simplistic argument that says, "The Internet should be regulated like broadcast." Broadcast is, in our First Amendment system—at least today—the medium of communications that is constitutionally most heavily regulated by the government—by the FCC and by Congress. The government very plainly said the closest analogy that the court should look at was broadcast. That single assertion alone by the government would have been enough to get the Internet industry—corporate America—highly concerned with what might happen out of this lawsuit.

CHRIS HANSEN: Everybody understood from the very beginning that the fight here was not about indecency or harmful-to-minors material on the Internet, although that was the way in which the fight was being played out. The fight was about what are the rules for free speech going to be on the Internet. What everybody had in mind was the disparity that the Supreme Court set up between the rules that apply to TV and radio, which were much more restrictive of free speech on the one hand, and on the other hand the rules that apply to books and magazines which are much more protective of free speech. I think everybody understood very early on that the fight was about which of those two models was going to apply in the context of the Internet.

ANN BEESON: [W]e were primarily arguing that the CDA was unconstitutional because it restricted speech that was protected for adults. We also argued and firmly believed that the law as written would have prevented young people—minors—from communicating speech that was even protected for them. There was not obscenity, but sex-related speech that teenagers have a right under the First Amendment to get to and that it's very important that they be able to access. That was one of the small differences between our case and the other one. We pushed that argument a little bit more.

JOHN MORRIS: Certainly, America Online and Microsoft and CompuServe and Apple didn't have a great corporate agenda to protect sexually oriented speech on the Internet. That was not their concern at all. Their concern was to not, through an uneducated and ill-considered court decision, send the Internet 98% of the way down the road toward broadcast-style regulation, which is very significantly regulated. They wanted to make sure that the court focused on the unique nature of the Internet, and focused on the way the Internet was not like television, which is what a lot of people thought. You know, it's electronic, you view it on a screen. There was a great concern that the courts in general needed to understand that this was diametrically at the opposite end of the spectrum from television.

CHRIS HANSEN: Many of the witnesses testified via affidavit. But the ones that we did bring in live, we chose very carefully—both toward illustrating the people who were at the greatest risk under this statute and were also the most respectable under the statute. The two clients who testified—the Critical Path AIDS Project guy who testified, Kiyoshi Kuromiya, and Patricia Nell Warren from Wildcat Press—were the ones designed to bring home to the court the valuable speech that would be at risk under the statute, and the respectability of our clients—both that they were genuinely at risk and that they were genuinely respectable.

PATRICIA NELL WARREN: I think in my case, I filled an area there that had some of the cultural overtones that they felt were important. I have been around a long time. I have done a lot of things. I have a resume that covers a lot of different ballparks in terms of what I've been involved in and what I've written about and what I've done over the years and maybe that was attractive to them. The fact that I am a businesswoman—that is important— a woman who owns her own publishing company. I think there were certain things there that may have made my name stand out on the list.

CHRIS HANSEN: Warren, who has written books for the gay and lesbian community and, indeed, for gay and lesbian adolescents, talked a lot about that. She, in fact, has a subpart of her Web site called Youth Art News which is specifically designed for gay and lesbian teenagers to exchange information—poems, drawings, short stories, and coming out stories. We thought that was incredibly valuable information. This case was not just about adults. This was also about teenagers.

PATRICIA NELL WARREN: They asked me a few questions about the credit card purchase process. That had been one of the points that I had made in my affidavit. If we would be required to verify the age of everybody who bought one of our books, this would be so costly for us that we would simply have to give up our Web site.

CHRIS HANSEN: The most moving testimony was probably Kiyoshi Kuromiya of the Critical Path AIDS Project who talked about how the AIDS prevention information on his Web site was literally necessary to save lives—that people would die if they couldn't get access to that kind of information.

JOHN MORRIS: I think that we understood even before the decision came out that the judges had gotten the Internet. As to whether they had bought our argument and agreed with our legal analysis, we weren't sure. Obviously, we were very optimistic. The court proceedings went very well, but I think we believed prior to the decision that the court really had, in fact, understood what was going on and understood how the Internet works. Certainly in our papers and in our oral presentation—our witness presentation—we made very clear that we think this is not like broadcast television. At the district court level I think we were comfortable with that.

CHRIS HANSEN: I was struck about how little the judges knew about the Internet [prior to the hearing]—how novel the issues were to them and how interested they were. It was very clear that all three of the judges were glad to be on the case, thought it was fun to be on the case, thought it was exciting to be on the case, and were fascinated by the kinds of testimony that they were hearing. They all asked lots of questions. They were a very active bench. But there was a sense in the room that everybody knew that this was really interesting and really important.

The effort to educate the district court's three-judge panel was successful. In June 1996, the court issued a wide-ranging ruling, striking down the Communications Decency Act (see court opinion excerpts at chapter's conclusion). Perhaps most remarkable was the court's articulation of its understanding of this new communication medium. This included sections on how the Internet is accessed, how communication on it occurs, the nature of the World Wide Web, the kinds of content available on the Internet, and the obstacles to age and credit card verification on the Internet. In all, the court enumerated 123 findings of fact about the Internet, followed by each of the judge's rationales for finding the government's defenses of the CDA inadequate, and the statute unconstitutional.

JOHN MORRIS: One thing that really excited our side about the district court decision is that the three judges at the district court level could have very easily done what is natural and what most judges do in most cases, which is to decide issues as narrowly as possible. It would have been relatively easy to write a 15-page decision striking down the Communication Decency Act on two or three specific, focused grounds. But the district court did not do that at all. It recognized that essentially it had been asked to be the first federal court to really look at the Internet at all closely anywhere in the country. It was being asked to set out a primer for the Internet and to try to articulate some first principles. We were very, very, pleased with the strength, breadth, and scope of the district court decision. I do have very strong memories of satisfaction in seeing over the course of a few weeks of trial—of courtroom presentation which happened over 5 days, although that was spread out over 3 or 4 weeks—and it was exciting and satisfying to realize that the court did understand it. The court really did get what we were saying. Again, we didn't have complete confidence that we would win, but we felt that the court would understand what we were trying to present. And that was a very satisfying result.

JERRY BERMAN: We were ecstatic with the opinion in the lower court—the opinions by all the judges—and the findings of fact which were accepted by the Justice Department which laid the framework for that decision. Coming out of Philadelphia, that opinion in my view is still, I would recommend it to anyone as a primer on how the Internet works and the characteristics of the new medium. And it has been used and taken on a whole aura. It has convinced a lot of people that decentralized user empowerment solutions are worth exploring across a range of issues.

Certainly nothing is a foregone conclusion, and I don't mean to suggest that—especially when it comes to the Supreme Court—but did you ever feel after the district court ruling and given what they did and the breadth of their opinions, that what would happen at the Supreme Court would very likely come down on your side?

CHRIS HANSEN: With the appropriate caveat you identify, the answer is probably, "Yes." The fact-finding that the three-judge court made was *terrific*. The Supreme Court is entirely capable of being dishonest about the facts, and ruling against you in spite of the facts, but it's harder for them. They have to *really* want to. I thought the three-judge court opinion fact-finding was as favorable as we could have hoped for. The case was postured—it was presented at the Supreme Court—in as favorable a posture as we could possibly hope for. I never had confidence that we were going to win, but I thought we had done as good a job as we could do. I thought that if we were going to lose, they were going to have to be dishonest about it. And that happens, but fortunately not as often as it might.

JERRY BERMAN: I was *not* confident. I wasn't confident because it's a very different court. It's much more conservative. [The district court ruling] was a very liberal decision.

Because of the nature of the expedited review provision that was written into the Communications Decency Act by Congress, the U.S. Supreme Court was required to hear *Reno v. ACLU* on direct appeal.

THE U.S. SUPREME COURT

MARJORIE HEINS: When it came to the Supreme Court, there were two people who wanted to argue it and were well-qualified to argue it—Chris [Hansen] and Bruce [Ennis]—and there was a contest. Everybody had agreed to this procedure. It's not unique. That's happened before

	when cases are consolidated or there may be two lawyers and they both want to argue it. Three people agreed to judge it. It's always awkward. They were both excellent. Naturally I wanted Chris to argue it.
JERRY BERMAN:	I thought the ACLU was putting its institutional ego in front of the merits and importance of the case. I would not rely on the ACLU in this case. Period. Under no circumstances were we going to rely on the ACLU's counsel. The best lawyer in town was Bruce Ennis. We hired him to win.
JOHN MORRIS:	In the end, it was decided by a moot court. Both Bruce and Chris Hansen prepared an oral argument. It was a private, confidential thing where a mock argument that Bruce Ennis and Chris Hansen both presented, the result of which that group of outside advisors decided that Bruce should argue the case. And that's what happened. Again, Chris Hansen would have done a great job, undoubtedly.
CHRIS HANSEN:	I thought Bruce was terrific. I thought he did a fabulous job, as always. He was a terrific lawyer.
JOHN MORRIS:	Bruce was truly one of the kindest, nicest, top-flight litigators that you can imagine, and one of the most diplomatic and courteous people that you could ever imagine being involved in a very fiercely contested litigation. There are lots of good lawyers out there in the world, but some of the good lawyers out there in the world can at times come off a little abrasively or a little harshly. And Bruce never did, although he certainly would argue any point vigorously that needed arguing. I think that level—that courtesy and professionalism—was a very important part of the whole dynamic that was created with the court in Philadelphia.
ANN BEESON:	At the Supreme Court you don't have the possibility of putting on any testimony or evidence and we were actually worried about that because we were afraid we wouldn't win them over so quickly if they didn't have a chance to look at it themselves.
JUDITH KRUG:	Every lawyer east of the Mississippi who works in or with, or even dabbles in the First Amendment was there. The lawyers' lounge was overflowing. The Court was absolutely packed. It was hilarious. I walked in and

said, "Oh, my God! The whole gang's here." It was
wonderful. It was exciting. There was an electricity in
the air. It was great. Our oral argument was March
19th. It was a combination of snow and rain in Washington. It was just awful. The cherry blossoms were
out and were as bedraggled as can be. Sitting in the
United States Supreme Court, and the thing I was
thinking about was, "This is *my* case! This is *my* case!
If I didn't raise the money I did, we wouldn't be here. If
I hadn't insisted that Bruce be the lead counsel, we
wouldn't be here."

JOHN MORRIS: At the Supreme Court level, there was a higher
level of anxiety because there wasn't any visual presentation. There wasn't a visual recording of the
demonstration below. It was entirely paper record.
It was one brief on our side and one oral argument,
and that was the sum total of our real, direct opportunity to educate the Court. But, frankly, the
Supreme Court works very hard, and they fully understood it even if we weren't there to kind of try
to hold their hand in getting to that understanding.
The initial full decision by the three-judge court in
the district court below spent a great deal of time
walking through what the complaint had walked
through—walking through how the Internet worked.
What the district court did itself became the
primer on how the Internet worked for a lot of
judges all around the country looking at a lot of issues. You see footnotes in cases—or you did back
then in '97, '98—you saw footnotes from judges
saying how the district court's decision in the *ACLU
v. Reno* case was how they got up to speed about
the Internet. The Supreme Court fully understood
that the district court had spent a lot of time understanding this, and I think it's pretty clear that
the Supreme Court themselves spent a lot of time.
Frankly, by 1997 when the case was argued at the
Supreme Court, the Supreme Court has very bright
law clerks. I'm sure that even at that relatively
early time—and I'm sure that even half of the law
clerks then were AOL subscribers or were on the
Internet somewhere. The Internet first really became popular on campuses, so I'm confident that
the law clerks played an important role in getting
the Supreme Court to fully understand how the
Internet worked.

ANN BEESON:	Everybody tries to second-guess what particular Justices will ask, and nobody ever does so successfully. We always set up—and we had several on this case—a moot court where we'd have the arguer practice their argument in front of a bunch of people who played the judges. And we'd jokingly try to play particular Justices, and never as I say, accurately predict what they'll actually ask. In this case, of course, we thought we'd have much more of an enemy in Justices Scalia and Thomas than we did, who ultimately voted totally with us and on our side.
JUDITH KRUG:	[Bruce] was asked a question by [Justice] Breyer, and that, I thought, clinched it for our side. The question was something like, "Do you mean if a father was with his son who happened to be 13 or 14, and the child accessed what somebody thought was indecent, that the father would be liable?" And Bruce said, "Well, sir, that's what the law reads." It was that question by Breyer that sort of clinched it for me, and I thought, "We are home free."

The thousands of people who were interested in the Supreme Court's pronouncements about the CDA and the Internet had a 3-month wait from the date it was argued in March 1997. The Court embraced the findings of the three-judge panel in Philadelphia. Justice John Paul Stevens addressed the key issue of age verification, citing the lower court's finding that there is no effective way to determine the identity or age of an Internet user (see Court opinion excerpts at chapter's conclusion). This was an important issue for Web site operators, who also claimed the cost of age verification could put them out of business. A number of other CDA problems were cited, including the law being vague and overly broad. The Court was concerned that in an effort to protect children, the CDA would have deprived adults of legal speech. Stevens cited a precedent in which the Court remarked that speech restrictions there amounted to "burning the house to roast the pig," and noted that the CDA similarly threatens to "torch a large segment of the Internet community." Likewise, despite the good intentions of the CDA to protect the welfare of children, Stevens wrote that "the level of discourse reaching a mailbox simply cannot be limited to that which would be suitable for a sandbox."

All nine Supreme Court Justices believed the CDA to be unconstitutional. Justice O'Connor, joined by Chief Justice Rehnquist, wrote a separate opinion in which she concurred in part and dissented in part. The opinion is construed by some as reserving the right to uphold a similar congressional effort in the future if it is better worded or if Internet technology develops to better enable enforcement of the law.

REACTIONS TO THE RULING

JUDITH KRUG: I was in San Francisco at a convention and we had John Morris at the Court, and he stood on the lawn of the U.S. Supreme Court and read us the decision as it came onto his computer, because that's how they released it. Bruce was on one pay phone and I was on the other pay phone. We were standing there holding hands yelling, "Yes! Yes! Yes!" We were crazy. It was wonderful. And all of a sudden [John] said, "Oh shit, I gotta leave because they're watering the lawn." That's hilarious ... We had an open air rally that afternoon in San Francisco. And as I'm telling you this, I'm pulling out this wonderful set of pictures of me and Bruce sitting on this flatbed truck at this rally. It was wonderful. It was a hell of a day. It was absolutely wonderful.

CHRIS HANSEN: Obviously, we were really pleased. I think the three-judge court decision at some level was more exciting and more pleasing because of the breadth of the decision. I remember reading that decision— a bunch of us were sitting in a room reading it together—and each one of us would reach a point in the decision and would stop and exclaim how wonderful that paragraph was, or this sentence was, and so on.

ANN BEESON: We were all sort of racing around, reading the opinion as we were simultaneously discussing it with one another in the office. Just, again, being amazed that all our hard work had paid off, and that we had managed somehow to convince all of the Justices, even those who had been very unfriendly, to issues about the protection of children before.

JOHN MORRIS: I think the Supreme Court did a hugely important thing in evaluating the Internet and recognizing that the Internet receives the same level of protection as print media. But it also did a very important thing in reaffirming its prior holding that you cannot reduce adult communications to the level of a child just to protect the child. The values of allowing adults to exchange constitutionally protected lawful speech, even if it's a little bit offensive to some people, is important enough that you can't unduly restrict that just to protect a child.

JERRY BERMAN:	What the Court said here is you don't need a Federal Internet Commission, at least for now. We're talking about a modium that fits tho characteristics of print. It's the first electronic medium that's treated as equivalent to print.
PATRICIA NELL WARREN:	Well, I was very happy that the Court decided the way that they did. At the same time, it's pretty clear that with the Supreme Court that when they make these decisions, people who are determined to have their perspective put in place for the whole country will simply then veer back and they will try another way. If you can't do it over the wall here, you're going to try to go over the wall another place.
CHRIS HANSEN:	[The two concurrences were] a hint to Congress that it wasn't time to give up entirely, and that there were ways to try to write a statute that would be consti- tutional, and that two of them at least would be will- ing to uphold the statute written in that way, and hinted at the possibility that some pieces of the stat- ute should have been found constitutional.
JERRY BERMAN:	I think the signal that it sent was this medium is dif- ferent. It's played a part in people paying more atten- tion to the Internet as a publishing venue. Because of this decision, the Internet has turned the computer clearly into a powerful communications medium, in part because it's so open. People reading the decision have said, "By George, we can open up on the Internet and we're not going to jail." People are understanding that you can't really control the Internet the way you control other things.
MARJORIE HEINS:	I guess I had mixed reactions, and that's because of [my] interest in getting the judges to really think about this very broad indecency standard that they had approved in *Pacifica*—at least for broadcasting— and the havoc it has wreaked in the field of censorship since then.
ANN BEESON:	One of the things that I think impressed us the most was the extent to which [the Justices] really had studied the record and were very concerned about our clients, and asked specific questions saying—the gov- ernment trying to focus on "Oh, all we're talking about here is pornography." The Justices just kept asking

again and again, "Well, what about the Critical Path AIDS site?" and "What are you telling me? That that content isn't explicit enough to be covered? It is, and what's he supposed to do?" I remember us all being very impressed by that.

JERRY BERMAN: The *ALA v. Reno* [part of the lawsuit] was indispensable because it's not clear whether the ACLU could have won this lawsuit given the need to explain, argue, and persuade the court that the Internet was different. So I think it was absolutely indispensable to the win—certainly to any win which would have established a vision for how the Court looks at the Internet as the most open electronic medium with the equivalency of print.

ANN BEESON: Would we still have won [without the *ALA* suit]? No doubt in my mind. I think we won the case because of the ACLU plaintiffs—real people truly threatened by the law, and because of all the facts and personal testimony about the Internet that we put into evidence. As you know, the ACLU has challenged many more Internet censorship laws (and much more narrowly crafted ones) since CDA, and have won all the cases even when ALA and the on-line businesses weren't involved. But the work of many additional talented lawyers, and the support of ALA and mainstream online businesses, was valuable for the CDA case.

THE LEGACY OF *RENO* AND THE FUTURE OF THE INTERNET

CHRIS HANSEN: I hope the legacy will be that it will be difficult, if not impossible, to censor speech on the Internet.

JOHN MORRIS: That doesn't mean, as Judge Dalzell suggested, that no regulation is constitutionally possible. As much as I might like that to be true, some regulation on the Internet is going to be constitutionally possible, but not in the kind of broad brush, kind of cumbersome fiat that Congress has tried.

CHRIS HANSEN: I do think that the longer you hold onto a medium like the Internet that is free of restriction, the harder it is to start rolling that back. It's easiest to impose restrictions at the very beginning. The fact that we held off restrictions at the very beginning I hope will last.

JOHN MORRIS: What is the legacy of this case? What's the long term impact? I think this decision will continue to be the starting point for 50 years—for a very long time it will be where courts start when they evaluate regulation of the Internet. But it will also be an important point in the whole development of lots of smaller parts of the First Amendment jurisprudence in terms of, for example, avoiding the dumbing down of communications just to protect children. I think it will withstand the test of time. I think it really sets up the framework for years to come.

JUDITH KRUG: Bruce felt that the decision was so strong—and, of course, the vote was as strong as it can get—that, in effect, the Court had said that this medium of communication is not only important, it is going to be vital to and integral to the 21st Century means of communicating. The Court, by its strong decision, has said that you're not going to be able to willy-nilly to try to censor or take other actions that would be detrimental to this communications mode. He also said that with this decision, we have set the standard. For the foreseeable future—and maybe into the far future— every legislative action and every litigated action is going to be held against the Communications Decency Act decision. And that is exactly what is happening. This decision set the standard, and that is the standard that we can live up to and that people are going to have to abide by because it's so strong.

MARJORIE HEINS: The specific rhetoric about protecting kids which drove the Communications Decency Act seems to continue unabated. There are people who are genuinely concerned about the upbringing of kids, but I don't know that I would necessarily count politicians among them. Most politicians are waving this banner of child protection because it's a hot emotional issue. They think it's to their advantage politically. The *Reno* decision didn't do very much in terms of engendering more sober thought about proper upbringing of children and ways in which control over the information they receive or guidance in their education might be accomplished.

PATRICIA NELL WARREN: If the ruling would have gone the other way, then the question would have been either to fold your tent and steel away into the night—namely take down your Web site for fear of being prosecuted, and there were Web sites that went down, even before the case was decided because people were very, very concerned—or they set up barriers where you had to somehow or other prove that you were over 18 to get in. They went through a certain drill even before the decision came down because they were that frightened. So after that, the decision would have been, "Are you willing to become a test case?"

JERRY BERMAN: I think [a loss] would have signaled that the Internet, despite its technological potential as an open medium, was going to be another regulated medium. You could turn to the government and in its discretion of acting on behalf of protecting children, the public interest and all that, it could set limitations on it. It would have made it very difficult for the Internet to thrive the way it has in terms of the number of Web sites and so on because it would begin to conglomerate the Internet.

CHRIS HANSEN: If the ruling had gone the other way, the Internet would have developed in a different way and, I think, in a less valuable way than it has. Whether it's developed in the way that it reaches its full potential, I don't have any idea. A loss would have been worse than a win is good. A loss would have really crabbed the Internet and constricted its development. A win has allowed it to develop freely. Whether it's developed well or poorly is a different question, but it has allowed it to develop freely.

ANN BEESON: I really think that if [the CDA] had passed [judicial scrutiny], the Internet might not have continued to expand the way it did and people would have been so constrained and so afraid of criminal prosecution, that the whole medium could have died. Every time there's a new medium that comes along, the first thing that happens is lawmakers try to control it, and they keep trying to control it until they succeed in some small way, at least. That's still going on with the Internet.

PATRICIA NELL WARREN: The Internet is at a very vulnerable point because they've been able to raise all these fears in peoples' minds. I think it's a mistake to try to handle this problem by legislation and government action because that's censorship. I think that parents ought to be doing more if that's how they feel. At a certain point you have to give parents a place to stand and say this is how I feel about what I want my kids to be seeing. They certainly have a right to put filtering things on their own computers at home, and the right to teach their kids certain things.

CHRIS HANSEN: I think the most significant thing was that of the three judges on the three-judge court that heard the trial, and the nine Justices on the Supreme Court—that's 12 judges—only one, as far as I know, at the time they heard the case had ever been on the Internet, even so much as e-mail. Nobody understood this medium. Nobody was using this medium. It was a new medium of communication and we were fighting about what the rules were going to be in a new medium of communication. The Internet has turned out to be an even more pervasive medium of communication than we all thought it was going to be. It's grown faster and grown in ways that none of us anticipated.

JOHN MORRIS: Has technology overtaken that suit and would the result be different? I think the result would not be different. A key element of the Internet is the ability for people to just go surf and browse willy-nilly wherever they want, and not to necessarily to have to go register to go look at a certain site, and not have to validate or verify that they are a certain age or that they're from a certain location. That nature and dynamic of browsing on the Web still continues today, and is still a dominant method of accessing content on the Internet—to be able to jump around to lots of different locations and get information without having to pre-register. That hasn't changed, and I think that was one of the most important factual elements that the courts looked at back in 1996 in terms of just understanding how the CDA back then would have changed the nature of the Internet. The CDA today would have the exact same debilitating effect on the Internet.

CHRIS HANSEN: I think the medium that it is most akin to is conversation. I've, over the years, more and more used the metaphor of conversation rather than books and magazines, in part because it is more off-the-cuff than books and magazines, much more spontaneous, much more interactive than books and magazines. And, in part, because it has the quality of conversation that nobody pays that much attention to what they're say-

ing. People don't worry that much about being careful.
So it's got a lot of hyperbole and a lot of excess and a
lot of casualness and a lot of misspellings and
mistypings. In my mind, it has become much more like
conversation. I do think one of the critical questions today that we didn't anticipate back then is whether that
part of the Internet is going to be drowned out by essentially the large corporate efforts to turn it into a
mall for sales. We just don't know the answer to that.

Bottom line, what was really at issue here?

ANN BEESON: I really, truly think it was about the very existence of
the Internet—whether this very powerful new medium
was going to be allowed to flourish, or whether it was
going to stagnate under very tight censorial government control. I think the very existence of the medium
was at risk. Even more particularly, the fact is, even if
we had lost, the big corporate interests and big media
companies would have probably been safe—felt safe
enough to continue to communicate. But all of the little guys, which is what makes the Internet so fascinating—the proliferation of content from regular
people and very diverse speakers who otherwise had a
very small audience, if any audience at all—all of that
content, the diversity of content and communication
would have been lost, I think.

CHRIS HANSEN: I think what was at issue was the amount of free
speech we were going to allow in the context of the
Internet. I think that's the principal thing that was at
issue. I do think there is a continuing debate in the
country as there has been over the last 25 or 30
years about speech about sex, and what to think about
speech about sex, and how much we should censor
speech about sex. As the prosecutors in the country
have largely stopped enforcing at least obscenity laws,
I think the people who believe that obscenity laws
should be enforced are becoming increasingly frantic to
pass other laws in the hopes that prosecutors would
enforce those other laws, because they can't get them
to enforce the obscenity laws.

JOHN MORRIS: The Internet really is a special and unique medium unlike anything we've seen before that really does offer
amazing potential for people to communicate with
other people, and to do so at a quite low cost. That

potential is both being realized and it's actually also somewhat being threatened. As the Internet becomes more commercialized, there's some question in my mind about whether it will continue to be as dynamic of a communications medium as it is. I think it will be. But I have some concerns about that. But I think that was the message: that the Internet really is something new and different and it needs to be protected in its state.

CHRIS HANSEN: If convergence occurs, it seems to me there will come a point when the Supreme Court will have to decide which of the two rules to use—whether the rules should be the broadcast rules, or whether the rules should be the Internet rules. And I don't think the result is pre-ordained. You know, the more cases we win on the free speech side—resisting censorship—the better in the sense that it creates a momentum toward free speech. And also the longer we live with free speech, the less scared we become of it.

ANN BEESON: You're going to get more and more situations where people are accessing Internet content through their cable lines and over TV. And what's going to happen at that point? We would argue that the way, so far as media are converging, it is going to continue to offer more and more control to the consumer and to the parent in terms of what content they look at and whether they affirmatively go and have to seek out content like you do on the Internet or whether there's just a couple of choices and you turn the TV on and it's there. We think that the ability to control it from the consumer point of view is going to increase and therefore anything the existing restrictions on broadcast should be re-thought and perhaps overturned.

JOHN MORRIS: The Internet both empowers speakers to reach out across the entire world and to speak with the same type of voice that huge corporate entities have been able to speak for many years. So it empowers individual speakers. But it also empowers listeners and parents and employers to control what speech is received on the receiving end.

PERSONAL REFLECTIONS

CHRIS HANSEN: I take the long view of all of this stuff that no issue is ever won, and no issue is ever lost.

ANN BEESON: The fact that our clients were so much at risk and there were so many, many literally millions of other speakers at risk—valuable speakers—made it an even more satisfying job to do.

PATRICIA NELL WARREN: There were certainly some anxieties on the part of my business partner and myself, thinking that if we lost, then what were we going to do? Would there be repercussions? When you're a small company and you push yourself into a high profile like that in a situation where there could be legal repercussions—it's one thing for Microsoft to have repercussions, for example. They have a lot of money and a lot of lawyers to fight it with. But a little company like ours, it would be very difficult. So there were certainly some anxieties. I think the fact that it went off fairly quickly was a help. I think that if it had gone on over a long period of time, it would have been more difficult.

ANN BEESON: I'm very definitely a First Amendment absolutist and the reason that I'm a First Amendment absolutist is that I haven't seen any other system that works any better. I'm certainly not a champion of certain kinds of speech at all, but I don't want the government being the one that decides what's good and what's bad.

CHRIS HANSEN: I don't think I quite anticipated the degree to which other people were paying attention to the case. When you get involved in one of these cases, there's an eye of the storm quality to them in the sense that you're dealing with the minutiae of litigation and the minutiae of briefing and the minutiae of what is practicing law these days. Much of it seems very detailed and almost trivial, very minor. Because you're so deep into it, it is not as easy to step back and see the big picture. We had a press conference here at the ACLU when we won the case, and I was shocked at the level of attendance and the level of attention the case got. Even though I thought it was really important, I hadn't quite focused on how many people thought it was important and how much attention was being paid to it.

ANN BEESON: We put together affidavits from three different teenagers, which I still believe are some of the most moving pieces of evidence in the case. One of them was from a high school student in Los Angeles who had been very much at risk, who had dropped out of school and who was involved in gangs, and was a very angst-ridden lesbian Hispanic girl who lived there. She had the good fortune to become affiliated with an arts-related project that encouraged students not just to write poetry and fiction and do other arts-related things, but also to put them up on the Internet. She had kind of discovered herself as a poet and had become a really quite incredible poet. She was publishing her poetry on the Internet. This whole thing had really turned her life around, both in that she had a venue for her own speech and also because it allowed her to connect with many other people like herself—young lesbians—across the country. I continue to be a champion of these teenagers, and felt that they were just as much at risk in terms of really losing a lot. Somehow because of that, there were over a hundred different high school students who found out about my involvement in the case and sent me personal e-mails telling me that I was their hero for defending this case and in particular for pushing the minors' rights point. I still get e-mail from high school students who are researching these issues for various classes, and I always find it very rewarding to respond to them. In those early days, in particular, it was just a great thing to have all of these teenagers backing me up and thrilled that we were also representing them.

Could you share with me how this case and working on it has impacted your life professionally?

ANN BEESON: Geez, Louise. I owe my entire livelihood to this case. It is all very serendipitous how I even got to work on it. This was my very first case. I had never tried a case before. It weighs on me much more in retrospect than it did at the time. It was a very exciting experience at the time. But having never experienced anything else (laughs), it was hard to appreciate that not every lawsuit was like this. You didn't always have cameras following you into the courtroom. I certainly knew personally what big issues were at stake and felt very lucky in many ways, and still do, to be able to be involved in such an important mission.

PATRICIA NELL WARREN: The real issue is for the individual human being. If I as an individual who believes in the American dream, and believes in free speech, and if I really think that our country has had a history of struggle to learn how to respect diverse viewpoints, then how can I live with myself to allow this to be done to me? If I let it be done to me, what kind of signal does that send to other people, especially young writers? Because young people do pay attention to these things, and when they see examples of people standing up for what they think and what they feel, that should be important to them. If they see a lot of us willing to eat dirt and bow our necks to the yoke, then that sends a terrible signal to those young people. So it really comes down to how I feel about myself and how I see myself and how I could live with myself if I had done that.

So was your involvement in all this worth it?

PATRICIA NELL WARREN: Oh yes! Absolutely!

When you began this entire effort could you have imagined that it would have unfolded as it did?

JUDITH KRUG: No, not in my wildest dreams. Realize that from the time this legislation was passed, which was February 6th, 1996, until we got a Supreme Court decision—we filed on February 26, 1996. The decision came down on June 26, 1997. That is only 16 months. Sixteen months! We changed the history of communication. It blows my mind.

**American Civil Liberties Union,
et al., v. Janet Reno, Attorney
General of the United States;
American Library Association,
Inc., et al.,
v. United States Department
of Justice, et al.**

UNITED STATES
DISTRICT COURT
FOR THE EASTERN
DISTRICT OF
PENNSYLVANIA

929 F. Supp. 824
Decided: June 11, 1996

OPINION BY: Dolores K. Sloviter;
Ronald L. Buckwalter; Stewart
Dalzell

ADJUDICATION ON MOTIONS
FOR PRELIMINARY INJUNC-
TION

I.

INTRODUCTION

Procedural Background

Plaintiffs contend that the two challenged provisions of the CDA that
are directed to communications over
the Internet which might be deemed
"indecent" or "patently offensive"
for minors, defined as persons under
the age of eighteen, infringe upon

rights protected by the First Amendment and the Due Process Clause of
the Fifth Amendment.

...

Section 223(a)(1)(B) provides in
part that any person in interstate or
foreign communications who, "by
means of a telecommunications device," "knowingly ... makes, creates, or solicits" and "initiates the
transmission" of "any comment, request, suggestion, proposal, image
or other communication which is
obscene or indecent, knowing that
the recipient of the communication
is under 18 years of age," "shall be
criminally fined or imprisoned."

...

Section 223(d)(1) ("the patently offensive provision"), makes it a crime
to use an "interactive computer service" to "send" or "display in a manner available" to a person under age
18, "any comment, request, suggestion, proposal, image, or other communication that, in context, depicts
or describes, in terms patently offensive as measured by contemporary
community standards, sexual or ex-
cretory activities or organs, regardless of whether the user of such
service placed the call or initiated
the communication."

...

As part of its argument that the CDA passes constitutional muster, the Government cites the CDA's "safe harbor" defenses in new @ 223(e) of 47 U.S.C., which provides:

(e) Defenses

In addition to any other defenses available by law:

(1) No person shall be held to have violated subsection (a) or (d) of this section solely for providing access or connection to or from a facility, system, or network not under that person's control, including transmission, downloading, intermediate storage, access software, or other related capabilities that are incidental to providing such access or connection that does not include the creation of the content of the communication.

(2) The defenses provided by paragraph (1) of this subsection shall not be applicable to a person who is a conspirator with an entity actively involved in the creation or knowing distribution of communications that violate this section, or who knowingly advertises the availability of such communications.

(3) The defenses provided in paragraph (1) of this subsection shall not be applicable to a person who provides access or connection to a facility, system, or network engaged in the violation of this section that is owned or controlled by such person.

(4) No employer shall be held liable under this section for the actions of an employee or agent unless the employee's or agent's conduct is within the scope of his or her employment or agency and the employer (A) having knowledge of such conduct, authorizes or ratifies such conduct, or (B) recklessly disregards such conduct.

(5) It is a defense to a prosecution under subsection (a)(1)(B) or (d) of this section, or under subsection (a)(2) of this section with respect to the use of a facility for an activity under subsection (a)(1)(B) that a person—(A) has taken, in good faith, reasonable, effective, and appropriate actions under the circumstances to restrict or prevent access by minors to a communication specified in such subsections, which may involve any appropriate measures to restrict minors from such communications, including any method which is feasible under available technology; or (B) has restricted access to such communication by requiring use of a verified credit card, debit account, adult access code, or adult personal identification number.

(6) The [Federal Communications] Commission may describe measures which are reasonable, effective, and appropriate to restrict access to prohibited communications under subsection (d) of this section. Nothing in this section authorizes the Commission to enforce, or is intended to provide the Commission with the authority to approve, sanction, or permit, the use of such measures. The Commission shall have no enforcement authority over the failure to utilize such measures.

...

II.

FINDINGS OF FACT

All parties agree that in order to apprehend the legal questions at issue in these cases, it is necessary to have a clear understanding of the exponentially growing, worldwide medium that is the Internet, which presents unique issues relating to the application of First Amendment jurisprudence and due process requirements to this new and evolving method of communication. For this reason all parties insisted on having extensive evidentiary hearings before the three-judge court.

...

The Nature of Cyberspace

The Creation of the Internet and the Development of Cyberspace

1. The Internet is not a physical or tangible entity, but rather a giant network which interconnects innumerable smaller groups of linked computer networks. It is thus a network of networks.

...

12. Individuals have a wide variety of avenues to access cyberspace in general, and the Internet in particular.

...

Methods to Communicate Over the Internet

22. Once one has access to the Internet, there are a wide variety of different methods of communication and information exchange over the network.

...

34. Purpose. The World Wide Web (W3C) was created to serve as the platform for a global, online store of knowledge, containing information from a diversity of sources and accessible to Internet users around the world.

...

46. A distributed system with no centralized control.

...

47. Contrast to closed databases. The Web's open, distributed, decentralized nature stands in sharp contrast to most information systems that have come before it.

...

[V]arious entities have begun to build systems intended to enable parents to control the material which comes into their homes and may be accessible to their children.

...

Internet software intended to empower parents to exercise individual choice over what material their children could access.

...

66. Another software product, SurfWatch, is also designed to allow parents and other concerned users to filter unwanted material on the Internet.

...

69. Plaintiffs America Online (AOL), Microsoft Network, and Prodigy all offer parental control options free of charge to their members.

...

74. The types of content now on the Internet defy easy classification.

...

75. The Internet is not exclusively, or even primarily, a means of commercial communication.

...

80. [U]nlike traditional media, the barriers to entry as a speaker on the Internet do not differ significantly from the barriers to entry as a listener.

...

81. The Internet is therefore a unique and wholly new medium of worldwide human communication.

...

84. It is possible that a search engine can accidentally retrieve material of a sexual nature through an imprecise search, as demonstrated at the hearing.

...

85. Once a provider posts content on the Internet, it is available to all other Internet users worldwide.

...

90. There is no effective way to determine the identity or the age of a user who is accessing material through e-mail, mail exploders, newsgroups or chat rooms.

...

93. Even if it were technologically feasible to block minors' access to newsgroups and similar fora, there is no method by which the creators of newsgroups which contain discussions of art, politics or any other subject that could potentially elicit "indecent" contributions could limit the blocking of access by minors to such "indecent" material and still allow them access to the remaining content, even if the overwhelming majority of that content was not indecent.

...

The Practicalities of the Proffered Defenses

Note: The Government contends the CDA makes available three potential defenses to all content providers on the Internet: credit card verification, adult verification by password or adult identification number, and "tagging."

Credit Card Verification

97. Verification of a credit card number over the Internet is not now technically possible.

...

101. Credit card verification would significantly delay the retrieval of information on the Internet.

...

102. Imposition of a credit card requirement would completely bar adults who do not have a credit card and lack the resources to obtain one from accessing any blocked material.

...

103. The Government offered very limited evidence regarding the operation of existing age verification systems.

...

107. Even if credit card verification or adult password verification were implemented, the Government presented no testimony as to how such systems could ensure that the user of the password or credit card is in fact over 18.

...

110. The Government's tagging proposal would require all content providers that post arguably "indecent" material to review all of their online content, a task that would be extremely burdensome for organizations that provide large amounts of

material online which cannot afford to pay a large staff to review all of that material.

...

116. Tags can not currently activate or deactivate themselves depending on the age or location of the receiver.

...

117. A large percentage, perhaps 40% or more, of content on the Internet originates outside the United States.

...

III.

CONCLUSIONS OF LAW

...

The government uses the term "indecent" interchangeably with "patently offensive" and advises that it so construes the statute in light of the legislative history and the Supreme Court's analysis of the word "indecent" in *FCC v. Pacifica Foundation*, 438 U.S. 726, 57 L. Ed. 2d 1073, 98 S.Ct. 3026 (1978). However, the CDA does not define "indecent."

...

B.

Preliminary Injunction Standard

...

Subjecting speakers to criminal penalties for speech that is constitutionally protected in itself raises the spectre of irreparable harm.

...

[T]he public interest weighs in favor of having access to a free flow of constitutionally protected speech.

...

C.

Applicable Standard of Review

The CDA is patently a government-imposed content-based restriction on speech, and the speech at issue, whether denominated "indecent" or "patently offensive," is entitled to constitutional protection.

...

Internet communication, while unique, is more akin to telephone communication, at issue in *Sable*, than to broadcasting, at issue in *Pacifica*, because, as with the telephone, an Internet user must act affirmatively and deliberately to retrieve specific information online.

Even if a broad search will, on occasion, retrieve unwanted materials, the user virtually always receives some warning of its content, significantly reducing the element of surprise or "assault" involved in broadcasting.

...

D.

The Nature of the Government's Interest

[T]he government has made no showing that it has a compelling interest in preventing a seventeen-year-old minor from accessing such images.

By contrast, plaintiffs presented testimony that material that could be considered indecent, such as that offered by Stop Prisoner Rape or Critical Path AIDS Project, may be critically important for certain older minors.

E.

The Reach of the Statute

Whatever the strength of the interest the government has demonstrated in preventing minors from accessing "indecent" and "patently offensive" material online, if the

means it has chosen sweeps more broadly than necessary and thereby chills the expression of adults, it has overstepped onto rights protected by the First Amendment.

...

[I]t is either technologically impossible or economically prohibitive for many of the plaintiffs to comply with the CDA without seriously impeding their posting of online material which adults have a constitutional right to access.

...

It is clear from the face of the CDA and from its legislative history that Congress did not intend to limit its application to commercial purveyors of pornography.

...

I conclude inexorably from the foregoing that the CDA reaches speech subject to the full protection of the First Amendment, at least for adults.

...

[T]here is no realistic way for many providers to ascertain the age of those accessing their materials.

...

BUCKWALTER, District Judge

A.

I believe that plaintiffs should prevail in this litigation.

...

[C]urrent technology is inadequate to provide a safe harbor to most speakers on the Internet.... In addition, I continue to believe that the word "indecent" is unconstitutionally vague, and I find that the terms "in context" and "patently offensive" also are so vague as to violate the First and Fifth Amendments.

...

[A]bove all, I believe that the challenged provisions are so vague as to violate both the First and Fifth Amendments, and in particular that Congress' reliance on *Pacifica* is misplaced.

...

It is a basic principle of due process that an enactment is void for vagueness if its prohibitions are not clearly defined.

...

Vague laws may trap the innocent by not providing fair warning.

...

The fundamental constitutional principle that concerns me is one of simple fairness, and that is absent in the CDA.

...

The thrust of the Government's argument is that the court should trust prosecutors to prosecute only a small segment of those speakers subject to the CDA's restrictions, and whose works would reasonably be considered "patently offensive" in every community.

...

DALZELL, District Judge

A. Introduction

I begin with first principles: As a general rule, the Constitution forbids the Government from silencing speakers because of their particular message.

...

The Government may only regulate indecent speech for a compelling reason, and in the least restrictive manner. *Sable*, 492 U.S. at 126. "It is not enough to show that the Government's ends are compelling; the means must be carefully tailored to achieve those ends."

...

D. A Medium-Specific Analysis

The Internet is a new medium of mass communication. As such, the Supreme Court's First Amendment jurisprudence compels us to consider the special qualities of this new medium in determining whether the CDA is a constitutional exercise of governmental power.

...

I conclude that the CDA is unconstitutional and that the First Amendment denies Congress the power to regulate protected speech on the Internet.

...

In this case, the Government relies on the *Pacifica* decision in arguing that the CDA is a constitutional exercise of governmental power.

...

The argument also assumes that what is good for broadcasting is good for the Internet.

...

Time has not been kind to the *Pacifica* decision. Later cases have eroded its reach, and the Supreme Court has repeatedly instructed

against overreading the rationale of its holding.

...

[T]he Court concluded that the law, like a law it had struck down in 1957, "denied adults their free speech rights by allowing them to read only what was acceptable for children."

...

[I]n *Turner Broadcasting System, Inc. v. FCC*, 512 U.S. 622, 129 L. Ed. 2d 497, 114 S. Ct. 2445 (1994), the Supreme Court implicitly limited *Pacifica* once again when it declined to adopt the broadcast rationale for the medium of cable television. The Court concluded that the rules for broadcast were "inapt" for cable because of the "fundamental technological differences between broadcast and cable transmission."

...

Turner thus confirms that the analysis of a particular medium of mass communication must focus on the underlying technology that brings the information to the user.

...

Over the course of five days of hearings and many hundreds of pages of declarations, deposition transcripts, and exhibits, we have learned about the special attributes of Internet communication. Our Findings of fact—many of them undisputed—express our understanding of the Internet. These Findings lead to the conclusion that Congress may not regulate indecency on the Internet at all.

…

To understand how disruptive the CDA is to Internet communication, it must be remembered that the Internet evolved free of content-based considerations.

…

The CDA will, without doubt, undermine the substantive, speech-enhancing benefits that have flowed from the Internet.

…

The diversity of the content will necessarily diminish as a result.

…

The CDA will also skew the relative parity among speakers that currently exists on the Internet.

…

Perversely, commercial pornographers would remain rela-tively unaffected by the Act, since we learned that most of them already use credit card or adult verification anyway.

…

At the heart of the First Amendment lies the principle that each person should decide for him or herself the ideas and beliefs deserving of expression, consideration, and adherence.

…

Both *Tornillo* and *Turner* recognize, in essence, that the cure for market dysfunction (government-imposed, content-based speech restrictions) will almost always be worse than the disease. Here, however, I am hard-pressed even to identify the disease. It is no exaggeration to conclude that the Internet has achieved, and continues to achieve, the most participatory marketplace of mass speech that this country—and indeed the world—has yet seen. The plaintiffs in these actions correctly describe the "democratizing" effects of Internet communication: individual citizens of limited means can speak to a worldwide audience on issues of concern to them.

…

[T]he Government's asserted "failure" of the Internet rests on the implicit premise that too much speech occurs in that medium, and that speech there is too available to the participants. This is exactly the benefit of Internet communication, however. The Government, therefore, implicitly asks this court to limit both the amount of speech on the Internet and the availability of that speech. This argument is profoundly repugnant to First Amendment principles.

...

[T]he Internet deserves the broadest possible protection from government-imposed, content-based regulation. If "the First Amendment erects a virtually insurmountable barrier between government and the print media," *Tornillo*, 418 U.S. at 259 (White, J., concurring), even though the print medium fails to achieve the hoped for diversity in the marketplace of ideas, then that "insurmountable barrier" must also exist for a medium that succeeds in achieving that diversity.

...

[I]f the goal of our First Amendment jurisprudence is the "individual dignity and choice" that arises from "putting the decision as to what views shall be voiced largely into the hands of each of us," ... then we should be especially vigilant in preventing content-based regulation of a medium that every minute allows individual citizens actually to make those decisions. Any content-based regulation of the Internet, no matter how benign the purpose, could burn the global village to roast the pig.

...

The Internet is a far more speech-enhancing medium than print, the village green, or the mails. Because it would necessarily affect the Internet itself, the CDA would necessarily reduce the speech available for adults on the medium. This is a constitutionally intolerable result.

Some of the dialogue on the Internet surely tests the limits of conventional discourse. Speech on the Internet can be unfiltered, unpolished, and unconventional, even emotionally charged, sexually explicit, and vulgar—in a word, "indecent" in many communities. But we should expect such speech to occur in a medium in which citizens from all walks of life have a voice.

...

[T]he CDA will almost certainly fail to accomplish the Government's interest in shielding children from pornography on the Internet. Nearly half of Internet communications originate outside the United States, and some percentage of that figure represents pornography.

...

Cutting through the acronyms and argot that littered the hearing testimony, the Internet may fairly be regarded as a never-ending worldwide conversation. The Government may not, through the CDA, interrupt that conversation. As the most participatory form of mass speech yet developed, the Internet deserves the highest protection from governmental intrusion.

Janet Reno, Attorney General of The United States, et al., Appellants v. American Civil Liberties Union, et al.

SUPREME COURT OF THE UNITED STATES

521 U.S. 844
Argued: March 19, 1997
Decided: June 26, 1997

COUNSEL: Seth P. Waxman argued the cause for appellants.

Bruce J. Ennis argued the cause for appellees.

OPINION: JUSTICE STEVENS delivered the opinion of the Court.

At issue is the constitutionality of two statutory provisions enacted to protect minors from "indecent" and "patently offensive" communications on the Internet. Notwithstanding the legitimacy and importance of the congressional goal of protecting children from harmful materials, we agree with the three-judge District Court that the statute abridges "the freedom of speech" protected by the First Amendment.

...

The Internet has experienced "extraordinary growth."

...

Individuals can obtain access to the Internet from many different sources, generally hosts themselves or entities with a host affiliation.

...

Anyone with access to the Internet may take advantage of a wide variety of communication and information retrieval methods. These methods are constantly evolving and difficult to categorize precisely.... Taken together, these tools constitute a unique medium—known to its users as "cyberspace"—located in no particular geographical location but available to anyone, anywhere in the world, with access to the Internet.

...

From the publishers' point of view, it constitutes a vast platform from which to address and hear from a world-wide audience of millions of readers, viewers, researchers, and buyers.

...

No single organization controls any membership in the Web, nor is there any centralized point from which individual Web sites or services can be blocked from the Web.

...

Though such material is widely available, users seldom encounter such content accidentally.

...

Systems have been developed to help parents control the material that may be available on a home computer with Internet access.

...

Age Verification

The problem of age verification differs for different uses of the Internet. The District Court categorically determined that there "is no effective way to determine the identity or the age of a user."

...

[A]t the time of the trial, credit card verification was "effectively unavailable to a substantial number of Internet content providers."

...

In sum, the District Court found:

"Even if credit card verification or adult password verification were implemented, the Government presented no testimony as to how such systems could ensure that the user of the password or credit card is in fact over 18."

...

The CDA's broad categorical prohibitions are not limited to particular times and are not dependent on any evaluation by an agency familiar with the unique characteristics of the Internet.

...

[U]nlike the conditions that prevailed when Congress first authorized regulation of the broadcast spectrum, the Internet can hardly be considered a "scarce" expressive commodity.

...

[I]t unquestionably silences some speakers whose messages would be entitled to constitutional protection.

...

We are persuaded that the CDA lacks the precision that the First Amendment requires when a statute regulates the content of speech. In order to deny minors access to potentially harmful speech, the CDA effectively suppresses a large amount of speech that adults have a constitutional right to receive and to address to one another. That burden on adult speech is unacceptable if less restrictive alternatives would be at least as effective in achieving the legitimate purpose that the statute was enacted to serve.

...

It is true that we have repeatedly recognized the governmental interest in protecting children from harmful materials. But that interest does not justify an unnecessarily broad suppression of speech addressed to adults. "Regardless of the strength of the government's interest" in protecting children, "the level of discourse reaching a mailbox simply cannot be limited to that which would be suitable for a sandbox."

...

In arguing that the CDA does not so diminish adult communication, the Government relies on the incorrect factual premise that prohibiting a transmission whenever it is known that one of its recipients is a minor would not interfere with adult-to-adult communication.

...

The District Court found that at the time of trial existing technology did not include any effective method for a sender to prevent minors from obtaining access to its communications on the Internet without also denying access to adults. The Court found no effective way to determine the age of a user who is accessing material through e-mail, mail exploders, newsgroups, or chat rooms.

...

The breadth of the CDA's coverage is wholly unprecedented.

...

The breadth of this content-based restriction of speech imposes an especially heavy burden on the Government to explain why a less restrictive provision would not be as effective as the CDA.

...

In *Sable*, 492 U.S. at 127, we remarked that the speech restriction at issue there amounted to "'burning the house to roast the pig.'" The CDA, casting a far darker shadow over free speech, threatens to torch a large segment of the Internet community.

...

[T]he growth of the Internet has been and continues to be phenomenal. As a matter of constitutional tradition, in the absence of evidence to the contrary, we presume that governmental regulation of the content of speech is more likely to interfere with the free exchange of ideas than to encourage it. The interest in encouraging freedom of expression in a democratic society outweighs any theoretical but unproven benefit of censorship.

For the foregoing reasons, the judgment of the district court is affirmed.

It is so ordered.

Afterword:
Of Dissent and Slippery Slopes

> If the First Amendment is to have an organizing symbol ... let it be the image
> of the dissenter. A major purpose of the First Amendment ... is to protect the
> romantics—those who would break out of classical forms: the dissenters,
> the unorthodox, the outcasts.[1]

Perhaps more than any other set of rights, those in the First Amendment transcend race, class, ethnicity, gender, age and even decorum. The right to express oneself is devoid of demographic characteristics. Just like the law itself, the First Amendment is blind. The cases examined within these pages help to illustrate this. The goal of this concluding section is to briefly examine some of the common threads that permeate the cases presented herein. It will be done by invoking a new perspective or two, but also by borrowing from the preceding pages as a reminder of some of the applicable viewpoints.

What we see in the rulings explored and analyzed here, and how the First Amendment is interpreted, serve as a framework. They are precedents to future decisions. As *Reno* co-counsel John Morris said with regard to that case, "I think this decision will continue to be the starting point for 50 years—for a very long time it will be where courts start when they evaluate regulation of the Internet." Many of these cases have had, and will continue to have, similar legacies. These and similar cases will serve as models for future cases. Already, many of them are cited and relied upon for the mod-

---

[1]Steven H. Shiffrin, The First Amendment, Democracy, and Romance 5 (1990).

els they provide. For example, rulings such as those in the *Ollman* and *Ne-braska Press Association* cases have served the judiciary with the tests they furnished. *Hustler v. Falwell* significantly contributed to the understanding of parody. The standards established in *Turner Broadcasting v. FCC* are repeatedly being used in subsequent cases. We learn from cases such as *Tinker*, *R.A.V.*, and *Reno* that no matter how well intentioned rules, regulations, or laws may be, they still must be constitutional and comport with the First Amendment.

Those people whose actions and beliefs were protected by the First Amendment in the cases profiled here include adolescents, an admitted racist, a political operative who was promised anonymity, established and conservative columnists, a liquor store owner deprived of the ability to advertise the price of his products, a pornographer who parodied a well-known man of the cloth, and an author whose online product was threatened by legislation targeting indecency. Every one of these individuals—and often those who opposed them, as well—have much in common. All of them paid a price of one kind or another, including some form of being ostracized by one community or another. "I think the common thread is very often a controversial position that with hindsight is the right position," says *R.A.V.* attorney Ed Cleary, "that it takes a certain amount of courage for whoever goes forward with it, that there's often misunderstanding during the case, and oftentimes that misunderstanding never totally dissipates. I think the common thread very often is that the people who pursue it do pay a price of sorts." That price can occur on a number of levels and demonstrates that the law consists of more than theoretical standards. "[Y]ou've got flesh and blood people here," says *Cohen* attorney Elliot Rothenberg. "It's not just ivory tower general legal principles. People are actually getting hurt."

These cases also involve people who to some extent were pawns of their circumstances and of history. While often passionate about their cause, none of them had any idea where the currents of history would carry them and their cases. "I've learned that ordinary people can have an impact," says Mary Beth Tinker. "It's just a fluke of history that there are these historical moments and ordinary people are just going along like we were. We certainly didn't set out to do anything like that." Moreover, history often forces the individuals at the heart of these cases into the distance. They are relegated to supporting roles. "History shows that they often fade into the background in terms of the fact that they were a willing party," says Cleary, "but they were a tool of history just like everyone else involved in the case."

The people at the center of these cases also share passion—a passion for their beliefs and a willingness to fight for them. That is, their link was a willingness to express their views, to speak their minds. They share a common bond with many of America's most prominent dissenters. Those people profiled within these pages were either dissenters themselves, or fought to protect the right to dissent. This includes not only the plaintiffs, but also attorneys like *R.A.V.*'s Cleary:

If you boil it down, to me it really came down to the right to dissent. I realize that a lot of people think that really wasn't what it was. But it was. You take some of the most serious issues that also happen to be group identities—race, religion, gender, etc.—and you attempt to stifle unpopular expression on one of those topics or group identities, and you could literally, I think, undermine the whole concept of freedom of expression. And I think there was a movement to do that. I think it was blunted. I think you'll still see it now in some places. Bottom line: it was the right to say unpopular things on hot topics. That's extremely important. Political speech isn't always going to be Democrat-Republican. Sometimes it's going to be on topics that we think, when we're at certain points in our history, are too sensitive to talk about. You have to make room for people to talk about them, even if that means putting up with the hateful diatribes that we get. So to me that was it: the right to dissent on sensitive topics and express yourself on those topics.

The First Amendment may be among the most "American" of rights, for its roots on this continent extend to a pre-constitutional, colonial era. The First Amendment embodies rights that were hatched prior to revolution. As expressed in these pages, the maintenance of those rights is a tradition that many contemporary attorneys believe they preserve through their work. It contains echoes of Paine, Jefferson, and the demand that representation is a prerequisite to taxation. These were the dissenters. To them, protecting dissent was commonsensical and self-evident. As James Madison wrote in *The Federalist* No. 51, one of the two main problems of republican government is protecting individuals and minorities from tyrannical majority factions of fellow citizens.[2] Historian Joseph Ellis suggests that labeling this group of revolutionary era political leaders the "Founding Fathers" is not a misnomer given that we continue to live their legacy.[3] They established the right not only for themselves, but also for others in the future, to dissent.

In his opening statement to the U.S. Supreme Court, Ed Cleary paid homage to the historical roots and value of the right to dissent: "The Framers understood the dangers of orthodoxy and standardized thought and chose liberty." His Supreme Court case, he says, was really about "the flip side of majority rule in the sense of how a single voice should be protected and should it continue to be protected. And that there's an anti-majoritarian element when it comes to the Bill of Rights. I think clearly the anti-Federalists understood that way back when, when they put those protections in."

"The connection between dissent and First Amendment jurisprudence is easy to grasp,"[4] writes Professor David A. Anderson. From the ideas developed by Radical Whigs and other religious and political dissenters in

---

[2]The Federalist No. 51, at 320–25 (James Madison) (Clinton Rossiter ed., 1961).
[3]Joseph J. Ellis, Founding Brothers: The Revolutionary Generation 12 (2000).
[4]David A. Anderson, *Metaphorical Scholarship*, 79 Calif. L. Rev. 1205, 1210 (1991).

18th-century England, Anderson tells us, our own First Amendment juris-prudence is richly peopled with memorable dissenters: World War I era so-cialists such as Jacob Schenck and Eugene Debs, the Jehovah's Witnesses, the communists of the 1930s, the anti-Semitic Jay Near, Klansman Clar-ence Brandenburg, and flag-burner Gregory Lee Johnson.[5] To that list, it is suggested here, names such as Tinker, Eckhardt, Haronian, Cohen, and Flynt should be added. As Vietnam War protestor John Tinker says, "Our opinion was different, and we thought it was important that we not just acqui-esce to the standard opinion." His co-plaintiff, Chris Eckhardt, concurs:

> The issue was an unpopular war, a wrong war, and an over-reaction on the part of some administrators and a conflict between those who would rather suppress creativity and freedom of expression against the minority and against principled, religious, ethical individuals who believe that they're do-ing what their constitution says they can do, and some authoritarians who would rather have law and order instead of democracy.

Thus the notion that dissent strengthens democracy. It is an integral ele-ment within the idea of a self-governing society. There is no more passion-ate advocate of dissent as a First Amendment value than Cornell University law professor Steven H. Shiffrin. "[I]f there is to be any central constitu-tional understanding," he writes, "it proceeds from a profound national commitment to preserving dissent, encouraging free minds, basking in the rich culture of diversity that follows from such preservation and encourage-ment."[6] Democracy and dissent run together. While dissent encourages in-dividualism, free will, and nonconformity, it also encourages community. In Shiffrin's view, the First Amendment should do more than simply accom-modate competing values; it should draw us into a community and "speak to the kind of people we are and the kind of people we aspire to be."[7] Be-cause dissent seeks converts and colleagues, it focuses on the community and attempts to draw people together. "Dissenters remind the community how far it has strayed from its prior commitments to free religion, political expression, and cultural iconoclasm. Respect for dissent, in this view, is in-strumental to preserving the shared liberal commitments of the American Community."[8] John Tinker is among those who recognize this bond be-tween dissent and a truly participatory democracy with an open market-place of ideas:

> [I]f we really believe in democracy—that a country should be controlled, run, governed—by its citizens, then we really have to reconcile our behav-

---

[5]*Id.* at 1211–12.
[6]Shiffrin, *supra* note 1, at 161.
[7]*Id.* at 159.
[8]Nicholas F. Gallicchio, *Creating a Community of Liberals*, 69 Tex. L. Rev. 795, 814 (1991).

ior with that, and that includes how we raise our kids and how we participate. If we're going to claim to be of the people, by the people, and for the
people—if that's the nature of our democracy—then we can't really shirk
our responsibility as citizens to pay attention to what's going on and to
make judgments about what's going on and then to work to be active, to
try to promote our points of view. To me, in the armband case, the most
important thing that comes out of that is that if we're going to have a democracy, then the kids should be taught that it's a democracy and should
be offered the opportunity to participate, to practice being participants in
a democracy.

At the same time, dissent suggests a community of individuals. Shiffrin
believes that "American democracy is inextricably tied to safeguarding dissent."[9] Dissenters themselves are "a reminder of our deeply shared respect
for freedom, individualism, tolerance, and other First Amendment values."[10] As Shiffrin writes, "The First Amendment's purpose and function in
the American polity is … to sponsor the individualism, the rebelliousness,
the antiauthoritarianism, the spirit of nonconformity within us all."[11] And
again, as John Tinker reminds us, this individualism actually enhances the
democratic dynamic within a community:

> I think that it's *entirely* appropriate in a democracy that students learn early
> to express their opinions and to go against the flow a little bit—to express
> their opinions even if they differ from the majority opinion. My opinion is that
> it's a *positive* thing to have that sort of a protest, especially a protest that is
> designed to be respectful of the rights of society to certain levels of decorum
> and order. I think for a democracy, the sort of protest that we had is very
> healthy and was much needed.

Shiffrin traces the value of dissent to Ralph Waldo Emerson, whose early
essays and lectures extolled the virtues of intellectual independence and
resistances of convention. Emerson celebrated the courage of the noncon-
formist and the dissenter, in turn "urging self-reliance and independence of
thought" and praising those willing to speak out against the tide.[12] The
Emersonian message is to trust your own intuitions, to speak out in favor of
your own ideas, and to oppose the "strait prison-like limits of the Actual,"[13]
to resist the conventions of the "old, halt, numb, bedrid world."[14] The acceptance of dissent as a value is a philosophy that trusts. To grant the free-

---

[9]William G. Buss, *Lighting a Flame Under the First Amendment*, 76 Iowa L. Rev. 871,
874 (1991).

[10]Gallicchio, *supra* note 8, at 814.

[11]Shiffrin, *supra* note 1, at 5.

[12]*Id.* at 78.

[13]Ralph Waldo Emerson, *The Protest*, in III The Early Lectures of Ralph Waldo Emerson:
1838–42 94 (R. Spiller & W. Williams eds., 1972).

[14]*Id.* at 89.

dom to dissent is to trust—trust of human spirit and wisdom. At the root of dissent is also the endorsement of change. "Change is the law of life," Emerson wrote, "and we consequently obey the law if we choose to live a life of change, to live life as welcomed change.... [O]nly conformists try to be fixed, and that in a democratic society, where change is allowed as a matter of principle, only conformists crave fixity."[15]

At the root of many of the cases and the actions of those who precipitated them that are profiled in these pages are basic but sometimes paradoxical questions: Can we accept the unacceptable? Can we tolerate the intolerable? "Is there room for speech that we hate, that we disagree with?" asks *R.A.V.* co-counsel Mike Cromett. If the conclusion is that the latitude does not exist, then we venture into some dangerous territory. According to Larry Flynt attorney Alan Isaacman, "[P]articularly in the First Amendment area—the free speech area—where it's so easy to fall victim to the attitude that, 'Well, this is so outrageous that what this person is saying, the courts or the government should stop them from being able say it.' Pretty soon you go down that slippery slope and they're telling you what you can say."

Law professor Frederick Schauer notes that these slippery slope arguments offer a common theme—the "contrast between a tolerable solution to a problem now before us, and an intolerable result with respect to some currently hypothetical but potentially real state of affairs."[16] Cases are sometimes argued by presenting a "what if" scenario—what might be called the "can of worms" approach. If a lower court decision and the law on which it was based are allowed to stand, it may be argued, an unacceptable result will unfold. Rulings are sometimes made to preclude the possibility of the scenario materializing. *Nebraska Press Association* attorney Barrett Prettyman, Jr. used this strategy in his oral argument, asking the members of the U.S. Supreme Court if the ban on the publication of information ought to extend beyond the media and to the general public, including ministers at the pulpit. Should their sermons be restricted? In effect, Prettyman was asking the Court if it really wanted to step onto that slippery slope.

Many of the cases examined herein are about the slippery slope. If a law is overbroad it will give the state the authority to regulate speech beyond the law's intended scope. *Reno v. ACLU* respondent Patricia Nell Warren noted the existence of the slippery slope: "When people start giving up territory under their feet and moving back, then the other side just gets more and more." *R.A.V.* co-counsel Mike Cromett helps with the understanding of the slippery slope principle and how it applied to his client's case: "If you're going to allow people to regulate speech that you don't agree with, it can't be too long before *your* speech—speech that *you* agree with—will be

---

[15]George Kateb, Emerson and Self-Reliance 154 (1995).
[16]Frederick Schauer, *Slippery Slopes*, 99 Harv. L. Rev. 361, 364–65 (1985).

limited, too. I think it's probably that slippery slope that we're afraid of. Once you decide that, where does it end?" Evan Lawson, the lawyer for 44 Liquormart, noted that his case involved a slippery slope argument. If a "liquor is special" philosophy had been accepted—the belief that advertising for alcoholic beverages could be regulated for the public's own good—then it begs the question what other products would ultimately be placed within that same rubric. And in *Nebraska Press Association*, where requiring the media to delay making public information they had lawfully obtained was at issue, the question of what was an "appropriate" delay arose. "It's a slippery slope if you start saying, 'Well, you can delay for a little while, but not too long,'" says Association attorney Barrett Prettyman. "Doesn't that vary from case to case? What's too long in a murder case? What's too short in a case involving the Pentagon Papers, for example?"

These pages have profiled some who expressed a sort of "institutional dissent"—a dissatisfaction with some aspect of the status quo. In some instances it was a retailer unhappy with a state law that prevented him from advertising the price of his products or an author being prevented from posting her writings on a Web site. As *Reno v. ACLU*'s Patricia Nell Warren says, she could not idly stand by while valuable works were being censored:

> The real issue is for the individual human being. If I as an individual who believes in the American dream, and believes in free speech, and if I really think that our country has had a history of struggle to learn how to respect diverse viewpoints, then how can I live with myself to allow this to be done to me? If I let it be done to me, what kind of signal does that send to other people, especially young writers? Because young people do pay attention to these things, and when they see examples of people standing up for what they think and what they feel, that should be important to them. If they see a lot of us willing to eat dirt and bow our necks to the yoke, then that sends a terrible signal to those young people. So it really comes down to how I feel about myself and how I see myself and how I could live with myself if I had done that.

These were people who challenged majoritarian legislation. In other cases it was someone like a Dan Cohen who successfully challenged press institutions in a community that he labeled a hotbed of conformity, or Bertell Ollman who unsuccessfully challenged a pair of recognized and established columnists. "[I]t's a matter of asking if I had access to other media," Ollman says, "where I might have presented another point of view where I might have engaged them in open debate about some of the questions—where I might have denied some of what they were accusing me of before the same audience. Of course, that wasn't the case."

We see a common thread of unpredictability in these cases—not only in the people whose actions were at the heart of these and similar cases, but also in the people who sit in judgment. Labeling judges and Supreme Court Justices as "conservative" and "liberal" verges on the irrelevant.

"[W]hen it comes to First Amendment law, I really do not think there's an ideological basis for the votes," Cleary says. "I think we should abandon labels when we look for votes on First Amendment issues." Perhaps one reason lies in Robert Novak's explanation of his case, *Ollman v. Evans and Novak*, when he says that for the judges on the D.C. Circuit, their "politics was stronger than their legal ideology."

Lastly, this notion of unpredictability is linked inextricably to the humanity embedded in these cases and in the law. People can and often do behave in irrational and unpredictable ways. Despite valiant attempts by scholars and litigators alike to lend an air of predictability to the law, forecasting results remains somewhat elusive. Aside from the tests, principles, and standards, there will always be humans who apply them, judge them, and perhaps most importantly, who challenge them by creating unanticipated circumstances. It is that—the essence of human behavior and all that accompanies that most complex of phenomena—as much as anything, that is at the center of these cases. While the law and its principles may be the heart of these cases, the people who made and shaped them are their soul.